THE GOLDEN WEB

A HISTORY OF BROADCASTING IN THE UNITED STATES

THE GOLDEN WEB

A History of Broadcasting in the United States

Volume II—1933 to 1953

ERIK BARNOUW

New York OXFORD UNIVERSITY PRESS 1968

CONTENTS

THE GOLDEN WEB

INTRODUCTION

The web of human things . . . that are not as they
were.   SHELLEY, *Alastor*

Until the late 1920's broadcasting in the United States was largely a story
of separate transmitter towers, each independent, each vying for attention
with countless others. This period has been chronicled in *A Tower in
Babel*, first of three volumes in this study. Even in that first era, broadcasting showed an unexpected ability to move and persuade, and precipitated
epic struggles for control.

Then a new element was added. Transmitters in various parts of the
country began broadcasting the same singer, the same speaker, the same
comedian, the same drama. To listeners it seemed a logical, rational step,
readily accepted. But in the process a new force had been added to the
nation's power constellation: the network. Within a few years it was a
dominant element not only in broadcasting but in many other fields. A far-
ranging shift in relationships and influences was under way.

What is a network? In a way it is—strangely enough—almost nothing, a
phantom. It is mainly a tissue of contracts by which a number of stations
are linked in operation. The linkage has been done largely through leased
telephone cables which the entrepreneur—the "network"—does not own.
Each of the stations so linked uses an air channel which is a public resource and which neither network nor station can own. Thus networks as
businesses would seem to rest on the flimsiest foundations. Yet they have
become a major power center—having, in an age of American hegemony,
world-wide ramifications.

This volume, *The Golden Web*, will trace the rise of the American net-

3

works during the years 1933–53. At the start of this period they were national distributors of voices and sounds; by its end they were distributors also of moving images, and reaching into international spheres. This would usher in an era dominated by television and the *pax Americana*, to be chronicled in a third volume.

The present volume, like *A Tower in Babel*, will examine what was broadcast, by whom, and why. Again the "why" will require us to scrutinize behind-the-scenes struggles, which tended to become more elusive—and more implacable—as the stakes rose. Again we shall find in action an extraordinary array of personalities—brilliant, arrogant, psychopathic, inspired, corrupt, dynamic, witty, relentless, tricky, ambitious. We shall also try to explore, insofar as we now can, their impact on our lives—on the web of human relationships, that are not as they were.

1 / EITHER / OR

Woe unto them . . . that lie upon beds
of ivory and stretch themselves upon
their couches . . . the houses of ivory
shall perish and the great houses
shall have an end.

Book of Amos

On a Sunday early in 1933 a minister told his congregation he would preach the next week on a text from Amos. It was the depth of the Depression; the minister was appalled at what he saw around him. There were breadlines of silent men and women. Many towns were bankrupt. Schoolteachers went unpaid, and in many towns school doors were closed. Yet the nation as a whole was rich in resources, and many individuals were affluent. As numbers of businesses collapsed, many others were strengthening their position. In many industries the concentration of power and wealth, evident throughout the 1920's, had been furthered by the Depression. All this had been in the minister's thoughts as he chose his text from Amos. He had in mind the prophet's warning: "The houses of ivory shall perish and the great houses shall have an end."

On the following Sunday he was gratified that crowds of people came to church, but their reactions to his sermon puzzled him. He learned later that they had thought he would be talking about *Amos 'n' Andy*.[1]

The incident epitomized some of the bizarre aspects of the moment, and the role of American broadcasting in it—a role due for change. It was a time of the breaking of nations. Throughout the world hunger amid promise of plenty was precipitating perilous action. In Germany it had brought Hitler to power; in cascades of rhetoric he foreshadowed military glory. In Italy the same pattern had been set by Mussolini, eyeing Ethiopia. Japan had begun a grab for China's resources. In the United States the despera-

1. *Social Service Bulletin*, February 15, 1933.

5

tion of the unemployed—fifteen million in number, according to some estimates—had swept into office Franklin D. Roosevelt, whose views were largely unknown and who was regarded by most business leaders with mistrust and hostility. As the President-elect faced his task, the national economy approached paralysis. In state after state banks closed their doors. Yet throughout these weeks millions sat spellbound nightly by two performers—a southerner and a mid-westerner—trained in the stereotypes of "blackface" minstrel comedy—*Amos 'n' Andy.*

Or if it was not *Amos 'n' Andy,* it was Kate Smith, singing again and again of the moon coming over the mountain ("every beam / brings a dream / dear, of you"); or the strenuous joke routines, mixed with unabashed sentimentality, of Eddie Cantor ("I love to spend / this hour with you / as friend to friend / believe me it's true") or the burlesque dialects of Jack Pearl ("vas you dere, Sharlie?"); or the giggle of Ed Wynn; or the parades of vaudeville acts on *Maxwell House Showboat* or *Vallee Varieties;* or hymn-singing at Seth Parker's; or mysteries of *Fu Manchu* or *Eno Crime Clues;* or the drama of *Roses and Drums, Moonshine and Honeysuckle,* or *Soconyland Sketches,* all celebrating a semi-mythical America of yesterday or never. The stale formulas of every field of entertainment were being tried on radio, and many were succeeding in winning audiences and, to an astonishing degree, boosting sales, particularly of drugs and packaged foods. Meanwhile they were winning for radio a loyalty that seemed almost irrational. According to social workers, destitute families that had to give up an icebox or furniture or bedding still clung to the radio as to a last link with humanity.

What did it mean? Perhaps, as a later observer put it, a new "tribal unity" was being forged by the nationally distributed voices.[2] Regardless of what these voices said or sang, perhaps they provided a sense of a shared life and destiny. Conceivably, even the hackneyed quality of the programming had a timely value. Perhaps, amid chaos, people looked to their past—or echoes of it.

Whatever the meaning, something new was becoming a central factor in American lives—network broadcasting. If more proof of its influence was needed, the incoming administration proceeded to provide it.

2. McLuhan, *Understanding Media,* pp. 297–307.

A REAL PRO

During 1933—on March 12, May 7, July 24, October 22—the new President gave four momentous "fireside chats." These broadcast talks became not only a Franklin D. Roosevelt specialty but milestones in politics and broadcasting. Differing in tone from the broadcasts of Hitler and Mussolini, who were heard in public appearances with a background of hysterical crowds, Roosevelt's "chats" implied a sharing of ideas in a sort of family council. One reflection of their impact was mail response. Until March 1933 one White House employee handled all presidential mail. This arrangement had sufficed even during the 1914–18 World War and the time of panic following the Wall Street crash. But during March 1933 a half million unanswered letters piled up at the White House, and assistants had to be hired.[3] Each "chat" swelled the deluge. People seemed to feel, according to various observers, that Roosevelt was talking to them directly as individuals, knew their problems, and was interested in them. Many people cut his picture from a magazine and propped it on a bookcase or on the radio.

Such reactions were not universal. To some his patrician tone seemed condescending and infuriating. This reaction could be found on the extreme left, where he was considered fascistic, and on the right, where he was seen as socialistic. But millions found in his calm, measured statements assurance that he was their representative and friend. Their response gave the President—at least for the moment—an incalculable political advantage. The fireside chats and the response they won helped propel through Congress with miraculous speed a broad legislative program—establishing the AAA (Agricultural Adjustment Administration), NRA (National Recovery Administration), FERA (Federal Emergency Relief Administration), and many other New Deal innovations. The country seemed to recover momentum; advocacy of more radical courses subsided.

A number of observers have described Roosevelt delivering his chats. After being wheeled into an improvised White House studio for the first broadcast, he delighted the radio personnel with questions about their preparations. Neither Coolidge nor Hoover had shown interest of this sort. Roosevelt remarked that the microphones looked different from those in

3. Schlesinger, *The Coming of the New Deal*, pp. 571–2.

Albany. He asked, "What's the CBS for?" [4] During the final moments of waiting, he chatted with Secretary of State Cordell Hull. Mrs. Roosevelt came in and sat with her knitting on her lap. When it was time to start, Carleton Smith of NBC touched the President's shoulder.

During his July chat, devoted to relief problems, Roosevelt created a small sensation by a simple human action that may have been sophisticated showmanship. He stopped and asked for a glass of water. After taking time for a sip—audible coast-to-coast—he told his listeners: "My friends, it's very hot here in Washington tonight." Later he asked the radio men whether this digression had been "all right." They told him it was terrific. He often asked their opinion on matters of delivery, and beamed if they approved. [5]

The radio men soon regarded him with admiration and spoke of him as "a real pro." Their network bosses at the time were largely anti-Roosevelt. A natural caution may have prompted announcers and engineers to express their admiration invariably in terms of Roosevelt as performer.

To Secretary of Labor Frances Perkins, watching Roosevelt deliver a fireside chat, he seemed totally unaware of those around him. She felt he was trying to picture in his mind the people he was talking to. "His face would smile and light up as though he were actually sitting on the front porch or in the parlor with them." The same quality was described in less friendly fashion by John Dos Passos: "There is a man leaning across his desk speaking clearly and cordially to youandme . . . leaning towards youandme across his desk . . . so that youandme shall completely understand. . . . " [6]

Among those who resented Roosevelt and his fireside chats were some who had reason to know what broadcasting could do, but whose interest took a different direction. These included advertising agencies, most of their clients, and the media men—including network executives—who looked to them for revenue. Their hostility to Roosevelt, and their determination to control the medium that had become his special instrument of power, became dominant motifs of the early New Deal era. The period was a vortex of crisscrossing currents and conflicts, sometimes reaching a

4. *Broadcasting*, March 15, 1933. Earlier CBS microphones, such as those Roosevelt had seen in Albany, had "Columbia" rather than "CBS." But the remark suggests—correctly—that CBS was still far from having a public standing comparable to that of NBC.
5. *Broadcasting*, August 1, 1933; John Charles Daly, in Brown and Bruner (eds), *I Can Tell It Now*, p. 97.
6. Perkins, *The Roosevelt I Knew*, p. 72; *Common Sense*, February 1934.

high pitch of fury. Among these an advertising oligarchy, which had risen to power throughout the 1920's, fought for its place in the sun.

THE LAND OF IRIUM

The acknowledged dean of advertising at the start of the New Deal was Albert D. Lasker, president and owner of Lord & Thomas.[1] Born in 1880, he had grown up in Galveston, Texas. His father was a German immigrant who had worked his way west as a peddler and had become the owner of a prosperous milling business, president of three banks, and a patriarch tyrannizing over a gaudy turreted mansion, resembling a castle on the Rhine. The boy Albert, who feared his father, soon showed a comparable sharpness. At twelve he launched a four-page weekly newspaper, the Galveston *Free Press*, which won enough readers and advertisers to last a year while earning the boy a weekly profit of $15—more than most adults earned at the time. It later won him a job as reporter for the Galveston *Morning News* at $40 a week. His father thought of newspapermen as drunkards and, to divert the boy from this fate, arranged a job for him in Chicago at the Lord & Thomas advertising agency, which owed the elder Lasker a favor. Here in 1898 Albert, aged eighteen, began his advertising career at a salary of $10 a week. He intended to stay briefly, but salesmanship became a game and a never-ending challenge to his sharp wits and combative nature. Besides, Lasker was so adept at winning new accounts that his salary and commissions soared, so that in 1903, at twenty-three, he could buy out old Mr. Lord, who was ready to retire; a few years later he also bought the Thomas share and became sole owner. Most of the income came from patented drugs—for a long time the leading account was Cascarets—but packaged foods and tobacco rose in importance. There were also miscellaneous items like Wilson Ear Drums, a cardboard hearing aid sold by mail at $5, which the Lasker advertising touch turned into a bonanza. By 1917 Albert Lasker, a young man in his early thirties, was personally taking home a million dollars a year from his advertising agency, which was considered the most prosperous in the world. Rumors of his wizardry reached the world of politics, and he was invited to Oyster Bay on Long Island to meet Theodore Roosevelt, who received him in khaki shirt, khaki pants, and boots. "They tell me you are America's greatest

1. It later became Foote, Cone & Belding. The following is based on Gunther, *Taken at the Flood*; Lasker, *Reminiscences*; and other sources as mentioned.

advertising man," T.R. said. Lasker answered, "Colonel, no man can claim that distinction as long as you are alive!" The exchange put them both in splendid spirits and helped launch a new phase of the Lasker career.

The first World War was at its height. Lasker was playing no part in it and wondered if he should. T.R. reassured him—Lasker could do more good at home. He could help save the nation from the international entanglements Woodrow Wilson was bound to drag it into. It was up to the Republicans to prevent that; for this, Lasker was needed. So he became assistant to Will Hays, chairman of the Republican National Committee, helping to fight the battle against the League of Nations; he became fanatical on the subject, putting some $30,000 of his own money into a pamphlet entitled *After the Peace, What?*, which was distributed in millions of copies. The anti-League work—credited with enormous success—lifted him into a position of leadership in Republican circles. With the nomination of Warren G. Harding for the presidency, Lasker became responsible for all publicity out of Marion, Ohio, for Harding's "front-porch" campaign, fostering the desired picture of Harding and stirring suspicions of the League. James M. Cox, the Democratic candidate, regarded Lasker as the most "sinister" force in the Republican machine.[2] With the triumph of Harding at the polls, Lasker entered the government as chairman of the U. S. Shipping Board. Sam Goldwyn asked him to come to Hollywood—beset by scandals—and assume the post of "czar," heading the newly formed motion picture association, but Lasker recommended his friend and associate Will Hays. In 1923 Lasker returned to Lord & Thomas. Had his ardor for advertising cooled? To dispel such a notion, he assembled his key men "for a few minutes"—and talked three days. His theme: the glories of advertising. His agency had slipped while he was away, but in a burst of energy he began pushing it back toward leadership. He won the Lucky Strike account, which soon brought in huge revenues. So did Pepsodent, Palmolive, Kotex, Kleenex. He was asked, how was Kleenex doing? "Fine! Women are beginning to waste it!" His personal earnings continued at a million or more per year. Near Lake Forest, a Chicago suburb, he began to build one of the greatest of great American homes at a cost of $3,500,000. It was a fifty-room, seventeenth-century French provincial manor house, set in a four-hundred-and-eighty-acre tract that included ninety-seven acres of formal gardens with six miles of clipped hedges and

2. Cox, a newspaper publisher, later became a broadcasting magnate and close friend of Lasker.

such extras as greenhouses, a one-hundred-by-forty-foot swimming pool with adjoining soda fountain, a theater, a twelve-car garage, a guest house, an eighteen-hole golf course, and fifty servants. A parade of the rich and powerful came and went.

When the crash came, followed by the Depression, Lasker felt it, but not too seriously. Some of his investments went sour, but his agency was in a state of almost dizzy prosperity. Walking down Park Avenue one day with his son, Lasker mentioned that he was seventeen million dollars poorer than he had been two years earlier but didn't feel any different. Two reasons were Pepsodent and Lucky Strike. Shortly before the crash Lasker had taken steps with these accounts that made his position almost impregnable.

With Pepsodent it had been largely *Amos 'n' Andy*. Lasker put the program on an NBC hookup for the toothpaste, and the company's sales tripled within weeks. But *Amos 'n' Andy* was not the sole reason. Pepsodent contained a detergent, sodium alkyl sulphate. Lasker decided to make it a mystery ingredient of fabulous power, and told his staff to invent a name having three vowels and two consonants; he gave no other instructions. They came up with irium. From then on it was *Amos 'n' Andy* and irium. "I invented irium," Lasker chuckled. "Tell me what it is!" Irium was backed by hard-selling commercials. NBC was still proclaiming that its policies called for "indirect advertising" only, but Lasker went on as he wished. For a time almost half of NBC's business was coming from Lasker. He persuaded Pepsodent to expand the campaign and accepted Pepsodent stock as partial payment for agency services. He became the second largest Pepsodent stockholder. As sales boomed, so did Lasker's wealth.

With Lucky Strike it was women. Until the mid-1920's few women smoked and fewer dared do it in public. Advertising had approached the possibility in gingerly fashion. In one advertisement a man smoked while a girl—trembling on the brink of emancipation?—said, "Blow some my way!" A simple economic fact lured Lasker further. If women could be induced to smoke, the market would double. He decided to begin with opera stars—foreign ones. They had the right aura of high life and daring. Soon advertising was proclaiming, of one soprano after another, that she smoked Lucky Strikes. Their mildness, said the ads, protected her priceless voice. As talking films appeared, screen stars were enlisted in the campaign. Meanwhile a theme of special feminine potency was added. "Reach for a Lucky instead of a sweet." The idea of cigarettes as an aid to figure control was novel and apparently effective. Conceived simultaneously by Lasker and his client George Washington Hill, president of American Tobacco, the campaign was backed by unprecedented budgets. In 1931, $19,000,000 went to advertise Luckies. On radio the sledge-hammer beat of B. A. Rolfe's orchestra—the Lucky Strike Orchestra—was accompanied by endless reiteration of the slimming theme.

George Washington Hill—a churlish, canny fellow who even in his office wore a tilted sombrero adorned with fishhooks, and who rode down Fifth Avenue in an open Cadillac manned by a bodyguard and decorated on the windshield with Lucky Strike packages—lived and breathed to increase Lucky Strike sales. All his waking hours were apparently spent in devising new schemes to that end. At Lord & Thomas he found willing lieutenants. On Saturday mornings Hill insisted that Lord & Thomas and NBC executives, male and female, join him at rehearsals of the Lucky Strike orchestra to foxtrot to the music and test its danceability. America should defeat the Depression by dancing its way out, said Hill.[3] Therefore such dignitaries as John Royal, NBC vice president in charge of programs, and Bertha Brainard, his stylish program manager, had to dance at the Saturday morning command performances. Meanwhile, the commercials got longer and more strident. NBC acquiesced, dancing to Hill's tune.

In 1932, while one firm after another announced across-the-board pay cuts, Lord & Thomas likewise cut all salaries 25 per cent. Employees must have thought their company, like many others, was hurting from the Depression. The impression was totally wrong. That year Lasker himself took home almost three million dollars from the agency operations. The average annual wage of a full-time worker in the tobacco industry was $614.12.

It was a period of rapidly shifting political winds, and this worried Lasker. Hitler and Mussolini worried him. Those men, he told a Lord & Thomas colleague, were bad news; people would be reading about Hitler and Mussolini instead of paying attention to advertising. Franklin D. Roosevelt also worried him. This Roosevelt had been running mate to James Cox in the pro-League Democratic presidential slate of 1920 and probably still harbored internationalist notions. But a greater fear revolved around

3. This idea was devised for him by Edward L. Bernays, public relations counsel. Bernays, *Biography of an Idea,* p. 388.

Roosevelt's advisers, such as braintruster Rexford Guy Tugwell. In the eyes of the advertising world, no figure threw more frightening shadows than Tugwell.

In the incoming Roosevelt administration Tugwell took the post of Assistant Secretary of Agriculture, but his interests were broader. He was especially concerned about what he called "the robbery of consumer deception" through misleading advertising. He thought it was time for "freedom from fakes." With his encouragement the Food and Drug Administration prepared a new food, drug, and cosmetic bill calling for precise information about contents—not only on labels but also in advertising. Although Tugwell had no part in the bill other than to encourage the preparation of it, it became known as the Tugwell bill. Enemies of the bill considered this good strategy because of Tugwell's professorial background.[4]

In the exhilaration of the early weeks of the New Deal, the Tugwell bill seemed to its sponsors reasonable and humane. The Food and Drug Administration staged a sort of horror show to dramatize the need. There were pictures of maimed people, victims of self-medication involving advertised products. Broadcasting circles did not at first take alarm at the bill's proposals. *Broadcasting* magazine thought they would get rid of "quacks and chiselers" and in the long run benefit everyone.[5] But advertising men held different views and soon impressed them on the broadcasting industry.

Perhaps they were worried about what would happen to irium, or to Lucky Strikes as slenderizer and throat balm. The Tugwell bill, Albert Lasker proclaimed, would lower the American standard of living and "menace human welfare." Others joined in the chorus. According to the patent medicine group known as the Proprietary Association, the bill was "grotesque in its terms, evil in its purposes, and vicious in its possible consequences." Frank Blair of Castoria, president of the association, called the bill "the greatest legislative crime in history." Others said it would "sovietize" the drug industry and cause waves of unemployment at advertising agencies, media organizations, and distributors. To underline this argument, drug manufacturers began inserting in contracts for advertising space and time a clause that made enactment of the Tugwell bill a cause for cancellation. Many broadcasters took note. At this time half the in-

4. Schlesinger, *The Coming of the New Deal*, pp. 355–7.
5. *Broadcasting*, September 15, 1933.

come of the broadcasting industry came from foods and drugs. The National Association of Broadcasters declared war on the Tugwell bill. *Broadcasting*, on reconsideration, decided the bill was badly drawn and should be defeated.[6] The anti-Tugwell campaign was a triumph. A revised bill was passed but with the teeth drawn: advertising was completely exempt from its provisions.

With each month of the New Deal, advertising agencies were more deeply drawn into politics. Lasker's clients were now more diverse than in earlier years. During the 1930's they included—besides food, drug, and tobacco products—such accounts as General Electric, RCA, RKO, Cities Service, Commonwealth Edison, Frigidaire, Goodyear. All felt New Deal anxieties, and these pressed on Lasker. Schemes to halt feared political trends were numerous and included such phenomena as the Liberty League. Some made use of radio. More than one involved Lasker and Lord & Thomas.

The Crusaders, headed by Fred G. Clark as "national commander," had started in the late 1920's to campaign for repeal of Prohibition, receiving help from various interested manufacturers. In February 1933, with big business in a state of the jitters about the incoming administration, Clark saw wider fields for crusades. The organization was revised "to oppose all forces destructive to sound government." Some months later a lunch meeting was held in Chicago, attended by about fifty business leaders, at which the commander broached the idea of a radio voice for the Crusaders to implement the opposition to destructive forces. A radio fund of $160,000 was quickly raised, subscribed largely at the lunch. Lasker gave $5000. Contributions came also from several of his clients: Kenneth G. Smith of Pepsodent, Lester Armour of Armour & Co., John Stuart and R. Douglas Stuart of Quaker Oats. Top-rung executives of DuPont, General Mills, National Biscuit Company, Corn Products, Heinz, Wrigley, Swift & Co., Sun Oil Company, Standard Oil Company of Indiana, A. B. Dick Company, and Montgomery Ward chipped in. The Columbia Broadcasting System agreed to provide free network time. The Crusaders set up a New York office, and the weekly broadcasts began in 1934 over 79 CBS stations— with Commander Clark at the microphone. Now and then he got suggestions from the donors as to what to attack—the AAA, the TVA, the Banking Bill—and he usually complied promptly. The commander later denied, during a Senate study of lobbying activities, that he had been trying

6. *Broadcasting*, October 1, 1933, to October 15, 1934.

to influence public opinion. The purpose, he said, was merely to "clarify public thinking." The inquiry revealed how doggedly he had bolstered the system he had built. To cement relations with William Paley, president of CBS, Clark telegraphed some instructions to the Crusaders staff:

GET IMPORTANT PEOPLE TO SEND LETTERS TO PALEY FLATTERING HIM ON THE CONSTRUCTIVE WORK HE IS DOING IN OFFERING THE CRUSADER BROADCASTS

He telegraphed the National Petroleum Association:

AM BROADCASTING OVER COLUMBIA NATIONWIDE NETWORK THURSDAY EVENING APRIL 11 AT 10:45 EASTERN TIME SUBJECT THE POLITICAL TAX RACKET IN WHICH I HIT GASOLINE TAX AND PETROLEUM TAX STOP WOULD GREATLY HELP IF OIL MEN AND THEIR EMPLOYEES ARE NOTIFIED TO LISTEN IN REGARDS

The broadcasts continued over CBS for five months, then shifted to a new network, the Mutual Broadcasting System.[7]

Another Lasker radio activity concerned California. Late in 1933 the novelist Upton Sinclair, known most of his life as a socialist, announced his decision to enter the Democratic primary as a candidate for governor. To coast-to-coast amazement, he won the primary with a vote that exceeded that of the front-running Republican candidate by 100,000. His election to the governorship was expected. But Republicans prepared for vigorous battle. Lord & Thomas was called to the rescue.

In Hollywood, where Lasker's friend Will Hays was "czar," the hierarchy was ready to help. Industry leaders announced they would leave the state if Sinclair were elected. Meanwhile they assembled campaign talent and money, with Louis B. Mayer, Republican state chairman, doing the fund-raising. At Metro-Goldwyn-Mayer each artist received a check already made out to the Republican party for a specific amount—$150 or $200 or more, depending on his salary bracket. All the artist had to do was sign it and fill in the date and the name of his bank. If he didn't comply promptly, a phone call followed.[8]

Sinclair's program was built around his so-called EPIC plan—End Poverty in California. This proposed to attack the problem of the one million Californians on relief. Sinclair wanted to use the state's credit to make idle lands and idle plants available to unemployed workers, so that they might

7. *Investigation of Lobbying Activities,* pp. 1731–86.
8. Hackett, *Reminiscences,* pp. 24–5.

grow food and make goods for their own use. The plan was outlined in Sinclair's book *I, Governor of California: And How I Ended Poverty;* a quarter-million copies of this were sold and these largely financed his campaign. Sinclair said he had received other offers of funds, but that most large offers had political strings and were rejected.

The Lasker-Hollywood magic went to work. "Hollywood Masses the Full Power of Her Resources To Fight Sinclair," reported the New York *Times.*[9] In the closing days of the campaign, Californians were bombarded with sensational material in all media, including radio and theatrical "newsreels." These depicted a panorama of derelicts streaming into California, explaining they were coming to share the Sinclair benefactions. The "Sinclair immigration," it was called. It worked in Russia, so "vy can't it work here?" asked a voice in Hollywood Russian. A photograph of "derelicts" used in the campaign was recognized as a shot from a recently completed Warner Brothers feature, *Wild Boys of the Road.* But the material succeeded in communicating a nightmare of endlessly swelling relief rolls. When the day came, Sinclair was defeated. Lord & Thomas had done its share. There was no doubt now: the advertising agency was in politics to stay.[10]

So was radio. The involvement took different forms, and was worldwide. When, in 1934, Austrian Nazis staged a *Putsch* in Vienna—in which Chancellor Dollfuss was killed—their first move was not toward a government building; instead they first seized a radio station, to broadcast their version of the truth. It was a symptom of the new strategic status of the broadcast word.

In the United States the advertising agencies which, like Lord & Thomas, had plunged early into broadcasting, were achieving an extraordinary position. In spite of the Depression they had brought the infant networks quick affluence and power. At the same time, the agencies themselves had entered a new phase of their history. In relation to network radio they were not mere time brokers and writers of advertising copy; they built and produced programs and—subject to only perfunctory network review—determined content. Thus they had in a few years come to control radio to an extent they would not have dared attempt with other media. The control was close-knit. In 1934 approximately one-third of net-

9. New York *Times*, November 4, 1934.
10. Schlesinger, *The Politics of Upheaval*, p. 119; Sinclair, *I, Candidate for Governor: And How I Got Licked*, pp. 25–9, 127–8; Kelley, *Professional Public Relations and Political Power*, p. 33.

work time was sold for sponsored programming, which occupied the choicest hours. More than half the revenue came from ten advertising agencies.[11] They were like-minded in their determination to protect the status quo against government innovations. This was implicit in many program decisions. With rare exceptions—such as *The March of Time,* the work of *Time* magazine—there was a blackout on current problems. The leading network, NBC-red, had not a single daily news series. NBC-blue had only Lowell Thomas. CBS had Boake Carter and (scarcely a newscast) Edwin C. Hill in *The Human Side of the News,* with occasional nonsponsored comments from H. V. Kaltenborn and others, largely in fringe hours. Most sponsors did not want news programming; those that did were inclined to expect veto rights over it. The center of the spotlight was firmly held by the vaudeville veterans, with Eddie Cantor leading the ratings[12] followed by Joe Penner, Ed Wynn, Burns and Allen, Al Jolson, Phil Baker, Jack Benny. In drama the current scene was represented by crime and love, always in a social vacuum. *First Nighter* led the drama ratings— except for *Amos 'n' Andy.*

In 1934 in the United States the Depression still appeared insoluble and overwhelming. That is, unemployment and relief rolls remained of disastrous proportions. Payrolls were 40 per cent below the 1926 level. Less well publicized was a different figure: dividends in 1934 were 50 per cent *above* the level of 1926. In the words of Raymond Swing, a journalist who would soon become a familiar radio voice, "Big business has adjusted itself to the Depression and is making money out of it."[13] He saw big business as a prosperous enclave in a wasteland struggling for survival. Those inside saw the outer danger—and tried to keep it out.

Standing guard over the enclave, manning the ramparts, were the advertising agencies. Their leader, their patriarch, was Albert D. Lasker. Numerous top advertising executives had served their apprenticeship under him.[14] He was an impressive figure whom no one could ignore; in a

11. Listed in order of volume: Blackett, Sample & Hummert; Lord & Thomas; J. Walter Thompson; Benton & Bowles; Erwin, Wasey; N. W. Ayer; Young & Rubicam; Batten, Barton, Durstine & Osborn; Ruthrauff & Ryan; Stack-Goble. *Variety Radio Directory* (1937–38) p. 731.
12. Crossley ratings. See *A Tower in Babel,* p. 270.
13. Swing, *Forerunners of American Fascism,* p. 24.
14. John Gunther mentions, among many others: William Benton of Benton & Bowles; Charles Erwin and Louis Wasey of Erwin, Wasey & Co.; Hill Blackett and Frank Hummert of Blackett, Sample & Hummert; Arthur Marquette of Sherman & Marquette; Emerson Foote, Don Belding, and Fairfax Cone, who later formed Foote, Cone & Belding. Gunther, *Taken at the Flood,* p. 211.

group all eyes were riveted on him. As he approached the middle years, he came to resemble an Old Testament prophet—but impeccably dressed. He was tall, spare, with an intense manner of speech, and always in motion. Ideas poured from him with such rapidity that he kept gasping for breath, interjecting little questioning grunts that seemed to be appeals for agreement. He had several nervous breakdowns. He once left Johns Hopkins hospital to attend a meeting at which important Lucky Strike decisions were to be made. Having settled matters to his satisfaction, he said: "Gentlemen, I have done all I can for you, uh? Good day, because I must return to Johns Hopkins to continue my nervous breakdown."

In 1934 he was on top of his world. His standing rose as the sponsored word extended its domain. He and his colleagues could look with satisfaction on the development of commercial broadcasting. But not everyone was satisfied. What was a boon to some seemed a threat to others. Various interests—including school, church, newspaper—felt their accustomed role in society hemmed in and even superseded. Many of their leaders had felt for some time that a stand must be made. The start of a new administration seemed a time for action—for counterattack. Thus the years 1933–35, which saw commercial broadcasters riding high, also saw determined assaults on the new power. The first came from the world of journalism.

THE PRESS ATTACKS

It was a short war with bloody moments.

Newspaper publishers began 1933 in an angry mood. It was bad enough that revenues were dwindling as readers and advertisers turned to radio. What was worse was that the newspaper world was itself furthering the disaster—first, by publicizing radio programs free of charge through listings and radio columns; and second, by providing news material free of charge for news broadcasts. This latter custom had been started years earlier to promote newspaper reading, but since then radio had become a competitor for advertising revenue, and might also turn into a serious news medium. The smashing success of the 1932 election-day broadcasts, which had forever doomed the newspaper "election specials," gave warning. The newspapers meant to heed the warning.

The American Newspaper Publishers Association, meeting in April 1933, passed a resolution that program logs should thenceforth be published only as paid-for advertising. That same month the Associated

Press voted to provide no more news to networks. Individual stations owned by AP member papers would be allowed to broadcast short bulletins, but must pay for them. The United Press and the International News Service adopted similar rules. Thus in the spring of 1933, news bulletins from AP, UP, or INS were available for a fee to some stations but not available on any terms to networks.

The networks faced a choice: they could give up the pretense of being news media—it was, at the time, scarcely more than a pretense except for special-event broadcasts—or gather their own news.

That fall both NBC and CBS made a start in the gathering of news.

The NBC effort was small, though surprising in results. Because of its leading position, NBC probably had less incentive than CBS toward reckless adventure. In any case, its effort consisted of the work of one man, A. A. ("Abe") Schechter. Originally hired by NBC to write publicity, he now became a news department and began to show what could be done by one man at a telephone. He asked publicity people at NBC affiliate stations to tip him off on local news events. Prompted by their tips or by newspaper stories, Schechter placed phone calls far and wide—to police chiefs, district attorneys, hospital directors, judges, governors. He discovered that virtually anyone except the President of the United States would accept a phone call "from NBC" at almost any time under almost any circumstance. During an uprising of Iowa farmers, which threatened to develop into a milk strike and to bring action by the national guard, a group of reporters waited outside the office of Governor Clyde Herring of Iowa for news of his decision. But a call from Schechter "from Lowell Thomas's office at NBC" was put through at once and Schechter got the story. Governor Albert Ritchie of Maryland didn't wait for calls; he got the habit of placing calls to NBC himself. During the murder-rape trial of the "Scottsboro boys" the judge on several occasions accepted calls "from NBC" in chambers and provided newsworthy comments on the case, helping Schechter to scoop all newspapers. The publicity world was an important Schechter source; he became the darling of press agents. He constantly rewarded the faithful with tickets or promises of tickets to Rudy Vallee broadcasts, which appeared to have incalculable value. Day after day Schechter gathered enough material for the Lowell Thomas program on NBC-blue plus an item or two for Sunday evening use by Walter Winchell—a gossip columnist on NBC-blue who was aspiring to a more significant news role. Roy Howard of the Scripps-Howard newspapers and United Press apparently thought that Schechter was taking items from newspapers and phoned NBC vice president Frank Mason, Schechter's superior, to express his suspicions. Mason, fearing the worst, called Schechter with nervous inquiries. "Are you sure that we are getting it all legitimately?" But Schechter always had a detailed log of phone calls: for every news item used there was at least one phone call.

His one-man news operation, launched on the spur of the moment, had its quarters in a storage room ("a kind of broom closet") at 711 Fifth Avenue, ventilated via an airshaft which also served the NBC carpentry shop. Each evening Schechter would pick wood shavings from his hair and head home to listen to Lowell Thomas, the authoritative newscaster with his worldwide sources.[1]

CBS, determined to match and outperform the firmly established NBC, made a more elaborate attempt at news-gathering—and got into trouble. Paul W. White, a former UP editor, was encouraged to set up a full-fledged CBS news organization. He established correspondents in all major cities, many of them "stringers"—reporters paid only for material actually used. White negotiated exchange arrangements with various overseas news agencies. Within weeks he had a functioning operation; the Kaltenborn and Carter broadcasts were kept well supplied with items. But precisely because the CBS efforts represented a large-scale challenge, newspapers began a determined CBS boycott. Sponsors of CBS programs began to experience a publicity blackout. Some considered canceling, or moving to NBC. CBS became fearful. Before the end of the year it had a chance to join in a compromise, and seized it. The compromise move was initiated by NBC.

In December 1933 the Hotel Biltmore in New York City was the scene of a meeting attended by representatives of NBC, CBS, and the National Association of Broadcasters on the one hand; and of AP, UP, INS, and the American Newspaper Publishers Association on the other. The result was a peace treaty, prudently called "the Biltmore program." [2] It virtually sabotaged—or tried to—the possibilities of broadcast news.

CBS agreed to disband its news service. NBC, it was understood, would refrain from building a news-gathering organization.

At network expense a Press-Radio Bureau was to be set up to supply broadcasters with bulletins from AP, UP, and INS, with no item to exceed

1. Schechter, *Reminiscences*, pp. 6–12; Schechter, *I Live on Air*, pp. 3–15.
2. White, *The American Radio*, p. 45.

30 words. These bulletins would be sufficient in quantity to make two five-minute newscasts daily—one in the morning at 9:30 or later; the other in the evening at 9:00 or later. The hours were intended to protect newspapers from radio competition. The bureau might authorize occasional bulletins at other times for news of "transcendent" importance; these bulletins would always be worded so as to refer listeners to newspapers for full information.

Radio commentators were to confine themselves to "generalization and background" and avoid spot news. This was later clarified: they were forbidden to use news less than twelve hours old. Non-network stations could join the plan by sharing the cost. Commercial sponsorship of Press-Radio Bureau bulletins was forbidden under any circumstances.

The Press-Radio Bureau, duly organized, announced a starting date of March 1, 1934. Patently designed to keep radio news on a leash, the plan was amended several times to meet indignant objections. Meanwhile many radio stations showed only scorn for the plan. Their attitude encouraged the formation of several independent news services to provide news to radio stations. One of these, Transradio, survived and prospered. A number of stations—including WOR, New York—subscribed to Transradio and scheduled extensive newscasts, many at hours forbidden under the Biltmore treaty. The Press-Radio Bureau had created a vacuum which was quickly filled.

The newspaper forces behind the Press-Radio Bureau, forgetting for a moment their zeal for freedom of the press, pondered how to get rid of the "outlaw" competition. The minutes of a Press-Radio Bureau executive meeting in March 1934—attended by Joseph V. Connolly of INS and Hugh Baillie of UP—tell us:

> Mr. Baillie declared that these outlaws should be squashed at the outset, and read a telegram from Mr. Howard in which he recommended the same procedure. Mr. Connolly said this was the attitude of INS and recommended that action not be put off. He further recommended that the question be settled in a friendly manner if possible. Mr. Baillie suggested that the newspaper, in a town where the radio station likes the outlaw service, try to make them see the light and if that wasn't possible make reprisals.[3]

But all this wasn't easy. Money intervened in various disconcerting ways. WOR, New York, seemed to be building a substantial audience with its

3. *Hearings: on Order No. 79 and No. 79A, FCC,* July-August 1941.

frequent Transradio newscasts and was even getting sponsors for them. Especially galling to the Press-Radio Bureau people was the fact that New York newspapers continued to carry the WOR program schedules. Didn't they understand the importance of making WOR "see the light?" The difficulty was that WOR, originally started by the Bamberger store of Newark, had been acquired (along with the store) by R. H. Macy, one of the most important New York department stores and leading newspaper advertiser. This apparently made newspapers think twice before squashing. The protests of the Bureau group availed nothing. Store-owned stations in other cities appeared to have a similar immunity. Roy Howard—a particular foe of radio—and others continued to talk about the need of "killing off outlaw news-gatherers," but by the end of 1934 it was clear they were losing the battle. The outlaws continued; Transradio thrived.[4]

An enticing complication entered the picture. Several potential sponsors, including Esso, began to express interest in sponsoring news broadcasts. The world was in turmoil and interest in news was growing. There were inquiries: would UP or INS be interested in supplying material? Ample funds would be available. There was talk of a four-times-a-day newscast to be called *Esso Reporter*. Such overtures prompted INS, at a Press-Radio Bureau meeting, to propose a startling new scheme for killing the outlaws: UP and INS would make their own news available for sponsored broadcasts.

On this high-comedy note, the anti-news treaty began to come apart. UP and INS began to sell their news to radio; eventually AP would follow suit. The Bureau continued for a few years to provide its impotent bulletins; they scarcely mattered. Meanwhile more and more newspapers applied for radio licenses or purchased existing stations; they were joining the enemy. News broadcasting grew; it had to. As Hitler mobilized and Mussolini moved troops into Somaliland, and rumblings came from Spain, the networks resumed news-gathering. Slowly they grew into news media. Half reluctantly they had met a challenge and moved forward.

TWENTY-FIVE PER CENT

Meanwhile they faced a still more serious threat, which had developed simultaneously. This had come from the world of education, with help from religious, labor, and farm groups.

4. Chester, "The Press-Radio War," *Public Opinion Quarterly*, Summer 1949.

Educators had been among the most avid broadcasting pioneers; in the early 1920's, scores of colleges and universities had launched stations. Financial pressures, unfavorable channel assignments, interference from other stations, and disgust over the increasing commercialization of the air had been factors edging educators out of the broadcasting spectrum. But some preferred to stay and do battle. Outmaneuvered for years by lobbyists for commercial broadcasters, they began their own pressure efforts, mainly through the National Committee on Education by Radio, organized in 1930.[1]

During the final months of the Hoover administration this committee labored unsuccessfully for the Fess bill, which called for reservation of 15 per cent of all channels for educational use. But with the victory of Franklin D. Roosevelt at the polls in 1932, the group raised its sights. Reform was in the air.

The news that Roosevelt wanted a new communications act to replace the Radio Act of 1927 stirred hopes. Actually, the administration had a limited purpose: to bring telephone and broadcasting under the same jurisdiction. Telephone matters had been under the Interstate Commerce Commission, which because of persistent railroad problems had generally been lax about the telephone. A "communications commission" was expected to correct this, as well as be alert to monopolistic trends, such as had plagued the first decade of broadcasting. Meanwhile the imminence of new legislation was seen by educators as their chance. To present their demands, they won two effective champions: Senator Robert F. Wagner of New York and Senator Henry D. Hatfield of West Virginia. The Wagner-Hatfield bill was offered as an amendment to the proposed communications act.

Among those who were indignant over the drift of broadcasting, none were more so than the militant group campaigning for Wagner-Hatfield. Many educators saw radio as an extraordinary educational resource that in a few years had been handed over to business control, with active help from the Federal Radio Commission. A flourishing rhetoric of "public service" had developed, but to the FRC this had been synonymous with service to advertisers. Educational broadcasters—considered by the FRC a "special interest"—had been squeezed into part-time channel assignments, in most cases confined to daytime hours and restricted to low power.

The Wagner-Hatfield bill proposed to meet this head-on. "To eliminate

1. See *A Tower in Babel*, pp. 261–4, 282–3.

monopoly," it provided that all existing station licenses would be "declared null and void 90 days following the effective date of this act." During the 90-day period a new distribution of channels would be made by the new commission, which would have to allot

> to educational, religious, agricultural, labor, cooperative, and similar non-profit-making associations one-fourth of all the radio broadcasting facilities within their jurisdiction.

These must be "equally as desirable as those assigned to profit-making persons, firms, or corporations."

The amendment had an additional and crucial provision. Many educational stations had been hard-pressed financially; some had begun to sell time to meet expenses. The Wagner-Hatfield amendment approved this by providing: "The licensee may sell such part of the allotted time as will make the station self-supporting." [2]

During the early months of 1934 educators and their non-profit allies put increasing pressure behind these proposals. The National Education Association gave the bill its blessing. Then, in May, a meeting on "Radio as a Cultural Agency" was staged in Washington. College presidents and deans, school superintendents, teachers, librarians, ministers, labor leaders, and representatives of parent-teacher groups met for two days of impassioned discussion. Dean Thomas E. Benner of the University of Illinois declared that the Depression had brought on a "sickness" of the national culture, and saw recapture of the radio channels as a necessary remedy.[3]

Later, in hearings before the Senate committee on interstate commerce, Father John B. Harney of the Paulist Fathers described the treatment given to educational radio as "beggarly and outrageous . . . in a country whose proudest boast is its devotion to the cause of education." He castigated the FRC for its frequent use of financial resource as a basis for allocating channels. "Oh yes—income, income—we will do everything we can for you." Such standards, he suggested, had created an "overlordship of mere commercialists whose dominant purpose is to accumulate wealth even at the cost of human decay." [4]

In an article published in *Forum* and entered in the *Congressional Record*, theatrical producer Eddie Dowling pictured the rise of commercial

2. *Congressional Record*, v. 78, pp. 8828–9.
3. Tyler (ed.), *Radio as a Cultural Agency*, p. 14.
4. *Federal Communications Commission*, pp. 185, 192.

broadcasting as a cultural disaster. For huge profits—protected by "swarming lobbies"—it had "sold its front page, sold its editorial page, sold anything and everything without reservation to keep that rich income coming in." [5]

Finally, on the Senate floor, co-sponsor Senator Hatfield attacked the commercial "pollution of the air." [6]

The bill won support and also determined opposition. "POWERFUL LOBBY THREATENS RADIO STRUCTURE," *Broadcasting* headlined, and castigated the "self-seeking reformers." [7] That Wagner-Hatfield should touch off indignation was to be expected. The bill would necessarily wipe out about a fourth of the commercial stations, all representing investments. Many of these had become bonanzas, while others showed signs of following the same course. Which would be blotted out? Nothing could have unified commercial broadcasters more effectively than the Wagner-Hatfield challenge. Some educators were dismayed by the anger it provoked; some blamed the backers of the bill for the growing rift between educator and commercial broadcaster. "A group of educators," said Levering Tyson, "did not throw down the gauntlet to the broadcasters; they just picked up a glove and slapped the industry in the face, and the scrap was on." [8]

In the Senate debate, opponents of Wagner-Hatfield shrewdly hammered at one issue. Among these was Senator C. C. Dill, often a spokesman for the local commercial broadcaster and co-author of the Radio Act of 1927. His purpose was to keep the pattern of the old law intact in the new. Many broadcasters, finding the Radio Act of 1927 congenial, shared this purpose. On the Senate floor Dill addressed himself to the advertising revenue authorized by Wagner-Hatfield. Dill expressed horror. Wasn't there too much advertising already? Wasn't everybody agreed on that? Now the educators proposed still more of it. "That," said Dill piously, "is not what the people of this country are asking for!" Thus he ingeniously turned the concern with "overcommercialization" into an argument for the status quo.

Yet he had touched a sensitive nerve. Educators themselves were far from united about this clause. Some disliked it. Their contradictory statements weakened the Wagner-Hatfield drive and opened the door to a

5. *Forum*, February 1934.
6. *Congressional Record*, v. 78, pp. 8829–36.
7. *Broadcasting*, May 15, 1934.
8. *Education on the Air* (1936), p. 63.

hallowed defensive maneuver. Clearly more study was needed, Dill told the Senate. The new commission should study the whole matter diligently, and be given instructions to that effect.

Wagner and Hatfield stuck to their guns. The FRC had had seven years for study and what had it produced? It was time, said Wagner, for Congress to set policy.[9]

In the end, in a fateful compromise, Congress handed the hot potato to the proposed Federal Communications Commission. The FCC was told to hold hearings and report back to Congress. Mollified by the clause, a number of legislators sympathetic to Wagner-Hatfield felt their obligations fulfilled. Under these circumstances Wagner-Hatfield came to a final floor vote and lost, 42–23. The compromise cleared the way for the Communications Act of 1934, which became law in the same week. It represented an almost total victory for the status quo. As requested by the Roosevelt administration, it transferred telephone jurisdiction to the new commission, but otherwise it was largely a re-enactment of the Radio Act of 1927.

The new seven-man Federal Communications Commission took office in July 1934, and that fall duly held hearings on the reserved-channel idea. For the National Association of Broadcasters, managing director Philip G. Loucks described commercial stations as so extraordinarily benevolent that any change in the existing system would be a disaster for the "vast majority of all religious, educational, charitable, civic and similar organizations." The networks testified on their contributions to education.[10] The reserved-channel campaigners also had their inning. Lee de Forest was quoted, describing current radio as a "huckstering orgy." But the drive had lost steam. The hearings were a formal interment of the cause. The FCC promptly reported back to Congress that commercial broadcasters had ample time for educational and other non-profit needs and were most eager to serve them. All that was needed now was "cooperation in good faith . . . under the direction and supervision of the Commission." To start it, the FCC called a conference, which created a Federal Radio Education Committee, which in turn appointed subcommittees which made studies and began issuing pamphlets about the possibilities of co-operative broadcasting. The activity went on for years.[11] To some it seemed that

9. *Congressional Record*, v. 78, p. 8831.
10. Curiously, NBC considered *Amos 'n' Andy* one of them, and as evidence arranged for the comedians to perform one of their sketches in person before the commission. *Education on the Air* (1949), p. 75.
11. Titles included *Local Cooperative Broadcasting, College Radio Workshops,* and

educators had been skillfully shunted into busy-work. This was true, but not the whole truth.

In winning their victory, networks and stations had made promises that were hostages. The very completeness of their victory put them glaringly in the spotlight. They would have to deliver. Dignitaries with such titles as "public service director" now became a feature at stations and networks, for liaison with non-profit groups. At some stations the same person was "publicity director," suggesting a prevalent constellation of values. But some of the public service directors had wide educational backgrounds and were anxious to develop programs of vigor and substance. Thankful for whatever combination of forces had brought them within the shelter of well-financed organizations but charged with pleasantly non-commercial duties, they worked zealously with the educator. They became a force for change within the broadcasting structure.

But behind all this was the plain fact that the educator had been defeated. Except for thirty-odd stations—of low power, and in most cases licensed for the daytime only—still operated by colleges and universities, the educator stood on the sidelines of radio. If he entered the main arena it was not as decision-maker but as suppliant. Final decisions were made by broadcasting executives whom he seldom, if ever, saw. The commercial broadcaster, holding the profitable channels, had become the dispenser of largesse, giving annual statements to the effect that he had donated "fifty-eight thousand dollars' worth of time" to non-profit causes, although in theory the air so price-tagged was publicly owned.

Among these top executives some seemed warmly inclined toward educators, churchmen, labor leaders, social workers, and the rest of the non-profit world. Others were condescending or openly scornful. In either case, final actions often seemed to depend on events elsewhere—in Congress or at the FCC. It was during the 1930–31 agitation over the Fess bill that CBS had launched its *American School of the Air* and that the *University of Chicago Round Table* began on WMAQ, Chicago. It was during the Wagner-Hatfield battle that this same series won a berth on NBC-red, and that NBC-blue became interested in an idea proposed by George V. Denny—a weekly *America's Town Meeting of the Air*. The timing suggested that these might be reactions to temporary pressures. What if the pressures subsided?

Public Service Broadcasting, all by Leonard Power; *The Groups Tune In*, by Frank Ernest Hill; *Forums on the Air*, by Paul H. Sheats.

All this focused special interest on the FCC, whose supervision was to bring on an era of "cooperation in good faith." What was the FCC prepared to do? What could it accomplish? And how?

The FCC inherited from the FRC an undistinguished tradition. The old commission had sometimes operated on a ward-heeler level, and ended its career in character. In its last two weeks, holding open house for friends, it granted nearly 150 applications for increases in power and changes in frequency. Many requests were approved within twenty-four hours of receipt.[1]

The new seven-member FCC that took office in July 1934 as defender of the public interest was an unknown quantity. It seemed generally conservative. Some members were clearly political appointees. Since the law required a bipartisan commission—not more than four could be of one party—political considerations necessarily came into play. Two members, Chairman E. O. Sykes and Commissioner Thad H. Brown, were holdovers from the FRC; the rest were new appointees.

Ironically, the most New Deal-minded of the new commissioners was a Republican, George Henry Payne. A Bull Mooser of earlier times, a scholar who had written a well-regarded *History of Journalism in the United States,* he brought to his task historical perspective on monopoly problems. Soon after his appointment he began making statements on the subject, as well as criticizing broadcasters for their programming, much of which he considered "silly and degrading." He seemed determined to do something about it. This brought a novel note of activism to the commission.

Payne told an audience at Harvard: "There is a belief that our predecessor, the old Radio Commission, was dominated by the industry it was supposed to control. I am very happy to say that such is not now the case. . . ."[2] But what could Payne, even if he found allies at the FCC, accomplish?

The tasks that faced the FCC in regard to broadcasting can be briefly summarized. Its powers were substantial, but limited. Its chief task was to act on applications for licenses and license renewals. It could say yes or

1. *Broadcasting,* July 1, 1934.
2. *Congressional Record,* v. 79, p. 8181.

no. By law no license could run for more than three years, so the task of
saying yes or no would come up at least once every three years for each
station. Actually, in the early months of the FCC, it came more frequently,
for the FCC at first followed the FRC practice of issuing six-month licenses.

A licensee, as under the old law, acquired no property right in the channel assigned to him. He had its use for the time of the license, and no
claim beyond it. He signed a waiver of "any claim to the use of any particular frequency or of the ether as against the regulatory power of the
United States. . . ." [3]

Toward the end of his license period he could apply for a renewal. If
the FCC felt the "public interest, convenience, or necessity" would be
served, it renewed the license.

Throughout the license period the FCC had no right to censor. It could
not forbid a broadcast or part of it.

But at renewal time the FCC could consider past performance—including programming—to decide whether "public interest, convenience, or necessity" would be served by continuation of the station. Disagreement developed later over this point, but in 1934 it was not disputed. *Broadcasting*
stated the case editorially. The commission, it said,

> cannot censor programs. But it can consider the merit of programs in
> passing upon applications of stations for renewal of their licenses, just
> as it did in deleting the stations operated by Brinkley, Baker and
> Shuler.[4]

If denied a renewal, a station could appeal to the courts. Since failure to
renew was rare, court decisions were rare, but tended to uphold the commission.

Thus the FCC's licensing power was essentially a life-or-death authority.

Its grimness was its main difficulty. A weapon so total was hard to use.
The tendency had been to renew licenses automatically, sometimes with
ceremonial reprimands.

3. *Communications Act of 1934,* Title III, Secs. 301, 304. See Appendix B.
4. *Broadcasting,* January 15, 1934. The cases cited were those of John R. Brinkley
(renewal denied, 1930), who used his station KFKB, Milford, Kansas, to promote
goat-gland rejuvenation operations; Dr. Norman Baker (renewal denied, 1931), who
used his KTNT, Muscatine, Iowa, to promote a cancer "cure" and assail the medical
profession; and Rev. Robert P. Shuler (renewal denied, 1931), who used his KGEF,
Los Angeles, for attacks on religious and other groups. In each case the commission
action was based on program content.

As the FCC took office, there were 593 broadcasting stations in the United States as well as 722 experimental stations of various kinds, including television and facsimile stations.[5] There were also various other kinds of stations, including amateur stations. Altogether some fifty thousand licenses claimed the FCC's attention. Within the broadcast band alone the bulk was so huge that the FCC inevitably made decisions about stations no commissioner had ever seen or heard. It had to exercise its life-or-death authority in a near-vacuum.

Thin strands of evidence were available. One consisted of complaints, which sometimes assumed unwarranted importance. A complaint went into the station file. "Any complaints?" was the question that came up as station renewals were considered, in batches. An innocuous schedule could mean prompt renewal. A provocative one could bring delays. At times the system seemed to encourage the crackpot.

Another strand was provided by questionnaires. It is not surprising that this device was used; it seemed to offer some index of station performance, and had been adopted by the FRC in its first year. Stations were asked to fill out report forms, which had become a fixture. Under the incoming FCC, the station had to report programming time devoted to various categories, such as "entertainment," "educational," "religious," "agricultural," "fraternal." These presumably helped the commission spot the presence or absence of public interest, convenience, or necessity.

The questionnaires—even with truthful answers—produced deceptions and obfuscations. What did it all mean? An "entertainment" item could be a thing of genius or trash. Formsmanship apparently required items under "educational," "religious," "agricultural," "fraternal," which were considered license insurance but could also be works of substance or trash. The report forms tended to put commission-station relations on a make-believe basis. Yet the size of the task probably made their use inevitable. No doubt they sometimes yielded useful data. The forms tended to get longer.

If such forms were in theory a basis for many decisions, the real basis was often different. According to Rosel Hyde, who in a commission career of decades rose from FRC file clerk to FCC chairman, relations with broadcasters in the early years were mainly "on a first-name basis."[6] Many licensees—or their Washington representatives—kept in close touch with commissioners. The commissioners knew the men, not the programs.

5. *FCC Reports* (1935), pp. 5–6.
6. Interview, Rosel Hyde.

This close relationship opened doors to corruptions subtle and unsubtle. Affable industry representatives were a constant presence. Two FRC commissioners, Henry A. Bellows and Sam Pickard, found their positions a springboard to CBS vice presidencies. Other commissioners, perhaps as a result of this, performed as though they were candidates for vice presidential berths. In July 1935 FCC employees had to be warned not to accept gifts or favors from the industry.

Besides yes-or-no decisions on licenses, the commission had to make decisions on power, hours of operation, and dial position. Here personal contact did its most telling work. Another set of decisions related to sales of stations. Theoretically a license could not be sold; the equipment was the only tangible merchandise. Yet approval had been given to sales in which the sales price was many times the value of the equipment. Clearly it was a coveted spot on the dial that was being bought, even though this might be camouflaged by terms like "good will." Equally clearly the practice had been encouraged by a tradition of prompt approvals.

The radio world as contemplated by the incoming FCC was a complex tangle. While much of it had a boom atmosphere, many low-power stations lived at subsistence level. The NRA code for the broadcasting field—the National Association of Broadcasters had a leading role in writing it—had set $15 per week as the minimum salary to be paid by small stations (i. e. having not more than ten employees) and $20 elsewhere. Low as these minimums were, they had forced many small stations to raise wages. At KWCR, Cedar Rapids, the owner was the only staff member getting more than the required minimum; every one else had to have a raise.[7] Most surviving educational stations also lived a marginal existence. High-powered stations, on the other hand, were likely to be money-makers—some, like WLW, Cincinnati, on an impressive scale. The networks were prosperous enough to have set other national network plans simmering, but two major efforts had collapsed in 1934.[8] The established positions of NBC and CBS, who had the dominant high-powered stations in major markets, made such ventures risky, although the Mutual Broadcasting Sys-

7. Interview, Leo Cole, Cedar Rapids. The station became WMT.
8. One was the Amalgamated Broadcasting System, headed by Ed Wynn. It had enlisted many artists but no sponsors. After lavish opening revelry and publicity it collapsed in a squabble over assets, which had dwindled to a Rolls Royce used to impress investors. The other was a project of George McClelland, former NBC vice president who resigned to form the new network. He was first rumored to have backing from William Randolph Hearst, then from Metro-Goldwyn-Mayer. His suicide ended the venture. See *Radio Art,* May 1, June 15, October 15, 1934.

tem, launched in September 1934, managed to survive. Regional networks were also being formed; most did little or no programming, and were intended as time-sale packages for regional sponsors. In large cities foreign-language broadcasting had become a thriving business. The main languages were Italian, German, Yiddish, Polish, but many others were represented. Such a station often dealt with each language group through a "time broker," who bought a block of time and resold it piecemeal to companies selling in his language market.

From this maelstrom of entrepreneurship complaints came to the commission in rising numbers. The chief subject was "false, fraudulent, and misleading advertising." Postal authorities had stepped up vigilance against fraud by mail, and this seems to have diverted some quack remedies into radio, as being safer territory. KNX, Hollywood, was famous for its parade of nostrums. Here an FCC field investigator reported forty violations of the Pure Food and Drug Act.[9] Complaints about stations also had to do with unfairness, bad taste, rigged contests, political bias, and other allegations.

While the ultimate weapon was non-renewal of a license, the FCC had at its disposal a device for exerting influence that had evolved under the FRC. When used, it usually aroused rage.

In the early 1930's the air bristled with lotteries. In answer to complaints, the commission said it had no right to forbid lotteries; that would be censorship. But a few days later it made an additional statement:

> There exists a doubt that such broadcasts are in the public interest. Complaints from a substantial number of listeners against any broadcasting station presenting such programs will result in the station's application for renewal of license being set for a hearing.[10]

The threat of hearings—and perhaps parades of hostile witnesses—was eloquent. Radio lotteries began to melt away. They were later outlawed by the Communications Act.

In 1934 the technique was used again. With repeal of prohibition, liquor advertising appeared on many stations. Protests followed: should radio be urging the young to drink whiskey? Again the commission said it could not forbid such advertising; that would be censorship. Again it followed with another statement. It reminded broadcasters that the radio audience included children. Therefore—

9. *Congressional Record*, v. 83, p. 149.
10. Quoted, Brindze, *Not To Be Broadcast*, pp. 166–7.

The commission will designate for hearing the renewal applications of all stations unmindful of the foregoing, and they will be required to make a showing that their continued operation will serve the public interest, convenience, and necessity.[11]

Once more the announcement had effect. Rather than face hearings, broadcasters canceled liquor advertising. A workable technique was evolving, which became known as the raised eyebrow.

It brought howls of anger. "Censorship!" said the broadcasters. They complained that the commission was telling them what *not* to do. Such hints or warnings, said ex-commissioner Henry Bellows, were a "flagrant violation of the very law" the commission was supposed to administer.[12] But the commission could argue—and did—that it was merely making clear its standards. To keep them secret until renewal time would scarcely be fair. Broadcasters had often demanded that the commission spell out its interpretation of "public interest, convenience, or necessity"—a phrase not defined in the law—and this had now begun, item by item. But how far could the raised eyebrow go?

The FCC, contemplating its task, must often have felt that its labor was a vast irrelevance. It considered renewals of hundreds of stations in cities and towns far and wide. In so doing, it glanced at "public service" claims: time for Red Cross, Junior Chamber of Commerce, Seventh-Day Adventists. Of some value—perhaps. But had they anything to do with what was riveting the attention of the American people?

The FCC was concerning itself with sideshows, broadcast in fringe periods to handfuls of listeners.

The Communications Act of 1934, re-enacting a 1927 law with only minor changes, was based on a premise that had been obsolete in 1927 and by 1934 was totally invalid: that American broadcasting was a local responsibility exercised by individual station licensees.

The myth held attractions. It dovetailed with the cherished idea of local autonomy in such matters as education. But while the law went on pretending that the autonomy existed in broadcasting, control had been ceded to others—executives at networks, advertising agencies, and sponsors, many of whom had no idea what was in a station license and did not think they had any reason to care. The main arena was scarcely touched by the licensing and renewal procedure.

11. *Congressional Record*, v. 78, pp. 2646–7.
12. *Harper's Magazine*, November 1935.

Day by day the FCC had evidence of the irrelevance of its work to that main arena.

In 1934–35 the United States faced tense issues at home and abroad. To some extent network radio was becoming a forum for probing them, but not yet in an organized or balanced way. *The University of Chicago Round Table* was attempting discussions in which opposing views were represented; on May 3, 1935, it was joined in this attempt by *America's Town Meeting of the Air,* scheduled as an experiment for six summer programs. But the idea of balance was still a rarity. Commander Clark's *Voice of the Crusaders* was still on the air, taking its cues entirely from its business backers. CBS scheduled a *Forum of Liberty* sponsored by *Liberty* magazine; on each program the executive of a major American corporation presented his views. Each received a dramatized introduction fulsomely narrated by Edwin C. Hill (of *The Human Side of the News*) and written by Merrill Denison. Each broadcast was preceded by a banquet in the Peacock Room of the Waldorf-Astoria where the guest tycoon found himself on a dais beside Bernarr Macfadden, millionaire health faddist who owned *Liberty* as well as *True Story, True Confessions, True Detective Mysteries,* and *Physical Culture.* It was expected that the guest tycoon would prove helpful to Macfadden's presidential ambitions and would meanwhile buy advertising in *Liberty.* The latter objective was achieved; more than one corporation offered to buy pages in *Liberty* if its president could have access to the *Forum of Liberty* network platform. The *Forum of Liberty* platform was, in a sense, being auctioned off to large corporations.[13]

CBS also broadcast the weekly *Ford Sunday Evening Hour.* Presumably sponsored to promote car sales, it offered classical music with "intermission talks" by Ford executive William J. Cameron. He eulogized Henry Ford and his ideas and philosophized on American institutions. Within this framework he managed to attack unemployment insurance, surplus profits taxes, and other New Deal measures or proposals. He spoke scathingly of government interference with business. The fact that Ford was refusing to subscribe to the NRA automobile code gave his words strong political meaning. Ford is said to have sent in two years more than five million copies of the talks to listeners asking for them. The talks aroused constant indignation from labor groups, which challenged Cameron's statistics and arguments but had no platform to answer him.

13. Interview, Merrill Denison.

Throughout 1935 international tension grew. It brought added pressures to American broadcasting. In March, Hitler ordered conscription. Germany became an armed camp. With huge rallies Hitler was stirring a popular delirium, while bringing all media in Germany under rigid control, purging opposition, and fomenting anti-Semitic violence. Over CBS Alexander Woollcott, critic and raconteur, was broadcasting a weekly Sunday evening series entitled *The Town Crier,* sponsored by Cream of Wheat. He devoted a program to acid comments on Hitler. His sponsor, perhaps troubled by listener protests, asked Woollcott to refrain from such broadcasts. Woollcott would not promise to do so, and the series was canceled. Woollcott said any one "with the courage of a diseased mouse" would have done as he did, but few were doing it. In the industry it had become an assumption that the company paying the bill could control content.[14]

Thus sponsorship and related censorship tended to exert editorial control over key periods.

Most sponsored programming on networks was "non-political" and was called "entertainment." To many people this term meant that the FCC need give it no thought; it was just for relaxation. But was its "non-political" nature perhaps a political fact of importance? Were relief and radio the equivalents of bread and circuses? To James Rorty, who had been a writer for the Batten, Barton, Durstine & Osborn advertising agency, American radio seemed "a conspiracy of silence regarding all those aspects of the individual and social life that do not contribute to objectives of the advertiser." [15]

To George Henry Payne—eventually to other commissioners too—there was something curious about the way the real arena of broadcasting had become a network domain over which the FCC had no control and which sold the time and its control to others even more remote. No matter how popular and skillful the resulting programming, was the slippage of control—away from the licensee and licenser—something to be pondered in relation to "public interest, convenience, or necessity?"

Such questions exercised Payne. Under lax administration, he told listeners in a broadcast over WEVD, New York, "private monopoly, without warrant of law, establishes itself and, too late, the public bestirs itself to recover ground that should never have been lost." [16]

---

14. Brindze, *Not To Be Broadcast,* pp. 111, 196–214.
15. Rorty, *Our Master's Voice,* pp. 73–4.
16. Quoted, Frost, *Is American Radio Democratic?,* pp. 137–8.

During the early months of the FCC numerous Payne speeches and statements were entered in the *Congressional Record*.[17] In Congress and at the FCC there began to be talk about monopoly trends and the need for a closer look at them and the mechanisms behind them.

Such talk made the industry edgy. Payne and his eyebrow were watched with uneasiness and resentment. How far would he go?

For the moment, not far. For the moment it was largely a skirmish of words. In the first months of the FCC, renewals and transfers slid through routinely. No stands were made—not yet.

Commercial broadcasting was firmly in the saddle. It had important victories behind it. Attacks from press and education had been routed. The legislative battle had ended in an industry triumph: a status quo undisturbed. Time sales were up. Sales of radio sets, which had slumped during 1931–32, had begun climbing again:[18]

1932	$200,000,000
1933	300,000,000
1934	350,000,000

In the fall of 1934 the annual meeting of the National Association of Broadcasters took place in Cincinnati. It was jubilation time. *Variety* reporter Ben Bodec had been at other NAB meetings, but found this one different. Even the year before, at White Sulphur Springs, the broadcasters had seemed a cautious bunch, uncertain of tomorrow. Most had stayed at the convention hotel, but at dinner time many went across the street for the fifty-cent blue plate special. In Cincinnati—one year later—it was a different universe. Cadillacs and beautiful girls were everywhere, and the liquor flowed. The broadcasters were on top of the world.[19]

Yet that world was due for change. Forces for change were at work everywhere: in the minds of people ground by years of Depression; in currents of violence sweeping through continents; also, in research laboratories.

17. *Congressional Record*, v. 79, pp. 14123, 8181; v. 80, p. 2454; v. 81 appendix, pp. 35, 817; v. 83, p. 149.
18. *Broadcasting Yearbook* (1939), p. 11.
19. Interview, Ben Bodec.

ABOUT READY

At the apex—as broadcasting entered 1935—sat David Sarnoff, president of RCA. His company owned two broadcasting networks, a worldwide message service, manufacturing facilities, and research laboratories that were devising future worlds. Over it all, Sarnoff had tight control.

In the brief time since General Electric and Westinghouse had been forced—in 1932, by government anti-trust action—to relinquish control of RCA, the company had virtually become a personal empire of David Sarnoff. Having risen from office boy to president through many jobs at all levels, he had reached the top with an extraordinarily detailed knowledge of every phase of the operation. Late in 1933 he had led his executive army and broadcasting personnel into the newly erected Radio City. Now established on its fifty-third floor, he was rapidly becoming a remote executive. The scope of the empire probably made this essential. He saw a few key executives; he delegated. If things went wrong, he ordered a gathering of data, made a rapid and exhaustive study and, when he felt ready, moved with full force, making shifts and changes as necessary, then withdrawing again to isolation.

Sarnoff had few friends. Among them was Albert Lasker. Sarnoff did not encourage intimacy. Even key executives were not inclined to pick up the phone and call Sarnoff about a problem. They addressed him in formal memos which—they knew—must not exceed a page, although his memos might run to many pages. On their memos Sarnoff might pencil brief answers—"Yes!"—"No!"—or "PSM," meaning "please see me." An appointment was a sort of audience. When angry, Sarnoff could show an icy reserve more frightening than an explosion of anger. The back of his neck would get red. When he spoke, it was usually without the slightest hesitation.[1]

The neatness of his desk suggested to visitors a well-organized mind. The neatness was a fifty-third floor feature. Sarnoff's executive style required a less orderly situation at lower levels. Asked by Edward L. Bernays—whom Sarnoff retained in 1936 as public relations counsel—for an organization chart, Sarnoff answered, "This is a company of men, not of charts." Sarnoff avoided defining lines of authority. He felt he could in this way encourage competition. It was as though he wanted to see who would scrap his way to the top, as he himself had done in a remarkably aggres-

1. Tebbel, *David Sarnoff*, p. 22.

sive and resourceful career. The technique had values, but Bernays found it damaging in its effects at NBC. People constantly pushed each other about, jockeying for position. "I have seldom seen such infighting and such waste of manpower, of time and energy." [2]

While physically close to NBC—in the same Radio City building—Sarnoff had a far more obsessive interest in the manufacturing and research activities of RCA, and the visions of tomorrow emerging from them. At NBC there was a resulting feeling of absentee ownership, and a growing morale problem. One complaint was that NBC profits—which were a subject of rumor, because RCA no longer published them separately—went into other RCA projects. This was true, but only meant that Sarnoff had less parochial concerns. He identified himself totally with the great future toward which he saw RCA moving. His ambitions were RCA's ambitions. Financially he did not reward himself in the baronial Lasker style. The important thing to Sarnoff was the firm control by which he could steer RCA toward visions taking shape in his mind. These visions were always clothed with an aura of rightness and destiny. Nothing must obstruct them.

Among elements of a future world taking shape in RCA laboratories nothing absorbed Sarnoff's attention more completely than television. For several years it had been "about ready." Under Vladimir Zworykin, a television laboratory pioneer, RCA made progress. So did others, and the possibility of patent struggles loomed, but Sarnoff was a veteran in such battles. Meanwhile, since 1932, NBC had been doing experimental telecasts from the Empire State Building. As 1935 began, Sarnoff felt the time had come for major moves.

Television could establish itself only if there were industry-wide standards, with set-makers and telecasters all using the same system. Sarnoff now wanted the FCC to adopt standards—based, he hoped and expected, on the RCA system—and to allocate the needed spectrum space.

In April 1935 Sarnoff made the dramatic announcement that RCA was ready to put a million dollars into television program demonstrations. The FCC, prodded by the RCA announcement, prepared for intensive study of the future of broadcasting—including television—with hearings to be held the following year. It invited testimony. In his usual meticulous fashion, Sarnoff was getting ready for his hour.

But there were thorns in his side. They included several inventors who,

2. Bernays, *Biography of an Idea*, pp. 436–7.

in an age in which corporation research seemed destined to take over the role of innovation, still insisted on inventing things on their own, in the Marconi tradition.

One was Philo T. Farnsworth. Child of a large Mormon farm family, Philo had never encountered electricity until he was fourteen and his family got a Delco system. He at once knew how it worked and applied electricity to his mother's handcranked washing machine. He became an ardent reader of electrical journals. In 1922 at high school in Rigby, on the upper Snake River in Idaho, he staggered his science teacher by asking advice on an electronic television system he was planning. The boy said he had been reading about systems involving mechanical wheels and considered those doomed; covering several blackboards with diagrams to show how it might be done electronically, he asked, should he go ahead? The baffled science teacher encouraged him. Philo, thin and with an undernourished, pinched look, worked his way through college with a patchwork of jobs including radio repair and, one year, work on a Salt Lake City community chest drive. He told George Everson, professional fundraiser from California who was helping organize the campaign, about his television ideas, and Everson took the youth back to California and set him up with equipment in an apartment—first in Los Angeles, later in San Francisco—while Everson belabored financiers for funds. Philo worked with the blinds drawn, stirring suspicions that led to a raid by police. They found strange glass tubes but not the expected distillery. Philo had his first successes in 1927 when he transmitted various graphic designs including a dollar sign, which Everson thought "jumped out at us on the screen." Switching to bits of film, they used the Dempsey-Tunney fight (the one in which Tunney was knocked down for the famous "long count") and Mary Pickford combing her hair in the silent *The Taming of the Shrew;* she combed it a thousand times that year for Farnsworth television. Applying for an electronic television patent, Farnsworth took RCA by surprise. Its attorneys contested the application, and in interference proceedings grilled Farnsworth for hours, but could not shake him. In August 1930 Philo Farnsworth, aged twenty-four, got his patent. Early in 1931 Vladimir Zworykin of RCA traveled to California to visit Philo's laboratory and have a look; he appeared impressed but was quoted as saying there wasn't anything RCA would need. Then Sarnoff came; RCA would not need anything young Farnsworth had done, said Sarnoff. But apparently RCA already felt it would have to come to terms with Philo Farnsworth.[3]

Another problem was Edwin Howard Armstrong. Armstrong had known Sarnoff since the days before the first World War, when the young Armstrong, commuting from his Yonkers home by motorcycle, had studied under Michael Pupin at Columbia and invented a new receiver circuit, which won him world fame—but no money—before he even graduated. The young Sarnoff had been among those who came to evaluate it; they got along. From then on their careers were strangely linked. During and after the war Armstrong invented other sensational circuits and in 1922 sold one to RCA and was suddenly a millionaire. RCA also got first refusal on his next invention.[4]

"I wish," said Sarnoff to Armstrong one day, "that someone would come up with a little black box to eliminate static." Marconi's invention of wireless had been in a little black box; Armstrong understood the implication and liked the challenge. He had been thinking along the same line.

The world lay before him. He married Sarnoff's secretary. He accepted a Columbia University research appointment at $1 a year and began working ceaselessly at his own expense in the basement of Philosophy Hall, occasionally emerging to read brilliant papers at scientific gatherings—a tall, lanky figure with a drawling voice. When he argued with opponents, he was inclined to demolish them, and he won important enemies, including De Forest. But mostly he just worked.

Ten years passed. Late in 1933 Armstrong took out four patents and notified Sarnoff that the little black box was ready. Sarnoff and various RCA engineers made the trip to the Columbia campus. What they found was not exactly a black box but two rooms full of equipment representing an entire new radio system—"frequency modulation," FM. Not just an invention, said Sarnoff at one point, but "a revolution."

RCA decided on field tests. In March 1934 Armstrong was invited to install his transmitter equipment in the Empire State tower. The FM receiver was placed seventy miles away on Long Island. The log of the first day, June 16, 1934, included a prophetic notation by an engineer. A new era, he wrote, "is now upon us." Results exceeded Armstrong's claims. De-

3. Everson, *The Story of Television: The Life of Philo T. Farnsworth*, pp. 15–160.
4. The following is based on Lessing, *Man of High Fidelity*, and other sources as mentioned. The circuit sold to RCA was the superregenerative circuit. See *A Tower in Babel*, pp. 47, 65–6, 77–8.

fying thunder and lightning, FM transmitted a range of sound never before heard, and was virtually static-free.

The tests went on, reports were written and studied. Armstrong waited. Then, in April 1935, he was "politely" asked to remove his equipment from the Empire State Building. That same month RCA announced its allocation of $1,000,000 for television tests. A wave of publicity heralded the imminence of television, as the FCC prepared for crucial decisions on the spectrum.

Armstrong became fearful. He had worked more than a decade on FM. Since receiving his patents, he had maintained public silence on the subject for two years, partly because he felt he owed this to RCA, and partly because RCA seemed the one organization able to accomplish the revolution FM called for. Now the sudden flurry of RCA television moves, accompanied by total silence on FM, confirmed a feeling he had already acquired: the company hierarchy wanted no part of frequency modulation. Was RCA intent on sidetracking—even sabotaging—his invention? Armstrong became convinced that it was.

He acted with resolution. He decided on a public demonstration, to be staged at the November 1935 meeting of the Institute of Radio Engineers. It was announced that Armstrong would read a paper on his latest work; the demonstration itself would be a surprise.

He prepared for months with the help of his friend Randolph Runyon, whose amateur station in Yonkers was adapted especially for the demonstration. Final checking was still in progress an hour before the meeting. As Armstrong began his paper, he gave no hint of what was in store. A message was handed to him: "Keep talking. Runyon has burned out generator." Armstrong kept talking. Finally a signal came that all was ready, and Armstrong drawled: "Now suppose we have a little demonstration." As the receiver groped through space, the audience heard a sound that would become familiar to FM listeners. In the words of Lawrence Lessing, Armstrong's biographer, there was a

> roaring in the loudspeaker like surf on a desolate beach, until the new station was tuned in with a dead, unearthly silence, as if the whole apparatus had been abruptly turned off. Suddenly out of the silence came Runyon's supernaturally clear voice: "This is amateur station W2AG at Yonkers, New York, operating on frequency modulation at two and a half meters." A hush fell over the large audience.[5]

5. Lessing, *Man of High Fidelity*, p. 209.

The demonstration included music and other items. A glass of water was poured in Yonkers. In New York it sounded like a glass of water—not, as in AM, like a waterfall.

In the spring of 1936, Armstrong presented to the FCC the case for spectrum allocations for FM. RCA, pressing solely for television allocations, was represented not only by Sarnoff but by C. B. Jolliffe, who a few weeks earlier had been the FCC chief engineer but was now suddenly an RCA executive. The RCA witnesses hammered at one theme: the readiness of television and its needs in the spectrum. They did not mention FM. The battleground was the upper frequencies, where both inventions needed elbow room. The battle was joined.

The policies pursued by Sarnoff throughout this period were in the interests of RCA as he saw them. He saw television as an invention "about ready" to take its place beside radio as a feature in every home. RCA had invested in television large sums from radio earnings, and counted on continued earnings to carry the work forward. FM was seen as an invention that could only disrupt the structure of radio and plunge it into years of readjustment and loss. FM posed a threat not only to the status quo in radio, but to funds needed for television. RCA was therefore not inclined to make any move helpful to FM. Because of RCA's position in the industry, its lack of interest loomed as a fatal road block. To Armstrong it was "sabotage" of a major invention.

When he asked the FCC for a license for an experimental FM station, the request was at first denied. With demonstration and argument, Armstrong persisted. He got his license. He cashed a block of his RCA stock and began to build a 50,000-watt FM station at Alpine, New Jersey, across the river from Yonkers. He himself climbed around the huge antenna tower, supervising each detail. It was the start of a long and bitter war. He was tackling a giant.

RCA prepared for its million-dollar television program demonstrations. It was not alone in the field. Farnsworth had won backing from Philco and moved to Philadelphia to continue his television experiments there. Another young genius, Allen B. Dumont, was making progress. In Los Angeles there were tests by the Don Lee organization. Various patent issues, still unresolved, would have to be settled before any commercial use was begun. Meanwhile experimenters pushed ahead.

To the Empire State transmitter, programs began to travel by cable from NBC studio 3H in Radio City. Less than two years old, this radio studio was made into a television studio with light grills and catwalks for technicians. It became the source of a diversity of productions, usually two per week, on Tuesdays and Thursdays. In the corridor, actors began to be seen with green make-up and purple lipstick. It became known that such things were necessary in the new medium; perhaps it would always be that way. Before long a green face no longer caused comment in Radio City cafeterias. It was, rather, a mark of status. Actors were plied with questions. Television was great, they said. The studio was hot beyond belief and people almost fried to death, but all that would be solved. There was no medium like it; it would sweep the country.

But history began to interfere. News about television began to be crowded off the front page by other matters.

By mid-1935 the New Deal was suddenly in deep trouble. In April it had enacted the WPA, a huge work program, because unemployment was still an overwhelming problem. WPA soon became, along with Mrs. Roosevelt, a target of anti-New Deal humor.

But no sooner had WPA been launched than the New Deal received staggering blows. Various New Deal measures had been challenged in the lower courts, and the cases were reaching the U. S. Supreme Court. In a series of stunning reversals, key measures were declared unconstitutional. They included NRA and later AAA.

In business circles there was rejoicing. On the *Ford Sunday Evening Hour* on CBS William J. Cameron hailed the NRA news with a rhapsody:

> Voices of millennial prophets and harbingers of doom, formerly heard by multitudes, have ceased even to be echoes! A whole system of law erected by lawmakers had been pronounced to be lawless. Constructed of baseless fancies and colored by rainbow hues, a perfect welter of gorgeously incompetent plans faded and melted at the first touch of reality. . . . Every attempt to subjugate our citizens as vassals of the state has failed. A vast sense of relief possesses the whole people.[6]

In the crisis precipitated by the series of reverses, debate suddenly centered on apocalyptic either/or alternatives. Radical feelings that had subsided during the first flush of the New Deal reappeared. To many observers, the middle way that had seemed for a time to hold promise had reached a dead end; only two roads now lay open. Some people—including many writers—favored the road of socialism and felt it must now be taken. To others another road, that of Hitler and Mussolini, seemed more

6. CBS, June 23, 1935.

promising. That the die was cast and the United States already moving down that road, ready to form behind a leader, was feared by many observers. There were several candidates for the role—all were voices of radio.

FASCIST REHEARSALS

Fascism, said Raymond Swing in 1935, was the scuttling of democracy to maintain "an unequal distribution of economic power." If democracy, which permits social conflict, fails to resolve its conflicts, then "fascism, the foe of social conflict, resolves them through the device of dictatorship." Dictatorship could be expected to vary from place to place in its choice of techniques to win and hold power.[1]

The fascist pattern that had evolved in Italy and Germany, and seemed to be developing elsewhere, called for a magnetic leader with a wide following. In each case he had seemed for a time to move in a socialist direction, mobilizing the people against poverty and despair. But in each case the leader had come to terms with finance capitalists. When Mussolini and Hitler became strong, wrote Swing, "big business made friends with the future and poured funds into their coffers." Swing observed that finance capital, both in Italy and Germany, had *not* found fascism a "comfortable resting place." Yet it seemed likely to him that in the United States, as elsewhere, backers would be ready to support a rising demagogue, in the hope that his power might be used in their interest.[2]

As potential American fascist leaders, Swing ruled out those various petty blusterers parading with uniforms and salutes and aping European models. They represented movie versions of fascism. The real threat would be found in popular movements seemingly headed elsewhere.

When Father Charles E. Coughlin—born in 1891 in Hamilton, Ontario, of an American father and a Canadian mother—was assigned in 1926 to the Shrine of the Little Flower in Royal Oak on the northern edge of Detroit, the church served only twenty-five families. Anxious to build its influence and improve its finances, Father Coughlin visited WJR, Detroit, and arranged to do some broadcasts from Royal Oak.[3]

According to his biographer, Charles J. Tull, Coughlin paid $58 per

1. Swing, *Forerunners of American Fascism*, pp. 14–18.
2. *Ibid.* pp. 18–22.
3. The following is based on Tull, *Father Coughlin and the New Deal*, and other sources as noted.

program for line charges but got the station time free. If so, this must have been for an experimental period. Station staff members have stated that Coughlin paid full commercial rates. Several religious groups paid for time on WJR; Sunday was its most profitable day.[4]

Coughlin at first aimed his broadcasts at children, then switched to adults, and with this came a change in themes. He addressed himself to the hopes and fears gripping the nation, and in so doing, began a process of self-discovery. He found there were buttons he could touch which produced floods of letters—often with contributions. The deluge of mail changed his picture of what he might be.

His subject matter involved a diversity of political strands, stemming from varied sources. Sometimes he spoke of the perils of communism, the "red serpent." Sometimes he pleaded for the remonetization of silver, and sounded like a Populist leader of the turn of the century. More often he castigated those of wealth and power, "dulled by the opiate of their own contentedness." As the Depression began, this became the dominant theme.

In rolling r's and broad vowels, he spoke scathingly of "unregulated capitalism." Human rights, he said, must prevail over "commercial rights greedily guarded by the few." Sometimes he attacked "international bankers," whose concern for investments seemed to him to threaten the well-being of the world. Property, he said, involved responsibilities; if those who controlled property neglected their responsibilities, the state must enforce them. Such words, in a time of paralysis, found wide response, and contributions rose. Coughlin organized a Radio League of the Little Flower—membership, one dollar a year—to stimulate the flow of funds. It was the beginning of an organized following.

Meanwhile he bought time on WLW, Cincinnati, the most influential station in the Midwest, and began negotiations with WMAQ, Chicago. Because WMAQ was at this time a CBS station, the matter was referred to network headquarters; the outcome was that Coughlin bought time on the CBS network. All these investments more than paid for themselves. The money flowed back in a rising tide of contributions, as the broadcasts grew more emotional.

As the Depression deepened, Coughlin increasingly berated President Hoover and international bankers. CBS now became alarmed; a phone call from Edward Klauber, its executive vice president, asked Coughlin to

4. Correspondence, Leo Fitzpatrick; Patt, *Reminiscences*, pp. 42–3.

desist from these subjects and to submit advance scripts. Coughlin promised that his next broadcast would deal with an entirely different subject—and it did. He used the broadcast—January 4, 1931—to ask his listeners whether CBS should be allowed to muzzle him. As a result CBS was overwhelmed with letters of protest—1,250,000 letters, according to some estimates. Coughlin, having showed his power, talked on—without submitting scripts. But the episode brought a turning point in his relations with networks. CBS improvised a *Church of the Air* series, with speakers on a rotating basis from various religious groups, on a free-time basis. Under the new policy Coughlin was eased off the network in April 1931. He found NBC likewise closed to him. But these rebuffs hardly slowed his progress. He was able to buy time on a group of stations including WOR, New York, and to lease telephone lines to link them. By the fall of 1932 he was on twenty-six stations at a weekly cost of $14,000. He needed a hundred stenographers to cope with his mail. Week after week he vehemently denounced Hoover and urged the election of Franklin D. Roosevelt. He sent advice to the campaigning Roosevelt: "Perhaps it would be wise in your Boston address to refer to 'that radio priest either from Michigan or from Florida' who spoke for the rights of the common man. A mention of this would certainly do you no harm in that particular spot."

In March 1933 Father Coughlin attended the inauguration of Franklin D. Roosevelt. At the Shrine of the Little Flower he built a 150-foot stone tower with a floodlit figure of Christ on the Cross. At the top of the tower was Coughlin's study, reached by a spiral staircase. Here, in the company of a Great Dane, he wrote his radio speeches. He was, said *Fortune*, "just about the biggest thing that ever happened to radio." He got more mail than anyone in America. A WOR poll voted him America's "most useful citizen." WCAU, Philadelphia, asked its listeners whether on Sunday afternoons they would prefer Father Coughlin or the New York Philharmonic. The vote ran:

Coughlin	187,000
Philharmonic	12,000

Bishop Gallagher of Detroit, Coughlin's superior, gave him resounding support. Had Coughlin lived in Russia before the revolution, said Bishop Gallagher, and "had he possessed the radio facilities," the revolution might not have taken place.[5]

5. *Fortune*, February 1934; *Broadcasting*, March 15, 1933; Schlesinger, *The Politics of Upheaval*, pp. 20–21.

Visitors to the tower studio found Father Coughlin genial and urbane. He sprinkled his dialogue with occasional hells and damns. As the Roosevelt administration began, Coughlin continued to send advice. On the air he took a proprietary tone, giving the impression he was close to the councils of the administration, with the result that presidential press secretary Steve Early wrote to one correspondent that "there is no connection whatever between the Shrine of the Little Flower and the White House." As to the Coughlin radio broadcasts, "I am certain the President has never heard one."

During 1933–34 money orders mailed to the *Golden Hour of the Little Flower* were being cashed by the Royal Oak post office at a rate of three thousand a month. Except for a summer intermission, the programs were heard weekly over twenty-eight stations, including two in Canada. In 1933 the time cost $226,000 and was bought through the Detroit advertising agency Grace & Holliday, which got 15 per cent. Receipts were probably $500,000 for the year.

Coughlin remained a Roosevelt supporter throughout 1933; in 1934 he shifted repeatedly from praise to damnation and back again. Late that year he organized the National Union for Social Justice. Many regarded it as the start of a third-party movement, noting that Coughlin, like Hitler, had combined the symbols "national" and "social." Meanwhile Coughlin pressed his views on the President. An absolute necessity, in Coughlin's view, was inflation through remonetization of silver. Congress leaned in that direction but Roosevelt did not. In an effort to block silver legislation, Secretary of the Treasury Morgenthau published a list of those who had made substantial investments in silver, and presumably had private reasons for wanting the legislation. On the list was the Radio League of the Little Flower. Coughlin angrily attacked Morgenthau as a tool of Wall Street and pointedly praised silver as a "gentile" metal. The incident marked a turning point in Coughlin-Roosevelt relations. A few months later, when the administration proposed to join the World Court, which Coughlin considered a tool of international bankers, he called forth a deluge of telegrams on Congress—200,000, according to his own estimate. The Washington telegraph offices could not handle them; some were routed to Baltimore and carried to Washington hourly in huge bundles on the interurban trains. The inundation unnerved Congress and apparently was a factor in stopping the World Court action. Administration officials became increasingly irritated with Coughlin. In February 1935 Coughlin

said that five million people had subscribed to his Social Justice platform
—a document that seemed to take several sides on several questions. The
following month General Hugh S. Johnson, former NRA administrator,
could not restrain his penchant for salty invective. On the air he assailed
Coughlin, and in the attack coupled him with another "pied piper," Senator Huey Long of Louisiana.[6] Over NBC the General said:

> You can laugh at Huey Long—you can snort at Father Coughlin—but
> this country was never under a greater menace. . . . Added to the
> fol-de-rol of Senator Long, there comes burring over the air the drip-
> ping brogue of the Irish-Canadian priest . . . musical, blatant bunk
> from the very rostrum of religion, it goes straight home to simple
> souls weary in distress. . . . Between the team of Huey Long and the
> priest we have the whole bag of crazy and crafty tricks . . . possessed
> by Peter the Hermit, Napoleon Bonaparte, Sitting Bull, William
> Hohenzollern, Hitler, Lenin . . . boiled down to two with the radio
> and the newsreel to make them effective. If you don't think Long and
> Coughlin are dangerous, you don't know the temper of the country
> in this distress!

In the administration General Johnson's broadcast was applauded but
also deplored. That he should have focused national attention on the two
demagogues, and at the same time pushed them together, was thought a
blunder. Senator Long, the more recent arrival on the national scene, was
gaining extraordinary momentum. A secret straw vote that summer taken
by the Democratic National Committee showed that an independent
ticket headed by Long could draw three to four million votes—presumably away from Roosevelt. What if—following the Johnson scenario—the
two movements coalesced? Had Johnson by his attack helped to bring it
about?

When Huey Long became a U. S. Senator in 1933 after four years as
state governor, he came with Louisiana in his pocket. No governor had
ever established a more total control over a state. By law he had made
even the appointment of local firemen, policemen, and teachers subject to
his approval. By taking over the assessment of property throughout the
state he had acquired another tool for rewarding friends and punishing
enemies. He was said to keep a "son-of-a-bitch book" to guide him; a fantastic memory helped him further. In the process of amassing his powers
he had reduced the state legislature to complete subservience and somehow kept it happy in this condition. Even after he went to Washington it

6. The following is based on Chase, *Sound and Fury,* and other sources as noted.

followed his instructions on what laws to pass, and did it jovially, without reading them. Huey Long's weapons were patronage control, corruption, an entertainingly flamboyant style—and something else. During his reign Huey had built more roads, schools, and hospitals than any previous governor. He had reduced electric and telephone rates. Under attack, his supporters could recite a catalogue of beneficences. Huey would be no menace, said Raymond Swing, if he had not achieved so much. One of Long's chief aides, Reverend Gerald L. K. Smith, put it this way: "I believe in the spoils system. You have to have power before you can serve the people effectively." Huey had power and used it—in grand style.[7]

Not long after he came to Washington radio listeners became familiar with the style. He had been a faithful Roosevelt follower during the New Deal honeymoon period, but the 1935 reverses found him a leader of the Senate opposition. A master of parliamentary tricks, he riveted public attention on himself. Broadcasting companies rushed to give him free time —especially NBC, which gave him three network periods in one two-week span.[8] He used this platform in a curiously personal and extraordinarily successful manner. Following a method he had used in Louisiana, he began:

> Hello friends, this is Huey Long speaking. And I have some important things to tell you. Before I begin I want you to do me a favor. I am going to talk along for four or five minutes, just to keep things going. While I'm doing it I want you to go to the telephone and call up five of your friends, and tell them Huey is on the air.

Long's use of this device produced steadily mounting audiences. Huey was a variety show by himself. Like Dr. Brinkley, he talked to the radio audience in a vernacular that carried no hint of condescension, and he could also quote Scripture in rippling streams. To the humble and pious he was one of them. He was the hillbilly come to power. He played on their fears and prejudices. He was often the clown, calling himself "the Kingfish" after the head of the lodge in *Amos 'n' Andy,* but the clowning served deadly purpose. In 1934 Long launched a Share-Our-Wealth movement; by mid-1935 there were said to be Share-Our-Wealth clubs in 8000 cities, towns, and villages. Gerald L. K. Smith, who organized this part of the Long machinery, claimed a club membership of seven million. Regardless of exact figures, the clubs provided a fantastic mailing list, an organization, and the spine for a political movement. The platform, promoted in

7. Swing, *Forerunners of American Fascism,* p. 84.
8. Bormann, "This Is Huey P. Long Talking," *Journal of Broadcasting,* Spring 1958.

every Long broadcast, called for a reduction of big fortunes from the top so that the national wealth could be shared; this would provide a $5000 nest egg for everyone, an annual income of at least $2000, limited work hours, a share in the pleasures and luxuries of life, and old-age pensions. It was natural that the "lyin' newspapers" and "smart-aleck" tools of the interests would scoff at all this, said Huey. He told a reporter, "It's all in Plato. You know—the Greek philosopher."

By 1935 the convergence of Long's Share-Our-Wealth and Coughlin's Social Justice movements became for Democrats a nightmare possibility. Signs pointed in that direction. Coughlin and Long were said to have met several times in Long's hotel room in Washington. What to do about this looming "coalition" was another question. In April, Secretary of the Interior Harold L. Ickes, like General Johnson, attacked the two radio demagogues over the air, but the President felt this had been "very unwise." [9]

During the following months, as Coughlin held massive rallies in a number of cities, Long was equally busy. He spoke four times on large radio hookups and dozens of times on local stations, while ceaselessly touring the country. Early in September newspaper reporter Francis Chase interviewed Huey in his Baton Rouge hotel, where the Senator received him, as was his custom, in flamboyant pajamas, reclining on a downy bed. Long told his interviewer that President Roosevelt was a back number now and the next election would find a new horseman in the saddle. Many believed him. To Raymond Swing he seemed "indeed plausible enough to Hitlerize America." But on September 10 Huey Long lay in the dust at his Louisiana Capitol, dead from an assassin's bullet. In Baton Rouge people ran through the streets in dismay. "The Kingfish has been killed!"

The news reached President Roosevelt at Hyde Park, where he was entertaining two visitors. Joseph P. Kennedy had brought Father Coughlin to try to heal the breach between the priest and the President.[10]

But the third-party idea had gained a momentum that could not be stopped. To Coughlin the assassination of Long seemed "the most regrettable thing in modern history." Reverend Gerald L. K. Smith, inheriting the Share-Our-Wealth clubs, mobilized them for action. That fall Coughlin broke irrevocably with the New Deal. In January 1936 he said that the National Union for Social Justice had units in 302 of the nation's 435 con-

9. Ickes, *The Secret Diary of Harold L. Ickes: The First Thousand Days,* pp. 352–3; Tull, *Father Coughlin and the New Deal,* p. 86.
10. Schlesinger, *The Politics of Upheaval,* p. 341.

gressional districts. They backed selected candidates in the primaries and were encouraged by results. In June the coalition became a reality with an agreement to back Representative William Lemke of North Dakota for President. A Union Party was formally created, backed not only by the Long and Coughlin forces but also by Dr. Francis E. Townsend, old-age pension crusader. Father Coughlin ranged up and down the land, denouncing "Franklin Doublecrossing Roosevelt" and predicting that the Union Party would pull nine million votes. If it didn't, he would leave the air.

To Republicans these developments were music. In June at Cleveland they nominated Alfred M. Landon, Governor of Kansas, who was pictured as a Kansas Coolidge, with Colonel Frank Knox of the Chicago *Daily News*—and former owner of WMAQ, Chicago—as his running mate. They felt they had reason for confidence.

In the same month the Democrats at Philadelphia renominated Roosevelt and Garner by acclamation.

By mid-summer the campaign reached a high pitch of bitterness. In Des Moines, Coughlin said: "Democracy is doomed, this is our last election. . . ." [11] It was either . . . or. . . .

RADIO AT THE RAMPARTS

The campaign of 1936 introduced new elements into radio.

Late in the previous year the Republican National Committee chose as its radio chief Hill Blackett, a Lord & Thomas alumnus who was one of the organizing partners of Blackett, Sample & Hummert. This young advertising agency had moved into first place in network billings as a result of its zealous concentration on daytime serials, which were becoming known as "soap operas" because many of the sponsors were soap companies.

When Blackett, riding the crest of soap opera successes, announced that the Republicans would convey their message through "modern radio technique," the networks became alarmed. Edward Klauber told the Republicans that CBS did not want political issues to hang on "the skill of warring dramatists." Political appeals, he said, should be intellectual.[1] NBC and CBS decided not to allow dramatization of political argument. Making an odd exception, CBS let *The March of Time* present a sample of what the

11. Schlesinger, *The Politics of Upheaval*, pp. 341–2, 629.
1. *Political Broadcasts*, p. 6.

Republicans wanted to do. But the taboo became moot in any case, because the Republicans recorded their dramas, entitled *Liberty at the Crossroads,* and found scores of stations ready to sell time for them. An excerpt:

MARRIAGE LICENSE CLERK: Now what do you intend to do about the national debt?

PROSPECTIVE BRIDEGROOM: National debt . . . me?

CLERK: You are going to establish a family, and as head of an American family you will shoulder a debt of more than $1017.26 . . . and it's growing every day. Do you still want to get married?

GROOM: You . . . er . . . er . . . er . . . I . . . What do you say, Mary?

MARY: Maybe . . . maybe . . . we'd better talk it over first, John. All those debts. When we thought we didn't owe anybody in the world.

JOHN: Somebody is giving us a dirty deal. It's a lowdown mean trick.

VOICE OF DOOM (*over music*):   And the debts like the sins of the fathers shall be visited upon the children, aye, even the third and fourth generation.[2]

Another innovation came from Republican Senator Arthur Vandenberg of Michigan. Scheduled to speak on CBS, he announced he would "debate" with President Roosevelt—or rather, with recorded excerpts of old Roosevelt speeches. CBS decided this would be "dramatization" and forbade it; then changed its mind and allowed it.[3] It was a difficult year for policy-makers.

Early in the year Earl Browder, leader of the Communist party, asked for time to reply to other party leaders who had broadcast. Under Section 315 of the Communications Act of 1934, a station allowing a candidate to "use" its facilities must give the same privilege to opposing candidates for the same office. Because Browder had not yet been formally nominated by his party, he was probably not a "candidate" in the sense of the Communications Act, but CBS decided to give him a fifteen-minute period, and at once received a torrent of abuse from William Randolph Hearst—via editorials in the Hearst press—and from publisher Bernarr Macfadden. CBS gave time to a conservative Republican, Representative Hamilton Fish of New York, to answer Browder. The Yankee Network of New England, although it had declined to carry the Browder talk, did carry the reply by Representative Fish. Asked why, John Shepard III, Yankee Network president, explained: "Because we believe in the American form of government."[4]

2. Quoted, *Time,* January 27, 1936.
3. *Broadcasting,* November 1, 1936.
4. *Broadcasting,* March 15, 1936.

Bernarr Macfadden, the health faddist, who was approaching his dotage, believed himself a contender for the Republican nomination for the presidency. He demanded that his advertising agency, Erwin, Wasey & Co.—Louis Wasey was another Lord & Thomas alumnus who had started a successful agency—arrange to broadcast his candidacy. The agency used as a vehicle the Macfadden-sponsored series on NBC-red, *True Story Court of Human Relations*. It arranged for Macfadden to read a Red Cross message and introduced him as "often mentioned for the Presidency."

President Roosevelt displayed a guile which became standard in later campaigns. He decided early to save his major thrusts for September and October; meanwhile he would spend the summer on "non-political" trips, visiting floods, laying cornerstones, dedicating dams. This might involve "non-political" broadcasts—not mentioning the campaign, not paid for, not involving a right of reply. Roosevelt valued such symbolic "non-political" events. Financial reasons may have influenced the strategy. Radio debts incurred by the Democrats in 1932 were actually not paid off until 1936,[5] and broadcasters were adopting a "cash in advance" policy for political time buyers.

The Roosevelt strategy of delay worried Mrs. Roosevelt. She wrote to James Farley that Landon's headquarters—so she had heard—was buzzing with radio plans. "They have continuity people writing for the radio, they have employed advertising people to do their copy. . . ." But the President stuck to his strategy.

Thematically the Roosevelt campaign of 1936 marked a sharp swing toward labor. The months following the death of NRA had brought a crucial turning point in the New Deal story.

The NRA had been an effort to foster industry-labor teamwork against Depression problems. Suspending anti-trust activity, it had virtually made trade associations a part of the government machinery. The idea had been to accept the bigness of big business as inevitable, but to encourage its cooperation with labor, under government supervision. The sudden demise of NRA had ended all that, and many segments of the business world had been delighted.

In an effort to salvage something, the administration had promptly re-enacted, in the Wagner Labor Relations Act, one element of the NRA: the guarantee to labor of collective bargaining rights—the feature most im-

5. *Broadcasting*, February 15, 1936.

portant to labor. Roosevelt also pushed ahead with plans for social security and a minimum-wage law. During 1935–36 these efforts forged a strong New Deal-labor coalition. Labor unions are said to have contributed three-quarters of a million dollars to the Democratic campaign, making possible much of its final radio drive. The stress of this "second New Deal" was *reform* rather than recovery. In reform lay the hope of saving American institutions, said Roosevelt. "Reform if you would preserve. I am that kind of conservative because I am that kind of liberal."

The final drive challenged the "economic royalists" who claimed they were saving the American way but were really—said Roosevelt—rallying to guard their powers and privileges. He compared them to an old gentleman in a silk hat who fell off a pier. A friend jumped in and saved him; the silk hat floated away. "Three years later the old gentleman is still berating his friend because the silk hat was lost." Such talk won roars from labor listeners but no friends among big business.[6]

In the early summer the election straw votes conducted by *Literary Digest* magazine showed a clear Landon victory. These polls had a history of accuracy. Two new and relatively unknown polling organizations, those of Gallup and Roper, showed different conclusions, but the *Literary Digest* poll received major attention. That summer Erwin, Wasey & Co., for its client the Goodyear Company, hastily built a radio series based on the *Digest* poll. Three times weekly over an NBC network the conservative commentator John B. Kennedy, scarcely concealing his delight, reeled off the latest *Digest* statistics. The figures provided the best tonic yet peddled on the air and created a bandwagon feeling among Republicans. Landon would win thirty-two states with 370 electoral votes, said the final broadcasts. Roosevelt, his forces splintering and crumbling, would carry sixteen states. Representatives from sponsor and agency came to stand in the control room and relish the cascade of figures. It made a heady dream while it lasted. In November it ended abruptly as 523 electoral votes went to Roosevelt, eight to Landon. The Union Party received less than a million votes and evaporated. The *Literary Digest* disappeared. Father Coughlin left the air—at least, temporarily. Oracles grew silent.

For the world of radio the landslide of 1936 produced an extraordinary change of atmosphere. It was crystal-clear now that the nation had rejected the either/or fixation and that it accepted Roosevelt's leadership. To preserve, it would welcome change. In that spirit radio had a new birth.

6. Schlesinger, *The Politics of Upheaval*, pp. 586–625.

2 / REBIRTH

History is a post-mortem examination.
It tells you what a country died of.
But I'd like to know what it lived of.
PETER FINLEY DUNNE, *Mr. Dooley*

The outburst of creative activity that came to radio in the second half of the 1930's was largely a CBS story. The first stirrings were at CBS, and while these eventually awakened much of the industry, the most brilliant moments were at CBS—in drama, news, and almost every other kind of programming.

A few years earlier none of this would have seemed possible. NBC, launched in 1926, had acquired most of the powerful stations, and had two chains going before CBS existed. NBC, born rich, had captured the leading concert and vaudeville stars and had the biggest corporations as sponsors when CBS was struggling and close to bankruptcy.[1]

That CBS had survived and caught up and was moving into the spotlight was in some measure the work of a youth who, in 1928 at the age of twenty-seven, had taken control of the company. His executive workmanship had been so smooth and effective that it soon raised the question, how had he done it? The question persisted because, along with other talents, William S. Paley had a genius for elusiveness.

He was born in Chicago in 1901 of Russian parents. His earliest memories concerned a house with a workshop in back, where cigars were made. It was a family business. His father, Samuel Paley, looked after the cigar-making, while an uncle, Jacob Paley, took care of selling and financial matters. The company had dramatic ups and downs and moved several times, but in the course of two decades turned into a dozen factories in

1. See *A Tower in Babel*, pp. 193–5, 219–24.

55

Pennsylvania, Delaware, and New Jersey, with the main plant in Philadelphia. This was the Congress Cigar Company, and it was a spectacular success story. The La Palina cigar, named after the family, was among its chief prides.

From the time William was a child, his father discussed business problems with him, as did his uncle. The boy had no plan other than to be part of the business.

It was a close-knit family and remained so in spite of success. During summer vacations William sometimes worked in the business, and at times was left in charge. While still a teen-ager he had to cope with a strike; he handled it smoothly, settling with the workers without giving too much.

He went to a military academy in Alton, Illinois, and briefly to the University of Chicago, then shifted to the Wharton School of Business at the University of Pennsylvania when the family moved to Philadelphia. Soon after graduation he became vice president of the Congress Cigar Company. Once when his father and uncle were in Europe on business, William decided to risk $50 per week on a *La Palina Hour* over WCAU, Philadelphia. Uncle Jacob, on returning, was indignant over his foolishness and made him cancel; but when letters came in, asking what had happened to the *La Palina Hour*, Uncle Jacob began to have second thoughts. When a family friend, Jerome Louchheim, bought CBS, the Paleys were among the few early sponsors. Soon they went further. Louchheim was in over his head and wanted to pull out, and in mid-1928 young William Paley asked him for a few days' option. He already had substantial funds in his own name but might need more, so he discussed it all with his father and uncle, and found them willing to help. Soon afterward, crossing the Atlantic, Samuel Paley told a fellow passenger, "I just bought the Columbia Broadcasting System for my son. I paid a quarter of a million for it." He hoped he had made a good bargain but wasn't sure.[2]

William Paley expected to need a few months in New York, putting the network in shape, before returning to the cigar business. But the work took hold of him. CBS was small, occupying one floor of the Paramount tower. It owned no stations. After some months it moved to larger quarters at 485 Madison Avenue and began growing.

2. Interview, Oscar Greene. Subsequent outlays brought the Paley family investment in CBS to approximately $1,500,000, including $400,000 for WABC, the New York outlet, which later became WCBS. This appears to have been the total Paley family investment in CBS. *Fortune*, June 1935.

The new president buckled down to long hours of daily work. One of the matters he studied was the relation of the network to its affiliates. After careful thought he decided to reorganize this. His plan was different from that used at NBC, which CBS had at first imitated. Among Paley's early moves, no other proved so crucial in the competition with NBC as his innovations in station relations.

NBC had always charged its affiliates for the *sustaining*—i.e. unsponsored—network programs they accepted. At first the fee was $90 per evening hour, which was later reduced—by 1932, to $50 per hour. The small stations found this burdensome and complained constantly.

Meanwhile NBC reimbursed stations for *sponsored* network programs they accepted. Acceptance was a matter for their decision. For those they accepted they received a flat fee. At first this was $30 per evening hour— later increased to $50 per hour. Large stations found this inadequate and complained constantly. Their dissatisfaction was a serious hazard. When attempting to clear time for new sponsored series, NBC often found small stations willing, large stations unwilling. The powerful WLW, Cincinnati, while listed as an NBC affiliate, often preferred to retain a sponsored local series in preference to a sponsored network offering. The plan kept relations with stations in a state of tension.[3]

In place of such patchwork arrangements, Paley developed a clean, fantastically simple plan.

He began by making the entire sustaining schedule *free* to affiliates. At any time during network hours—ten to twelve hours daily—the affiliates could plug into CBS without cost, using its offering of the moment. The affiliate was under no obligation to use any of the sustaining programs, but could use all. To many stations the arrangement was a windfall, particularly as the Depression deepened. It was also convenient, eliminating much haggling and bookkeeping.

In exchange for the bonanza, Paley wanted something: an option on any part of the affiliate's schedule, for sponsored network series. He found little resistance to this.

The option meant that Paley could sell time to a network sponsor without any uncertainty as to clearance. He could sign a contract with a sponsor for time coast to coast, then instruct the affiliates to clear the time. At first, this required only two weeks' notice.

3. Testimony by William S. Hedges at FCC hearings, *Broadcasting*, December 15, 1938.

Sponsors paid for each station according to its established rates. Network and station divided the receipts, with the larger share going to the network because of its substantial costs, which included AT&T line charges. The formula for dividing receipts was spelled out in the affiliation agreement, and varied from station to station according to the bargaining power of the station. Stations generally received about 30 per cent of the time-sale revenue. This was earned without any effort on the part of the station. It had only to stay on the air.

The neatness of the plan was characteristic of Paley. The occasions for dispute had been pared to a minimum. Best of all, from the point of view of network finances, was the fact that it smoothed dealings with network sponsors.

CBS grew rapidly on the strength of the plan. When Paley took over in 1928, CBS had nineteen stations. By 1935 it had ninety-seven stations. It could not rival NBC-red in total wattage, but it could call itself "largest" in number of stations. Several important NBC affiliates—WJR, Detroit; KSL, Salt Lake City; WRVA, Richmond—were lured to CBS by the attractions of the contract.[4]

This CBS plan with all its attractions also held the germ of later monopoly troubles for the network. Paley had, in effect, persuaded affiliates to cede control to him: the option gave control. Although each station by the terms of its license was responsible for what it broadcast, each CBS station had in fact surrendered control over its schedule.

If this was not at first seen as a problem, it was because the Federal Radio Commission had generally ignored such matters; because the time actually pre-empted under the option was at first too small to be thought of as "control"; and because programming obtained under the option was generally better than what a station could produce itself. Under these circumstances the option did not seem at odds with "the public interest." Only later did the full implications become apparent.

Meanwhile the option strengthened CBS and focused attention on the skills of William Paley. He handled negotiations with an ease that baffled observers. The casual simplicity with which he could answer crucial questions—going straight to the point—threw seasoned bargainers off stride. There was no excitement, no tension.

When Adolph Zukor of Paramount wanted to acquire a 49 per cent share of CBS, Paley set a value of five million dollars on this proposed

4. Hedges, *Reminiscences,* pp. 86–8.

share. Old Mr. Zukor assumed it was a bargaining figure and suggested another. But the twenty-seven-year-old Paley had already decided *not* to bargain; he did not want to seem uncertain of the value of CBS. To hold quietly to his own valuation seemed to him, at this stage, more important than a few million dollars. Zukor was flabbergasted and ended by offering the young man the presidency of Paramount, with an arrangement that would pay him a half million or more a year. But William Paley had found his arena.

He soon began a search for a number two man. He liked to blue-print actions and avoid minutiae. Retaining Edward L. Bernays as public relations counsel, he asked his advice. Bernays had on his staff Edward Klauber, a former newspaperman of recognized talents whom he—Bernays—did not especially like. He explained to Paley that Klauber was not right for a small office but would be fine in a growing organization like CBS. Paley agreed that Klauber was the man. Klauber quickly became Paley's indispensable buffer and aide. He promptly decided to save Paley money by canceling the Bernays retainer.[5]

The Paley-Klauber alignment became the basis of a brilliantly streamlined leadership. Klauber seemed to take deep satisfaction in his role. Unpleasant tasks like high-level firings were always handled by Klauber. In time of dispute, Klauber took the spotlight. The odium was always on Klauber; he seemed to welcome it. And he endured the wear and tear. Protective toward his boss, Klauber administered the organization with a strong hand. Lyman Bryson, who later joined CBS as educational counselor, once heard Klauber criticize the executive ability of a young staff member by saying: "He has too many of the instincts of a father." Bryson admired Klauber's judgment, but felt he never let the instincts of a father interfere when he considered CBS interests to be at stake.[6]

Klauber's newspaper background—he had been night city editor of the New York *Times*—became invaluable to CBS. It was under Klauber's firm guidance that Paul White began to build an effective CBS news organization.

Most CBS people dealt with Paley through Klauber. News commentator H. V. Kaltenborn was hired by Paley but seldom saw him after that. Paley seemed to Kaltenborn "a big boy . . . smooth-faced, round-faced." On the few occasions they met, Paley was "never peremptory." Bryson consid-

5. Interview, Edward L. Bernays.
6. Bryson, *Reminiscences*, p. 216.

ered Paley "diffident," but others were more apt to stress the easy assurance that made Paley so effective as negotiator. Bernays found him self-indulgent. Paley's bachelor apartment, according to Bernays, had racks for a hundred neckties and a hundred shirts, and Bernays considered this excessive.[7]

Paley, avoiding the spotlight, was meanwhile getting an extraordinary education. Day by day he found himself tangled in problems never mentioned at the Wharton School of Business. While exercising his talent for salesmanship, and trying to organize things in a workmanlike way, he found himself called on to be the guardian of "freedom of speech," "freedom of the press," "freedom of religion," not to mention "public interest, convenience, or necessity." Every week seemed to bring a new political, social, or religious crisis.

It had seemed logical to sell time to Father Coughlin, especially after the powerful Senator Arthur Vandenberg of Michigan wrote a letter of endorsement.[8] Who could have anticipated the reverberations? Who could have guessed the pitfalls of scheduling a *Ford Sunday Evening Hour* with William J. Cameron as intermission philosopher; or of scheduling *Voice of the Crusaders*—recommended by good clients? From each of these problems CBS eventually disengaged itself. Klauber bore the brunt, while Paley evolved policy. In each case he made long-range decisions designed to avoid similar problems. CBS would no longer sell time for religion—but would maintain a free-time *Church of the Air,* rotating its pulpit among various groups. CBS would no longer (except during campaigns) sell time for political argument—but would plan a balanced-discussion series like *The University of Chicago Round Table* and *America's Town Meeting of the Air.* Lyman Bryson, assistant to Denny on the *Town Meeting* series, joined CBS for this purpose and eventually developed *People's Platform.*

From each of these crises Paley emerged with praise from all sides, which often used the words "shrewd" and "statesmanlike." In Paley these two qualities were often hard to distinguish from each other.

In the early 1930's CBS was under attack for its many laxative commercials. On May 13, 1935, Paley announced that laxatives and other products involving "questions of good taste" would thenceforth be banned. The pol-

7. Bernays, *Biography of an Idea,* pp. 427–8.
8. Interview, Judith Waller. Father Coughlin's first contacts with CBS were with Miss Waller at WMAQ, Chicago.

icy would take effect "as rapidly as present commitments with clients expire."

Immediately the chairman of the FCC hailed Paley for his "wise leadership," and CBS was reported getting an "avalanche of praise," which continued for months.[9]

But there was another thread to the story. Until the mid-1930's many sponsors left the air each June for a "summer hiatus." This was considered a low-listening period. Networks had tried without avail to stop the annual exodus.

In his laxative announcement Paley said he would honor existing contracts. A laxative manufacturer, by exercising the renewal option in his CBS contract, could stay on for some time, and would now be protected from new competition. But if he left for the summer, his tenure would end. That summer the laxatives saw good reason to stay. The year in which CBS got its "avalanche of praise" for banning laxatives turned out to be one of its best laxative years—the best, some say. Eventually the laxative ban was forgotten.

From every crisis CBS seemed to surge ahead.

While self-effacing, Paley apparently disliked being alone. Someone always had to go along in the taxi. It might be Klauber but more likely it was Lawrence Lowman, an old school friend and now CBS vice president, who had become Paley's link with New York society; or Paul Kesten, a sunken-eyed intellectual, who wrote smart promotion pieces.

During these years CBS took the lead in proclaiming the gospel of radio. Its promotion items were a sharp contrast to those of NBC, which were usually ornately designed and stuffy in style. The CBS brochures turned out by Kesten looked like volumes of verse or de luxe editions of the sayings of Marcus Aurelius. With their wisdom set off by broad margins of white space, the booklets became conversation pieces decorating executive coffee tables. And they reflected the Paley style.

A Kesten item of 1935, *You Do What You're Told*, caused a stir at advertising agencies. Its theme was that people do as told. It conceded that this flicks the pride—"without which none of us can breathe"—but then asked questions. When the dentist says, "Open your mouth," you open, don't you? When your wife says, "Tuck her in tight," you tuck, don't you? When the Western Union messenger says, "Sign here," you sign, don't you?

9. *Broadcasting*, May 15, 1935; *Radio Art*, June 1935.

So too with—"have a cigarette"—"listen to this"—"watch your step"—"turn left at the end of the corridor"—"don't go yet"—"shake hands with Jim Brown"—"come right in."

The point, said the booklet, was that voices of affection and authority were involved in each of these, and that was true also of radio—in contrast to other media. Where such voices are involved, said the booklet, it is a basic rule that

> Seven times
> Eight times
> Nine times out of ten
> People do what they're told.[10]

Scores of advertisers wanted to try it.

In *The Very Rich* CBS gave evidence that even the well-heeled were more responsive to radio than to other media and that it might be a good way to sell Cadillacs. The idea was a thought-provoking surprise.

In 1935 *Fortune* magazine took note of William Paley and could scarcely restrain its enthusiasm.

> Mr. Paley as a businessman is a theme that practically brings tears to the eyes of his Directors—never in all their lives, they say, have they been associated with anybody so clever at business. Not only is he a master advertiser and feeler of the public pulse, but these gentlemen say he is the greatest organizer, the best executive, the quickest thinker, the coolest negotiator they have ever seen.

A later article spoke of the men around him. CBS executives, said *Fortune*, "would mix well with Anthony Eden, Adolphe Menjou, or Oscar of the Waldorf, they are that suave." Their style was all "grace and swift maneuver." [11]

In 1935 William Paley made important moves—statesmanlike/shrewd—that helped set the stage for a renascence.

CBS was prosperous. It had finished a year in which a gross of $19,300,-000 had yielded a profit of $2,270,000. It had rising prestige and influence in related fields. Columbia Concerts Corporation, of which CBS owned 56 per cent, was handling approximately half the artists touring the United States.

At the same time CBS, like much of radio, was under attack. The channel-reservation battles, in Congress and at the FCC, had created pressure for action. There was also the FCC monopoly talk. Paley was

10. *You Do What You're Told*, pp. 3–7.
11. *Fortune*, June 1935; March 1938.

ready to defend the CBS record in any forum, but he knew it was vulnerable on a number of points. The dominance of important parts of the schedule by advertising interests was one of them. Meanwhile the other part of the schedule, the sustaining part—approximately two-thirds of the network hours—represented an opportunity that was scarcely being used. While it already included some notable material—like the New York Philharmonic, the *American School of the Air,* and the beginnings of a news service—much of it was filler material. For many hours of the day, "programming" meant scheduling orchestras into unsold periods to fulfill obligations to affiliates. Yet those periods could be thought of in another way: an unexplored frontier, available for experimentation. It could yield new ideas. It could provide a balance that would answer criticisms. It might even, thought Paley, help the network in time recapture control over sponsored programming.

Paley decided to open the frontier. Therefore he placed an advertisement:[12]

Wanted—

A BIG MAN

*for an important
creative and executive post in*

RADIO BROADCASTING

A brilliant flair for entertainment, a capacity for bold, broad-gauge creative work in program-building are essential. This man will head a large department in one of the biggest organizations creating radio programs, today. His job will be to create *new* radio programs for some of the most important advertisers on the air. Radio experience, advertising agency experience—either or both would help. Neither is essential.

He must have, in addition to his own creative ability and imagination, sufficient flexibility to cover the whole range of musical and dramatic possibilities. He must be able to organize other people to help him, to find them if necessary; to use their suggestions; to take rough or complete ideas from others and build them into good shows.

12. *Printers' Ink,* May 16, 1935.

This man must be familiar with sources of talent, and with the best in opera, moving pictures, the theatres, night clubs and so on. And he must be thoroughly responsible in all his dealings with talent and with the buyers of talent.

His opportunity will be one of the best in the whole field of radio broadcasting. *Replies confidential.*

Address "X," Box 93, P. I.

It ran in *Printers' Ink,* the New York *Times,* and the New York *Herald-Tribune.* Via a weird comedy it led to a brilliant choice—weird, because it all happened by mistake.

The advertisement brought six hundred applications. Carefully and painfully these were reduced to six finalists. Their dossiers lay in a folder on Klauber's desk. They were to have appointments with Klauber and perhaps Paley.

William B. Lewis had not even answered the advertisement. Raised in St. Louis, he had entered the University of Missouri, but disagreements with his stepfather prompted him in the mid-1920's to quit college and leave home to tackle New York City. After ten years in various advertising agencies he and a friend decided to start a new agency, but at the last moment the friend pulled out, and Lewis launched a disaster. Fortunately his wife had a job and kept him afloat, but he had to liquidate the firm and look for work. In *Fortune* he read about William Paley. The rise of CBS seemed an exciting story. Lewis managed to learn Paley's home address and wrote him a long letter, expressing a desire to work for CBS. Receiving the letter at home Paley took it with him to the office and dropped it casually on Klauber's desk. By mistake it got into the file of finalists. Not knowing why, Lewis found himself summoned to interviews for the position of CBS program chief. Nothing in his record identified him as the supershowman CBS was seeking. He was a school dropout and, at the moment, a failure. His connection with showmanship was tenuous—almost non-existent. But he made a favorable impression and was hired. Early in 1936 William B. Lewis became CBS vice president for programs, in charge of opening a frontier.

NOT FOR SALE

William B. Lewis—he was originally called Wilbur but changed it—was dark-haired and handsome with a square jaw, and could look enormously interested in what people said to him. His face could light up. "You've got an idea there!" He had little originality but quickly recognized it in others, and he set them going.

Irving Reis, a studio engineer, suggested a series with a title like *Columbia Workshop,* in which experiments would be tried. "Good idea!" Lewis said, and promptly scheduled it. Reis had been suggesting it at CBS for months. It was first broadcast in July 1936.

Reis had been studio engineer on various series including *Buck Rogers* and was fascinated by technical challenges. The *Buck Rogers* serial was broadcast from a twenty-first-floor studio that had given trouble with air-conditioning noises. At a bend in a duct the air gave a *whooosh* that had been difficult to dampen. Later, when it became necessary to suggest a rocket traveling through outer space, Reis remembered the duct and put a microphone in the bend. Whenever Buck Rogers was on the move, this microphone was opened, producing a low and unearthly roar. Millions knew exactly what it was—a spaceship.

Some of the early *Columbia Workshop* programs evolved from such technical challenges. A few had to do with *filters.*

In the 1920's and early 1930's a voice heard over a telephone was a baffling problem to radio directors. They would have an actor talk into a hat or box or the wrong end of a megaphone, all with totally irrelevant results. An actual telephone circuit was too cumbersome. The final solution, a filter, emerged in various forms at various stations. It was generally a small box through which a microphone circuit could be shunted. The box had dials on its surface. Its inner mechanism could remove upper or lower tones or a combination of them, to give an *incomplete* reproduction —as given by a telephone. The dials allowed the engineer to vary the effect, creating varieties of incompleteness.

Playing with filter settings became a grand diversion. Someone would exclaim: "Hey! That's a leprechaun!" Sure enough, once the idea was rooted, the sound seemed like nothing *but* a leprechaun. Such games brought home to directors and writers an essential aspect of radio. Many effects became definitive only through context provided by a writer. But once clinched by a word, such effects could be compelling. Some scripts were written on the inspiration of such discoveries. The filter made thoughts, talking serpents, ghosts, invisible men, voices of conscience.

One *Columbia Workshop* script presented a ghost called Benjamin Sweet who, with a friend, could haunt old associates once a week. Since the world was heard from the point of view of the ghosts, it seemed wrong for the ghosts to be filtered. So the process was reversed: the ghosts were heard normally and the voices of the "real" world were heard filtered as through an ectoplasmic curtain. This *Columbia Workshop* script became a separate series, *The Ghost of Benjamin Sweet.* Other *Workshop* experiments were based on echo chambers, and on sound effects used as bridges or symbols as well as supports for realism.

Supervised by an ex-engineer, it was natural that some early *Columbia Workshop* plays stressed technical devices. The emphasis would not continue. World events intruded sharply. In July 1936, at the time the *Workshop* was beginning, a military group under Colonel Francisco Franco started a revolt against the elected socialist government of Spain. He was aided by Mussolini and Hitler, who had just formed the Rome-Berlin Axis. The *Workshop* was soon touched by the world tensions created by these events.

That fall Reis received in the mail a half-hour script entitled *The Fall of the City,* by Archibald MacLeish. "Archie" MacLeish was a former Yale football and water-polo player who had become a successful lawyer and then turned into a poet. After winning a Pulitzer Prize for *Conquistador,* a long poem about Cortes, he veered toward contemporary themes with *Frescoes for Mr. Rockefeller's City* and *Panic,* a verse play about the Wall Street crash. These led naturally to a verse play for radio, *The Fall of the City.*

As soon as Reis read the play, he sensed that radio was entering a new chapter in its career. The play portrayed a city that seemed both mythical and compellingly real. Much of the action took place in the crowded city square. One of the principal characters was a Radio Announcer, speaking from the square.

ANNOUNCER: We are here on the central plaza.
      We are well off to the eastward edge.
      There is a kind of terrace over the crowd here.
      It is precisely four minutes to twelve.
      The crowd is enormous: there might be ten thousand:
      There might be more: the whole square is faces.

For reasons not specified, the people of this city anticipate—perhaps even welcome—subjugation by an approaching conqueror. Trembling at his approach, some accept the inevitability of their enslavement. A prophecy is heard:

The city of masterless men
Will take a master.
There will be shouting then:
Blood after!

As the conqueror approaches, the city breaks into tumult.

VOICES: Order must master us! . . .
Freedom's for fools:
Force is the certainty!
Freedom has eaten our strength and corrupted our virtues!
Men must be ruled!
Fools must be mastered!
Rigor and fast
Will restore us our dignity!
Chains will be liberty!

At the end of the play, the armor-clad figure of the conquering leader dominates the plaza. The people prostrate themselves before him. His visor opens, but the people do not see it. The Announcer sees it. In the space beyond is nothing. The helmet is hollow.

Seeing the great crowd prostrate before the empty armor, the horrified Announcer murmurs:

ANNOUNCER: They wish to be free of their freedom: released from their liberty:—
The long labor of liberty ended!
They lie there! . . .[1]

Reis, able technician but not yet a seasoned director, knew well the challenge he faced in *The Fall of the City*. It seemed to go to the heart of the terror of its time.

Reis began to ask for things. He wanted an acoustical atmosphere resembling that of a city square. He wanted to assemble a huge crowd. William Lewis was willing. Arrangements were made to broadcast the program March 4, 1937, from the Seventh Regiment Armory in New York City. A crowd of students and faculty from the College of the City of New York was recruited; they would be the people of the city of masterless men who would take a master. Because the production seemed likely to be complex without precedent, Reis asked for still more. Other CBS directors were pressed into service. William N. Robson, whose work at KHJ in Los Angeles had attracted attention and who had been brought east by Lewis,

1. MacLeish, *The Fall of the City*, pp. 4, 7, 30–32.

was recruited to direct the crowd. Brewster Morgan, already an experienced CBS director, would direct the cast. Earle McGill, also a staff veteran, would direct the sound effects. Reis became co-ordinator, a sort of symphonic conductor, controlling the pace and cuing each element.

The cast included well-known actors like Burgess Meredith; also unknowns like Orson Welles, who had been on the air but almost always anonymously. Welles portrayed the Radio Announcer.

The scale of the production pushed Reis into added complexities. In the vast armory the crowd drowned the Welles reportage. In the middle of the armory a small studio had to be set up for him and his microphone, shielding him from the crowd. This *isolation booth*—the idea had been used in other productions—had to have a glassed window through which Reis would cue Welles.[2]

A special control booth was also needed. Special lines into the armory involved a host of problems.

All this invited periodic panic, which was further fanned by events. On Saturday, when rehearsals in the armory began, gentlemen with tennis racquets—"from Park Avenue" according to Robson's recollection—insisted they had the place reserved for their tennis game. On Sunday at six o'clock, as the ensemble was beginning a late dress rehearsal, the big armory doors swung open and truck after truck of a National Guard unit rolled in. Someone had failed to cancel maneuvers.[3]

Scheduled for Sunday at 7 P.M., the program competed with Jack Benny on NBC-red, whose program—sponsored by Jell-O—had just ousted Eddie Cantor from leadership in the "Hooperatings."[4] Even so, *The Fall of the City* must have been heard by millions. They heard something that, by the very texture of its sound, gripped the attention and chilled the marrow. Orson Welles, its principal voice, established himself as one of the great performers of radio.

The Fall of the City had an historic impact in several ways. In the printed edition MacLeish included a sort of manifesto, calling on poets to recognize in radio a medium made for their needs. Were they really satis-

2. The term *isolation booth* was later used in television quiz programs for a booth of similar design but different purpose—to isolate contestants from audience hints.
3. Robson, *Reminiscences*, p. 9.
4. Hooperatings were introduced in 1935 and soon superseded Crossley ratings as the dominant rating system. Both were based on telephone calls, but Hooper used a *coincidental* method, noting only what the listener said he was listening to at the time of the call, whereas Crossley had used a *recall* method, noting what the listener mentioned having heard during a period of a few hours.

fied with writing "the thin little books to lie on the front parlor tables?" The poet had once spoken to the many, not the few. Books had isolated him. Radio, establishing a new age of the spoken word, could restore him to the great audience. If the poet would examine radio—commercial radio —he would find it had developed tools "which could not have been more perfectly adapted to the poet's uses had he devised them himself." Let the poet not look hopefully to the stage. The eye, said MacLeish, is a realist, whereas the ear "is already half poet."[5]

Of special value to the poet, as MacLeish saw it, was the narrator. Here MacLeish was prophetic, for much radio experimentation would revolve around narrators and their use.

Even before the manifesto appeared, poets heard the MacLeish call. Almost immediately after *The Fall of the City*, a stream of verse plays began arriving at network offices. It continued unabated—and involved well-known names. Alfred Kreymborg and Stephen Vincent Benét turned to radio. To CBS came a script—handwritten in green ink—by W. H. Auden. It was about horse-racing. He got $100 for it, which he shared with a friend who had been able to provide him with information on betting procedures.[6] Kimball Flaccus supplied a rhapsody on the Fulton Fish Market. Among later recruits were Maxwell Anderson and Edna St. Vincent Millay. The flood went on for years.[7]

MacLeish was prophetic in another way. In *The Fall of the City* a radio announcer broadcast to the world an eye-witness description of the arrival of a conqueror. No announcer had done any such broadcast. But H. V. Kaltenborn was in Europe and moving about amid the mounting turbulence. A younger man, Edward R. Murrow, was also there, arranging broadcasts for short-wave relay to the CBS *American School of the Air*. They were like actors moving into place for a MacLeish scenario.

To William Lewis the *Columbia Workshop* triumph brought deep satisfaction. William Paley was delighted. CBS rate cards carried by time salesmen to advertising agencies listed the *Columbia Workshop* period as "withheld from sale." It was a characteristically shrewd move. The period opposite Jack Benny was considered unsalable at CBS, as it was at NBC-blue. If things changed, the "withheld from sale" sign could always be moved to another period, along with the program.

5. MacLeish, *The Fall of the City*, foreword, ix-xiii.
6. Interview, Davidson Taylor. Many unsponsored dramatic programs at this time were produced with budgets of less than $500.
7. See Kaplan, *Radio and Poetry*.

At NBC the *Columbia Workshop* success brought repercussions. John F. Royal, vice president in charge of programs, got complaints from RCA president David Sarnoff and in turn chivied his English-born script chief Lewis H. Titterton. The CBS upsurge became a daily obsession in Radio City.

MARQUEES

John F. Royal had made his name in vaudeville. After a time as press agent for the magician Houdini, Royal had run Keith-Albee theaters in Boston and Cincinnati and eventually Cleveland, where he had stepped over into radio as manager of WTAM, Cleveland. This powerful station, an NBC-red affiliate, was so richly supported by Midwestern sponsors and was so independent about clearing time for network series that NBC saw no solution but to buy the station.[1] Thus NBC also acquired Royal and brought him to New York as vice president. As a long-time obstacle to NBC network operation, he was especially prized. His ties to vaudeville proved rewarding. NBC's early acquisition of a long roster of headline singers and comedians gave it a head start and a leadership that seemed unshakable—until the mid-1930's. CBS now began to look like a problem.

Royal reacted in vaudeville tradition. He saw the NBC-CBS situation in terms of competing marquees. He watched the marquee across the street. Any strong move called for a similar but more spectacular countermove. This began a period of rivalry that often seemed childish, but bore some rich fruit. In the summer of 1937, when William B. Lewis at CBS announced an unprecedented Shakespeare series to be directed by Brewster Morgan—starring Burgess Meredith as Hamlet, Walter Huston as Henry IV, Edward G. Robinson as Petruchio, Brian Aherne as Henry V—John Royal instantly got in touch with the declining but still celebrated John Barrymore, and announced a Barrymore Shakespeare series.[2] Since the CBS series was scheduled for Monday evenings, Royal also scheduled the Barrymore series on Monday evenings; the listener had to choose. Both

1. Hedges, *Reminiscences*, p. 58.
2. According to one account, Royal phoned an NBC West Coast representative, and the conversation went: "Where's Barrymore?" "Are you kidding? He's in the gutter." "Well, go find that gutter, and get in there with him and get him out of it!" For the series NBC constructed a waist-high railing that surrounded the microphone like a fence. Reporters said it was for Barrymore to hold onto; NBC said it was to keep him the right distance from the microphone. Barrymore achieved several brilliant performances. Slate and Cook, *It Sounds Impossible*, pp. 82–4.

series were scheduled in summer "hiatus" periods vacated by winter sponsors—periods that in earlier years had been virtually wasted.

Meanwhile the marquee battle raged elsewhere. To counter the CBS success with Sunday broadcasts of the New York Philharmonic, Royal in 1937 proposed to Sarnoff that an NBC Symphony Orchestra be formed, drawing outstanding musicians from all over the world, and that the great Arturo Toscanini be invited to form it. As emissary, Samuel Chotzinoff discussed it with the maestro and found him interested.[3]

To counter the good will CBS had won with the *American School of the Air,* NBC made plans for an NBC *University of the Air* under James Rowland Angell, retiring president of Yale University. Poetry likewise became a battlefield. At CBS William B. Lewis scheduled a Sunday afternoon poetry series to be produced by a new discovery, Norman Corwin, whom Lewis respected so highly that he named the series *Norman Corwin's Words Without Music.* NBC countered with an Alfred Kreymborg series of *Fables in Verse.* In all these projects NBC and CBS were using the wilderness soil of unsold periods to grow new crops, of value yet to be determined.

Meanwhile Royal fretted about *Columbia Workshop* and hounded Titterton on the subject. Then one day Titterton phoned with an urgent suggestion. He had been talking to a writer-director who might be the answer —Arch Oboler.

ANOTHER ARCHIE

At the University of Chicago and later, Arch Oboler observed the rise of radio with excitement—and impatience. He proceeded to write fifty radio plays before anyone showed the slightest interest. Then, late in 1933, a telephone call from Clarence Menser, NBC production head in Chicago, told him that his *Futuristics* had won favor and had been chosen for a very special honor. In New York NBC was moving into Radio City; a

---

3. The negotiations produced many legends. Toscanini made the unusual, canny demand that the contract specify net earnings after taxes. As tax rates rose rapidly, the NBC gross payments needed to produce the stipulated net rose beyond foreseeable estimates. During one negotiation in Rome, when Chotzinoff was visiting the maestro and Signora Toscanini, the apartment was bitterly cold. They wore their overcoats but were still frozen to the marrow. At the lady's suggestion—so the story goes—they all got into bed with their coats on; covered by a large quilt, they continued their earnest discussions. The NBC Symphony project, though conceived by Royal, was credited to Sarnoff in NBC releases.

mammoth on-the-air dedication was planned, with numerous pickups. Chicago would do a coast-to-coast broadcast of *Futuristics*. Oboler would get $50.

The young man was dismayed about the fee. He had worked very hard on it, he explained. Menser mentioned the great honor, and the deal was concluded. Later Oboler came in to suggest an experimental series exploiting the potentialities of radio. He brought possible scripts, some dealing with dictators and the fall of nations. Oboler was told the radio audience was not mature enough for such material, but he was offered something else—the horror series *Lights Out,* broadcast over the network every Tuesday at midnight. Oboler became its writer and later its master of ceremonies. He tackled the work avidly and wrote sixty scripts, some of which dealt with out-of-this-world dictators and the fall of galaxies. One program is said to have been so frightening that it drew 50,000 letters of protest.

On *Lights Out* Oboler had the tutelage of its previous writer, Wyllis Cooper, who made him aware of undreamed facets of the medium. Along with others, Oboler came to consider Cooper one of the innovating geniuses of radio.[1] Oboler began to experiment with narration, occasionally in a stream-of-consciousness form.

Oboler was a prodigious and swift worker. Having a dozen friends in for a social evening, he might withdraw about 11 P.M. to tackle a script, then rejoin them at 1 A.M. with script in hand. He loved to sit listening to sound-effects records; some exploded into script ideas. In a typical Oboler *Lights Out,* a chicken heart grew constantly larger in the course of a scientific experiment, until it overwhelmed the world. At the end of the play the last survivors were cruising in a small plane six thousand feet above the chicken heart. The plane then sputtered, failed and came down with a ghoulish, dull splash. The beat of the all-encompassing heart continued as the play ended.

Past and future alike fascinated Oboler. On his stationery he felt he should have, as a crest, a dinosaur rampant on a field of spiral nebulae. His imagination electrified co-workers, especially sound technicians. In one program they had to turn a man inside out. The task was solemnly divided into three components: for *flesh* sounds, a technician put his arm in a length of inner tube, grasped the end firmly, and yanked; for *blood-and-guts* sounds, warm spaghetti was attacked with bathroom plunger;

1. Interview, Arch Oboler.

for *bones crunching*, Lifesavers were ground between the teeth, very close to the microphone.[2]

On *Lights Out* Oboler became a sure craftsman, but he chafed at the confinement to horror. Chicago network executives were on the alert against any intrusion of the current world; people were not considered ready for it. Oboler left for a few months of service in Hollywood, during which he contributed some spectacular short sketches to variety hours. Then one day he turned up at Titterton's office in New York with a recording he had made with friends—directing it himself and using a rented disk recorder. It was entitled *The Ugliest Man in the World* and featured Raymond Edward Johnson. Oboler carried equipment to play it for Titterton. After about a minute, Oboler found Titterton suddenly lifting his telephone. To his secretary he said in his quiet, peppery voice: "I don't want to be disturbed for the next half hour." Afterwards, according to Oboler's recollection, he was kept waiting while Titterton phoned Royal and went upstairs to confer with him. Later a contract was signed. Oboler was to get $150 a week for writing and directing a weekly series of plays; this was later raised to $250. The series was to occupy the Sunday 7–7:30 period on NBC-blue, opposite Jack Benny. When it came time to select a series title, Titterton suggested *Arch Oboler's Plays*. Oboler was flabbergasted. Titterton, like Lewis, believed that the growth of the medium would depend, in the long run, on writers.

The Oboler *forte* was melodrama. His determination to make it yield contemporary meaning had only intermittent success, but his virtuosity as a radio technician aroused intense interest. His direction was precise. The start or finish of a musical theme or sound effect was always pinpointed to the syllable. He began getting phone calls from celebrated actors and actresses, offering their services. Such a call came from the world-famed Alla Nazimova. The fee was no issue, she said; she would accept the standard $21. For her he wrote an overtly anti-Nazi play, *Ivory Tower*. NBC had tremors but approved it. Nazimova, who was determined to perform the play, had marquee value. Another investment in sustaining time was paying unexpected dividends.

2. Beaumont, "Requiem for Radio," *Playboy*, May 1960.

HAYSTACK

When H. V. Kaltenborn headed for Spain to look at the Franco rebellion —rapidly becoming an international struggle—he was paying all his own traveling and living expenses. He was a CBS news analyst doing two broadcasts a week, unsponsored and in fringe periods. He had been on CBS six years, always unsponsored except for three months under Cunard Line auspices. He was not considered commercial material. His CBS salary was $50 per broadcast, bringing him a total of $100 per week. He was fifty-eight years old.[1]

Travel cost him far more than his CBS pay but was important to him. His main income came from lecture bookings throughout the United States. Air exposure plus constant travel maintained his market value as a lecturer. The travel enabled him to make the kind of statement that punctuated his talks on and off the air: "Now, I stood alongside the desk of the President of the United States at a press conference last week, where he said definitely that he believed in the Civil Service, and I believe he does . . ." (CBS, March 1, 1936). "Two weeks ago, I was flying over the locks of the Panama Canal . . ." (CBS, January 17, 1937). "Politically they are, as the President of Czechoslovakia said to me, illiterate" (CBS, March 20, 1938).[2] These promotional parentheses made friends squirm but successfully conveyed the picture of a newsman in relentless motion. Very likely he had, in fact, talked with more world leaders than any other radio newsman. They included Hitler and Mussolini.

In France, near the Spanish border, Kaltenborn found a neck of land projecting into Spain. Because the battle of Irun raged beyond the border, the French had evacuated the strip, but Kaltenborn and a French engineer managed to establish themselves on it. A river marked the border. The strip was between the opposing armies and sometimes bullets whistled overhead. But there was also an evacuated farmhouse with a telephone. Kaltenborn was determined to broadcast for the first time from Europe to America—via short-wave—the sounds of war. A circuit was developed leading via Paris and London to a British short-wave transmitter.

Hugging a haystack, Kaltenborn and his engineer found their micro-

1. The following is based on Kaltenborn, *Reminiscences,* and other sources as mentioned.
2. Quoted, Chester, *The Radio Commentaries of H. V. Kaltenborn.* The scripts are in Kaltenborn, *Papers,* at the Mass Communications History Center, Madison, Wisconsin.

phone picking up the battle sounds. Overhead passed French planes, guarding the border. Kaltenborn notified CBS in New York that he was ready. "Hold up," said the reply. Several sponsored programs were coming up. The Battle of Irun had to wait for an unsold period. Finally it was broadcast.

During the following months, with cars rented at fantastic prices in Hendaye—at his own expense—Kaltenborn made trips into areas held by the government and to others held by Franco's rebels. He returned to France for his CBS broadcasts, which became a chronicle of a war and of rising personal indignation. Britain, France, Germany, Italy, and Portugal had signed a "non-intervention" agreement which effectively kept Britain and France inactive even though the others were blatantly violating it. The United States was meanwhile tied by its arms embargo law, precipitated by a Senate munitions investigating committee of the mid-1930's, which had stirred wide indignation by its revelations of huge profits made by American munitions makers—"merchants of death"—during the 1914–18 World War. This arms embargo had at first won general acceptance. But as the Spanish republic bled in a struggle for survival, the embargo became to Kaltenborn and others a symbol of tragedy and horror. On September 27, 1936, he said over CBS:

> I know of my own observation that German planes, Italian planes, Italian airmen, Portuguese supplies have come in to the rebel armies of Spain and that would seem to be, on the face of it, a definite violation of the non-intervention agreement signed by those powers. . . .

January 10, 1937:

> We have, in effect, given a decisive advantage to the rebels in Spain. Ours is the only country from which the legal Spanish government can obtain certain kinds of supplies . . . the rebels in Spain get all they want from Germany and Italy. . . .

March 14, 1937:

> Non-intervention is and has been a mockery from the beginning. . . .

March 28, 1937:

> Of course the rebels would have been beaten in two months if it had not been for German and Italian help. From the first, fascist help for the rebels far outweighed French or Russian help for the loyalists. That help has now created a sharp European crisis . . . and France and Britain continue their namby-pamby non-intervention policy. . . .

Kaltenborn told listeners that he had seen hundreds of Italian prisoners in loyalist jails.

A dramatic aspect of the Kaltenborn broadcasts was that they contrasted sharply with other versions of the war, in terminology as well as point of view. The Hearst press seldom spoke of "rebels," preferring "insurgents" or "the Franco regime." Instead of "loyalists" or "the legal Spanish government" it preferred "the reds." Many other papers, perhaps in part for headline convenience, adopted "reds." This terminology probably helped convey an impression of a government under a respectable general coping with an insurrectionary rabble. (When Kaltenborn spoke of "rebels," some listeners may have thought he meant the reds.) Thus a battle of terminology reflected, and further intensified, a cleavage that was bringing deep divisions to America as to Europe.

Kaltenborn was soon speaking of the war as "part of the fascist international drive for power." But suddenly the spotlight shifted.

ACROSS THE GOAL LINE

Edward R. Murrow had joined CBS in 1935 as director of talks after journalist Raymond Swing had declined the job. Swing wanted to broadcast, and this was to be a supervisory, not an on-the-air job.

Murrow, handsome and lean, was still in his twenties. As president of the National Student Federation he had organized debates between American and European universities. Later, for the Institute of International Education, he had helped place refugee scholars at American colleges. This background helped him in his new job, and he set about it impressively.

As signs pointed to a wider war in Europe, Edward Klauber felt CBS must have a new European director. The position had been held by César Saerchinger, who had first organized CBS broadcasts from Europe,[1] but he had resigned, feeling the work had no future. When Klauber asked William B. Lewis to propose candidates for the job, Lewis suggested Murrow, but Klauber at once rejected the idea, saying Murrow was too important as director of talks.

A few weeks later Klauber surprised Lewis by saying: "I've thought of exactly the person we need for that European job—Edward R. Murrow."

1. See *A Tower in Babel*, pp. 247–50, 280.

Lewis agreed it was a brilliant suggestion, and in 1937 Murrow headed for Europe to organize the work.

On August 20, 1937, in Berlin, journalist William L. Shirer wrote in his diary:

> I have a job. I am to go to work for the Columbia Broadcasting System. That is, *if* . . . I have a job *if* my *voice* is all right. . . . Who ever heard of an adult with no pretenses to being a singer or any other kind of artist being dependent for a good, interesting job on his *voice?* And is mine terrible.

> It has been quite an evening. I met Edward R. Murrow, European manager of CBS, in the lobby of the Adlon at seven o'clock. As I walked up to him I was a little taken aback by his handsome face. Just what you would expect from radio, I thought.[2]

At first the work included cultural events such as concerts, as well as newscasts. In March 1938 Murrow was in Warsaw lining up a program for the *American School of the Air* while Shirer was in Vienna for the same purpose. Then Shirer telephoned Murrow: "The opposing team has just crossed the goal line."

"Are you sure?"

"I'm paid to be sure."

With these words Shirer told his boss that the expected *Anschluss*—Hitler's seizure of Austria—had begun.[3] German troops were crossing the border. It was agreed that Shirer should at once fly to London to broadcast the story. Murrow himself flew to Berlin, where he chartered a twenty-seven-seat Lufthansa transport for $1000. He was determined to reach Vienna, and it was the only plane he could get on any terms. He became its sole passenger. In Vienna he took a streetcar into the city. He was there to describe by short-wave the fall of a city. On March 13, 1938, he broadcast his first news report to American listeners.

> This is Edward Murrow speaking from Vienna. It's now nearly 2:30 in the morning and Herr Hitler has not yet arrived. No one seems to know just when he will get here, but most people expect him sometime after ten o'clock tomorrow morning. . . .

> I arrived here by air from Warsaw and Berlin only a few hours ago. From the air, Vienna didn't look much different than it had before, but

2. Shirer, *Berlin Diary*, pp. 78–80.
3. Woolley, *A Rhetorical Study: The Radio Speaking of Edward R. Murrow*, pp. 35–6.

nevertheless it's changed . . . they lift the right arm a little higher
here than in Berlin and the "Heil Hitler" is said a little more loudly.
. . . Young storm troopers are riding about the streets, riding about
in trucks and vehicles of all sorts, singing and tossing oranges out to the
crowd. Nearly every principal building has its armed guard, including the one from which I am speaking. . . . There's a certain air of
expectancy about the city, everyone waiting and wondering where
and at what time Herr Hitler will arrive.

Thus listeners were introduced to a voice that spoke with a quality of its
own—a strength used with dramatic understatement. Listeners were introduced to something else too. On the same broadcast they heard reports
from William L. Shirer in London, Edgar Ansel Mowrer in Paris, Pierre
Huss in Berlin, Frank Gervasi in Rome, and Robert Trout in New York.
The "news round-up," a CBS creation, was born in crisis.[4]

The CBS news team began to maneuver with extraordinary swiftness
and precision. On Sunday March 19 Murrow continued his Vienna story—
from London.

Later Herr Hitler arrived, made a speech, took the salute of the big
parade, and Austria ceased to exist. Vienna became a provincial town;
faithful party members, most of them Germans, were placed in all the
important posts. It was called a bloodless conquest and in some ways
it was, but I'd like to be able to forget the haunted look on the faces
of those long lines of people outside the banks and travel offices.
People trying to get away. I'd like to forget the tired futile look of the
Austrian army officers, and the thud of hobnail boots and the crash of
light tanks in the early hours of the morning on the Ringstrasse, and
the pitiful uncertainty and bewilderment of those forced to lift the
right hand and shout "Heil Hitler" for the first time. I'd like to forget the sound of the smashing glass as the Jewish shop streets were
raided; the hoots and jeers aimed at those forced to scrub the sidewalk.

Well, those are a few of the things that happened in Austria. People
in London are wondering when similar things may happen again.

That "similar things" would happen seemed certain. But who could react
adequately to that certainty? A moment later Shirer was reporting from
Paris:

I strolled down the Grands Boulevards and also the Champs Élysées
on my way to the studio tonight. They were filled with people, rush-

4. Bliss (ed.), *In Search of Light,* pp. 4–5.

ing to the movies or to their favorite cafés. Both are filled as they always are on Sunday night. The only sign of extraordinary events was that everybody was buying newspapers, pausing in the street to read about the prospects for peace or war. I return you now to New York.[5]

Day by day, as Murrow and Shirer returned them "to New York," listeners braced themselves for new developments. Hitler did not keep them waiting long. He began mounting threats and fulminations against Czechoslovakia. Murrow added new members to the CBS European staff. Technical preparations were also made. During the Vienna broadcast Murrow's voice had been routed via a short-wave transmitter in Berlin. In a Czechoslovakian crisis this might not be possible. CBS engineers therefore proceeded to help the Czechoslovakian government develop a short-wave station so that direct communication with the United States would be possible. It was all very deliberate, like wiring a parade route. CBS newsman H. V. Kaltenborn, who had returned to the United States, later recalled: "We had everything ready when the Munich crisis began." Kaltenborn himself was ready for an extraordinary role.[6]

For eighteen days, September 12 through 29, the world was gripped in tension shared minute by minute through radio. From a packed stadium in Nuremberg, backed by the roar of scores of thousands of voices, Hitler screamed threats against Czechoslovakia, demanding cession of its Sudetenland. Troops moved into position. In Prague gas masks were distributed, and at the airport and the railroad station Shirer saw would-be refugees looking for transportation. The French cabinet was deadlocked, not sure if it would meet its treaty obligations to the Czechs. President Roosevelt sent a plea to Hitler. British Prime Minister Neville Chamberlain wired Hitler: "I propose to come over at once to see you with a view to trying to find a peaceful solution." He would gladly come the very next day, Chamberlain said. "Good Heavens!" ("Ich bin vom Himmel gefallen!") exclaimed Hitler as he read the eager message. Chamberlain flew to Hitler; at the latter's aery in Berchtesgaden Chamberlain listened to a tirade, then heard the key question: would Britain agree to cession of the Sudetenland? Chamberlain was responsive; he at once approved the idea in principle. But he must first talk to the French and others. Returning to England, he made himself salesman of the German plan. A message went to the Czechs, saying that the French and British recognized "how great is

5. CBS, March 19, 1938.
6. Kaltenborn, *Reminiscences*, p. 202.

the sacrifice thus required of the Czechoslovak government in the cause of peace." The Czechs rejected the notion; the proposed cession would leave them defenseless. But they were ignored; the plan went forward. Hitler and Chamberlain met again at Godesberg. Hitler asked for more territory, and Chamberlain agreed. Shirer was baffled at their cordiality as they stood together. Hitler maintained the pressure. At the Berlin Sportpalast he went into paroxysms of rage, hurling insults at President Eduard Beneš of Czechoslovakia. The Czechs remained stubborn. Russia said it would back the Czechs if France did likewise. A Chamberlain note urged Beneš to yield, implying that if war broke out Czechoslovakia must bear the onus. In a broadcast heard in the United States, Chamberlain defended his role: "How horrible, fantastic, incredible it is that we should be digging trenches . . . because of a quarrel in a faraway country between people of whom we know nothing!" Then a climax: Hitler, Mussolini, Daladier, and Chamberlain headed for Munich to settle the details. The Czech ambassador in London, Jan Masaryk, made inquiry as to whether Czechoslovakia would be represented. No, he was told, Hitler would not stand for it; but in the end a Czech was allowed "in the next room." The great men assembled and affixed their signatures. Daladier looked wretched. Chamberlain returned to London. From a second-story window at 10 Downing Street he told a crowd that it was "peace with honor . . . peace in our time." The British wanted desperately to believe it. In Parliament Winston Churchill called it an "unmitigated defeat," but was shouted down.[7]

During this eighteen-day period millions of Americans kept track of these events through short-wave pickups and commentaries. According to *Variety*, CBS made 151 short-wave pickups to NBC's 147 and a lesser number by MBS. All the principals—Hitler, Mussolini, Chamberlain, Daladier, Beneš, Masaryk—were heard on the air. On CBS it was Kaltenborn who threaded the drama together—translating, commenting, interpreting, explaining as he felt the need. The CBS-Kaltenborn coverage stole the radio spotlight. It was the greatest show yet heard on American radio.

For eighteen days Kaltenborn was almost constantly on the air, doing at least eight-five separate broadcasts, some lasting two hours. He was uniquely equipped for the task. He could understand and instantly translate German or French. The principal actors were all known to him. "All

7. Shirer, *The Rise and Fall of the Third Reich*, pp. 520–67.

my life," he said, "I had prepared for this particular event without know-ing it." At each development he assessed its importance without hesitation. He virtually lived in Studio 9 at CBS, 485 Madison Avenue. Between cli-maxes he slept on a cot. With each new bulletin on the news ticker, Paul White rushed to wake him. "A flash, Hans!" As Kaltenborn rose, White pressed the button that turned on Kaltenborn's microphone. Instantly other CBS programs were off the air. An attendant brought the new bulle-tin. Kaltenborn read it at once on the air and then commented on it. Dur-ing the final days of the crisis, as the broadcasts dealt with the Munich meeting, a violent storm swept through the northeastern parts of the United States, contributing to a sense of apocalyptic struggle.

In contrast to the policy during the Battle of Irun, CBS now gave the Kaltenborn broadcasts priority over all commercial commitments. Pro-gram after program was canceled.[8]

The year that led to Munich had seen mounting interest in news broad-casts. Commentaries were started by Dorothy Thompson on NBC-red and by General Hugh S. Johnson, former NRA administrator, on NBC-blue. A weekly commentary was begun by Raymond Swing on WOR, New York, and soon became a five-times-a-week MBS feature. Swing, who started at a salary of $40 per program, was warned not to dream about a sponsor; such things could not happen. But his ratings rose so astonishingly that he *did* begin to think about it.[9] Then came Munich, changing the whole out-look for radio newsmen. NBC began to look for "someone like Kalten-born." So did MBS. Its publicity writer, Lester Gottlieb, who had been an office boy at Simon & Schuster, remembered an editor there who had seemed knowledgeable. As a result editor Quincy Howe—courtesy of the office boy—became an MBS commentator. Meanwhile General Mills de-cided to sponsor H. V. Kaltenborn. Raymond Swing likewise achieved the impossible—sponsorship by White Owl cigars. Swing was puzzled to find that even friends thought more of him now that he had his cigar sponsor. Marketplace acceptance seemed to raise his standing in their eyes.

The status of the radio commentator was suddenly an extraordinary

---

8. Kaltenborn, *Reminiscences*, pp. 201–4; Kaltenborn, *I Broadcast the Crisis*, pp. 9–12.
9. Swing was known to listeners at this time as Raymond *Gram* Swing. He had mar-ried the feminist Betty Gram, a follower of Lucy Stone, who believed in retaining her maiden name in marriage. As a journalist Swing found it awkward to travel with a lady having a different name, and persuaded her to become Betty Gram Swing while he became Raymond Gram Swing. After their divorce he dropped the *Gram* but found it clinging to him long afterward in fan mail and radio columns.

thing. Swing was received by Secretary of State Cordell Hull for discussion of the implications of Munich. President Roosevelt was apparently considering taking some credit for preserving peace, because of his appeals to Hitler. Swing warned: "Munich stinks! It will stink throughout history. And anyone who identifies himself with it will stink. . . ." Such talks with world leaders would not be unusual for radio newsmen.[10]

Kaltenborn turned suddenly into an all-purpose celebrity. His staggering virtuosity was material for topical humor. NBC news chief A. A. Schechter, paying tribute to Kaltenborn's prowess as an ad-libber, said: "You could wake Kaltenborn up at four o'clock in the morning and just say 'Czechoslovakia'—one word—and he'd talk for thirty minutes on Czechoslovakia."[11] Kaltenborn, though seldom showing a glint of humor, was invited for a huge fee to appear on an Eddie Cantor series sponsored by Camel cigarettes. Knowing his aversion to speaking commercials, the Eddie Cantor writers tried to extract humor from it. Having introduced Kaltenborn as "the greatest news commentator of our time, Columbia's gem of the ozone," Cantor continued:

CANTOR: Mr. Kaltenborn, in those hectic days from September 12th to the 29th, when you were broadcasting day and night, you were under great tension. What did you do to ease that tension—you know, to relax?

KALTENBORN: Oh, I drank coffee.

CANTOR: Yes, but you just can't keep drinking coffee.

KALTENBORN: Oh no, no. Sometimes I drank soup. Then when I'd get really nervous, I'd—

CANTOR: You'd let up, huh?

KALTENBORN: No—I'd lie down and rest a while.

CANTOR: But Mr. Kaltenborn, what did you do when you got jangled nerves?

KALTENBORN: Oh, I turned off your program!

CANTOR: Look—when you felt your nerves were on edge—didn't you—

KALTENBORN: No, I didn't.

CANTOR: Just a moment, please . . . R. J. Reynolds Tobacco Company, makers of Camel Cigarettes: will you admit your boy is trying?[12]

Kaltenborn spoke rapidly. He sometimes started a broadcast at 150 words per minute but was likely to end at 200 words per minute. His clipped delivery and individual speech mannerisms made him an ideal subject for amateur-hour impersonations. *Russia* was pronounced in three distinct syllables—RUSH-she-uh. At lectures he was sometimes told he

10. Howe, *Reminiscences*, p. 91; Swing, *Good Evening*, pp. 195–203.
11. Schechter, *Reminiscences*, p. 23.
12. November 21, 1938, *Camel Caravan*. Kaltenborn, *Papers*.

sounded vindictive on the air, but benign in person; that he sounded English but looked German; and that he was much taller than had been expected.[13]

Few events in history did more for radio's prestige than the Kaltenborn Munich broadcasts. Even James Rorty, frequent and scathing critic of American radio, joined the chorus of praise with an article in *The Nation* entitled "Radio Comes Through." He found Kaltenborn "brilliantly illuminating." In addition, he sensed that the barrage of broadcast statements by world leaders had added a totally new dimension to world diplomacy. "For the first time, history has been made in the hearing of its pawns." [14]

All this had been, once more, the reward of pioneer work in unsold time. Network news operations, long a marginal activity, had produced the most spectacular episode in broadcasting history. It was soon followed by another—closely related—almost as strange.

NEW JERSEY INVADED

While the ferment in network programming—especially sustaining programming—was being stirred by events in Europe, it was also stirred by developments at home. The Depression was creating its own fever and culture.

The Federal Theater, launched in 1935 to put unemployed theater people to work,[1] became an enterprise of scant budgets and shabby playhouses, but also of experiment and ideas. At the same time the labor movement, burgeoning after the Wagner Act of 1935, was producing a theater movement of its own, yielding the exuberant musical *Pins and Needles* of the International Ladies Garment Workers Union as well as the shows in summer camps of the labor movement, like Camp Unity and Camp Tamiment—which were fostering such talents as Danny Kaye. These camps were part of the "borscht circuit"—the camps and hotels of the Catskill Mountains and adjoining areas, which were bursting with activity in drama and music. Interacting with this was a widespread surge of folk music, bringing to the fore such figures as Woody Guthrie with his dustbowl ballads, and the Negro music of Huddie Ledbetter—"Lead-

13. Chester, *The Radio Commentaries of H. V. Kaltenborn*, p. 465.
14. *The Nation*, October 15, 1938.
1. Unemployed theater workers were estimated at twenty to thirty thousand in New York City alone. Flanagan, *Arena*, p. 20.

belly." Alan Lomax, who in 1937 took charge of the folk music archive of the Library of Congress, played an important role in furthering this surge —eventually, via radio. On Broadway the intellectual, proletariat-minded Group Theater was another Depression product. And finally came the Mercury Theater, a spin-off of the Federal Theater.

Such activities were almost totally ignored by sponsored programming but began to push into the frontiers of unsold time, especially at CBS. It was at CBS that Alan Lomax—sent to musical supervisor Davidson Taylor by Harold Spivacke of the Library of Congress—found a welcome and an invitation to produce a folksong series on the *American School of the Air*. CBS also found time for a Federal Theater series. Meanwhile William B. Lewis announced another and more spectacular venture: *Mercury Theater on the Air*, under Orson Welles and John Houseman. Scheduled Sundays at 8 P.M. eastern time opposite the Edgar Bergen-Charlie McCarthy series, it had its debut in mid-1938.

Orson Welles, born in Chicago in 1915, was already widely quoted at the age of six.[2] His father was an inventor, and his mother a musician. The boy lived among musicians, painters, and actors, who treated him like an adult. He was taught magic by Houdini. He was considered a fine cartoonist and did brilliant things with a puppet theater. He did not go to school until he was ten, but by then he had read all of Shakespeare and some Nietzsche. He could not add, but there would always be people to do that for him. The Todd School in Woodstock, Illinois, virtually reorganized its curriculum around him. Its headmaster Roger Hill became his friend and collaborator. Orson graduated in 1930 and started a sketching tour of Ireland. After seeing a performance at the Abbey Theater in Dublin, he tried out for a part, got it, and was asked to stay as guest star; no one suspected he was only sixteen. Heading for the New York theater, he found his Irish triumphs meant nothing, and he returned to Chicago and a time of frustration. He sold a few stories to pulp magazines. But at a party he met Thornton Wilder, who had heard of his Irish successes and gave him a note to Alexander Woollcott which won him a New York start. After a tour with Katharine Cornell he played briefly in *Panic*, the Archibald MacLeish verse play about the Wall Street crash, directed by John Houseman. This started a Welles-Houseman partnership; they formed a Federal Theater producing unit and astonished New York with a virtuoso *Dr. Faustus*

2. The following is based on Noble, *The Fabulous Orson Welles*, and other sources as noted.

and a Negro *Macbeth* in a Haiti setting. When their next venture, Marc Blitzstein's opera *The Cradle Will Rock,* was halted by Federal Theater executives as too radical, the Welles-Houseman team decided to start the Mercury Theater. Its first production—*Julius Caesar* in fascist-style uniforms acted against a bare brick wall—was so electrifying that it quickly led to a CBS offer.

Welles, a youth of protean energies who had been supplementing his theater earnings with radio appearances on *The March of Time, The Shadow,* and *The Fall of the City*—sometimes to help finance theater projects—at once showed an imaginative grasp of the possibilities of radio. He made varied use of narration—a tool that was still considered poisonous in commercial circles. A radio *Julius Caesar* used narrative passages from Plutarch spoken by H. V. Kaltenborn, who thus guided listeners through another crisis in power politics. In most productions it was Welles himself who narrated. His voice could produce organ tones but also narrative passages of amazing rhythmic dexterity. He was especially successful with first-person narration, putting the aural spotlight fully on one character and often producing a narration as charged with emotional richness as any dialogue scene.

When script writer Howard Koch began work on the H. G. Wells story *The War of the Worlds,* the project seemed unpromising. It was for a time dropped from the schedule in favor of a George Bernard Shaw play, but clearance problems with Shaw put *The War of the Worlds* back on the list. To counteract its old-fashioned quality, the story was transferred to the United States, with the landings of the Martians placed in New Jersey. John Houseman, an astute editor, supervised the writing but feared that few would take the play seriously enough to listen to it.

Orson Welles was rehearsing a new Mercury Theater stage production, working on the Sunday series, and making flying trips to a girl in Chicago. Each week the early radio rehearsals were directed by Paul Stewart, with a stand-in in Welles's role. Welles would return in mid-week, listen to a recording of the Tuesday rehearsal, then take over the direction. In the case of *The War of the Worlds,* CBS had by this time asked for thirty-eight script changes. The Museum of Natural History was changed to "National History Museum." National Guard was changed to "Militia." U.S. Weather Bureau was changed to "Government Weather Bureau" or to "meteorological bureau." The purpose was to emphasize a fiction atmosphere. CBS was already worried that the program might seem too real, although the Mercury Theater group was only worried that it might seem too absurd.

With the changes made, the program went on the air on Sunday evening, October 30, 1938—a month after Munich.

ANNOUNCER:　The Columbia Broadcasting System and its affiliated stations present Orson Welles and the Mercury Theater on the Air in *The War of the Worlds* by H. G. Wells. Ladies and gentlemen: the director of the Mercury Theater and star of these broadcasts, Orson Welles.

WELLES:　We know now that in the early years of the twentieth century this world was being watched closely by intelligences greater than man's and yet as mortal as his own. We know now that as human beings busied themselves with their various concerns they were scrutinized and studied, perhaps almost as narrowly as a man with a microscope might scrutinize the transient creatures that swarm and multiply in a drop of water. Across an immense ethereal gulf, minds that are to our minds as ours are to the beasts of the jungle, intellects vast, cool, and unsympathetic, regarded this earth with envious eyes and slowly and surely drew their plans against us. In the thirty-ninth year of the twentieth century came the great disillusionment.

It was near the end of October. Business was better. The war scare was over. More men were back at work. Sales were picking up. On this particular evening, October 30, the Crossley service estimated that thirty-two million people were listening to their radios.

ANNOUNCER:　For the next twenty-four hours not much change in temperature. A low pressure area over the northeastern states, bringing a forecast of rain, accompanied by winds of light gale force. Maximum temperature 66, minimum 48. This weather report comes to you from the Government Weather Bureau.

We now take you to the Meridian Room in the Hotel Park Plaza in downtown New York, where you will be entertained by the music of Ramon Raquello and his orchestra.

At this point many listeners were puzzled. They did indeed seem to be listening to a second-rate orchestra in a hotel pickup—whether real or fictional, who could say or care? But within seconds it was interrupted.

ANNOUNCER:　Ladies and gentlemen, we interrupt our program of dance music to bring you a special bulletin from the Intercontinental Radio News. At twenty minutes before eight, Central Time, Professor Farrell of the Mount Jennings Observatory, Chicago, Illinois, reports observing several explosions of incandescent gas, occurring at regular intervals on the planet Mars. The spectroscope indicates the gas to be hydrogen and moving toward the earth with enormous velocity. Professor Pierson of the observatory at Princeton confirms Farrell's observation, and describes the phenomenon as "like a jet of blue flame shot from a gun." We return you to the music of Ramon Raquello.

(*Music: up. Sound of applause*)

ANNOUNCER: Now a tune that never loses favor, the ever-popular "Star Dust."
ANNOUNCER 2 (*interrupting*): Ladies and gentlemen, following on the news given in our bulletin a moment ago, the government meteorological bureau has requested the large observatories of the country to keep an astronomical watch on any further disturbances on the planet Mars. Due to the unusual nature of this occurrence, we have arranged an interview with the noted astronomer, Professor Pierson. We are ready to take you to the Princeton Observatory at Princeton where Carl Phillips, our commentator, will interview Professor Richard Pierson, famous astronomer.
PHILLIPS: Good evening, ladies and gentlemen. This is Carl Phillips speaking to you from. . . .

Minutes later an object was reported to have landed in a farm near Grovers Mill, N.J. In a purported pickup from that location, listeners heard an announcer describe a creature emerging from the object, sending out rays that caused barns, automobiles, and woods to burst into flame. This "eye witness description" suddenly ceased "due to circumstances beyond our control." Switches to other points followed, including one supposedly from Washington, D. C. Other Martian landings were reported.[3]

To the control room of the CBS studio a phone call came from a police station. "What's going on up there?" Another policeman was seen outside the studio, peering through the porthole window. He began to enter but was pushed out by an actor. These were the first hints to those in the studio that their activities were snowballing into something quite different.[4]

All over the United States people were telephoning newspapers to ask what they should do. The New York *Times* alone is said to have received 875 calls. The Associated Press sent out an explanatory bulletin to its member papers. Police stations were also swamped with calls. Priests had calls from people seeking confession. But many people were not waiting to make telephone calls. By 8:30 cars were racing along highways between New York and Philadelphia. Police were helpless. Some people dug old gas masks out of closets. Sailors on shore leave in New York were sum-

3. "The War of the Worlds," *Mercury Theater on the Air,* CBS, October 30, 1938.
4. Interview, Paul Stewart.

moned back to their ships. Outbreaks of panic occurred throughout the country. In Indianapolis a woman rushed into a church service screaming that the world was coming to an end; she had heard it on the radio. The service broke up hurriedly. A power failure in a town in the state of Washington convinced its inhabitants that the end had indeed come. In various parts of the country, as people rushed about in a panic, some said they had seen the Martians.

It was a brilliantly produced broadcast, with an impact not foreshadowed by anything in radio experience. Its relation to war fears was avidly discussed. Dorothy Thompson called it "the news story of the century—an event which made a greater contribution to an understanding of Hitlerism, Mussolinism, Stalinism, anti-Semitism, and all the other terrorisms of our time than all the words about them that have been written by reasonable men." The event was in many ways a re-enactment of *The Fall of the City:* men had rushed to prostrate themselves before an empty visor.

For years the panic participants were kept busy answering questions of researchers. It became "the first panic . . . studied with the research tools now available." [5]

The panic had one immediate effect on broadcast policy. Interruptions for fictional news bulletins became taboo in broadcast drama.

As CBS and the FCC conducted post-mortems, the panic seemed for a moment to have doomed the Mercury Theater series, but instead established its commercial value. Sponsors, including the Campbell Soup Company, became interested. The 8–9 P.M. period on CBS, long considered worthless because of the Charlie McCarthy competition, likewise won commercial status. Perhaps it could start a stampede to Campbell soups. *Mercury Theater on the Air* became *Campbell Playhouse.*

The broadcast was a high point in the radio renascence. The years 1936–38 had produced on the air a mounting creative excitement in which Reis, MacLeish, Robson, Oboler, Corwin, Kaltenborn, Murrow, Shirer, Swing, Houseman, Koch, and others had taken part. Their work had been a by-product of commercial affluence and been financed by it, but had been done almost entirely in unsold time, as a result of an executive decision to use that time for more than fill-in purposes.

These men had helped to bring into existence a sustaining program world impatient with formula, zestful for experiment. This world had

5. Cantril *et al., The Invasion from Mars,* pp. vii, 47–84; Allen, *Since Yesterday,* pp. 261–3.

shown surprisingly little relationship with commercial program activities. Its productions used the same studios, were served by the same engineers, and to some extent called on the same actors. But the writers and directors tended to be different.

Those in the commercial program world lived under an advertising agency hierarchy, those in the sustaining program world under a network hierarchy. There was some interaction and crossing over, often for personal financial reasons. But during 1936–38 the groups lived largely separate lives. They passed each other in network corridors but had little reason for contact.

To the commercial directors, sustaining people were a species of dependent relatives living on marginal pay. To the sustaining people, the commercial people were not free souls.

The sustaining people worked by preference in the tensions of their time. They tended to be journalists even when writing drama or poetry. A straight line ran from MacLeish's city through Kaltenborn's haystack— through the chicken heart—through Vienna—through Munich—to the New Jersey flatlands.

With some exceptions the world of commercial programming during 1936–38 was startlingly different.

WE PROUDLY PRESENT

In the vast pageant of sponsored programming of 1936–38, representing investments by several hundred network sponsors and thousands of local ones, marketing considerations were a potent influence. With 80 per cent of network revenue coming from drugs, foods, tobaccos, soaps and other household goods, the pressure for a mass audience was overwhelming. By 1938 sponsors were spending $150,000,000 for time and further millions for talent.[1]

In this pageant there were some programs that seemed more related to the sustaining than to the commercial world. These were special cases, reflecting special circumstances. A few are worth noting.

When Du Pont began sponsoring the history series *Cavalcade of America* in October 1935, the company was at low ebb in public relations. The Senate investigation headed by Senator Gerald P. Nye of North Dakota, on profits in the 1914–18 World War, showed that Du Pont had made 40

1. *Broadcasting Yearbook* (1939), p. 12.

per cent of propellant powders used by the Allies and had derived $1,049,-888,787 from war contracts, for a wartime profit of $237,908,339.64—all of which had sent Du Pont stock from $125 to $593.[2] The report had horrified the nation and helped bring on the 1935 Neutrality Act and arms embargo. (Intended to discourage aggression, they had apparently had the opposite effect in Spain.)

For Du Pont the Nye report was traumatic. It was the chief reason for *Cavalcade of America* and the policies governing it. In this history series, produced for Du Pont by the Batten, Barton, Durstine & Osborn advertising agency, wars were shunned. The emphasis was on humanitarian achievements, explorations, inventions. Though international struggles were occasionally mentioned—they were difficult to avoid—battle scenes were not permitted. The sound of a shot was taboo. Even explosions were for many years forbidden. The atmosphere was pacifist and highly idealistic. The progress of women was frequently celebrated.

The earliest *Cavalcade* programs were divided into segments on different topics. This fragmentary approach was abandoned in the fall of 1936. From that time half-hour biographical dramas dominated the schedule and began to attract talented young writers—among them, Arthur Miller.

Arthur Miller had grown up in Harlem and Brooklyn in polyglot neighborhoods. His father made women's coats and had seen prosperity, but this went "into the ashcan" as the Depression came. Arthur began delivering bakery rolls each morning before school—4:30–7:30 A.M. He later worked in a warehouse to make money for college. At the College of the City of New York, which he attended briefly, there were not enough seats in the library, and many students studied on their feet. He applied to the University of Michigan, which had a very low tuition; was rejected, but wrote a letter to the Dean that reversed the decision. This first literary achievement led to others. He had seen only two plays in his life, but they excited him and he wrote one, which won a prize. Later he won another. His writings came from the ferment around him. War seemed on its way in Europe. Pacifism was strong on campus, and many students were taking the "Oxford pledge" not to go to war. After college Miller returned to New York and in 1938 became a writer for the Federal Theater, getting $22.77 a week and working on a play about Montezuma. He became increasingly interested in history. On the side he sold a script to *Columbia Workshop*, then learned about *Cavalcade of America*. In less than a year he was off

2. *Munitions Industry*, v. 3, pp. 20–22.

CBS

President Franklin D. Roosevelt in fireside chat.

TODAY ON THE RADIO

THURSDAY, NOV. 16, 1933.

OUTSTANDING EVENTS ON ALL STATIONS.

12:30-1:30 P. M.—Farm and Home Hour; "Radio as an Aid to the Government," Postmaster General James A. Farley—WJZ.

4:15-4:45 P. M.—From London; Speaker, Sir Herbert Samuel, Former Secretary of State for Home Affairs—WJZ.

6:15-6:30 P. M.—"The Red Cross," Major Gen. J. G. Harbord—WEAF.

8:00-9:00 P. M.—Vallee Orchestra; Play, "Strictly Dishonorable," With Margaret Sullavan and Tonio Selwart; Collins and Peterson, Comedians, and Others—WEAF.

8:30-9:00 P. M.—Shilkret Orchestra; Alexander Gray, Baritone; William Lyon Phelps, Narrator; "America Looks Ahead," Governor Wilbur L. Cross of Connecticut—WABC.

9:00-10:00 P. M.—Family Welfare Committee Dinner, Hotel Astor; Speakers, Former Governor Alfred E. Smith, Mrs. Dwight Morrow, Ogden L. Mills—WOR.

9:15-10:15 P. M.—Kate Smith, Songs; George Gershwin, Piano; Harry Richman, Songs; Helen Morgan, Songs; Morton Downey, Tenor; Renard and Daly Orchestras—WABC.

10:30-11:00 P. M.—Rockefeller Center Program; Speakers, Colonel Arthur Woods, Major Gen. James G. Harbord; Grace Moore, Soprano; Tito Schipa, Tenor—WJZ.

A 1933 program listing. Note that the NBC-red network (WEAF) offers no news, relying mainly on vaudeville and concert material. The NBC-blue network (WJZ), with Lowell Thomas, and CBS (WABC), with Boake Carter, have the beginnings of a news schedule. NBC-red, with *Vallee Varieties* followed by *Showboat* and Paul Whiteman, holds Thursday evening leadership. All network programs are live. New York *Times*, Thursday, November 16, 1933.

WMCA—570 Kc

7:00 A. M.—Exercise Class
7:30—Business Advice
8:00—Roy Shelley, Songs
8:15—Vagabond Poet
8:30—Organ Music
8:45—Current Events
9:00—Novelty Trio
9:15—Dental Health Talk
9:30—Health Talk
9:45—John Quine, Songs—Shopping—Ruth Adams
10:00—Health Information
10:15—Betty Gould, Organ
10:30—Jeannie Carroll, Songs
10:45—Studio Program
11:00—Health Talk; Music
11:15—Shopping Talk
11:30—Italian Program
12:00—A. M.—Chuck Richards, Songs; Stock Quotations
12:15 P. M.—Market Technic—Talk
1:05—Walter Garbutt, Songs
1:15—News; Music
2:00—Matinee Club
2:15—Health Talk
2:20—Sports Talk
2:30—Apps Players
3:00—International Duo
3:30—Stock Quotations
3:45—Market Technic—Talk
3:50—Elizabeth Fehr, Piano
4:00—Tea Time Concert
4:30—News Digest
4:45—Gertrude Thomas, Songs
5:00—Children's Program
5:15—Carrie Lillie, Songs
6:00—Studio Musicale
6:30—Feltxl Orch.
6:45—Fallon Orch.
7:00—Sports—Clem McCarthy
7:15—News Dramatization
7:30—Doris and Rennie, Songs; Danch Orch.
8:00—Three Funsters
8:15—Argentine Orch.
8:30—Metropolis—Drama
9:00—Concert Orch.
9:30—Ozark Mountaineers
10:00—Della Baker, Soprano; Redfern Hollingshead, Tenor
10:15—Hockey—Rangers vs. Detroit
10:45—Dance Music
11:15—Jerry Lester and Pietro Gentili, Songs
12:00-2:30 A. M.—Dance Music

WEAF—660 Kc

6:45 A. M.—Exercises
8:00—Gene and Glenn
8:30—Cheerio—Inspirational Talk and Music
9:00—Gould and Shefter, Piano Duo
9:15—Three Scamps, Songs
9:30—Childs Orch.
10:00—Variety Musicale
11:00—Josef Stopak, Violin; Josef Honti, Piano
11:15—Frances Lee Barton
11:30—U. S. Navy Band
12:00—Fay Ferguson, Piano
12:15 P. M.—Organ Recital
12:30—Orchestral Concert
1:30—Pedro Via. Orch.
2:00—Pirates of the Stratosphere—Sketch
2:30—Russian Choir
3:00—From London: Is America Calling?—Burlesques of American Entertainers
4:00—Three X Slaters, Songs; Male Chorus
4:30—Puccini's Opera Gianni Schicchi, by Juilliard School of Music Students
5:30—Adventures of Dr. Dolittle—Sketch
5:45—Nursery Rhymes; Lewis James, Tenor; Milton J. Cross, Readings
6:00—NRA Talk
6:05—Cugat Orch.
6:15—The American Red Cross—Major Gen. James G. Harbord
6:30—Associated Glee Clubs of New York
7:00—Mountaineers Music
7:15—Billy Bachelor—Sketch
7:30—Lum and Abner
7:45—The Goldbergs—Sketch
8:00—Vallee Orch.; Play—Strictly Dishonorable, With Margaret Sullavan and Tonio Selwart; Tom Howard, Comedian; Collins and Peterson, Comedians, and Others
9:00—Captain Henry Show Boat Concert
10:00—Whiteman Orch.; Deems Taylor, Narrator
11:00—Frances Alda, Soprano; Concert Orch.
11:30—Hollywood Tribute to Radio City; Patsy Ruth Miller, Fay Wray, Mae Clark, Richard Arlen, Jack Oakle, and Others

WOR—710 Kc

6:45 A. M.—Gym Classes
8:00—Talks; Music
9:00—Edward Nell, Songs
9:15—Kath'rin 'n' Calliope
9:45—Beauty School
10:00—Food—A. W. McCann
10:30—Beauty—Nell Vinick
11:15—Cookery Talk
11:30—Thrift—Ann Stevens
11:45—Inspirational Talk
12:00—Stanley Meehan, Tenor
12:15 P. M.—Lina Di Flore, Piano
12:30—Children's Books—Monica Selwin-Tait
12:45—Studio Orch.
1:55—Bartlett Orch.

1:00—Health Talk; Music

1:30—Theatre Club
1:45—Freddy Ferber and Edith Handman, Songs
2:00—The Psychologist Says—Dr. Arthur Frank Payne
2:15—Comedy and Songs
2:30—Genevieve Pitot, Piano
2:45—Talks; Music
3:00—Bridge Talk
3:15—Show Boat Boys
3:30—Byron Holiday, Songs
3:45—Freudberg Orch.
4:00—Beneath the Skin—Dr. I. Strandhagen
4:15—Studio Music
4:45—Jimmie Brierly, Songs
5:00—Studio Orch.
5:05—Program Resume
5:15—Gypsy Ensemble
5:30—Studio Music
5:45—Open Sesame—Sketch
6:00—Uncle Don
6:30—Happy Landings—Talk
6:45—Frances Hunt, Songs
6:50—Stories of Life
7:00—Sports—Ford Frick
7:15—News—Gabriel Heatter
7:30—Terry and Ted—Sketch
7:45—Al and Lee Reiser, Piano Duo; John Kelvin, Tenor
8:00—De Marco Girls; Frank Sherry, Tenor
8:15—Talk—Percy Waxman
8:30—Lone Star Rangers
9:00—Family Welfare Committee Dinner, Hotel Astor; Speakers, Former Governor Alfred E. Smith, Mrs. Dwight Morrow, Ogden L. Mills
10:00—Saxophone Quartet
10:15—Current Events—Harlan Eugene Read
10:30—The Jolly Russians
11:00—Weather Report
11:02—Moonbeams Trio
11:30—Childs Orch.
12:00—Bestor Orch.

WJZ—760 Kc

7:30 A. M.—Dance Band
8:00—Morning Devotions
8:15—Don Hall Trio
8:30—Lew White, Organ
9:00—Dance Orch.
10:00—Edward MacHugh, Songs
10:15—Clara, Lu 'n' Em
10:30—Today's Children—Dramatic Sketch
10:45—Marcella Shields and Walter Scanlon, Comedy; Pollock and Lawnhurst, Piano Duo
11:00—George Bass, Violin; Ennio Bolognini, 'Cello
11:15—String Ensemble
11:30—Stokes Orch.; Jesters Trio; Ward and Muzzy, Piano Duo
12:00—Commodore Quartet
12:15 P. M.—Cyril Tobin, Violin
12:30—Farm and Home Hour; Speaker, Postmaster General James A. Farley
1:30—Molina Orch.
2:00—Greetings to the World; Students at International House
3:00—Southernaires Quartet
3:15—Rochester Philharmonic Orch.; Guy Fraser Harrison, Conductor
4:00—Betty and Bob—Sketch
4:15—From London; Speaker, Sir Herbert Samuel, Former Secretary of State for Home Affairs
4:45—Ruth Lyon, Soprano; Edward Davies, Baritone, Concert Orch.
5:15—Work of the Grenfell Juniors—Sir Wilfred Grenfell, Missionary
5:30—Singing Lady
5:45—Little Orphan Annie
6:00—Mitzi Green's Party—Mitzi Green, Mary Small, Marilyn Mack, Baby Rose Marie, Pops and Louie
6:30—Songs of the Church
6:45—News—Lowell Thomas
7:00—Amos 'n' Andy
7:15—The Three Musketeers —Sketch
7:30—Michael Bartlett, Tenor; Alfred Lustgarten, Violin
7:45—Mario Cozzi, Baritone
8:00—Captain Diamond's Adventures—Sketch
8:30—Adventures in Health—Dr. Herman Bundesen
8:45—James Melton, Tenor
9:00—Death Valley Days—Sketch
9:30—Wayne King Orch.
10:00—Concert Orch.
10:30—Rockefeller Centre Program; Speakers, Colonel Arthur Woods, Major Gen. James G. Harbord, Tito Schipa, Tenor; Marcel Rodrigo, Baritone; Grace Moore, Soprano
11:00—Explorers Club Program: Speakers, Colonel Theodore Roosevelt, Captain Bob Bartlett, Vilhjalmar Stefanson, and Others
11:30—Waring Orch.
12:00—Same as WEAF

WNYC—810 Kc

9:00 A. M.—Music Moods
9:15—Weather; Ship News
9:30—Masterwork Hour
10:30—Information Bureau
10:45—Joseph Marte, Music
11:00—November in the Garden—Montague Free
11:15—Margaret Hall, Songs

11:30—Educational Talk
11:45—Electricity: A Heal Agent—Dr. H. Goodma
12:00—Mazie Corr, Songs
12:15 P. M.—Your Police Department—James S. Bol Commissioner
12:30—Stan Lee, Guitar
12:45—Song Recital
1:00—Studio Musicale
2:00-3:00—Silent
3:00—Kay Curtis, Songs
3:15—Traveling With Y. M. C. A. Guide—Alb K. Dawson
3:30—Eugene Mott, Tenor
3:45—Family Welfare Talf Charles G. Meyer
4:00—Marguerite Zender, Songs
4:15—Department of Mar kets—here F Ryan, Con missioner
4:30—Music School Settlement Concert
5:00—Dangers of Pneumon —Dr. Abbott Allen
5:15—Ward Eggleston, Son
5:25—Police Alarms
5:30—Max Olanoff, Violin

WABC—860 Kc

7:30 A. M.—Organ Reveil
8:00—Salon Musicale
9:00—Eton Boys quartet
9:15—Chamber Music
9:45—'ystery Chef
10:00—Bill and Ginger, Son
10:15—Talk—Ida Bailey Al
10:30—Robison Buckaroos
10:45—Studio Music
11:30—Tony Wons; Keens and Phillips, Piano Du
11:45—What You Should Know About X-Ray—Dr William H. Meyer, N. Post Graduate Medicai School
12:00—Voice of Experience
12:15 F. M.—Connie Gates Songs
12:30—News; Music
1:00—Marie, the Little French Princess—Sketch
1:15—Reis and Dun, Song
1:30—Easy Aces—Sketch
1:45—Painted Dreams— Sketch
2:00—Ann Leaf, Organ
2:15—Romance of Helen Trent—Sketch
2:30—School of the Air
3:00—Metropolitan Orch.
3:30—Morale and the Uner ployed Student—Colonel H. Edmund Bullis ot N tional Committee for Mental Hygiene
3:45—Curtis Institute Mu sicale
3:30—News Flashes
4:35—American Legion—Ta'
4:45—Happy Minstrel
5:00—Skippy—Sketch
5:15—Hall Orch.
5:30—Jack Armstrong, All American Boy—Sketch
5:45—Stamp Adventurers Club—Sketch
6:00—Buck Rogers—Sketch
6:15—Bobby Benson—Sketch
6:30—Football Dope—Eddi Dooley
6:45—Little Italy—Sketch
7:00—Myrt and Marge
7:15—Just Plain Bill—sketc
7:30—Jeannie Lang and Pa Small, Songs; Denny Orch.
7:45—News—Boake Carter
8:00—Elmer Everett Yess Sketch
8:15—Singin' Sam
8:30—Shilkret Orch.; Alex ander Gray, Baritone; William Lyon Phelps, Narrator; America Look Ahead—Governor Wilbur L. Cross of Connecticut
9:00—Kostelanetz Orch.
9:15—Kate Smith, Songs; George Gershwin, Piano; Harry Richman, Songs, Helen Morgan, Songs, Morton Downey, Tenor; Renard and Daly Orchs.
10:15—Deep River Orch.
10:30—News Bul etins
10:45—Concert Orch.; Glady Rice, Soprano
11:15—Phil Rega n, Tenor
11:30—Jones Orch.
12:00—Nelson Orch.
12:30 A. M.—Lyman Orch.
1:00—Light Orch.

WEVD—1,300 Kc

7:00 A. M.—Studio Music
7:45—Morning Devotions
8:00—Psychology—Dr. Jaco List
8:15—Exercises
8:30-9:00—German Musicale
3:00 P. M.—Variety Music
3:30—Music Store—Sketch
3:45—Italian Musicale
4:00—Cichetti Ensemble
4:15—Studio Music
4:30—Variety Musicale
5:30—Helen Steele, Songs
5:45-6:00—Helen Lanvin, Contralto; String Ensemble
8:00—The Human Side of the Courts—Judge Benja min E. Greenspan
8:15—Piano Recital
8:30—Dunne Band
8:45-9:00—The London Eco nomic Conference—Pro fessor Francis Desk of Columbia University
10:00-11:00—Mildred Ander son, Contralto; String Ensemble
10:30-11:00—Hamlet—Play
12:00—Dance Music

TV: ABOUT READY...

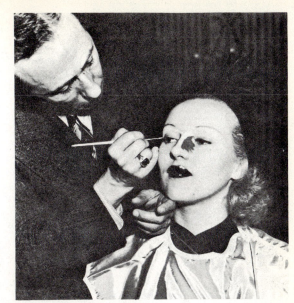

Betty Grable gets green make-up (1937) required for primitive television cameras.

Mobile unit (1937) starts roaming New York streets in search of news events.

Fire telecast (1938) via mobile-unit relay—as seen on television tube.

FM: NOT JUST AN INVENTION...

Edwin H. Armstrong, inventor, 1918.

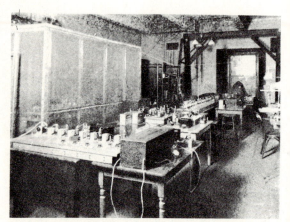

FM in the making: Armstrong's laboratory, 1935.

Columbiana

Columbiana

Columbiana

Armstrong builds demonstration FM transmitter tower at Alpine, N.J.

The tower completed: W2XMN, Alpine, 1938.

Father Charles E. Coughlin.

National Archives

Senator Huey P. Long.

Wide World

FACSIMILE. During 1937-39 the newspaper-by-radio was considered at the breakthrough point. Above, a 1939 RCA facsimile receiver.

After the Martian invasion: Orson Welles holds a press conference.

Wide World

FAKE RADIO 'WAR' STIRS TERROR THROUGH U.S.

DRAMA: CBS, 1938

Orson Welles: "I had no idea...."

Arch Oboler directing *Arch Oboler's Plays.*

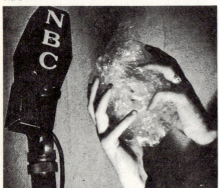

Fire!... crackling of cellophane.

Agnes Moorehead in *The March of Time*

the Federal Theater payroll and living on *Cavalcade*. He became "the utility man for the program," and developed a gratifying sense of expertise. Batten, Barton, Durstine & Osborn would sometimes call him Thursday to ask if he could get a script written or revised by Monday. He always could. Some of his scripts pleased him, as did the subjects. He was earning several thousand dollars a year. It was a kind of subsidy, enabling him to work on other projects.[3]

The circumstances that made the interests of a boy from the slums, social-minded and pacifist, coincide for a time with those of the Du Ponts of Delaware—whose gunpowder seemed totally forgotten in favor of "better things for better living through chemistry"—were curious but part of the pattern of the time. Other young writers of similar interest found a welcome at *Cavalcade*. Norman Rosten had studied with Miller at the University of Michigan, had written a radio verse play under the inspiration of *The Fall of the City*, and followed Miller to *Cavalcade*.

Cavalcade of America had an audience that would not have satisfied many major sponsors. During the 1930's its Hooperating seldom rose above 7, at a time when top comedians had ratings of 30 or above, and some drama programs topped 20. But *Cavalcade of America* won favor with educators, the group that had been most vociferous about "merchants of death."

Cavalcade scripts were reviewed by Yale historian Frank Monaghan. Its samplings of history were usually accurate, although highly selective. The labor movement was never mentioned. For a dozen years no Negro hero appeared.[4] The abolitionist John Brown received favorable treatment; however, where Brown told the court that condemned him to death, "Had I interfered in behalf of the rich, the powerful, the intelligent, the so-called great . . . it would have been all right," the drama omitted "the rich."[5] Such adjustments were looked on as a concession to good manners. The series shied away from almost everything in the twentieth century except inventions and women's rights. But the idealism with which it retold many stories of the American past, at a time when many people had lost faith in its institutions, won it awards and wide praise. This had been precisely its task. On the air it virtually represented American history.

3. Miller, *Reminiscences*, pp. 1–15.
4. When the series finally presented a biography of a Negro—November 15, 1948—it chose to honor Booker T. Washington, who felt the Negro should "keep his place" until better educated.
5. *Cavalcade of America*, December 11, 1940.

Also standing somewhat apart were the series of Mary Margaret Mc-Bride and others who followed in her path.

The McBride series became something quite different from what it had been meant to be. When WOR, New York, first put her on the air after auditioning fifty women, she was given very specific instructions. She would be called "Martha Deane" and would be a grandmother with six children and many grandchildren—all imaginary. They were all named and described; she was to memorize the details. Her job was to talk collo-quially and dispense philosophy. She could refer to the children and grandchildren both in philosophizing and in doing her commercials. She found it all very difficult. Her alleged son Johnny was supposed to have twins named Penny and Jenny, and girls named Judy, Josie, and Jessie. She kept getting them mixed up. Within three weeks she jettisoned the whole tribe—on the air. In a moment of despair she blurted out:

> I can't do it! . . . I'm not a grandmother! I'm not a mother. I'm not even married . . . It doesn't sound real because it isn't. The truth is I'm a reporter who would like to come here every day and tell you about places I go, people I meet.[6]

She was no longer a radio grandmother but she was still Martha Deane. As Martha Deane she worked tirelessly, sometimes reading three books in a night. She attended dinners only if she thought they would yield mate-rial. She was endlessly making notes.

Oddly, she still thought and talked of "Martha Deane" as someone sepa-rate. Other people did too. A college professor wrote to her and wanted to meet her. When he did he seemed bored with her but kept telling her what a marvelous person Martha Deane was. Mary Margaret McBride stood uncomfortably in awe of Martha Deane. But gradually the self-confidence of Martha Deane seeped into Mary Margaret McBride. When she moved from WOR to a network—first CBS, later NBC—she was able to become an institution in her own name.[7]

The rise of Mary Margaret McBride epitomized the gradual triumph of the ad-libbed over the written interview. At NBC early network policy had frowned on ad-libbing, which had existed mainly in descriptions of news events, particularly in sports. The risks of ad-libbing seemed fear-

6. McBride, *Out of the Air*, p. 19.
7. The name Martha Deane, owned by WOR, was assigned to others: first Bessie Beattie, then Marion Young Taylor.

some, and most network interviews were completely written, permitting editorial control. The practice produced drab and stilted dialogues. Lower-budgeted local programming had no time for such procedures, and ad-libbing was common in studio programs and sidewalk interviews. It some-times generated a humanity impossible in rehearsed conversations, and gradually drove such material from the networks.

The career of Mary Margaret McBride was built on a unique ability to draw others out. When she talked with people she could almost make them forget they were on the air. She played the unknowledgeable one, asking questions that seemed naïve but were not. Often her guests told more of themselves than they had ever meant to. The best-known authors began to make publication-day pilgrimages to her program, not only be-cause it meant book sales but because they felt invigorated by it. Mrs. Roosevelt came to chat about life in the White House, and revealed such homey details as the Emperor Haile Selassie having to take his shoes off after a public occasion, and wiggling his toes in blessed relief. Historian Carl Van Doren was a frequent visitor to the program. The ad-lib proce-dure made Mary Margaret McBride fairly free of editorial control. As po-tential sponsors waited in line for her program, she became one of the most independent of radio artists.

Her influence became legendary. At a time when carrots glutted the market, Lloyd Morris tells us, some talk by Mary Margaret McBride made daily sales leap from two to ten carloads.[8]

In 1938 Mary Margaret—millions came to know her by her given names—was in her second year as a network feature. She was only be-ginning. Her program and others of similar trend—Marion Young Taylor as "Martha Deane" was among them—sought to keep listeners in touch with the world around them.

A diversity of other sponsored programs occupied daytime hours. Some dispensed advice—on love ("Beatrice Fairfax" for Silver Dust); on cook-ing ("Betty Crocker" for General Mills); on home decorating ("Betty Moore" for Moore Paints)—while some philosophized or read poetry (Tony Wons, Ted Malone). A daytime variety-hour tradition was devel-oping: the Don McNeill *Breakfast Club* was well established; Arthur God-frey, having built a local reputation in the Washington area, was begin-ning a network series.

But while some of these had substantial audiences, the daytime hours

8. Morris, *Not So Long Ago*, p. 476.

were dominated not by them but by something entirely different: the day-time serial.

By the end of 1938 daytime serials had conquered millions of listeners and scores of sponsors and were beginning to arouse intense interest among sociologists. Thirty-eight sponsored women's serials occupied day-time hours,[9] and the number was still growing. Almost all were humorless as a matter of policy. Their language was correct. Most characters, even the uneducated, talked in complete, rather formal sentences. Sensational events were interspersed with much philosophizing. The plots, though highly charged, moved at a snail's pace; a tense dilemma might be held for weeks.

There was evidence that listeners during daytime hours fell into two groups: serial listeners and others. A woman who listened to a serial was likely to listen to other serials also, but not to reality-oriented programs like that of Mary Margaret McBride. People who listened to Mary Marga-ret McBride ignored serials. The two groups seemed to breathe different environments. This apparent split was thought-provoking, but its precise meaning could not be clearly established.[10]

Critics spoke of serials as "fantasy" but listeners did not think of them in that way. They thought of them as "real." So—apparently—did leading serial producers.

In 1938 Blackett, Sample & Hummert, the leading advertising agency in total time purchases as well as the leading serial producer, generally had a dozen serials on networks, while testing others on local stations. It also produced evening programs such as *American Album of Familiar Music* and *Waltztime*. The serials were produced for the agency by Frank Hum-mert and his assistant Ann Ashenhurst, who in 1935 became Mrs. Hum-mert. The Hummerts later formed a separate unit to produce the serials; withdrawing from advertising duties, they moved their work from Chi-

9. Of these, the following were the work of Blackett, Sample & Hummert: *Arnold Grimm's Daughter, Backstage Wife, Betty and Bob, David Harum, John's Other Wife, Just Plain Bill, Lorenzo Jones, Our Gal Sunday, The Romance of Helen Trent, Stella Dallas, Young Widder Brown.* The following were produced by other agencies: *Aunt Jenny's Stories, Bachelor's Children, Big Sister, Central City, Girl Alone, The Gold-bergs, Her Honor Nancy James, Hilltop House, Houseboat Hannah, Jane Arden, Joyce Jordan—Girl Intern, Life Can Be Beautiful, Ma Perkins, Mary Marlin, Myrt and Marge, The O'Neills, Pepper Young's Family, Pretty Kitty Kelly, Road of Life, Scat-tergood Baines, Stepmother, This Day Is Ours, Those Happy Gilmans, Valiant Lady, Vic and Sade, Women in White, Your Family and Mine.*
10. For a later, detailed study of this split see Lazarsfeld and Stanton, *Communica-tions Research 1948–1949,* pp. 73–108.

cago to New York. Their growing operation was soon compared to the literary factory of the elder Alexandre Dumas, who is said to have had dozens of anonymous writers working for him. The Hummerts defined the formula for each serial in a detailed memorandum, then wrote synopses of sequences for which others "filled in the dialogue." The pay for this was standardized: in 1938 the writers received $25 per script—$125 per week for a 5-a-week series. Some writers found they could turn out several simultaneously. The writers worked anonymously and owned no rights in their work. They seldom saw the Hummerts—some, never. Communication was generally through written instructions or through six "script readers" responsible for checking.[11] The Hummerts tended to become recluses, sometimes working at their home in Greenwich, Connecticut, a place never seen by most associates. In New York a Park Avenue restaurant shielded a corner table with ferns to give the Hummerts privacy. Frank Hummert, a lean, gangly man of folksy quality, was as likely to order shredded wheat as the *plat du jour*. The much younger Mrs. Hummert was petite, chic, and high-strung.

The Hummerts were serious about their work. Mrs. Hummert once told a new writer, Manya Starr, "I want you to put God on every page." When the writer asked drily, "Who's going to play the part?" she was promptly fired.[12] The Hummerts considered genuineness the most important characteristic of their programs, and felt that *Just Plain Bill* exemplified this. Bill was a barber who had married "out of his station." Speaking to a college group, Mrs. Hummert elaborated:

> So we put this man of the Middle West—the fact that he was from the Middle West makes him a great favorite; people seem to like characters from that section best—in this situation. Here he was talking to his assistant: "My daughter is coming home today. I haven't seen her in eighteen years. She's been East with her aunt, in fine finishing schools, and doesn't even know I'm her father. Is she going to be too good for me?"[13]

The Hummerts often seemed to begin with a basic dilemma, such as a social gap. This was apparently the "reality" they were after. Then they spun fantastic webs of plot around it, which went on for years. *Our Gal*

11. New York *Post,* January 30, 1939.
12. Interview, Manya Starr.
13. Hummert, *The Woman's Daytime Serial,* p. 1. This lecture, delivered at Columbia University January 11, 1939, was apparently the only such talk given by her. Delivered without notes, it had been fully memorized.

Sunday was similarly founded on a gap, which remained unchanged through years of elaborate plotting. The formula was described in each episode:

> . . . the story that asks the question: can a girl from a little mining town in the West find happiness as the wife of a wealthy and titled Englishman?

In similar vein, *Backstage Wife* portrayed a simple girl who had married a Broadway idol, and could worry year after year about the gap between them, and about the beautiful actresses intent on capturing him. *John's Other Wife* was essentially a carbon copy, with a business tycoon replacing the Broadway idol. *The Romance of Helen Trent* featured another kind of gap: she was a woman whose marriage had come to an end and who was remaking herself for a new life.

For all these series the folksy Frank Hummert and the chic Ann Hummert mapped the plotting. Writers were forbidden to deviate. The Hummerts specified how many days each plot development should take. Plots were usually planned in sequences of three or four weeks. Before the end of a sequence the next was introduced as a subplot. Each episode began and ended in trouble; sunny stretches were in the middle. A Friday ending was expected to be especially gripping, to hold interest over the weekend. A serial was not conceived in terms of beginning or end; such terms had no meaning. It ended when sponsorship ceased. Until that day there were endless variations of a basic, insoluble dilemma.

The central characters of serials fell into two categories: (1) those in trouble and (2) those who helped people in trouble. The helping-hand figures were usually older. *Big Sister*, produced by the Ruthrauff & Ryan advertising agency, was first planned to revolve around a younger helping-hand character, but the series failed to take hold while it pursued this formula. When the heroine was plunged into a long-held and seemingly insoluble problem—she fell in love with a man married to an insane woman—the rating climbed quickly.

What did serials mean to their listeners? A hundred interviews with listeners—mainly housewives—by social psychologist Herta Herzog left her surprised at the number who seemed to accept the stories as real, or who at least spoke of them in those terms. "I like to hear how he cures sick people," said a listener about the doctor in *Road of Life*. "It makes me wonder whether he could cure me." The more complex a listener's own problems, the more serials she tended to follow. The average serial listener listened to 6.6 serials. None listened to less than two; one listened to twenty-two. Most said they had never been bored by their favorite serials. Almost one-third spoke of planning the day around serials. Listening was apparently a solitary occupation—with private meanings—but in some cases led to phone calls. A New York woman called a friend in New Jersey each day "after my sketches" to talk about them. However, few listeners discussed the stories with husbands or children. Many seemed to look to serials for guidance. An unmarried woman said: "I like family stories best. If I get married I want to get an idea of how a wife should be to a husband." A mother said: "Bess Johnson shows you how to handle children. She handles all ages . . . I use what she does with my own children." Serial addiction clearly affected buying habits. "I am kidded by everybody because my pantry shelf is full of radio brands. The programs help me, so I've got to help the products." A woman used a face cream advertised on *The Romance of Helen Trent* "because she is using it and she is over thirty-five herself and has all those romances." Of the women interviewed, 61 per cent said they used merchandise advertised on the serials they followed.

While listeners looked to a serial for help, they also tried to give help. Letters, almost always addressed to the characters by name, warned against other characters or suggested solutions of problems.

Many women expressed a sense of dire dependence on serials. "I can hardly wait from Friday till Monday, when the stories come on again." Asked how long a serial should run, a woman answered: "I want the story to go on for years so that my family can grow up right along with it." Another, misunderstanding the reason for the question, said anxiously: "They're not going to stop them, are they? I'd be lost without them!" [14]

In 1938 negotiations were under way to test Hummert serials over Radio Luxembourg under American sponsorship, aimed at the British market.[15]

By 1938 over 5,000,000 words a year were being written for Hummert serials alone—the equivalent of fifty full-length novels. They were drawing over 50,000,000 letters a year, many enclosing boxtops or coupons. Some merchandising plans were related to story events. A character invented a can opener, which was later offered for boxtops. Garden seeds

14. Herzog, "On Borrowed Experience," in *Studies in Philosophy and Social Science* (1941), pp. 65–91.
15. Hummert, *The Woman's Daytime Serial*, p. 4.

were a frequent boxtop offer. A housewife could say: "Look at my Ma Perkins peonies—they're doing fine!"

Merchandise offers played a similarly important part in children's serials, of which six were on national networks at the end of 1938.[16] Like women's serials, they had a following of addicts. The Blackett, Sample & Hummert advertising agency was also active in this field, producing *Little Orphan Annie.*

To some observers the radio serials—especially women's serials— seemed dangerous, encouraging listeners to seal themselves in a world built around their own frustrations and fantasies, with diminishing contact with reality. To others the serials seemed a source of emotional support, friendship, guidance.

Without question they were a smashing business success, contributing to the growing power of network radio.

But the main strength of radio still lay in the evening hours. Here the kings were still—as they had been most of the decade—stars from vaudeville and musical comedy along with newcomers working in the same tradition. The cluster of comedians heading the ratings remained remarkably constant. They seemed to cut across age groups and socio-economic strata. They provided universal therapy. Edgar Bergen, the leader at the moment, was balm for all introverts. Shy himself, he had apparently found in his wooden dummy, Charlie McCarthy, a vehicle for expressing feelings he dared not otherwise express. Charlie could be a monster of impertinence, disdaining even his ventriloquist. With female movie-star guests, Bergen's alter ego could be the brashest philanderer. This ventriloquist-dummy team became a brilliant embodiment of struggles between the introvert and extrovert within us.

Bob Hope, always high in the ratings, was psychologically related to Charlie McCarthy. He was a court jester, a dweller among the mighty, but allowed to tweak their noses. Through him every office worm was less a worm.

Jack Benny, always near the top, delighted by patently exhibiting pettinesses most people hide. His penny-pinching was his most endearing shame. One of his triumphant moments came in a sketch in which he was held up. The robber said: "Your money or your life!" There was silence—a long, long, long silence. Finally the studio audience got the point. A laugh

16. *Dick Tracy, Don Winslow of the Navy, Jack Armstrong, Little Orphan Annie, Terry and the Pirates, Tom Mix.*

began, and built. Jack Benny, always in control, waited. Then he said, "I'm thinking it over," and got a thundering roar.

As Benny gave atonement for petty vices of all men, Gracie Allen was a joyous scapegoat for mental shortcomings. She took them all on her shoulders, shortening the electric cord to save electricity, putting salt and pepper in one shaker so that if she picked the wrong one, she would always be right. With her all losers triumphed.[17]

All the comedians were aided by subsidiary characters, some of whom built a vast following. Bob Hope was long abetted by Jerry Colonna. Jack Benny had his "Rochester" and others. Edgar Bergen, in addition to creating Charlie McCarthy, developed the rustic Mortimer Snerd. Fred Allen invented a windbag Senator Claghorn, played by Kenneth Delmar, and other characters who later became regulars on "Allen's Alley." All stirred insatiable curiosity: listeners had a sense of knowing them intimately but wanted to see them. The combination of intimacy and elusiveness may help to explain the longevity of radio comedians.

The 1938 cluster of comedy leaders, all sponsored, also included Bing Crosby and Bob Burns; Al Jolson; Al Pearce and his Gang; Fibber McGee and Molly; Phil Baker and the Andrews Sisters; Ben Bernie and Lew Lehr; Tommy Riggs and Betty Lou; Pick and Pat; Joe Penner; Joe E. Brown. Mining the same vein were *Vallee Varieties;* a Kate Smith variety hour; a George Jessel variety hour.

Almost all of these did their broadcasts before studio audiences, whose reactions were considered part of the show. This had been true since the first influx of vaudeville talent.[18] A number of NBC's Radio City studios had for this reason been planned for large audiences. CBS had only one large studio at 485 Madison Avenue but had taken over several Broadway theaters vacated by Depression. Echoing with the roar of laughing crowds, these theaters gave the impression of a continuing vaudeville tradition.

Tickets for such broadcasts were distributed through the sponsor and his distributors and dealers and became an important part of the merchandising process. Throughout the United States they were cherished business favors. Planning a vacation trip to New York—or Hollywood—meant asking someone at Bristol-Myers if he could get two tickets for the

17. Quoted, Gracie Allen memorial broadcast, CBS, August 30, 1964.
18. According to John Royal, the insistence of Ed Wynn and Eddie Cantor played an important part in establishing the studio audience. Both had suffered early agonies in performing in empty studios. Interview, John Royal.

Fred Allen show. Once there, the traveler sat in an audience with hundreds of out-of-towners, applauding loudly, because Aunt Meg at home was listening and knew he was there. Over the audience hung mikes to build the laughter and applause, and in a special warm-up session the announcer even made the audience rehearse: "Come folks, I can't hear you! You can do better than that!" He held up the sign: "APPLAUSE!"

Some said the radio had killed vaudeville, but it could also be said that vaudeville had taken over radio or, more accurately, that the sponsor had taken over both.

Several comedy-vaudeville series sought attention through cooked-up feuds. There were "feuds" between Jack Benny and Fred Allen; Charlie McCarthy and W. C. Fields; Ben Bernie and Walter Winchell; Bob Hope and Bing Crosby. They fostered a tradition of gay insult:

CROSBY: As I live, ski snoot!
HOPE: Mattress hip!
CROSBY: Shovel head!
HOPE: Blubber!
CROSBY: Scoop nose!
HOPE: Lard!
CROSBY: Yes, dad! [19]

Music on variety programs was beginning to feel a rising Benny Goodman swing vogue, but there was a lot of sweet music, and often poem-reading to go with it. Oddly, comedian Jimmy Durante had given this an important boost. In 1934 he had been sued—and NBC with him—for "shouting and reciting" without permission a poem by Alfred Kreymborg. The court, finding for Durante and NBC, had ruled that poems could be read on the air without any permission.[20] So poem-reading went on without inhibition, and attracted strangely diverse exponents. Sammy Kaye had a Sunday evening network series called *Sunday Serenade* and also toured in personal appearances. One night on a bus leaving Cincinnati his band listened to *Moon River*, a WLW late-night program of organ music,

19. Ulanov, *The Incredible Crosby*, p. 157.
20. The decision was based on the letter of the copyright law. *Performance* rights were mentioned among rights controlled by copyright owners of plays and lectures, but were not mentioned in the case of books. To be sure, a book copyright owner controlled *adaptation* rights, but the court felt that Durante had not adapted the poem, only "shouted and recited" it. A 1952 amendment to the copyright law finally changed the situation by giving owners of non-dramatic material control of performance rights.

close harmony, and poems. "Listen to that!" said Sammy Kaye eagerly to his publicity man George Gingell. "I want to do that!" "Where?" "On the *Sunday Serenade.*" "You're out of your mind." "No, I'm not. I want to do it! Now, you find me some poetry." Father's Day was imminent, so at the next stop Gingell visited stores and pored over Father's Day greeting cards in search of poems. Not satisfied, he wrote one, inventing a pseudonym out of embarrassment. "Exactly what I want!" said Kaye. He began using poems on all his "swing and sway" broadcasts and even in theaters, with the orchestra bathed in blue light. Eventually Kaye published the *Sunday Serenade Book of Poetry,* which was mostly Gingell and Longfellow, and plugged it on every broadcast. It sold and sold.[21]

Standing somewhat aside from the radio-vaudeville world, but very much a vaudeville product, was Walter Winchell. With Eddie Cantor, George Jessel, and others, he had formed a Newsboys Sextet that had started their careers in 1910. Even in vaudeville days Winchell had been a "keyhole reporter," contributing tidbits to *Vaudeville News.* His inside-information talents had attracted publisher Bernarr Macfadden and led to a column in the *Evening Graphic,* which became a springboard to the New York *Mirror,* and to Hearst syndication and radio. The inside story became his career, but by the mid-1930's he no longer had to scramble for material. As he sat at his special table near the entrance of the Stork Club, "items" came to him. They also flooded in by wire, phone, and mail. For good measure he maintained a car with short-wave radio and, by some mysterious police department dispensation, red lights and a siren. He sometimes beat firemen to fires and policemen to scenes of crime. All became items, transmitted to the public in special Winchell language. Marrying couples had "melded" or "sealed" or "lohengrined" or "merged" or "middle-aisled; separating couples had "soured" or "curdled" or were "telling it to the judge" or had "Reno-vated" or were "on the verge." Since 1933 his Sunday evening radio series sponsored by Jergens Lotion had kept a huge audience constantly on edge. Shouting in strident voice at top speed, it seemed to confirm a theory held at many advertising agencies that the main requisite for radio was not a pleasant voice but an unmistakable one.

Winchell, always signing off "with lotions of love," had achieved an exceptional sponsor-identification quotient. NBC research showed that an overwhelming majority of Winchell listeners knew who sponsored him. It

21. Gingell, *Interview,* p. 12.

also showed that Winchell-addiction affected buying habits. According to the NBC figures:[22]

> 19.8 per cent of those who listen to one Winchell program a month use Jergens Lotion
>
> 30.2 per cent of those who listen to two or three Winchell programs a month use Jergens Lotion
>
> 51.2 per cent of those who listen to four Winchell programs a month use Jergens Lotion.

During his broadcasts Winchell bounced up and down in an old arm-chair. Loosening his collar and tie, pushing his hat back on his head and shouting "Flash!" he beat at a telegraph key with meaningless bops and bashes. "It stimulates me to do it myself!" he explained. In fear of violence, he carried a gun.[23]

In 1938 Winchell, to the discomfiture of his sponsor, was getting increasingly interested in politics and international affairs. He sometimes praised President Roosevelt. He fomented indignation against "Ratzis." He castigated isolationists. While this stirred controversy and made his sponsor restive, it also raised a question—previously posed by disputes over Father Coughlin and William J. Cameron and others—of whether a speaker booked for one kind of task, such as religious discussion or philosophy or Broadway chitchat, should become an all-purpose oracle. Did the discussion of international issues on a coast-to-coast network at the choicest hour on Sunday evenings call for "qualifications?" Winchell's huge rating thrust such questions aside.

The protests of his sponsor raised still another question. To what extent should a cosmetics manufacturer be permitted to assume the role of news editor?

Related to the dominance of variety during 1936–38 was a burst of contests and games. Led by the *Major Bowes Amateur Hour,* which became a network offering late in 1935, the mania included *Professor Quiz* (1936), *Hobby Lobby* (1937), a *Gateway to Hollywood* audition series (1938), *Information Please* (1938), *Kay Kyser's College of Musical Knowledge* (1938), *True or False* (1938), and other bees and quizzes. Activity of this sort spilled into news departments. A. A. Schechter at NBC found his Hollywood news chief wiring him a suggestion for a news feature:

22. *And with Lotions of Love,* p. 1.
23. *Current Biography* (1943), pp. 832–6.

OFFER DIAPER CHANGING CONTEST FOUR PROMINENT ACTORS ACTRESSES
FOUR MEN HAVE CHALLENGED THE FOUR WOMEN TO DIAPER CHANGING
CONTEST PLANNING LUNCH BEFOREHAND AT WHICH ONLY BABY FOOD
WILL BE SERVED WINNER JUDGED ON BASIS OF NEATNESS DISPATCH
COMFORT SPEED . . . ARE YOU INTERESTED.[24]

The activity found local echoes. WJSV, Washington, D. C., reported a
Zasu Pitts impersonation contest in which Zasu Pitts herself placed second. WGAR, Cleveland, reported a singing contest between two singers,
one in a bathtub, the other in a studio.[25]

Moving into competition with variety and games during 1936–38 was a
growing roster of sponsored drama. Two trends were notable. *Grand Central Station* (1937), *On Broadway* (1937), and *Curtain Time* (1938) were
not written under contract but invited contributions from writers anywhere. The formula had been explored by the Aubrey, Moore & Wallace
advertising agency of Chicago for its two series *First Nighter* (1930) and
Grand Hotel (1933) and had proved fruitful and durable. These were all
half-hour series without continuing characters; they could use a diversity
of material. While conventional in taste—*First Nighter* demanded
"WHOLESOMENESS . . . excessive sophistication is OUT" [26]—these series
offered an "open market" that encouraged many writers to try the medium. In one season *First Nighter* appears to have bought three scripts
from a prisoner in Michigan State Penitentiary.[27]

A more powerful 1936–38 trend in drama was a move toward Hollywood. This had begun slowly but was developing into a surge. At the start
of the decade relations between radio and the Hollywood world had been
minimal. Early corporate links such as those between CBS and Paramount, and between RCA and RKO, had had almost no effect on programming. In 1932 all major studios except RKO had adopted a policy of keeping their contract talent off the air. Hollywood strategy, for the moment,
was to ignore radio.

One day in 1933 Raymond Rubicam of the Young & Rubicam advertising agency stopped Donald Stauffer, its radio vice president—and an early
March of Time director—in the agency corridor. "Don, why hasn't anyone
ever done a show about Hollywood?" Stauffer had no idea. When the
Borden Company showed interest, the question was pursued. So total was

24. Schechter, *I Live on Air*, p. 96.
25. *Variety*, December 14, 1938.
26. *Suggestions for Radio Playwrights*, p. 1.
27. Correspondence, Michigan State Penitentiary.

the lack of contact with the Hollywood hierarchy that the agency made its approach through a fan magazine—*Photoplay*. Through its mediation, *Forty-five Minutes in Hollywood* had its debut in February 1934. *Photoplay* also had a central on-the-air role. With lavish publicity buildup, a *Photoplay* editor interviewed a screen star on the air in a written, studio-approved interview about a forthcoming film. This was followed by an excerpt from the film, *not* performed by the film star—the studios would not allow it—but by an anonymous radio actress, usually a *March of Time* performer skilled in impersonation. When Arlene Francis, a *March of Time* veteran, played a Bette Davis scene on *Forty-five Minutes in Hollywood,* it resulted in a phone call to Bette from her mother, congratulating her on her fine radio acting.[28]

Because the program plan fitted itself completely into the Hollywood publicity apparatus—promoting films, stars, companies, and Hollywood as an institution—it was accepted by all major companies except MGM. Young & Rubicam became a Hollywood-oriented agency, following with *Silver Theater* (1938), *Screen Guild Theater* (1938), and a later *Hollywood Star Theater*. Meanwhile the mighty Louella Parsons, paralleling the efforts of *Photoplay,* had helped the Ward Wheelock advertising agency to launch a *Hollywood Hotel* (1934) for Campbell's soups, and the J. Walter Thompson agency had launched *Lux Radio Theater* (1934), presided over by Cecil B. DeMille. It started lamely but by 1938 had a Hooperating rivaling that of many comedians, and had become a major Hollywood promotion vehicle. The taboo on radio appearances had by this time weakened, especially when a promotion purpose was involved.

Throughout this period films were turning increasingly to radio for material and talent. By 1937 the Paramount contract list included Jack Benny, Burns and Allen, Bing Crosby, Fibber McGee and Molly. Films began using stories from *Silver Theater, Big Town* and other series. Hollywood recruited Irving Reis, Arch Oboler, Orson Welles, and others. Radio lore became a basis for many films. The Winchell-Bernie feud turned into a Twentieth Century-Fox film, *Wake Up and Live.* The McCarthy-Fields feud became the Universal Pictures film *You Can't Cheat an Honest Man.* The Benny-Allen feud became Paramount's *Love Thy Neighbor.* Films were planned or announced based on *Hobby Lobby, Information Please, Professor Quiz, Dr. Christian, Grand Ole Opry, The Long Ranger, The Green Hornet.* Each success furthered the process.

28. Interview, Donald Stauffer.

The Hollywood attitude was, of course, ambivalent. While drawing on radio, it feared the rise of radio and preferred to look down on it. The ambivalence was reflected in a brilliantly acid verse with which Gene Lockhart welcomed Orson Welles to Hollywood:

> Little Orson Annie's come to our house to play,
> An' josh the motion pitchers up an' skeer the stars away
> An' shoo the Laughtons off the lot an' build the sets an' sweep
> An' wind the film an' write the talk an' earn her board-an'-keep;
> An' all us other acters, when our pitchur work is done,
> We set around the Derby bar an' has the mostest fun,
> A-list'nin' to the me-tales 'at Annie tells about,
> An' the Gobblewelles 'll git YOU   .
> Ef you DON'T WATCH OUT! [29]

The ambivalence was also reflected in the million-dollar campaign launched by Hollywood in 1938. The sum was raised to promote the film industry through advertising. No money was earmarked to buy radio time —to the annoyance of many broadcasters. The slogan adopted for the campaign was "Movies Are Your Best Entertainment." [30] This was quickly dropped when the initials were found to spell MAYBE.

The growing involvement of sponsored drama with Hollywood tended to widen the gap between commercial and sustaining radio. While sustaining drama drew on the Depression ferment and gathering war clouds, commercial drama moved in other directions, implicit in Hollywood's monopolistic structure.

Hollywood in 1938 was at the apex of its career as a controlled market. Eight companies, collaborating closely, ruled the industry—its production, distribution, and exhibition. Owning most of the first-run theaters, they had extended their control to other theaters through "block booking," under which a theater generally agreed to take the full output of one or more companies. Sooner or later almost every theater, to obtain films, had had to accept the block-booking system, and thus to surrender control over its choice of films. By 1938 only a fringe of theaters existed outside the system.[31]

29. Quoted, *Current Biography* (1941), pp. 909–12.
30. *Broadcasting*, August 15, 1938.
31. In the late 1930's the eight companies—Loew's (including MGM), Paramount, RKO, Twentieth Century-Fox, Warner Brothers, Columbia Pictures, United Artists, Universal—took in approximately 95 per cent of film rentals. While all engaged in block booking, only the first five owned theaters. Among theaters outside the system, some showed low-budget Western and gangster films from Republic Pictures and

While the eight companies competed in many ways, their joint activities were more significant in determining the production climate. They had joined in framing a censorship code, by which they hoped to persuade state censor boards to go out of business. They had not succeeded in this but had developed their own code into a powerful censorship system. It included self-righteous, absurd, and sinister aspects. The code administrators required that wrongdoers be shown coming to grief—in one way or another. This was demanded in the name of religion, but the rule seemed to proclaim a devious God who worked vengeance through landslides and automobile wrecks. The administrators had obsessions which became law. Feminine "cleavage" was a forbidden sight on the screen of the late 1930's. In bathrooms, toilets must not be seen. Double beds were discouraged. Rules and precedents multiplied. Sitting on the edge of a bed, a couple could kiss, but the girl's feet must not leave the floor. However, such absurdities diverted attention from more serious issues. The monopoly control over theater programming gave the Production Code Administration —or "Hays office"—the power of a national censor of the screen. Its ban on specific subject matter—miscegenation, for example—acquired the force of law, with long-range social implications. It was law privately instituted, privately enforced, beyond the reach of voters.

The Hollywood stance was non-involvement in social issues: "If I want to send a message, I'll call Western Union." In effect, the stance was a commitment to the status quo—an attitude reinforced by world-wide markets.

The industry could exert strong conservative pressures, both subtle and overt, on the lives of its artists. In 1936 MGM star Melvyn Douglas, returning by steamer from Europe, sat at the Captain's table and was appalled to hear pro-Hitler talk from midwestern businessmen. They felt Hitler had put things in order and that the United States needed someone similar instead of "that cripple in the White House." The experience stirred Douglas to political activity and to association with a Hollywood anti-Nazi committee. Months later he received a midnight phone call from an MGM executive in its foreign department. "Melvyn, I have something to ask you, and I hesitate because I know how strongly you feel in this matter. There are two Metro pictures in which you play which are being held up in Berlin now for distribution. The government censor won't allow

Monogram; a handful showed foreign films. Conant, *Antitrust in the Motion Picture Industry*, pp. 33–83.

them to be shown because of things you have said about Hitler and the German regime, in this country. But we have been informed by our Berlin office that if you will retract those statements publicly, the pictures will be distributed." The easy neutralism behind this suggestion was chilling to Douglas. He was unwilling to retract, and this probably won him a reputation for being unco-operative.[32] The episode provides a revealing glimpse of the film colony of the time: a restless, glittering concentration of talent, held on a taut leash.

The great man at MGM was Louis B. Mayer. An old-time Hoover friend, first White House visitor during the Hoover administration, Republican party chairman for California, he was also the highest salaried man in the United States.[33] Early in the Depression, while MGM still paid dividends, Mayer with tears in his eyes had asked MGM artists to accept a 50 per cent pay cut. "I'm not the kind that asks. I give. But now I have to ask you to save this industry." [34]

Another potentate in the Hollywood leadership was Will Hays, former Republican national chairman, who had recruited Albert Lasker for the anti-League campaign and the Harding drive, and was now Hollywood "czar" at $250,000.

Sponsored drama, moving into the Hollywood orbit, was inevitably adopting its mores, taboos, and outlook. It drew increasingly on the Hollywood talent pool—brilliantly agile, and challenged by restrictions to spectacular variations of formula. Formula itself became, as in the Restoration theater, a fount of virtuosity and a way of life. This became as true of Hollywood radio drama as of film. Some of the plays written by True Boardman for *Silver Theater* were illustrations of this: precise, skilful farces that seemed written on the head of a pin.[35]

The rise of Hollywood radio poured funds into the film community but enriched the networks even more. The continued expansion of network programming—East and West, commercial and sustaining—was creating an extraordinary boom culture around the network centers.

32. Douglas, *Reminiscences*, pp. 25–8.
33. Salary in 1937: $1,161,753.
34. Hackett, *Reminiscences*, p. 25.
35. See Boardman, "Expert Opinion," in Wylie (ed.), *Best Broadcasts of 1938–39;* and Boardman, "For Richer—for Richer," in Wylie (ed.), *Best Broadcasts of 1939–40.*

STUDIO WORLD 1936–38

The broadcasting world of the late 1930's sensed it was living on the verge of world catastrophe but showed little outward sign of it. While the awareness was reflected in some programming—mainly unsponsored—the prevailing urge was to ignore it, perhaps with the hope that the storm would pass. Meanwhile there was boom. The hurly-burly of confident enterprise seemed destined to go on forever.

At the major studio centers thousands of performers swarmed day and night. Every season brought a new influx of ingenues, expectantly criss-crossing waiting rooms and corridors. Mothers of child actors, with their charges in tow, were constantly in evidence. When not engaged in watch-ful waiting at the studios, they visited advertising agency offices, pressing for appointments and auditions. The boom nourished strange performing specialties. In New York, Bradley Barker made a living from animal noises. So did Donald Bain, whose eight-page printed brochure offered "realistic imitations of North, Central, and South American, African, and Asiatic birds, insects, barnyard animals, wild animals . . . If you don't see what you want here ask for it." [1] He had made the bird sounds for the Frank Buck feature film *Bring 'em Back Alive* but now lived by radio. Two girls, Sally Belle Cox and Madeleine Pierce, made baby-crying ca-reers. Each walked around the studio world with a suitcase containing a pillow to muffle cries, and a clean pillow-slip for each performance. They were said to be bitter rivals. Sally was a more spectacular new-born baby, but Madeleine could take a child to kindergarten age. A number of tal-ented midgets, including Walter Tetley and, somewhat later, the brilliant Sara Fussell, were in demand for child roles; their use avoided child-labor regulations and problems over rough language and late hours.

The chaos of performers—and casting messages for them—encouraged CBS receptionist Doris Sharpe to leave her $30 a week job to form Radio Registry, a phone-message service. She soon had a dozen phones in action with a bevy of girls taking messages and tracking down performers at restaurants, beaches, bars, and hideouts.

Unionization of performers, spurred by the Wagner Act, had been well started by AFRA—the American Federation of Radio Artists. By 1937 it claimed two thousand members; new recruits poured in. Writers were or-

1. *Catalog of Sound Effects Made by Donald Bain*, p. 1.

ganizing a Radio Writers Guild as a member guild of the Authors League of America but were making slow progress. Air credit, though already won by some writers, was opposed by advertising agencies on the ground that it would "destroy the illusion."

All programs on NBC and CBS were produced live. Both networks had policies forbidding the use of recorded elements other than sound effects. Sound effect disks were produced by several companies including Gennett and Speedy-Q. Most haunting of all such disks was a pre-diesel recording of the New York Central's Twentieth Century Limited; it kept the steam locomotive in radio drama for years after it had vanished from the national scene. Speedy-Q's Night Noises, with its instant rural peace, was another favorite. MBS, unlike NBC and CBS, permitted recordings of speech. It used them in such programs as year-end reviews, but the network was considered second-rate because of this. In similar programs the older networks used skilled impersonators, in the *March of Time* style.[2]

Most coast-to-coast evening programs on NBC and CBS had to be performed twice—once for the East and Midwest, and three hours later for the West. The "repeat" broadcasts meant business for nearby restaurants and—to some extent—bars. They kept the studios humming until late hours. They often produced production crises by running long or short. They were pitfalls for alcoholics.

In radio drama, music was important. Many dramatic programs had orchestras for bridges and backgrounds, and these supported talented composers and musicians. But the Hammond electronic organ, appearing in the mid-1930's, was thinning their ranks. After replacing an eighteen-piece orchestra on the *True Story Court of Human Relations* in 1935, the Hammond was quickly adopted by daytime serials and mystery programs. Musicians faced dwindling employment from other causes: in local programming, recordings were making the live musician seem obsolete. The

2. A 1937 event dramatized the limitations of the NBC-CBS policy. Announcer Herbert Morrison of WLS Chicago, an airship enthusiast, had persuaded his station to let him cover the May 6 arrival of the German Zeppelin Hindenburg after a transatlantic flight with many notables aboard. During his broadcast—of which a recording was made for file purposes—the ship burst into flame near the mooring mast, and Morrison became hysterical as he described people leaping from the flaming ship. "Oh my," he wept, "this is one of the worst catastrophes in the world . . . all the humanity!" Some hours later NBC suspended its anti-recording rule—apparently for the first time—to permit the extraordinarily moving record to be broadcast over NBC-blue.

president of the Chicago Federation of Musicians, James C. Petrillo, was urging musicians to discontinue all recording. Those who made recordings, musicians were saying, would play at their own funerals.[3]

Another struggle was brewing in radio music. Most copyrighted music was controlled by ASCAP—the American Society of Composers, Authors, and Publishers, founded in 1914. Most radio stations used this music under blanket licenses, which during 1935–39 called for payment to ASCAP of 2⅛ per cent of the station's gross revenue from time sales. In 1937 ASCAP began talking about a sharp increase, to take effect after 1939. Broadcasters, long indignant over ASCAP, prepared for battle. Within the NAB—originally formed for the specific purpose of combating ASCAP [4]—long-discussed plans reached the action stage. With a war chest subscribed by broadcasters, a move was begun to build a rival group of publishers and song writers—to be controlled by broadcasters. It was formally inaugurated in 1939 as Broadcast Music, Incorporated—or BMI. The move was helped by divisions within ASCAP. ASCAP's formulas for distributing collected copyright fees among its own members were favorable to long-established song writers, unfavorable to new writers—even those with current hits. Thus the BMI promoters found young song writers available to them. The ASCAP monopoly was faced with a determined and well-financed challenge; a BMI-ASCAP confrontation lay ahead.

As the struggle loomed, the networks continued to expand in drama, news, and special events, and to lessen their dependence on music.

In the burgeoning radio world the Negro had a dwindling role. In the early 1930's, when musical programs held the spotlight, a number of Negro orchestras and singing groups were broadcast regularly. A few remained, like the Southernaires with their Sunday program of spirituals. Also, stars like Marion Anderson and Dorothy Maynor appeared occasionally on concert programs. But with drama replacing music as the radio staple, the Negro found himself edged out. The drama was almost lily-white. Negroes who applied for auditions found only occasional servant roles, given to those who sounded sufficiently "Negro." "Wonderful" Smith, who eventually acquired a role on the Red Skelton series, said: "I had difficulty sounding as Negroid as they expected." Johnny Lee, who became a comedy-lawyer on *Amos 'n' Andy*, said: "I had to learn to talk as white people believed Negroes talked." According to actress Maidie Nor-

3. Lichtenfield, *Interview*, p. 14.
4. See *A Tower in Babel*, pp. 119–21.

man, "I have been told repeatedly that I don't sound like a Negro." But when she applied for other roles she was rejected without a reading. The actor Frank Silvera, who played occasional radio roles, considered the stereotype "a link in a heavy chain" shackling the Negro to the past. But the stereotype was proving durable. *Amos 'n' Andy* held popular as well as critical esteem. The stereotype also seemed, to some extent, capable of evolving. Eddie "Rochester" Anderson, who joined the Jack Benny program in 1937, was the old formula on all counts—a servant with tendencies to "drink, dice, wenching, and razor-toting." But some observers noted with satisfaction that he was also smart and sassy, while his boss was foolish, stingy, somewhat effete.[5]

Audiences, on the whole, were unaware of such issues. To comedy and variety shows studio audiences trooped by thousands day after day. Some drama programs also welcomed audiences. Even forum programs, like *American Forum of the Air* (MBS) and *America's Town Meeting of the Air* (NBC-blue), attracted crowds. At NBC in Radio City there were studio tours. Actors rehearsing in a third-floor studio would suddenly see a roomful of people peering down from an upper-level observation room. These were the "forty-centers," making the Depression-priced guided tour. The uniformed pages and girl guides answering questions were mostly college graduates and post-graduates and at times included stars-to-be like Gregory Peck and Eva Marie Saint. They pointed out the great actors, directors, musicians, writers; on another floor, newscasters, commentators.

This bustling world brought the networks $56,192,396 in time sales during 1937, of which $15,962,729 was passed on to affiliate stations and station-groups and $8,428,860 as commission to advertising agencies. The industry as a whole, said Commissioner George Henry Payne, was making a 350 per cent per year profit on its investment. Tens of millions in talent fees also fed the boom. The centerpieces of the pageant were the commercials written by hundreds of writers at advertising agencies, at salaries well above those of sustaining dramatic writers. These commercials were continually reviewed by network policy readers and sometimes by the Federal Trade Commission. During the fiscal year ending June 30, 1938, the FTC reported reviewing 1,069,944 pages of commercials from networks and stations. According to *Broadcasting*, the FTC found "only 1,544

5. Edmerson, *A Descriptive Study of the American Negro in United States Professional Radio 1922–1953*, pp. 28–75.

prospective cases involving allegedly false or misleading advertising."
These brought hearings and the signing of a steady stream of cease-and-
desist stipulations—concerning campaigns that had meanwhile, in most
cases, run their course. Major sponsors and agencies took these procedures
in stride. Beyond the agencies lay a vast premium industry. Fifty-six per
cent of all network programs were said to involve premium offers. In
"merchandising" tie-ups the faces of radio characters smiled from cereal
packages, comic strips, pencil boxes, shirts, hats, glassware, guns, holsters,
lunch boxes, games, dolls.[6]

A growing trade press supported every part of this bursting empire.
Associated with it was a huge, expanding publicity and talent-
management industry. "My dear admirer," replied Baby Rose Marie—
"darling of the air"—in a printed letter to all admirers who wrote her in
1938, "Many, many thanks for your kind letter and I want you to know I
sincerely appreciate your writing to me. It is friends like you who keep me
on top of the radio world." [7]

Vulgarities were plentiful. The American Bar Association was so appalled at the coverage of trials in various parts of the country that in 1937
it adopted, in its Canon 35, the principle that microphones and
photographers should be barred from courtrooms. A major cause of its
indignation had been the 1935 Hauptman trial in Flemington, New Jersey,
for the kidnapping of the Lindbergh baby. On that occasion microphones
were present only at the verdict, but throughout the trial radio had helped
turn the area into a midway. Jurors in their hotel rooms had heard the
cacophony of broadcast speculations from an improvised studio below. At
least two pundits—Gabriel Heatter and A. L. Alexander—had won fame
through marathons of high-voltage talk. A. L. Alexander had managed to
install a microphone in the sheriff's office and once talked three hours and
eleven minutes without pause. Lowell Thomas broadcast from a poolroom
opposite the courthouse. The American Bar Association considered the
dignity of the court threatened by the carnival atmosphere.[8]

Another sort of furor was caused by the 1937 appearance by Mae West
on the Charlie McCarthy series. She and the wooden dummy played a

6. *Broadcasting*, May 1, 1937; June 1, 15, December 1, 1938.
7. She was a twice-a-week feature over NBC-red at 6:30 p.m. Eastern time.
8. Waller, *Kidnap*, p. 302; *Broadcasting*, January 15, 1935. A curious by-product of
the Lindbergh trial was the *Make Believe Ballroom*, devised by Martin Block, a
$25-a-week announcer for WNEW, New York, to fill intervals between bulletins from
Flemington. It hung on after the trial, and later became a source of wealth.

sketch about Adam and Eve, written by Arch Oboler. She filled out the dialogue with oohs and grunts that brought thousands of angry letters, many of which found their way into the *Congressional Record*.[9]

A zany attention-getter of 1938 was a radio campaign for the Texas governorship. A flour manufacturer, W. Lee O'Daniel, had long sponsored a hillbilly program over the Texas Quality Network. He himself delivered the commercials, along with doses of poetry and philosophy. One day he asked listeners if he should enter the primary for governor. Soon afterwards he broadcast the news that he had received 54,499 "yes" replies and a few that said "no" on the ground that he was too good for the governorship. He began a whirlwind tour with sound truck, all the time plugging his flour and singing his commercial theme-song, "Please Pass the Biscuits, Pappy!" He said he had no idea if he could win but added: "Boy! It sure is good for the flour business." He won the primary and in 1938 was elected governor of Texas.[10]

Every corner of radio seemed to explode with activity. New York's bouncing Mayor Fiorello La Guardia scored such a success reading comics over New York City's WNYC during a 1937 newspaper strike that Coty offered to sponsor him at $2000 per week. The New York City corporation counsel, when asked for advice, reported that the city could buy almost anything but was only authorized to sell junk. Did the Mayor wish his program so classified?[11]

In California a cemetery reviewed with pride its ten years of radio sponsorship. Radio was credited with having improved its business. Its commercials were topical: for Mother's Day, the theme was that mothers are sensible and prefer "advance cemeterial arrangements"; at the time of the coronation of George VI of England, Inglewood Cemetery was compared favorably with Westminister Abbey as a burial place.[12]

With the growing dominance of programming from New York and Hollywood, drama production was declining in most other cities. During 1936–37 San Francisco, once the chief West Coast radio center, saw an exodus of talent bound for Hollywood. Chicago continued as a drama center, but with a shrinking roster of programs. Detroit survived by syndicating recorded drama series, mainly *The Lone Ranger* and *The Green*

9. *Congressional Record*, v. 83 pp. 560–62.
10. *Broadcasting*, August 1, 1938; Michie and Ryhlick, *Dixie Demagogues*, pp. 46–55.
11. Whalen, *Reminiscences*, p. 20. The Coty offer stimulated many suggestions about city finances. A wit suggested: why not a city fire truck called *L'Aimant?*
12. *Broadcasting*, August 1, 1937.

Hornet, both produced by station WXYZ. They were considered naïve by network personnel, but held an audience of addicts. Both featured superheroes who fought crime, not within the law but as a private occupation. Each had a "faithful" sidekick: the Lone Ranger was aided by the Indian Tonto; the Green Hornet, by the Japanese Kato.[13]

At many college campuses a radio innovation was taking hold. At Brown two undergraduates, George Abraham and David W. Borst, had shown in 1936 that a campus heating system or power system—or any campus-wide metal network—could be used as the antenna of a flea-powered broadcasting system. With power of two to ten watts one could obtain radiation of a few dozen feet from any part of this network, so that the station could be picked up in any dormitory room. Stations of this sort quickly sprang up at Wesleyan (Conn.), Harvard, Swarthmore, Cornell, Princeton, Columbia, Connecticut College, and elsewhere. The student broadcasters picked any available spot on the broadcast dial, assuming the FCC had no jurisdiction over radiation confined to a campus. At some colleges a dean learned of a station on his campus by tuning in, to his surprise, a *Jazz Lab* or *Music To Study By* announced by a student voice. The FCC was uncertain of its proper role, but technical slip-ups by some stations persuaded it to assume jurisdiction. One station was heard miles away because its programs were somehow radiating from city telephone wires. But the stations were meanwhile becoming an institution, attracting local record-shop, delicatessen, and barbershop sponsorship, and before long, national sponsors, including cigarette companies. Advertising agencies took a paternal interest. The Brown innovators began to plan an Intercollegiate Broadcasting System, with offices in New York for the sale of advertising.[14]

All segments of the radio empire had Washington-relations problems. For many organizations—major networks, stations, sponsors—this meant full-time lobbyists. Lobbying battles were also fought through associations like the American Association of Advertising Agencies, the Association of National Advertisers, and the National Association of Broadcasters. The NAB acquired its first paid president in 1938 and was pressing for a government probe of ASCAP. Staunch allies in Congress formed another battle line. According to Kenneth Crawford, Washington insiders regarded

13. Buxton and Owen, *Radio's Golden Age,* pp. 143–4.
14. The IBS was formed in 1939. For the early history of these stations see *Saturday Evening Post,* May 24, 1941.

Bennett Clark of Missouri as "the Senator for Listerine," Josiah Bailey of North Carolina as "the Senator for Vick's VapoRub," and James Mead of New York as the Congressman "for Doan's Kidney Pills." [15]

Standing astride this world of bursting activity were the networks, conscious of growing power, never certain how it should or should not be used, evolving policies case by case. The stakes increased and problems got larger. Meanwhile they pushed into new arenas. By 1938 thirty-eight short-wave stations, privately operated, were beaming programs throughout the world, and commercial sponsorship was expected to be authorized soon by the FCC. A number of companies were experimenting with facsimile broadcasting—newspapers sent by radio and received by special facsimile receivers, which listeners kept supplied with paper. Some stations were transmitting such newspapers at night over their regular frequencies; the listener found his newspaper by his set in the morning. A Crosley facsimile receiver went on sale in 1938 at $79.50.[16] In 1938 CBS became the owner of Columbia Records, which had once owned it. The network talent-booking subsidiaries were still expanding. Columbia Artists was beginning to represent writers and directors as well as performers. An NBC subsidiary was operating series of concerts in fifty-seven cities. CBS was building a television studio at Grand Central Terminal. An NBC television mobile unit was roaming the streets of New York.

The growth meant power. In 1938 nothing seemed capable of stopping it. But a challenge was taking shape.

The "second New Deal," which had started in 1935, took an interest in anti-trust activity, which had lapsed during the NRA years. In 1938 this brought two government actions affecting broadcasters—one very directly.

The FCC began a study long urged—of "chain broadcasting" and monopoly problems said to be developing from it. A few weeks later the U. S. Department of Justice brought an anti-trust suit against the dominant motion picture companies, charging conspiracy in restraint of trade. The potential impact of this suit on the broadcasting field was not immediately apparent.[17]

---

15. Crawford, *The Pressure Boys*, p. 75.
16. New York *Times*, January 23, 1939. Stations engaged in facsimile broadcasting at the start of 1938 were: KSD, St. Louis; WGN, Chicago; WSM, Nashville; WOR, Newark; WHO, Des Moines; WGH, Newport News; KFBK, Sacramento; KMJ, Fresno.
17. Known as the "Paramount" case, the suit also involved Loew's (including MGM),

At first the trade press in each industry tended to take these actions lightly. American radio, said *Broadcasting,* "is admittedly the best in the world. Since the bleatings of the opposition can only be stilled by what the headline writers call 'probe,' it is best that one is being undertaken. Even though there is no dirty linen, laundry day still comes around." [18]

For networks it was new incentive to push the pioneer work in unsold time that was already winning wide acclaim. At CBS this now brought to the fore a writer-director of exceptionally versatile talent.

BALLAD

When CBS vice president William B. Lewis late in 1938 offered Norman Corwin a Sunday half-hour to experiment with poetry productions, one of the first Corwin presentations was a group of nursery rhymes.

NARRATOR: Old Mother Hubbard
    Went to the cupboard
    To get her poor dog a bone.
    (*Biz: cupboard noises*)
    But when she got there—
HUBBARD: Well, I declare
    The cupboard is bare.
NARRATOR: And so the poor dog had none.
DOG: (*sad yipping*).
HUBBARD: Now, stop your whining, dear. I'll go right
    down to the baker's and get you some bread.
DOG: Okay.
NARRATOR: She went to the baker's
    (*Door opens, closes*)
    To buy him some bread
    But when she came back
    (*Door opens, closes*)
    The poor dog was dead.
HUBBARD: Why are you lying there so quiet?
DOG: I'm dead.
HUBBARD: Oh dear. . . .[1]

The broadcast had a response that seemed totally out of proportion to the simplicity of what Corwin had done. His offering had aural surprises; at

RKO, Twentieth Century-Fox, Warner Brothers, Columbia Pictures, United Artists, Universal. The litigation continued for a decade.
18. *Broadcasting,* April 1, 1938.
1. *Norman Corwin's Words Without Music,* CBS, December 18, 1938.

the same time it apparently tugged at submerged memories. Corwin found verse contributions flooding in on him. Meanwhile he made "word orchestrations" of works of Edgar Lee Masters, Carl Sandburg, Stephen Vincent Benét, and others. The poets themselves were enthusiastic about the presentations; they began to visit his broadcasts and even to contribute "radio poems."

On Christmas day, 1938 Corwin for the first time presented work of his own—a half-hour play in verse, *The Plot To Overthrow Christmas*. Its reception at once won it the status of a Christmas perennial. On the morning after the broadcast a "handsome and well-spoken man" came bounding into Corwin's office. Searching around the CBS building, he had had some difficulty in locating Corwin. He was Edward R. Murrow, in from Europe; he had caught the show and said he considered it the nearest thing to W. S. Gilbert he had heard. They chatted an hour; it was the beginning of a long friendship, which on one occasion became a collaboration.[2]

The Plot To Overthrow Christmas, a holiday prank, had one foot in the world of international plots, conspiracies, and *coups d'état*. In addition, like all Corwin programs, it was an experiment in—and a playful comment on—the radio medium. Along with its main narrator it had another —a "footnote" voice.

NARRATOR: Now it happened in Hades,
    Ladies,
    And gentlemen,
    It happened down there that the fiends held a meeting—
    The fiends held a meeting for the purpose of defeating Christmas.
    With the aid of a fade, a fade on the radio,
    We'll take you there, with a hi and a hey-di-ho,
    To hear first-hand the brewing of the plot
    Down in the deepest Stygian grot.
SOTTO VOCE (*confidentially*): Grot is a poetical term for grotto.
    (Whenever you hear my *voce sotto*
    Or *sotto voce*, whichever you prefer,
    It's just I, taking pains to make quite sure
    That nobody makes a poetical allusion
    Which may in any way create confusion.)
    I return you now to the voice you were hearing
    Before I had to do this interfering.
NARRATOR: As I was saying: in this Stygian *grot*

2. Corwin, *Interview*, p. 14.

The notables of Limbo hatched a plot,
And what went on in that sulphurous hole
We'll soon pick up by remote control. . . .
Don't be surprised if you're deafened by thunder
Just as we start our journey under;
You'll hear earthquakes and all the commoner
Varieties of natural phenomena.
And so, below, via radio (*fading*)
To the regions where legions of the damnèd go.

(*Sound: clang of Chinese gong; two thunder peals; oscillator at high pitch before thunder is entirely out. Bring pitch gradually down as—*)

(*Board: fade in echo chamber*)[3]

Corwin followed his Christmas frolic with a script of burning anger. Vittorio Mussolini, serving in his father's air force, had described the explosion of a bomb on the ground below as a thing of beauty, "like a budding rose unfolding." *They Fly Through the Air* was Corwin's reaction. It was chosen by the Ohio Institute for Education by Radio as the outstanding broadcast of the year. This was followed by a documentary "verse brochure," a tribute to his chosen medium—*Seems Radio Is Here To Stay.* In a printed edition it served as a CBS promotion piece and became something of a collector's item.

Corwin's first series was called *Words Without Music* because its minimal budget barred the use of music. In spite of scant means, the series had attracted extraordinary attention. The result was a new series—with a new budget.

In mid-1939—while the world was waiting for a new Hitler explosion—CBS commissioned Corwin to start work on *Pursuit of Happiness,* a variety series to be devoted to Americana. Supported by a large orchestra and with Burgess Meredith as master of ceremonies, it began that fall. It catapulted Corwin into national prominence.

Norman Corwin had been born in Boston in 1910. He attended public school and did not go to college. Further education was provided by work at newspapers and radio stations. At the Springfield *Republican* he was film critic and sports reporter, sometimes unsettling readers with columns in verse, and also handled newscasts over a local station. Later at WLW, Cincinnati, he did more newscasting.

3. Corwin, *Thirteen By Corwin,* pp. 89–90.

In the mid-1930's WLW, one of the stations of the Crosley Radio Corporation, was the only American station authorized to operate at 500,000 watts. Calling itself "The Nation's Station," it covered the Midwest. It probably commanded more listeners than any other American station. On his arrival in May 1935, Corwin was tried as 11 P.M. newscaster. He was to select material from the Transradio teletype, adapt it to his own delivery, and broadcast it. His assignments also included a program of stock market reports and a miscellaneous question-and-answer program. After a week the business manager told Corwin the station was delighted with his work and wanted him to stay. Corwin put its enthusiasm to the test by asking a $10 a week raise; this was promptly given, bringing him to $50 a week. His future at the station seemed assured.

During his second week, memoranda flowing to his desk included one which read: "No reference to strikes is to be made on any news bulletin broadcast over our stations." A few days later came a similar memorandum: "Our news broadcasts . . . will not include mention of any strikes. This also includes student strikes and school walkouts." Another memorandum invited WLW personnel to make suggestions to management. Corwin, in no sense protesting, decided to make a suggestion. He pointed out that if, at some future time, newspaper headlines told of a spectacular strike, it would seem strange for WLW to ignore it. Would not listeners lose some of their confidence in WLW? Two days later the business manager, summoning Corwin, told him that the station had regretfully decided to abolish his job. Corwin did not immediately connect the action with his modest suggestion. But leaving, he took the WLW memoranda with him. Subsequently, at the urging of a friend, he turned them over to the American Civil Liberties Union, which later found important use for them.[4] Meanwhile Corwin got a job in New York City writing publicity for Twentieth Century-Fox and, as diversion, did poetry broadcasts over WQXR, New York. These attracted the attention of William Lewis at CBS and led to *Norman Corwin's Words Without Music* and *Pursuit of Happiness*.

On *Pursuit of Happiness* Corwin presented a rich diversity of material, much of it stemming from ideas and organizations generated by the Depression. From the "borscht circuit" he introduced comedian Danny Kaye in his first radio appearance, as well as Betty Comden and Adolph Green.

4. Corwin, *Interview*, pp. 3–9.

He presented the "talking blues" of dustbowl balladeer Woody Guthrie and other folk singers brought to public attention by Alan Lomax at the Library of Congress. Continuing the tradition of *The Fall of the City*, Maxwell Anderson and Kurt Weill contributed a short radio opera on Magna Carta, in which Walter Huston appeared as singing narrator. But the item of most extraordinary impact stemmed from the Federal Theater—"Ballad for Americans."

Originally written for the musical revue *Sing for Your Supper*, with music by Earl Robinson and words by John Latouche, the "Ballad of Uncle Sam" (the original title) seemed headed for oblivion when the Federal Theater was abolished by Congress in June 1939—shortly after the debut of the musical. But Earl Robinson brought the number to CBS for *Pursuit of Happiness*, playing it for Norman Corwin and a group of program department executives. They retitled it "Ballad for Americans," made some cuts and revisions, and decided to offer its solo singing role to the Negro baritone Paul Robeson. The choice seemed so ideal that CBS agreed to pay more than its previous "top" *Pursuit of Happiness* fee. With Paul Robeson's voice flowing with extraordinary power and momentum, "Ballad for Americans" had its broadcast debut in November 1939. The ballad began:

> In '76 the sky was red,
> Thunder rumbling overhead,
> Bad King George couldn't sleep in his bed,
> And on that stormy morn
> Old Uncle Sam was born.

Later the song asked a question: did the people all believe in liberty in those days? The great voice sang:

> Nobody who was anybody believed it,
> Everybody who was anybody, they doubted it. . . .

But in the end the song expressed a faith:

> Out of the cheating, out of the shouting,
> Out of the windbags, the patriotic spouting,
> Out of the uncertainty and doubting,
> Out of the carpet-bag and the brass spittoon
> It will come again,
> Our marching song will come again:

We hold these truths to be self-evident,
That all men are created equal,
That they are endowed by their Creator
With certain inalienable rights,
That among these are life,
Liberty,
And the pursuit of happiness.[5]

At the studio-theater where the program was broadcast, an audience stood on the seats and roared and cheered and would not stop. "Ballad for Americans" was embarked on a dramatic and strange career. It was chosen as featured song for the Republican National Convention of 1940. At Lewisohn Stadium in New York, to the music of the Philadelphia Orchestra, it was again cheered by standing crowds. It was repeated over CBS. It was called by *Broadcasting* "an American epic." [6]

But that was only one thread in the story of "Ballad for Americans." It made its impact at a unique moment; the acclaim was part of that moment. The later story was part of another era.

Paul Robeson, a man of magnificent physique, had been an outstanding student and athlete at Rutgers and had subsequently won world fame as a concert singer and actor. He had also been a vigorous critic of the American treatment of the Negro. Traveling to the Soviet Union, he had been welcomed and later said he found no racial bias there. His sympathetic attitude toward communism was freely expressed in the following years.

That CBS in 1939 engaged Robeson unhesitatingly for "Ballad for Americans" and even agreed to the highest fee for the series reflected a wide respect for Robeson. It also reflected a moment in world politics.

FRONT

In America the Depression had spurred liberal thinking. It had also been a spur to various radical groups. Usually hostile to each other as well as to liberals, they become more unified after 1936—largely because of Spain.

There were many reasons for this. Leftist schisms had revolved to some extent around the role of force. Communists and socialists could agree somewhat on goals but disagreed on means. Socialists put faith in the ballot. Communists, while not scorning it, pictured it as impotent at the

5. "Ballad for Americans" by John Latouche and Earl Robinson. Copyright 1939 Robbins Music Corporation. Copyright renewal 1967 Robbins Music Corporation, New York, N. Y. Used by permission.
6. *Broadcasting*, August 1, 1940.

crucial hour. Any socialist victory at the polls, they said, would be contested with force by entrenched capitalists.

The Spanish fascist revolt against an elected, predominantly socialist government seemed almost a dramatized commercial to prove the communist argument. Debate became obsolete as liberals, socialists, and communists—in Spain, America, and elsewhere—were suddenly working together to aid the embattled Spanish republic.

With the American, British, and French governments standing aside on various grounds, hope for the survival of the Spanish republic centered for a time on help trickling from Russia. Among anti-fascists everywhere, Russia's standing rose.

Then came Munich. This time Britain and France did not merely stand aside but helped to dismember Czechoslovakia. Again Russia, expressing readiness to fulfill its treaty obligations, seemed the only hope for the survival of a democratic republic. Once more Russia rose in standing—among a diversity of people who included liberals and socialists, as well as communists.

Their new unity was soon symbolized by the fantastic International Brigade serving in Spain, which by 1938 had drawn 40,000 volunteers from America, Britain, France, Germany, and Poland to aid the loyalists. Including many from the arts, they were slaughtered by thousands. They came, said W. H. Auden, to "present their lives."

Their unity was further symbolized by committees formed to back the cause—via financial help, propaganda work, medical supplies, petitions to Washington, relief for refugees. There was an American Committee for Loyalist Spain, a Medical Bureau for Aid to Spain, a North American Committee for Spanish Democracy, and many others.

Communists took a leading role in organizing many of these, and many were later known as "communist fronts." But they started with diversified boards. The North American Committee for Spanish Democracy had Secretary of the Interior Harold Ickes as honorary chairman and Bishop Francis McConnell as chairman. The fact that its directors also included communists did not seem outrageous—merely understandable. The committee is said to have sent "shiploads of grain and food" to Spain and to have organized film showings.[1]

The ability of the Spanish war to unify diverse elements was illustrated by an unusual meeting. Socialist leader Norman Thomas and communist

1. Baldwin, *Reminiscences*, pp. 360–65.

leader Earl Browder met one day in the office of lifelong pacifist Roger Baldwin, head of the American Civil Liberties Union, to plan effective aid to the Spanish loyalists. Baldwin did not see this as a strain on his pacifism; it was a defense of a legal government. And he saw no objection to working with others in a cause that seemed right and crucial. "Few in my liberal world," he recalled later, "objected to association in the communist-led fronts." He himself was a board member of the most powerful of all "fronts," the American League Against War and Fascism, which at his suggestion changed its name to American League for Peace and Democracy.[2]

The "front" spirit extended to many areas of activity, as exemplified by the National Negro Congress, which included liberals as well as communists; and the League of American Writers, which included radio and screen writers of diverse views. It was addressed by Archibald MacLeish on the crucial role of the Spanish war.

The news of every day spurred the sense of urgency. Hitler, a few months after Munich, marched into the remnant of Czechoslovakia. Spain and Czechoslovakia—they were the great spurs to group activity, enlisting deep idealism. Paul Robeson went to Spain to sing for loyalist troops. Dorothy Parker, screen writer, was there to help organize aid. In an interview years later, when asked about Spain, she began by saying: "Must we go into that?" Then she added: "It's the proudest thing I've ever done—that time in Spain. I was for a time with the proudest people I've ever known. Well it happened, it happened, it happened, they were overthrown. You knew darn well it was going to happen, even when you were there. . . ."[3]

During those months Russia and the communist parties were identified with causes which non-communist liberals were ready to call their own. In the process Russia and the communists acquired a "liberal" tinge and became respectable—even popular. On October 23, 1938, not long after Munich, H. V. Kaltenborn did his CBS broadcast from Cincinnati—a city considered conservative, with a strong German heritage. He began:

> Good evening, everybody. I am sitting here in the studio of WKRC in the city of Cincinnati where I have just spoken to an audience of two thousand people. An interesting thing happened in the course of my address. The mention of Soviet Russia was applauded. . . .

2. *Ibid.* pp. 212, 353–66.
3. Parker, *Reminiscences,* p. 14.

Kaltenborn had referred to the role of Russia during the Munich crisis as "straightforward," but he had scarcely expected an outburst of approval.[4]

The year following Munich made a high-water mark in the standing of Russia and what she represented. American communists were using the slogan, "Communism is twentieth-century Americanism." It almost seemed plausible. Earl Browder was appearing on radio forums and round tables.

When studio audiences wildly cheered pro-communist Paul Robeson in "Ballad for Americans," they were expressing a mood that would not have been possible a few years earlier—or later.

The crisis unity was already being undermined. From Russia came news of treason trials that seemed to be part of a large-scale purge. Reports were at first fragmentary but disturbed many liberals and cast a shadow over communist parties. In Spain the anti-fascist coalition, approaching defeat, began to break into bitter factions. The rancor had world-wide echoes. A more serious blow came late in August 1939 with the Hitler-Stalin "non-aggression" pact, setting the stage for their joint action against Poland. Some observers sought to rationalize the Russian action as a necessary response to the perfidy of Munich, but this was scarcely heartwarming. Then, on November 30, 1939, Russia invaded Finland. It was a decisive blow to the hard-won standing of communists. Liberals began to desert the "popular front" organizations by hundreds and thousands. Many of the organizations collapsed overnight. An empire of letterheads was disintegrating.

Meanwhile attention shifted elsewhere. On the morning of September 1, H. V. Kaltenborn was again at his post as guide to a crisis. A Hitler speech to the Reichstag was broadcast. Kaltenborn told his CBS listeners it amounted to a declaration of war against Poland, and an expression of hope that England and France would stay out. Then, in a pickup from England, a lugubrious Chamberlain was heard announcing that England would fulfill her obligations to Poland. By one o'clock in the afternoon, eastern time, American listeners knew it meant war. The broadcast ended:

ANNOUNCER: We should like to express our appreciation again at this time to the makers of Oxydol, sponsors of *The Goldbergs;* the makers of Ivory Soap, sponsors of *Life Can Be Beautiful;* the makers of Chipso, sponsors of *The Road of Life;* the makers of Crisco, sponsors of *This Day is Ours.* . . .[5]

4. Kaltenborn, *Papers.*
5. Quoted, Chester, *The Radio Commentaries of H. V. Kaltenborn,* p. 303.

The months that followed brought to the broadcasting world one of its strangest intervals. The quick defeat of Poland was followed by a mysterious lull in action—a "phony war," some called it. Throughout this time frantic preparations went on everywhere in the world for an era of carnage that seemed certain to come. At the same time—perhaps in the hope that peace might yet be plucked from imminent chaos—there was a feverish burst of business-as-usual.

EDGE OF CHAOS

During 1939 and the early months of 1940 the clash of opinion grew more bitter, and bewildering new alignments took shape. The use to be made of the power of radio became an increasingly tense issue. The coming of a great war was a factor in every step and transaction. These months brought a war-production boom, and huge preparations for a time of turmoil. Yet amid all this, there was determination to complete long-planned projects.

One sequence of events concerned television. David Sarnoff, RCA president, was also a member of the planning committee for the 1939 New York World's Fair. He had long been determined that commercial television, with programs on a regular schedule, should have its debut at the fair. The FCC had seemed ready to give the go-ahead.

In the course of the preparations Sarnoff had in 1936 installed a new NBC president: Lenox Lohr, a military engineer who had headed—with financial success—the Chicago Century of Progress Exposition. In choosing an army man, Sarnoff probably felt on safe ground; in another time Owen D. Young, in transporting Major General James Harbord into the RCA presidency, had acted similarly. But Lohr was scarcely a happy choice. Sarnoff confided to public relations counsel Edward L. Bernays that Lohr showed little *saichel*, or shrewdness. Would Bernays please do something about it?

Bernays visited the Lohr estate in Irvington-on-Hudson for a family dinner. After dinner the new NBC president invited Bernays to accompany him to the basement—to discuss, Bernays assumed, network problems. But the basement was the setting of a model railroad. For the rest of the evening the president demonstrated his favorite pastime as trains zoomed around banked curves and negotiated complex switches.[1]

1. Bernays, *Biography of an Idea*, pp. 435–6.

At the network Lohr was ill at ease and expressed his puzzlement by appointing "coordinators"—some of them army associates—who increased the organizational confusion.

Meanwhile plans for the long-awaited debut of television went forward. An experimental pickup from the unfinished fair grounds was scheduled for February 26, 1939. Selected for this special honor was a telecast of *Amos 'n' Andy* in blackface make-up. On April 30 came the formal opening, in which Franklin D. Roosevelt became the first President to appear on television.[2] David Sarnoff also spoke, and a new era was proclaimed. RCA sets with five-inch and nine-inch tubes went on display, later followed by sets with twelve-inch tubes. In some, the tube was seen via a hinged mirror. Prices ranged from $199.50 to $600. Crowds came and, in amazement, stared at the programs. Every day brought new items. The NBC schedule usually included one program a day from Studio 3H in Radio City—still the network's only television production studio; one program a day from the mobile unit; and assorted films, from a special film-facilities room at Radio City.

The studio programs included plays, bits of opera, comedians, singers, jugglers, puppets, and kitchen demonstrations—usually salad-mixing, because it was really too hot for cooking. Three cameras were used. The ritual of live television was already well developed. The control room had head-phone communication with studio technicians. A continual stream of cryptic jargon flowed over the intercom wires—abbreviated instructions for adjusting camera angles or distances. This was punctuated with: "Take one! . . . Ready two . . . take two!" Visitors from the theater found the continuous chatter bewildering and astounding; did no one ever listen to the performers? Visitors from the film world were equally amazed at the notion that shooting and editing could be done simultaneously. In the studio the performers still worked in heat that stung the skin. Actors took salt tablets. The big cameras swung slowly. "When I am on the television set," said Earle Larimore, who starred in *The Unexpected* on May 3, 1939, "I think of those cameras as three octopuses with little green eyes blinking on and off, their silvery forms moving ponderously."[3] The actor always felt hemmed in. Everything had to be played "close." He had to cultivate microscopic gestures.

---

2. Herbert Hoover appeared on an AT&T experimental telecast in 1927; he was Secretary of Commerce at the time.
3. Porterfield and Reynolds (eds.), *We Present Television*, p. 179.

The mobile unit was somewhere every day. On May 17 it showed a Columbia-Princeton baseball game from Baker Field. Its single camera stood near the third-base line, sweeping back and forth across the diamond and conclusively proving its own insufficiency. By the time the unit went to Ebbets Field for a double-header between the Brooklyn Dodgers and the Cincinnati Reds, it had acquired a second camera. Sometimes the mobile unit went to Ridgewood Grove in Brooklyn for second-rate wrestlers or boxers, or merely picked up ice skating at Rockefeller Center or planes landing at La Guardia airport or interviews with visitors to the World's Fair. It was all equally amazing. High points of 1939 were a fashion show from the Waldorf-Astoria and pickups from the sidewalk and lobby at the Capitol Theater for the world premiere of *Gone With the Wind*.

The mobile unit consisted of two huge buses; one was a studio crammed with equipment for field use; the other housed the transmitter that relayed the program to the Empire State tower for rebroadcast by the main transmitter.

The films included sponsored travelogues, old cartoons, government documentaries: *Jasper National Park, Washington—Shrine of Patriotism, Miracles of Modernization, Donald's Cousin Gus, Millions for Safety.*[4]

CBS and Dumont were also telecasting in New York in 1939–40, and Dumont had sets on the market. In May 1940 twenty-three stations were telecasting in the United States. In Los Angeles, Don Lee was especially active, having experimented throughout the 1930's.

In all of this there was awe and excitement but along with these, a sense of doom. The FCC had authorized only "limited" commercial operation, which meant that stations could invite sponsors to do program experiments and defray their cost, but could not sell time. In May 1940 even this "limited" authorization was rescinded because of conflicts about technical standards; television went back to "experimental" status. The following year it finally went fully "commercial," but soon afterward schedules were reduced from fifteen hours per week to four hours per week. The boom was being put in storage. Precious materials and electronic assembly lines were needed, not for television but for war. RCA's own assembly lines worked at full speed. One reason was a Navy item related to television and in production since 1939, but with a name not yet to be spoken, even in a whisper—radar. Most television stations left the air. Six hung on with

4. *Ibid.* pp. 51–241.

skeleton programming to serve the 10,000 sets—they would soon be museum pieces—that had already been sold. New sets disappeared from the market. A few went into police stations for the training of air raid wardens. In New York the NBC studio telecasts began to demonstrate the duties of the warden. Groups of volunteers at police stations watched and listened. Television, in modest fashion, had gone to war.

A parallel sequence of events involved international short-wave broadcasting.

Among the entrepreneurs beaming short-wave programs throughout the world in 1939 were NBC, CBS, Westinghouse, General Electric, Crosley. The thirty-eight active stations were "experimental" but could rebroadcast domestic programs including commercials. They pressed constantly for permission to sell time. Finally on June 1, 1939, the FCC gave the authorization. NBC's first short-wave customer broadcasting to South America was United Fruit—a radio pioneer and once part owner of RCA.[5] Subsequent short-wave sponsors were Standard Oil of New Jersey, Adam Hats, S. C. Johnson and Son, the Astor Hotel, the Waldorf-Astoria, Columbia Pictures, Paramount, RKO, Universal Pictures, and Warner Brothers. Each paid $25,000 a year for a daily fifteen-minute program. In 1940 John F. Royal was put in charge of NBC's international short-wave projects and traveled through Latin America to pursue an additional angle: authorized local rebroadcasts under commercial sponsorship, with a fee to NBC.

To all this there was always opposition at the FCC and in Congress—at first mild, then increasingly strenuous. Commissioner George H. Payne argued that the United States needed an international *government* voice far more than it needed product salesmanship. By 1937 the air was already bristling with a short-wave war of words in countless languages representing many nations—but with the United States unrepresented. A proposal to establish government short-wave stations was favored by President Roosevelt but strongly opposed by the radio industry. This aroused Commissioner Payne to anger:

> Every other nation in the world is prepared to see that the world understands its point of view—and yet this nation, where the greatest development of radio has taken place, is absolutely without control over the commercial interests within its own borders and outside its borders is at the mercy of every propagandizing nation.

5. See *A Tower in Babel*, pp. 29n, 42, 72–3, 88–9, 161.

The proposal had been blocked, said Payne, by "misguided captains of industry" who played on congressional fear that it would be an "entering wedge of government control and operation" of all broadcasting. Their real motive, Payne said, was a desire to devote the channels to nostrum peddling. But good will abroad, he argued, would not be won through sale of nostrums. He felt the situation could lead to a major scandal, as serious as Teapot Dome in the misuse of a national resource.[6]

Among nations making extensive use of short-wave broadcasts was Germany. A German News Service at 204 Park Avenue, New York City, was said to be supplying program logs of German short-wave stations to seventeen camps in the United States where goose-stepping was going on.[7]

By mid-1940 the commercial short-wave stations were said to be getting 10,000 letters per month from Latin America. CBS, like NBC, was lining up Latin-American affiliates to be supplied via short-wave broadcasts; Paley himself made a South American tour to further this development. CBS and NBC defended their commercial operations as an aid to hemispheric unity. Their programming would show, said NBC, "the dividends that democracy pays."[8]

But war finally proved more persuasive. In 1941 the federal government began to take over blocks of time on various short-wave stations; then it took control of the stations for the duration of the emergency. The short waves had gone to war.

A similar sequence took place in frequency modulation.

The experimental 50,000-watt FM station W2XMN that Edwin Armstrong, after initial rebuff by the FCC, was allowed to build at Alpine, New Jersey, finally reached full-power operation in early 1939. Then its performance was so magical that a runaway boom seemed to start. Armstrong had commissioned General Electric, at his expense and on his specifications, to build twenty-five FM receivers for his demonstrations. GE became so enthusiastic that it became a leading FM proponent and prepared for mass production of sets. On Mt. Asnebumskit in Massachusetts the Yankee Network built a station that proved almost as astonishing as Alpine. The summer of 1939 was momentous in high fidelity annals. Armstrong's demonstrations and crusading were reaching a break-through

6. Address at Harvard, January 11, 1937; quoted, *Congressional Record,* v. 81 appendix, p. 817.
7. *Congressional Record,* v. 81 appendix, pp. 8557–8.
8. *Broadcasting,* August 1, October 1, 1940.

point. That fall the FCC had before it some 150 applications to build FM stations. Because these called for more spectrum space than the FCC had assigned to FM, they precipitated another spectrum battle, with opposition from television interests—especially RCA. This time, with a new FM Broadcasters Association firmly behind him, Armstrong won the day. Channel 1 was removed from the television band and assigned to FM. Various manufacturers joined the bandwagon, preparing to make FM sets under Armstrong license. They included Freed, Stewart-Warner, Stromberg-Carlson, Western Electric, Zenith. Even RCA, through Sarnoff himself, began overtures for an Armstrong license; but he wanted RCA to have a special cash-settlement deal (rather than a royalty arrangement) and Armstrong was unwilling to give it. Meanwhile, in May 1940, the FCC authorized commercial operation of FM, and followed this with a decision that television should have FM sound. Armstrong was jubilant. A lifetime of struggle seemed to be moving toward a triumphant climax. But the boom did not come. War-time priorities suddenly halted set manufacture. FM stations, with scarcely the beginning of an audience, faced a perilous future. Armstrong, a World War I Signal Corps veteran, was meanwhile being consulted about army problems. In a burst of generosity he made FM patents royalty-free for military needs and plunged into the army work. FM was proving the ideal and only solution for communication in mechanized warfare. Soon every American tank, jeep, command car went forth equipped with FM. FM had gone to war.[9]

Another sequence involved superpower.

Since 1934 WLW, Cincinnati, owned by Powel Crosley, Jr., had been allowed to broadcast "experimentally" with 500,000 watts, while no other station in the United States was allowed more than 50,000 watts. The meaning of "experimental" was not clear. On acquiring its superpower, which made it virtually a network in itself, WLW raised its time charges to $1200 per hour and became enormously profitable. In 1936 it grossed more than $2,500,000 for a probable profit of $500,000.[10] Smaller stations as far away as Canada protested WLW's superpower on the ground of interference with their signals. But the more powerful broadcasting companies, far from protesting, applied and lobbied for the same privilege and seemed confident they would get it.[11]

9. Lessing, *Man of High Fidelity,* pp. 234–52.
10. *Fortune,* March 1938.
11. In 1938 fifteen 50,000-watt stations were pressing the FCC for 500,000 watts:

Who was Powel Crosley, Jr. and how had he come to play a central role in the superpower issue?

As a young man, in 1916, he had started a small automobile accessories business. When the United States went to war the next year he had an idea: he designed a radiator cap with a flag-holder for a small American flag. He did a glorious business in patriotic radiator caps and was off to success.[12] He branched into other things, including canoes and phonograph cabinets, and by 1921 was grossing $1,000,000 per year. That year he also helped his son put together a radio set and a 20-watt amateur transmitter, on which they sent out phonograph music. Crosley began to get ideas about mass-producing cheap crystal radios and by Christmas 1921 had one on the market—the Harko, priced at $20 but later reduced to $9 plus earphones and antenna. By early 1922 the main business of the American Automobile Accessories Company was radios. By mid-1922 it was turning out 500 sets a day. That same year the amateur station grew into WLW.

Because Crosley had made his initial plunge into low-cost radios of limited range, he wanted WLW to have the highest possible power. Owners of Crosley radios might not be able to get *other* stations, but he at least wanted WLW to come booming in. Midwestern Crosley owners were likely to be full-time WLW listeners. In April 1923, with 500 watts, WLW already called itself the "world's most powerful broadcasting station." In 1924 it went to 1000 watts, in 1925 to 5000 watts. Within months after that, Crosley announced his intention of getting a 50,000-watt transmitter; in 1928 he persuaded the Federal Radio Commission to approve it. Only three other such stations—KDKA, Pittsburgh; WEAF, New York; WENR, Chicago—were authorized at the time. Soon after that, Crosley began agitating for 500,000 watts.

The prestige of WLW sold fantastic quantities of Crosley radios. Crosley was able to buy out other manufacturers and their patents[13] and by 1928 did a gross business of $18,000,000 for a profit of $3,605,973, and acquired a second Cincinnati station, WSAI. He also moved into other ventures—patent medicines, a scalp massager, a tire patch, a refrigerator

KDKA, KFI, KNX, KSL, WBZ, WGN, WGY, WHAS, WHO, WJR, WJZ, WOAI, WOR, WSB, WSM. *Broadcasting*, May 1, 1938.

12. The following is based on Lichty, *The Nation's Station*, and other sources as mentioned.

13. In 1925 he bought AMRAD of Medford, Mass. (see *A Tower in Babel*, pp. 35–6); in 1927, the De Forest Company of Jersey City.

with in-a-door shelves. The refrigerator paid off handsomely. He bought the Cincinnati Reds baseball team. He planned a small car to sell through department stores.

While manufacture was always his chief interest, Crosley was finding that WLW, the favorite of all owners of low-priced sets, could yield huge sponsor revenue. WLW became an enormous, bustling station. It was long housed in the Crosley factory, but scarcely an artist ever saw Powel Crosley. He took little interest in the operation of the station except to issue occasional edicts. Executives who dealt with him found him arrogant.[14] Editorial policies were consistently anti-labor. WLW gave time for an *Ohio School of the Air* under the auspices of the Department of Education of the state, but its instructor in Modern Problems found his scripts and reading recommendations censored by WLW, which on one occasion also cut him off the air.[15]

For many years Crosley's relentless drive for higher and higher power met little resistance in Washington, in spite of protests from lesser stations. In 1938 Charles Michelson was on the Crosley payroll handling Washington relations, apparently at the same time as he served the Democratic National Committee as publicity director. According to Stanley High, writing in the *Saturday Evening Post,* Michelson was "a powerful spokesman in the administration's inner councils" on behalf of Crosley.[16] But some resistance began to develop. Senator Burton K. Wheeler considered superpower a "potentially dangerous" weapon. Commissioner George Henry Payne held a similar view, and felt that Crosley's one-sided editorial policies were a relevant consideration. When Crosley appeared at an FCC hearing in 1936, Payne questioned him about his directives barring news of strikes. Crosley denied any such directive.[17] Unfortunately for Crosley, the FCC had photostats of them, provided by the American Civil Liberties Union—which had had them in its files since receiving them from Norman Corwin.

Some broadcasters apparently considered Payne's injection of such issues into the superpower hearings an outrage. *Broadcasting* called it "the most brazen piece of political demagoguery we have ever seen perpetrated at a public hearing on radio . . . bureaucracy at its worst." It had,

14. Interview, William S. Hedges.
15. *The Social Frontier,* May 1936.
16. *Saturday Evening Post,* February 11, 1939.
17. *Report on Social and Economic Data Pursuant to the Informal Hearing on Broadcasting,* p. 86.

said *Broadcasting*, "not the remotest connection with the subject of allocations or superpower."[18] Not everyone agreed. In 1938 the U. S. Senate
adopted a resolution offered by Senator Wheeler opposing any power over
50,000 watts. In 1939 WLW's experimental use of 500,000 watts was
finally ended; the station went back to 50,000 watts. The superpower ad-
vocates, however, were not quite ready to give up. In 1940, with war in
the air, they pressed the issue again, asking for 500,000 watts "as a defense
measure."[19] The idea failed to arouse patriotic response, and died.

While these various disputes were hastened to a resolution by world
events, the nation's attention was increasingly on radio. News broadcasts
were winning a growing audience—and stirring increasing contention.

Two weeks after the declaration of war by Britain and France, Roosevelt called Congress into special session to ask for a change in the neutrality law. He wanted to be allowed to sell arms to England and France on a
cash-and-carry basis. This was urged on the ground that it would help
keep the United States neutral. The proposal squeaked through Congress
but unleashed a nationwide torrent of debate, bringing unprecedented
tensions to broadcasting.

The "isolationists" accused Roosevelt of wanting to lead America into a
re-enactment of the 1914–18 blood bath—and one that would, once more,
settle nothing. These "isolationists" included a strange new alignment of
forces:

> Conservatives like Senator Robert Taft and Senator Arthur Vanden-
> berg, especially strong in the Midwest and reflecting a traditional
> aversion to European entanglements. (They appeared on many radio
> forums and round tables.)

> Liberals like Senator Burton Wheeler and Senator Robert La Fol-
> lette, Jr., who reflected a disillusionment over World War I, which had
> choked off liberal reform and led to the Palmer raids and the Harding
> era. (They too appeared frequently on radio forums and round
> tables.)

> Followers of Father Coughlin, particularly strong among Irish-Amer-
> icans because of resentment of Britain, but also attracting an anti-
> Semitic following. (Coughlin, changing his mind about retiring, had
> returned to the air, again with a line-up of stations purchased at com-
> mercial rates.)

18. *Broadcasting*, October 15, 1936.
19. *Ibid.* October 15, 1940.

Pro-Germans like Charles Lindbergh, who had visited Goering in Germany, witnessed his air-power demonstrations, accepted a Nazi decoration, and who looked on Britain and France as decadent and saw nazism as "the wave of the future." (His views became known in a network radio talk in September 1940.)

Italian-Americans still impressed with Mussolini. (Some foreign-language stations were said to reflect considerable pro-Mussolini sentiment.)

Socialists like Norman Thomas, who felt little identity of interest with a British empire that still refused independence to India and that had played a leading role in choking the Spanish and Czechoslovakian republics. (Thomas, being anti-Soviet and representing a small, idealistic constituency, was occasionally welcomed on forums and round tables.)

Communists, for whom Chamberlain's Britain likewise represented imperialism, reaction, and an obstacle to their hopes. (At the moment they had almost no access to the air, but every one else was expressing their anti-intervention views.)

Some businessmen felt that Hitler would win the war and that America should be prepared to do business with him. Throughout this time the German embassy was spending large sums on the distribution of literature in the United States and was getting help from many sides. According to German embassy documents, the MBS commentator Fulton Lewis, Jr., offered suggestions for a message from Hitler to Roosevelt, expressing desire for an "honorable peace treaty with England." According to the embassy report:

Lewis added that Roosevelt would, of course, make a rude and spiteful reply; that would make no difference. Such an appeal would surely make a profound impression on the North American people and especially in South America. . . .[20]

Late in 1939 the assorted "isolationist" groups, ranging from the solidly respectable to extremist fringes, appeared to represent a majority of the American people. In October 1939 the American Institute of Public Opinion conducted a poll on the question: "Do you think the United States should do everything possible to help England and France win the war, even at the risk of getting into the war ourselves?" The answers ran: *yes,* 34 per cent; *no,* 66 per cent.[21]

20. From *Documents on German Foreign Policy,* quoted in Shirer, *The Rise and Fall of the Third Reich,* p. 985.
21. Cantril (ed.), *Public Opinion,* p. 967.

Nevertheless Roosevelt, feeling that a Hitler victory would be disastrous to the United States, was determined to give England and France such help as he could wrest from Congress. The debate grew in bitterness.

Network executives were increasingly nervous about this. Every expression of opinion seemed to arouse fury. Paley had reached the conclusion that opinion should be confined as much as possible to round tables and other programs providing balanced discussion. Sale of time for the arguing of views had already been ruled out by CBS, except in campaigns. Paley felt that the broadcaster should also refrain from pushing his own opinions. "We must never have an editorial page," he said as early as 1937. "We must never try to further either side of any debatable question." [22] By the same token, he had reached the conclusion that a radio newsman should not push opinions—his or any one else's. Many of Paley's major headaches had been caused by opinion-pushers—Father Coughlin, Commander Clark, William J. Cameron. They caused nothing but trouble. All this led to a determined effort to define and enforce CBS policies about opinion-pushing.

One problem was Kaltenborn, who insisted on expressing his opinions. This may have played a part in keeping him unsponsored for years. The Munich crisis had won him sudden fame and a sponsor, but the problem continued. The sponsor, General Mills, had publicly pledged him "complete freedom in news selection and in expression on that news";[23] nevertheless, a General Mills executive had soon afterward requested him to avoid discussion of Spain. Kaltenborn refused, and the contract ended after its first thirteen-week period.

Paley's concern over such problems generated a CBS policy: CBS would have news *analysts*, not *commentators*. A news analyst, in CBS doctrine, was a newsman who analyzed the news but promoted no view. A commentator was an opinion-pusher—not wanted on CBS.

Klauber was delegated to discuss this with Kaltenborn. In the very months that Kaltenborn was being hailed as radio's greatest commentator, Columbia's "gem of the ozone," he was constantly pressed by CBS not to be a commentator but an analyst.

To Kaltenborn the distinction seemed unreal and false. He had no objection to being called a news *analyst*, but to him it meant the same as *commentator*. As for influencing opinion—even the selection of one news

22. *Broadcasting*, December 15, 1937.
23. CBS, January 1, 1939.

item over another tended to influence opinion. Terminology and tone of voice influenced opinion. The newsman could scarcely help influencing opinion. To pretend otherwise was a charade. But the pressure on Kaltenborn continued. He later recounted:

> Vice President Edward Klauber would call me up to his office for a friendly heart-to-heart talk. . . . "Just don't be so personal," he'd say to me. "Use such phrases as 'it is said,' 'there are those who believe,' 'the opinion is held in well-informed quarters,' 'some experts have come to the conclusion . . .' Why keep on saying 'I think' and 'I believe' when you can put over the same idea much more persuasively by quoting someone else?" [24]

To Kaltenborn such arguments pointed up that the *analyst* idea was pretense. He could not accept the theory, but perhaps was influenced by it in practice. In 1940 Wendell Willkie, a businessman new to politics, was moving into contention as a presidential possibility. Kaltenborn, after listening to a Willkie speech, drafted a comment for his next broadcast.

> I listened to Wendell Willkie's speech last night. It was wholly admirable.

He then crossed this out and substituted:

> Millions of Americans of both parties listened to Wendell Willkie's speech last night. Most of them agreed that it was a wholly admirable speech.[25]

That same year NBC ended its diligent search for "someone like Kaltenborn" by hiring Kaltenborn. Somewhat to the relief of CBS, he transferred to NBC. But NBC and MBS were moving toward a position similar to that of CBS. In a joint statement on war coverage, the networks declared:

> News analysts are at all times to be confined strictly to explaining and evaluating such fact, rumor, propaganda, and so on, as are available. No news analyst or news broadcaster of any kind is to be allowed to express personal editorial judgment or . . . to say anything in an effort to influence action or opinion of others one way or the other.[26]

Most commentators never quite accepted this doctrine. In 1941 they formed an Association of Radio News Analysts, choosing its name in ap-

24. *Radio Daily*, September 16, 1943; also Kaltenborn, *Reminiscences*, p. 207.
25. Chester, *The Radio Commentaries of H. V. Kaltenborn*, pp. 504–5.
26. Quoted, Dryer, *Radio in Wartime*, pp. 164–5.

parent concession to network policy, but Kaltenborn as its first president resolutely declared that the association was "entirely made up of radio commentators." [27]

Network policy constituted a kind of neutrality law for radio. In 1941 the FCC enunciated a somewhat similar doctrine, emphasizing the need for neutrality by licensees. Reprimanding Boston station WAAB for its one-sidedness (but renewing its license) the FCC declared:

> A truly free radio cannot be used to advocate the causes of the licensee . . . the broadcaster cannot be an advocate.

This statement, known as the "Mayflower doctrine," was later denounced by industry spokesmen as FCC tyranny, but at the time seemed an echo of views developing within the industry.[28]

The National Association of Broadcasters had itself expressed such views in a code adopted in 1939. Like previous NAB codes, it was a statement of principles without enforcement machinery. Its purpose was largely tactical—to head off interference by others. But presumably its statements had considerable backing. The 1939 code, which also included recommendations about children's programs and the length of commercials, made the following proclamations on news and public affairs:

> Since the number of broadcasting channels is limited, news broadcasts shall not be editorial. . . .
>
> Elucidation of the news should be free of bias. . . .
>
> Time for the presentation of controversial views should not be sold, except for political broadcasts. . . .

The code also ruled out solicitation of membership on the air, whether in sold or unsold time.

These ideas won considerable approval. Their application was closely watched.

Some of the forty-four stations selling time to Father Coughlin dropped his broadcasts because of the code, but others continued to carry them, including some NAB members. Presumably they did not consider the programs controversial and were prepared to overlook the element of membership solicitation.

27. *Education on the Air* (1942), p. 71.
28. It was named the "Mayflower doctrine" after the Mayflower Broadcasting Corporation, which had sought to replace WAAB as licensee.

Some labor unions complained that the code was given as a reason for refusing them time. Some were told they could not buy time because they were controversial. Others were told they could not have time—free or otherwise—because a union broadcast would in effect be a membership solicitation.

A more dramatic test of the code came in connection with the America First Committee, the organization around which the leading isolationist sentiment coalesced. It included many nationally known figures and in 1940 engaged the Batten, Barton, Durstine & Osborn advertising agency to produce a series of recorded programs opposing aid to Britain. Many stations at first hesitated to sell time for these programs on the ground that the issue seemed controversial, but BBD&O managed to clear this up by a phone call to Ed Kirby, public relations director of the NAB. America First agreed to describe itself as "non-partisan" and this, the NAB decided, would make the programs acceptable under the code. The programs presented addresses by America First adherents, and choir music.[29]

At the networks, and especially at CBS, the turmoil of the time encouraged disengagement, neutrality, non-involvement. The policy fitted the personality of Paley, and the CBS manner became a projection of his: smooth and unruffled, with a modern look, but basically conservative. As tensions grew, the conservatism took an increasingly strong hold.

William Robson, director of *Columbia Workshop*, took a vacation in Mexico and returned with a beard. A few days later William Lewis said: "Klauber says to get rid of the beard."

"Bill, you must be kidding."

"No, Klauber says we don't want people around with beards."

Robson invited a number of people to dinner at his apartment near CBS, and afterward Mrs. Robson brought vice president Lewis a bowl of warm water and a razor. Lewis shaved the beard ceremoniously.[30]

Audience surveys reflected a constant increase in sets-in-use. A *Fortune* poll showed that more people were relying on radio for news than on newspapers. Farm tractors were appearing with radio as standard equipment. As 1940 began, sponsors were renewing contracts "almost 100%," and new sponsors were signing in "unprecedented numbers." War contracts were spurring business; employment and retail sales were rising.

29. *Broadcasting*, October 15, 1940.
30. Robson, *Reminiscences*, pp. 13–14.

This should, said Paley, "be the greatest year in the history of radio in the United States." [31]

Network staffs meanwhile continued to grow. In Paris, Eric Sevareid, a newspaperman working for United Press and the Paris edition of the New York *Herald-Tribune,* got a phone call from Murrow asking if he would like to try radio reporting. "I think this thing may develop into something," Murrow told him. "There won't be pressure on you to provide scoops or anything sensational. Just provide the honest news, and when there isn't any news, why, just say so. I have an idea people might like that." Sevareid decided to try. Late in 1939 another UP man, Larry Lesueur, joined Murrow from New York. NBC had Fred Bate in London, William C. Keirker and Max Jordan in Germany. In the spring of 1940 Jordan found increasing censorship problems in Berlin. Every broadcast script had to have three approvals: (1) propaganda office; (2) foreign office; (3) military censor. Copies of the script were required for all three. Moscow was not permitting any broadcasts at all by foreign correspondents. London was the easiest place for a reporter.[32]

On the home front CBS engaged Elmer Davis for a nightly news analysis—soon celebrated for dry, candid wit. He was scheduled unsponsored in a peak listening period of five minutes—8:55 to 9 P.M.—wrested from one of the most valuable commercial hours. If the move was shrewd, riveting mid-evening attention on CBS, it also appeared statesmanlike.

In April 1940 Hitler began his westward *Blitzkrieg.* Denmark took a day, Norway about two weeks. Luxembourg, Belgium, and the Netherlands fell in eighteen days, France in fifteen. From an enveloping French chaos came several brilliant broadcasts by Eric Sevareid, then silence.

On June 21 American listeners heard William Shirer of CBS and William C. Keirker of NBC describe an extraordinary scene in a clearing in a forest of elms, oaks, and pines near Compiègne, France. To this clearing, by order of Hitler himself, a war trophy was brought: the old Wagon-Lits railway coach in which the World War I armistice had been signed by defeated Germany. It had long stood in a nearby museum built with funds donated by a Mr. Arthur Fleming of Pasadena, California. German army engineers quickly demolished the museum wall with pneumatic drills and

31. *Fortune,* August 1939; *Variety,* February 1, 1939; *Broadcasting,* January 1, August 1, 1940.
32. Sevareid, *Not So Wild a Dream,* p. 107; *Broadcasting,* June 1, 1940.

pulled the old coach into the clearing, to the spot of the 1918 humiliation. Then came Hitler and his top generals in ceremonial uniform. The Fuehrer, hardly able to contain himself, strutted as he entered the coach for the signing. Shirer and Keirker, at their microphones at the edge of the clearing, watched and later described the scene. According to *Broadcasting* they were the only correspondents on hand; others, expecting the big news to break at the center of power, had rushed to Berlin. Said Shirer over CBS: "What a turning back of the clock, what a reversing of history . . . !"[33]

Sevareid, on a refugee ship edging out of Bordeaux crammed with fleeing Poles, Czechs, Austrians, Hollanders, heard the Shirer broadcast. Around the ship, starting for England, bombs were falling.

As the Germans massed on the English Channel, Americans began to hear, night after night, a voice from London. Murrow—calm, never arguing, never urging an opinion—began to refer to himself as "this reporter." He narrated—and in so doing, had historic impact.

THIS REPORTER

In mid-1940 the American networks were making some twenty foreign pickups a day. The extraordinary organizations they had built during the preceding months—especially at CBS under Paley-Klauber-White-Murrow leadership—now showed their brilliance. For the moment the star performer was Edward Murrow. He was where bombs were falling and told about it in a manner few listeners could ever forget.

He opened his broadcasts: "This is London." It became a trademark.[1] He was soon describing a city of shattered buildings. On August 18, 1940:

> There were two women who gossiped across the narrow strip of tired brown grass that separated their two houses. They didn't have to open their kitchen windows in order to converse. The glass had been blown out. There was a little man with a pipe in his mouth who walked up and looked at a bombed house and said, "One fell there and that's all."

33. Shirer, *The Rise and Fall of the Third Reich*, pp. 975–8; Hohenberg, *Foreign Correspondence*, p. 336; *Broadcasting*, June 22, 1940; Wylie (ed.), *Best Broadcasts of 1939–40*, pp. 340–45.

1. The phrase appears to have been first used on September 22, 1938. See Bliss (ed.), *In Search of Light*, p. 7. The following excerpts are from this collection of Murrow scripts and from other sources as noted.

Soon the CBS London building was bombed. On September 18 Murrow reported: "The top floors lie in the street." Later both CBS and NBC buildings had bomb hits. One office looked "as if some crazy giant had operated an egg-beater in its interior." Murrow spoke of the sound of the falling bomb: "That moan of stark terror and suspense cannot be encompassed by words." Nor could the relief on finding that "you could pick yourself up out of the gutter without the aid of a searcher party." Occasionally periods of silence—of waiting—could be more terrifying than the noise of action.[2]

Murrow was conscious of how crucial the role of radio might be. When Neville Chamberlain was succeeded by Winston Churchill in the spring of 1940, Murrow said the new prime minister had "the advantage of being the best broadcaster in this country." Mr. Churchill could inspire confidence, said Murrow, and "preach a doctrine of hate that is acceptable to the majority of this country." Murrow was well aware that his own task as broadcaster permitted no note of hate or even of persuasion. He was aware that most Americans wanted no part of the war, and that any hint of an effort to involve them would be attacked. His role was that of reporter, and he held to it.

But how could he adequately report what he saw? "How do you report suffering to people who have not suffered?" He spent many nights on rooftops practicing ad-lib descriptions of flaming air raids. He searched for meaningful phrases. "It's a bomber's moon tonight." He prowled endlessly around the city, and told what he saw. On September 3, 1940:

> Today I went to buy a hat—my favorite shop had gone, blown to bits. The windows of my shoe store were blown out. I decided to have a haircut; the windows of the barber shop were gone, but the Italian barber was still doing business. Some day, he said, we smile again, but the food it doesn't taste so good since being bombed. I went on to another shop to buy flashlight batteries. I bought three. The clerk said, "You needn't buy so many. We'll have enough for the whole winter." But I said, "What if you aren't here?" There were buildings down in that street, and he replied, "Of course we'll be here. We've been in business here for a hundred and fifty years."

Americans were hearing from many orators that Britain was decadent, a spent force. Murrow did not argue with them; he merely reported. But his words left little doubt that Britain would fight on.

Throughout the battle of Britain, Murrow alarmed associates with the

2. *Broadcasting*, October 1, 1940; April 21, 1941.

risks he took. He drove around the bomb-scarred countryside with reckless speed. Elmer Davis after a visit to England reported: "I had heard of the horrors of war but I didn't know they included Ed Murrow's driving." Davis was also "faintly scandalized" that anyone without the slightest newspaper experience could be so fine a reporter.[3] In later months Murrow flew combat missions.

Throughout the time that Murrow was making his reports, they had a bearing on a struggle he dared not mention. The months of the London blitz were also the months of a presidential election campaign. The networks, throughout the time of dazzling foreign coverage, were also coping with a hard-fought political struggle.

CAMPAIGN 1940

Like every presidential campaign since the birth of radio, that of 1940 left footnotes in the annals of broadcasting.

When the Republicans swung to Wendell L. Willkie at their Philadelphia convention in June, at about the time the fighting in France collapsed, they were hedging their bets. The men who had been the leading candidates—Taft, Dewey, Vandenberg—were all committed isolationists. Willkie, the dark horse, had the advantage of being an unknown quantity. He was also a beguiling radio personality. His background was that of a utilities executive, but he had overlaid this image with other images. He had made a charming appearance on *Information Please* and performed impressively on *America's Town Meeting of the Air*. He had written an article for the *New Republic*. Thus he had various images to attract varied hopes. New to politics, he had uttered few words that could be used against him.

He had a pleasant, friendly sound on the air, with a Hoosier quality. His distinctive speech habits aroused interest. He skipped vowels. He spoke intently of his *flosophy*, his *princples*—the things in which he *blieved*—which were the *oppsite* of Roosevelt's ideas, which were *obslete*, and a *clamity* to the *Unistates*. These ellipses conveyed an eagerness that was infectious. He sometimes stumbled and backtracked, but that only proved he wasn't a smoothie, and people liked it. His ruffled hair gave the same impression.[1]

3. Murrow, *This Is London*, introduction by Davis, p. viii.
1. *Broadcasting*, September 1, 1940.

Willkie was regarded by Roosevelt as a formidable opponent but made his quota of mistakes. In his big labor speech broadcast from Pittsburgh before a union audience, he made one point with telling success. Roosevelt's Secretary of Labor was Frances Perkins, a former social worker, efficient and with a quiet courage, but in no sense a representative of organized labor. Willkie promised: "I will appoint a Secretary of Labor directly from the ranks of organized labor." This drew a large ovation. Then Willkie tried to top his success: "And it will not be a woman either!" This too won cheers, but Roosevelt told Frances Perkins it was a "boner." She got many letters from women expressing resentment over Willkie's comment.

The Democratic convention, held in Chicago a month after the Republican meeting, featured a diabolical innovation in radio technique. The prospect of a third term for Roosevelt was resented by many in the party, including James Farley, who had long been the President's political mentor. Politicians lived on expectations, said Farley, and for many politicians—including, apparently, himself—the third term meant deferred expectations. However, the third term was strongly supported by others, among them Mayor Kelly of Chicago, and this led to a strange stratagem.

Kelly placed a host of loyal men in the basement of the convention hall at microphones connected to loudspeakers in the hall above. The men in the basement could hear the convention proceedings by radio. At every mention of Roosevelt's name, they released a "bedlam of cheers," which were given good volume on the upstairs loudspeakers. Delegates and home listeners heard an enthusiasm that did not really exist in the convention hall. On the third day the boys-in-the-basement arrangement became known and was ended amid anger and vituperation.[2]

Both party platforms had planks which, in vague rhetorical terms, called for a "free" radio. Perhaps intended as anti-FCC mortar fire, they meant little to voters but suggested the close ties already existing between the radio industry and party leaders.

Roosevelt, following the same strategy as in 1936, held back in the early months of the campaign, while Willkie vigorously attacked the "arrogance" of a third-term bid and the "socialistic" tendencies of the New Deal. Willkie was endorsed by almost all newspapers, including the influential New York *Times*. Having achieved enormous momentum, Willkie was anxious to match blows with the President. "Bring on the champ!" he cried. He clearly felt frustrated by the President's long silence and, in the

2. Perkins, *The Roosevelt I Knew*, pp. 116–29.

absence of opposition, shouted himself hoarse. He also kept repeating himself, while Roosevelt appeared to be completely preoccupied with defense preparations and the study of intelligence reports from London, Moscow, Tokyo, Chungking, and elsewhere.

Until the last days of the campaign Willkie was cautious about international problems. Already backed by most isolationists, he had little to gain from isolationist themes, although he made some use of them in the final hours. His strategy tended to remove international issues from the campaign—to Roosevelt's relief.

Roosevelt in his final campaign broadcasts, perhaps taking a cue from radio comedians, made extraordinarily successful use of his audiences. Speaking from a crowded Madison Square Garden on October 28 he mentioned various isolationist backers of Wendell Willkie. One was Bruce Barton, BBD&O co-founder and apostle, who had built a successful career by identifying business success with spiritual leadership.[3] On the urging of clients he had run for Congress in 1937 from Manhattan's "silk stocking district" and had become a House of Representatives isolationist leader. His agency had produced the America First radio programs. Roosevelt in his Madison Square Garden broadcast linked Barton's name euphoniously with those of two other isolationist Republicans: "Martin, Barton, and Fish." Repeating the phrase, he got the enormous audience to chant it with him. In a broadcast from the Boston Arena three days later, he only had to mention "Martin . . ." when the audience resoundingly supplied: ". . . Barton, and Fish!" When Willkie heard that chant, he said later, he had an idea he was licked.[4]

The campaign marked the debut of Robert Sherwood, Pulitzer Prize playwright, as a speech writer for Roosevelt. He worked with Harry Hopkins and Samuel Rosenman on major broadcasts from Cleveland, New York, and Boston, and subsequently on many others. But all speeches were, in the end, Roosevelt's own.

The major political parties spent about $2,250,000 on radio in the 1940 campaign.

The Communist party had candidates on the ballot in nineteen states but found many stations unwilling to sell air time. In Cincinnati the manager of WCKY, L. B. Wilson, said:

3. See *A Tower in Babel*, p. 203.
4. Sherwood, *Roosevelt and Hopkins*, v. 1, p. 233.

The Communist Party has not enough money, nor can it ever have enough money, to buy one minute on WCKY.

In place of candidate Browder the station broadcast a "patriotic drama." [5]

Communists had acquired an ambiguous legal status. The Smith Act, passed in June of 1940, made it illegal not only to "teach" the overthrow of government but even to "conspire to teach" it. Until then the guiding principle had been that words are protected by the freedom of speech guarantee of the First Amendment except in situations where—as Justice Oliver Wendell Holmes put it—they would create a "clear and present danger that they will bring about the substantive evils that Congress has a right to prevent." [6] The Smith Act, over protests from many legal authorities, swept this guideline aside. Propaganda and even the planning of propaganda appeared to become punishable. Many radio stations interpreted the law to mean that any communist political campaign was an illegal conspiracy with no claim under the equal-time provisions of the Communications Act.

It should be noted that liberal groups protesting the Smith Act included the American Civil Liberties Union, which had as its purpose the defense of the Bill of Rights. Yet the ACLU decided in the same year to bar communists from its own board. Some liberals protested this too; but others argued that in civil rights cases involving the Smith Act or similar acts the ACLU would be compromised by having communists on its board. Even communists, they said, could be better defended by non-communists. This argument won the day at the ACLU but ironically moved the organization in a direction similar to that of the Smith Act itself, making the communists a political pariah, virtually confined to clandestine teachings.

Throughout the campaign the Gallup and Roper polls showed Willkie trailing, but in the final weeks he appeared to close the gap. On election day, November 5, the early returns were close.

In New York City the NBC and Dumont television stations provided coverage of election returns—the first in television history. NBC personnel included Leo Rosenberg, the man who had read returns over KDKA in the historic broadcast of November 2, 1920.

In winning a firm victory, Roosevelt was especially delighted that he carried—376–302—his own district in Dutchess County, New York—a Republican stronghold. Late on election night townspeople brought a ban-

5. *Broadcasting*, October 15, 1940.
6. *Schenk v. United States*, 249 U. S. 47 (1919).

ner: "Safe on 3rd." The electoral college vote was: Roosevelt, 449; Willkie, 82.[7]

LIFELINE

As the United States election ended, Britain still faced its most grueling hour. Hitler, angered by Britain's "criminal" resistance, began saturation bombing of one town at a time. Coventry was leveled with more than a thousand killed or injured. Many expected this would be followed by invasion from the Continent—probably by early spring. Britain braced for the expected event. On December 24, 1940, Edward R. Murrow told his CBS listeners:

> Christmas Day began in London nearly an hour ago. The churchbells did not ring at midnight. When they ring again, it will be to announce invasion. . . . The rooftop watchers are peering across the fantastic forest of London's chimney pots. The anti-aircraft gunners stand ready. . . . The fire fighters and ambulance drivers are waiting, too. The blackout stretches from Birmingham to Bethlehem. . . .

On that day Murrow for the first time signed off, "So long and good luck." A variation of this—"Good night and good luck"—later became his regular closing.[1]

Britain was approaching bankruptcy. Cash transactions could carry her no further, and now Roosevelt, with the election behind him, made a carefully planned move. He told a press conference: "Suppose my neighbor's home catches fire, and I have got a length of garden hose. . . ." You would not haggle about wanting fifteen dollars for the hose, Roosevelt said. You would tell your neighbor to take the hose and put out the flames, and give the hose back later. With this homely figure of speech Roosevelt introduced the idea of Lend-Lease, which he urged in a "fireside chat" on December 29 and presented to Congress. The United States would lend Britain ships, planes, and other items—that is, a garden hose. Actually it would not be a mere loan: as *quid pro quo* the United States would take over various British bases.

When Lend-Lease got through Congress two months later, Murrow reported what it meant to Britain psychologically and in practical terms. At the same time he tried to suggest the urgent need for quick delivery. The best invasion weather was approaching. On March 9 he broadcast:

7. Sherwood, *Roosevelt and Hopkins*, v. 1, p. 246.
1. Bliss (ed.), *In Search of Light*, p. 44.

> One thing that is not doubted is that the decisions taken in Washington between now and the time the crops are harvested will determine the pattern of events for a long time to come.[2]

While the voice of Edward Murrow was providing a link between two worlds, another voice was playing a similar, equally crucial role. However, few Americans knew of it; there was no reason why they should.

Raymond Swing had for some years broadcast a weekly program from New York for the British Broadcasting Corporation. He was its American commentator. His painstaking analyses of American affairs had built a wide following in Britain. As Britain approached its hour of desperation, the Swing link assumed historic importance. Britons hung on his words. He offered hope but never garnished it with false hope. He pictured precisely the forces in conflict. The day-to-day ramifications of the isolation battle were perhaps more vividly real to Britons than to Americans. In Parliament he acquired a large following: members organized a "Swing club" to listen together. Churchill listened regularly and sent cables of comment. King George VI asked an aide to get him an autographed photo of Swing. In mid-1941 Swing flew to England in an unheated Lend-Lease bomber, visited Churchill, and was honored at a luncheon attended by 267 guests, including eighteen government ministers. Forty-five national leaders sat at the speaker's table. George Bernard Shaw sent handwritten regrets, saying that "spectral back numbers" should not take up Swing's time, but "you may assure him that I always listen with special attention when he broadcasts." The BBC regularly short-waved Swing's commentaries internationally for rebroadcast throughout the Commonwealth. When he visited India years later, Swing was astonished to find he was well known there. The *New Yorker* called Swing's voice the best-known in the world, and it may have been—certainly among professional broadcasters.

Swing prepared his broadcasts with the most tenacious care. To check details he had access to almost any government leader. He regularly phoned Secretary of War Henry Stimson, Secretary of the Interior Harold Ickes, Secretary of Labor Frances Perkins. At the Navy Department Adlai Stevenson, assistant to Secretary Frank Knox, was always available. At the White House it was Harry Hopkins. Swing worked ten hours on each commentary. He had four assistants for research and office work but did all writing himself. He rehearsed each commentary.[3]

2. *Ibid.* p. 47.
3. Swing, *Good Evening*, pp. 194–211.

While Murrow was primarily a reporter, answering *what* and *how,* Swing was in every sense a commentator, examining *why.* He did not hesitate to express opinions, but criticized with a compassion that was almost agonizing. He called the French action at Munich "treachery," but when he had explored the ramifications of the moment, he left listeners feeling: "In those shoes, I might have done likewise." Swing was less quotable than other commentators; his quality was less in phrasing than in structure. Each broadcast was a minutely balanced entity full of internal tensions. He was the most scholarly of all commentators.

He spoke with a hushed urgency that seemed compelling to admirers. But executive vice president Klauber at CBS is said to have disliked Swing's voice and ruled him out as a CBS news analyst. The ban may have originated with Paley and may have stemmed from the fact that Swing was more than a news analyst.

Swing, along with Kaltenborn and others, took a firm stand against commercials spoken by newsmen. He insisted on absolute separation of news and commercial message, at a time when the news field was vulgarized by Gabriel Heatter and others who specialized in the "clever" integration of sales talk and news, and by sponsors who rejoiced in the practice.

Fortunately, Swing's sense of responsibility toward his commentary was to some extent infectious. Preparing his talk on the Nazi invasion of Luxembourg, Belgium, and the Netherlands, Swing was so tortured by the thought of a middle commercial for White Owl cigars that he offered to step aside for some other newsman. Instead White Owl decided to waive the middle commercial, and it never returned to any Swing broadcast. When he later acquired Socony Vacuum as sponsor, the contract ruled out middle commercials.

This contract also had a clause guaranteeing Swing editorial control. Before signing it, Swing wondered whether the sponsor fully understood it. He asked for an appointment with John A. Brown, president of Socony Vacuum. They had lunch and then repaired to Brown's office for a talk. "I want it to be understood," said Swing in his hushed, earnest voice, "that I have the freedom to criticize Standard Oil in my broadcasts if I consider it to be in the public interest." The president sat still for a few moments. Swing suspected that the blood was running cold in his veins. Brown then asked whether Standard Oil would be entitled to reply. Assured that it would, Brown agreed.[4]

4. *Ibid.* pp. 222–3.

By mid-1940 Swing, although heard over MBS, the weakest of the national networks, was established as one of the leading news voices in America. But to Britain, through his weekly unsponsored broadcasts for the BBC, he was far more—a lifeline in its loneliest hour.

Then suddenly that loneliness was ended.

WORLDWIDE

In June 1941 Hitler, having failed to destroy British defenses, wheeled eastward to attack Russia. His aim was to remove a potential threat and seize Russian oil fields and food resources. His swift moves slashed deep into the Soviet Union. The Soviet retreat left "scorched earth."

Politically these events brought a new upheaval in alignments in the United States. Among recent isolationists, many hoped Hitler would quickly destroy the Soviet Union; others, that Russia would bleed the Hitler might. Bedfellows split up.

For radio it meant activity rapidly expanding toward global dimensions. In the CBS lineup Larry Lesueur was sent by northern convoy via Archangel to the Soviet Union, and short-wave pickups from Moscow began. During 1941 Howard K. Smith joined CBS and went to Berlin. Charles Collingwood joined, working first in England. Others were stationed in Stockholm, Athens, Bucharest, Budapest. Asia, too, was receiving attention. CBS sent Cecil Brown to the Far East. The Chinese, like the Russians, were retreating into the interior; since 1939 Chungking, a mountain stronghold, had been their capital. Scrambling into caves at the air-raid siren, its population was under constant Japanese attack. Meanwhile Japanese troop movements were seen in many parts of eastern Asia.

The worldwide news system developed by CBS was watched over day by day by Paul White. He had a staff of fifty. The full-time men in major capitals were supported in other places by "stringers," available in emergency. From his desk, White could contact his farflung correspondents by pressing buttons. A short-wave listening staff kept him informed about broadcasts of other countries. UP and INS news came spilling in from tickers.

White listened avidly to the broadcasts of his correspondents and was quick to cable comments and criticisms. After a broadcast he cabled Eric Sevareid that he had gotten "furtherest limbward," which meant—in cablese—as far out on a limb as any CBS correspondent should go. Such admonitions were frequent. There must be no foisting of opinions on others. Tone was as important as content. Even while uttering words that involved the death of thousands, or tens of thousands, or hundreds of thousands, the CBS newsman must not—so Sevareid learned—"display a tenth of the emotion that a broadcaster does when describing a prize-fight." [1]

Considering the attention centered on Murrow during the battle of Britain, it is not surprising that his manner—harmonizing well with CBS instructions—became the basis of a CBS style. With variations in vocal texture, other correspondents tended to echo his deliberate, measured delivery. The style had quiet dignity. It avoided stuffiness and also the condescension of folksiness. It permitted pungent phrases but always mildly spoken. It abhorred the ornate, the strenuous, the frenzied. It favored short, concise statements.

During the half decade that the CBS news organization was developed, spreading its influence throughout the industry, radio news style—both in bulletins and analyses—underwent a transformation. Paul White later traced the changes in his book *News on the Air*. At first radio news echoed written journalism. An opening sentence usually gulped down the full story, in curiously inverted sequence. The style hung on in wire-service bulletins used on many stations:

> AT A BRITISH PORT—Bringing a welcome cargo of more than 4,000,000 eggs, 120,000 pounds of cheese, and 1000 tons of flour, the first food ship to ferry across the Atlantic under the terms of the lease-lend act has arrived here.

Radio had learned to handle it thus:

> The first lease-lend food ship from America has reached a British port. The ship carried four million eggs, 120 thousand pounds of cheese, and 1000 tons of flour. [2]

The CBS team became a genuine all-star line-up. Any one of them could, at the moment of challenge, perform brilliantly. There was jealousy, but also admiration and camaraderie. Lesueur in a slip of the tongue from Moscow described an incident as creating a "teapest tempot." Murrow promptly cabled Paul White: "Please purchase suitably inscribed, old-fashioned enameled single-handled teapest tempot and present to Lesueur." [3]

1. Sevareid, *Not So Wild a Dream*, pp. 111, 132.
2. White, *News on the Air*, pp. 8–9.
3. *Current Biography*, (1943), pp. 441–3.

If the calm style of CBS newsmen was meant to avoid the *appearance* of trying to shape opinion, it succeeded. If, however, CBS intended that opinion should not be shaped, it surely failed. Murrow influenced many, and consciously or unconsciously must have wished to. It was not merely to transmit data that he haunted rooftops. So it was with Shirer, Sevareid, Lesueur, and others. The absence of argumentation was one of the keys to their success: argumentation produces its antidotes. Argumentation ("foisting") could also bring prompt rebuke and action from White. Murrow and his colleagues offered something akin to drama: vicarious experience of what they were living and observing. It put the listener in another man's shoes. No better way to influence opinion has ever been found. Archibald MacLeish, in words addressed to Murrow, put it this way:

> You burned the city of London in our houses and we felt the flames that burned it. You laid the dead of London at our doors and we knew the dead were our dead—were all men's dead—were mankind's dead—and ours. . . .[4]

The CBS news organization, poised for world action, was perhaps the most splendid product of the renascence that had begun at CBS in the mid-1930's. But the surge carried in other directions also. Throughout 1941 the drive for national preparedness quickened. President Roosevelt invited Archibald MacLeish, who was already serving as librarian of Congress, to head a governmental Office of Facts and Figures. MacLeish asked CBS vice president William B. Lewis to head its radio activities. From Washington William B. Lewis phoned Norman Corwin and enlisted him for its first radio project. MacLeish wanted to foster a strong sense of the American heritage. December would mark the 150th anniversary of the adoption of the Bill of Rights. MacLeish, with the President's enthusiastic backing, wanted to make this an occasion of large meaning. Corwin was asked to write and direct a one-hour broadcast.

Work began. There would be major stars—Orson Welles, Lionel Barrymore, and others. On December 7 Corwin was on the transcontinental train *The Chief* somewhere between Chicago and Kansas City, headed for Hollywood. He asked the porter if it was possible to rent a radio. The porter looked at him as if he were insane. "Haven't you heard the news?" "What news?" "The Japs have attacked Pearl Harbor." Radios, it seemed, were in demand. Corwin assumed his broadcast would be canceled and tried to phone Lewis from Kansas City, but all Washington lines were

4. Quoted, Friendly, *Due to Circumstances Beyond Our Control*, p. xvi.

busy. From Hollywood he finally succeeded. "Certainly we're going on," said Lewis. "It's more important now than ever. That's the way the President feels about it." [5]

The program would be on all four networks simultaneously on December 15. President Roosevelt would conclude the program. The circumstances made it possible to assemble an extraordinary cast.[6] The dramatic portions would come from Hollywood under the direction of Corwin. In New York the Philharmonic, conducted by Leopold Stokowski, would play the national anthem.

On December 7 Edward Murrow, who was in the United States for a short rest, was to have dinner at the White House along with his wife Janet. Assuming the dinner was canceled, he put in a call. Of course it wasn't canceled, Mrs. Roosevelt told him. They would all have to eat anyway. Edward and Janet Murrow ate with Mrs. Roosevelt; the President would see Murrow later. At midnight he and the President had a long talk. Murrow told a few things about London; then the President gave Murrow details about the catastrophic damage in Hawaii. Was it off-the-record information? Was the President giving him informaton for a scoop? The President did not say. Murrow used nothing of what he had learned.[7]

At stations throughout the country, there were moments on that day that people would never forget, and by which they would measure segments of their lives. At WMSD, Muscle Shoals, Alabama, student John L. Slaton was serving as part-time announcer.

> Being a part-time announcer . . . I happened to catch this Sunday trick. I was in the newsroom at the time, tearing off UP copy to prepare a newscast when the bell on the teletype began jangling; and subconsciously, of course, you always just count the number of rings of the bell to see if it's a bulletin or a flash or whatnot, and the darn thing just kept ringing. I thought the machine was out of order. So I went to look at it.[8]

The station did not sign off at the usual time that day but stayed on the air around the clock. Thousands of broadcasters had such a day.

Seventy-nine per cent of all homes in the United States tuned in as Roosevelt went before Congress on December 8, spoke of a day that

5. Corwin, *Interview*, pp. 22–4.
6. Edward Arnold, Lionel Barrymore, Walter Brennan, Bob Burns, Walter Huston, Marjorie Main, Edward G. Robinson, James Stewart, Rudy Vallee, Orson Welles.
7. Woolley, *A Rhetorical Study: The Radio Speaking of Edward R. Murrow*, p. 61.
8. Slaton, *Interview*, p. 4.

would "live in infamy," and asked for a declaration of war. There was one dissenting vote. On December 11, to the surprise of many, Germany and Italy declared war on the United States. Congress in joint session declared that a state of war existed between the United States and the Axis partners. There was no dissent. The United States was entering the war with a startling sense of unanimity. On December 15 *We Hold These Truths* was broadcast over CBS, NBC-red, NBC-blue, and MBS to the largest audience ever to hear a dramatic performance. According to Crossley estimates, more than sixty million Americans heard it. It became an appeal for unity—on the basis of principles the nation stood for. Historic vignettes threw light on old struggles and the liberties at stake in them; but in its first moments the drama plunged the listener into Washington of 1941. Backed by Bernard Herrman music that interlaced the words with the energy of a city in motion, a "citizen"—played by young Corporal James Stewart—said:

CITIZEN: Have you ever been to Washington, your capital? Have you been there lately? Well, let me tell you, it's a place of buildings and of boom and bustle, of the fever of emergency, of workers working overtime, of windows lighted late into the night. It's a handsome city, proud of its sturdy name, proud of the men who've stopped there and made decisions; proud of its domes and lawns and monuments.
(*Music: level drops*)
(*Traffic background is sneaked in*)
CITIZEN: Of course, too, Washington is like other cities you have seen—has street cars, haberdasheries, newsstands, coffee shops, and slums. At busy intersections there are neon traffic signs which, when the light's against you, say:
SIGN: (*very flatly*): Don't walk.
CITIZEN: And when the light changes:
SIGN: Walk.
CITIZEN: It's a tourist city. . . .
The tourist goes to see the Capitol, the White House, the museums; sees all about him statues and inscriptions—more sayings than he's ever seen before—wise sayings, profound sayings. At Union Station, for example—
DEPOT: A man must carry knowledge with him if he would bring home knowledge.—Samuel Johnson.
(*Music: filigree after each of these. We do not stop for them.*)
CITIZEN: The Archives Building—
ARCHIVES: What is past is prologue.
CITIZEN: The Supreme Court—
COURT: Justice, the Guardian of Liberty.

CITIZEN: But one of the best is in the Library of Congress—
LIBRARY: The noblest motive is the public good.—Virgil.
    (*Music: a respectful chord*)
CITIZEN: The tourist thinks that over. . . .
TOURIST: The noblest motive is the public good.
CITIZEN: . . . and with this in mind he climbs the marble stairs inside the
    library—to come at length upon a case containing a handwritten docu-
    ment.
TOURIST (*reading slowly*):   The engrossed original of the Constitution of the
    United States of America.
CITIZEN: He sees the manuscript is aging, that its words are worn as though
    from use. The writing's dim; it's hard to make out . . . it's getting on in
    years. . . .

Thus, with a zestful overture, Corwin fused past and present. At the end
of the program Corporal James Stewart introduced President Roosevelt.[9]

With this program—magnificently produced and directed—Corwin became a sort of unofficial laureate. His first assignment had been to dedi-
cate a war. Other assignments followed.

During a half-decade of steady growth and adventure, radio had developed as a medium of expression. Its canvas had broadened and its palette
grown richer. Expanding audiences looked to it with expectation. Its personnel was maturing. The growth would continue; some of the most remarkable achievements of radio—and virtually all of television—lay
ahead. But for the moment war was the framework for action.

It pushed broadcasters toward new worlds, bringing new problems—
and old ones in new disguises.

9. The script was published in pamphlet form and also appears in Corwin, *More by
Corwin;* and Weiser (ed.), *The Writer's Radio Theater 1941.*

3 / CRUSADE

Faces along the bar
Cling to their average day:
The lights must never go out,
The music must always play. . . .
W. H. AUDEN

A fever was in the air. Trains were crowded, phone lines jammed. Wrangling had been replaced by consensus—at least, on needs of the moment. Energies were released by this, and a sense of purpose prevailed. There were appointments, committee meetings, mass meetings, parades.

One of the most-played songs was "God Bless America." There was irony in this. Irving Berlin had written it in 1918 but decided it was too "sticky" and put it away. Twenty years later he got it out of a drawer and let Kate Smith use it on the air. By 1941–42 it was everywhere and was not considered too sticky.[1]

A mass migration into radio war assignments had begun before Pearl Harbor and now became a stampede. Dedication merged with other feelings, conscious or unconscious. For some, the prospect of release from frustrating assignments played a part. Some felt their professional futures demanded a move to the new center of action. Motives intertwined. In broadcasting as in other fields, a worldwide scrambling resulted.

The departure of a high executive from his haunts was likely to stir speculation. The company president had recommended him, it was said, for a key government position. Was the president sacrificing a top man to the war effort? Or was the man expected to be a friend in high places? Or was the president seizing a chance to ease him out—as too liberal? Or too incompetent? The migration swelled.

A number of government radio activities swung into action simultane-

1. Letter from Irving Berlin in *Fact*, January-February 1965.

ously. One concerned censorship. On December 16 an Office of Censorship was created with Byron Price of the Associated Press as director. He appointed John Harold Ryan assistant director in charge of radio. Ryan had been general manager of a group of stations owned by his brother-in-law, George B. Storer.[2]

By January 15, 1942, the Office of Censorship was ready to announce its plans. Censorship was to be *voluntary*. Radio scripts could be submitted for review if broadcasters wished, but it was not required.

Along with the voluntary submission plan, the office announced directives and suggestions. Weather news was to be abolished. (Be careful about announcing cancellation of sports events.) Also banned was news about troop, ship, or plane movements, war production, fortifications, casualties. Abolition of man-on-the-street interviews and other ad-lib programs was urged.

The voluntary system was an experiment and a surprise. Many broadcasting leaders had assumed that New Deal "bureaucrats" would at the first opportunity take over the industry under the emergency powers of the Communications Act. A number of military leaders favored such a course, but the administration did not. While amateur stations were at once silenced, as in World War I, domestic commercial broadcasting continued with minimum disruption. It was an experiment—it could, of course, be abandoned if it proved unfeasible.

Quizzes, games, request programs, amateur hours tended to disappear. Programs like *America's Town Meeting of the Air* changed their procedure: questions from the floor were no longer asked ad lib but were passed in writing to the moderator, who reworded them as he read them.

Few programs submitted scripts to the Office of Censorship for review. Those that did included *The March of Time* and its imitators, such as *We The People;* also the Drew Pearson and Walter Winchell programs. These submitted their script precisely because they aimed at sensational news. Pearson at one time learned that the government was giving five or six destroyers to the Soviet Union—a fact classified as secret at the time. He wanted to break the news on his Sunday night broadcast. The Office of Censorship urged him not to—the destroyers were en route and might be attacked. They argued by phone until seconds before broadcast; then

2. See *A Tower in Babel*, p. 270. Ryan later became president of the National Association of Broadcasters.

Pearson hung up. The censors listened to his broadcast with bated breath. He did not use the item.[3]

On another occasion MBS broadcaster Arthur Hale on his *Confidentially Yours* series referred to Pasco, Washington, as the site of atomic research. Most people, including Hale, were unaware that atomic research had military implications, but presumably enemy agents knew it. Military leaders were furious about the incident and demanded abolition of the voluntary system. They wanted a military censor posted at every station. This incident presented the voluntary review plan with its most serious crisis, but the plan survived.[4]

The foreign-language stations, which in 1942 numbered more than a hundred, presented thorny problems. Some stations—WHOM, Jersey City, for example—carried broadcasts in as many as ten languages, and sold time through numerous "time brokers." [5] No official at the station could understand half the programs it was broadcasting. The complexity of this problem was illustrated by the case of an Italian announcer at a foreign-language station who was said to echo Axis propaganda even while dutifully urging the purchase of United States war bonds. According to *Variety*, he promoted the bonds by urging the soundness of the investment: "These bonds are backed by the greatest 'have' nation in the world which has 85 per cent of the world's gold opposed to the have-not nations." Democracy at some of these studios, *Variety* concluded, was paved with "slippery bananas." [6]

That the government's voluntary censorship plan survived in spite of such problems was in many ways remarkable, and a reflection of an exceptional wartime consensus.

Another government activity involved short-wave monitoring. Early in 1941 the FCC set up a division to listen to and analyze foreign short-wave broadcasts. After Pearl Harbor it acquired special importance and was named Foreign Broadcast Intelligence Service.[7]

---

3. Fetzer, *Reminiscences*, p. 86. Fetzer, an assistant to Ryan, later succeeded him as chief radio censor.
4. *Ibid.* pp. 87–9.
5. WHOM broadcast in German, Greek, Italian, Lithuanian, Norwegian, Polish, Russian, Spanish, Yiddish, and occasionally English. *Variety*, June 8, 1942.
6. *Variety*, May 27, 1942.
7. For a few months after its formation it was called Foreign Broadcast Monitoring Service.

At four listening centers[8] it recorded short-wave broadcasts on plastic disks, which were kept for archive purposes. Selected material was transcribed and translated. War agencies received weekly reports, as well as special reports with such titles as *Radio Tokyo's Racial Propaganda to the United States, Underground Movements and Morale in Japan, Berlin's Claims of United Nations Shipping Losses, New Nazi Portrait of the American Soldier,* and *Reactions to the First Bombing of Japan.*

Stations monitored included official stations of many countries and also "black" stations—those which were not what they purported to be. A station calling itself "The Station of All True Americans" was heard in the United States at 8:30 each evening, pretending to come from the Midwest. Its main speaker, "Joe Scanlon," had a Midwestern accent. The station always began with "Stars and Stripes Forever" and signed off with "The Star-Spangled Banner." It specialized in attacks on President Roosevelt, items designed to stir race tensions, and items to shock. A home-bound transport was said to have landed at Hoboken with a load of nurses pregnant by army officers. Information was offered on officer attendance at foreign brothels. The station built up an impression of genuineness by referring to alleged difficulties with the FCC over its "disclosures." Then, on June 10, 1942, it announced triumphantly: "Before we continue the program tonight, we would like to inform you that the Federal Communications Commission has renewed our license and given us a new wave length, commencing June 15." Presumably freedom of speech had been vindicated. Many people believed the station to be located in Maine, but FCC long-range direction finders finally placed it in Germany. It remained on the air until 1944.[9]

All major warring nations were apparently involved in "black" broadcasting. The Foreign Broadcast Intelligence Service kept track of sixty such stations. They included a German-language station pretending to represent an anti-Nazi army group in Germany and spreading damaging rumors about storm troopers; an anti-Nazi "Catholic" station; and an English-language station attacking Churchill and purporting to represent Britons favoring friendship with Hitler.

8. Portland, Oregon; Kingsville, Texas; Guilford, Maryland; Santurce, Puerto Rico. Later, listening was also done in London.
9. On the other hand, stations operating illegally without a license were from time to time tracked down within the United States. They included a prewar station that regularly signed off with "Heil Hitler!" and was found in Peoria, Illinois. *Broadcasting,* May 5, 1941.

The first director of the Foreign Broadcast Intelligence Service was Lloyd Free of Princeton University; he was succeeded during 1942 by Robert D. Leigh, who had been president of Bennington College. Harold Graves of Princeton was assistant director. Goodwin Watson of Teachers College, Columbia University, joined before Pearl Harbor to supervise the work of analysis. Also recruited for this work were Bernard Berelson, Saul K. Padover, Otto Klineberg, John W. Gardner, David B. Truman, Frederick L. Schuman, and other scholars. It provided essential information to war agencies and to our allies and was highly valued.[10]

Another government activity concerned broadcasts to other nations. In June 1942 an Office of War Information was established under Elmer Davis. He appointed playwright Robert Sherwood to head the OWI international branch, which in the fall took over programming on a number of existing short-wave stations and rushed plans for twenty-two additional stations. Joseph Barnes, formerly of the New York *Herald-Tribune,* took charge of programming; he was joined by Edward W. Barrett and John Houseman.

While their task was to address people of other countries,[11] they became temporarily enmeshed in another problem. Americans in uniform were already in action at many distant bases, and short-wave broadcasts from the United States seized their interest. Letters from distant servicemen began reaching American short-wave stations early in 1942, before the OWI was formed. Requests for "jive" music came from General Chennault's Flying Tigers, stationed in Kunming, China. Soon afterward requests came from troops under siege in Bataan; then from troops training in New Caledonia. Such pressures resulted in the series *Command Performance,* which was conceived in the War Department in the spring of 1942 and which eleven short-wave stations agreed to carry. It placed the faraway soldier or sailor in the position of royalty, able to summon any entertainer he wished. Its title alone seemed to ensure success. No artist said "no" to this "command performance." The series at once drew mail from service men and women in such scattered places as Iceland, Hawaii, and Brazil.

The OWI international division, taking over the short-wave stations to perform a propaganda function, inherited *Command Performance* and an

10. Graves, *Statement of Harold N. Graves, Jr.,* pp. 26–8; Leigh, *Statement of Robert D. Leigh,* pp. 8–10; *New Nazi Portrait of the American Soldier,* p. 7.
11. Except South America, which was under the jurisdiction of the Co-ordinator of Inter-American Affairs.

involvement with farflung serviceman audiences. But the needs of the armed forces were not really its proper concern, and it soon found it could not satisfy them.

At some bases men were not waiting for attention from the United States. At Kodiak, Alaska, servicemen put together a low-powered station from junked Signal Corps equipment and began to address the base with available troop talent, phonograph records, and news plucked from short-wave broadcasts. Early in 1942 they began writing to Hollywood stars asking for recordings of their broadcasts in the United States. The stars ran into wartime mailing restrictions and began phoning the War Department in Washington for permission to send recordings "to that army radio station in Alaska." In this way the War Department received its first inkling that it had a station in Alaska. The FCC, likewise unaware of it, wondered briefly whether it was a "black" enemy station masquerading as an army station. At Nome, Alaska, another low-powered station meanwhile took shape—built on the same principle as campus stations. It too began clamoring for material.

This spontaneous activity generated the idea of a large network of troop-serving stations. A factor that pushed the plan forward was an army report that men in New Guinea were regularly tuning in to Tokyo Rose, who offered the best swing music available along with intriguing low-voiced sex talk and skillful propaganda. In Europe an Axis Sally was playing a similar game. In mid-1942 Thomas H. A. Lewis, vice president of the Young & Rubicam advertising agency in charge of its Hollywood office and supervisor of *Screen Guild Theater* and other series, was asked to organize a network of troop stations as a War Department project. Thus the Armed Forces Radio Service was conceived. The mapping of a fantastic worldwide radio system began. It took over *Command Performance*.

With the job of broadcasting to troops detached from that of broadcasting to the people of other lands, the OWI international division concentrated on its original assignment. But a mutual involvement continued. Obviously other nations—including enemy nations—would eavesdrop on anything broadcast to or by troops. This invited the thought that items planted in Armed Forces Radio Service broadcasts could usefully confuse an enemy. OWI-AFRS liaison continued for this purpose.[12]

Another government activity concerned information broadcasts to the

12. Kirby and Harris, *Star-Spangled Radio*, pp. 42–5; De Lay, *An Historical Study of the Armed Forces Radio Service*, pp. 40–110.

American public. Many agencies became involved in this, including the War Department. Edward Kirby, public relations director of the National Association of Broadcasters, transferred to the public relations division of the War Department in 1941. He was an effective catalyst, with a talent for rapid-fire action. It was his demand for a troop-morale idea that generated *Command Performance*, and he set it in motion. In the early stages of the war, before jurisdictions were laid out, Kirby's office branched in many directions.

Among those who joined his staff was Louis G. Cowan. As a student at the University of Chicago, Cowan had fallen under the spell of Professor Harold Lasswell and acquired a feverish philosophic interest in all problems relating to communication. After college he found little chance to put his enthusiasms to work. He did publicity for *Kay Kyser's College of Musical Knowledge*. Then, turning to independent production, he conceived and launched *The Quiz Kids*, which was a quick financial success. For Cowan, who had money, this was gratifying but not precisely what he yearned for. When war came, he happily delegated *The Quiz Kids* to others, took an apartment in Washington, and offered himself as a dollar-a-year man to Kirby. Kirby soon found diverse tasks for him.[13]

One assignment found him on a strange errand to New York City for a lunch meeting with Mr. and Mrs. Frank Hummert of the daytime serials. This curious mission also involved Truman Gibson, a Negro lawyer. The lunch was arranged in a private dining room of the Gotham hotel to avoid incidents with headwaiters. The subject was the Negro soldier.

The American army was fully segregated. Awareness of this was instantly thrust on draftees. There came a moment on troop trains headed south—most training camps were there—when a sergeant appeared at the end of the car. "Colored to the rear!" Many northerners lived in cities that were segregated in fact if not by law; but now they saw the system buttressed and glorified with the full force of federal, state, army, and navy authority. Amid talk of fighting for democracy, the experience cut deeply. To many Negroes the war brought sharp unrest. There was high-level agitation for change, but it moved slowly. Throughout army and navy—at all levels, in all parts of the country—there were those who favored the status quo, and were determined to bolster it at every opportunity. It served their purposes that the Negro should be called a coward. Tales to

13. Cowan, *Reminiscences*, pp. 9–68. He later became president, CBS Television Network.

this effect were fed into the air in a steady stream by "the Station of All True Americans" as well as by Axis Sally. How combat such stories?

The fear of Negro advancement, Louis Cowan felt, was strong in lower middle-class American groups uncertain of their own status. The serials reached such groups. Could the Hummerts help?

The lily-white Hummert world of troubled heroines scarcely seemed ideal for such a purpose, but the Hummerts—who were clearly disturbed by the problem presented to them—wanted to try. In several serials they began to introduce threads of plot and message.

In the summer of 1942 the character of Franklin Brown, a young Negro in military training, was introduced into *Our Gal Sunday*. He appeared intermittently during furloughs—and mainly as a subject for conservation between Sunday and Henry, the titled Englishman, about the loyalty of the Negro to his country. More elaborate was the effort made in *The Romance of Helen Trent*. Its heroine, while preventing a truck loaded with war goods from falling into an abyss, fell into the abyss herself and was rescued by a Negro doctor, for whom she later found a job as staff physician in a war factory. The plot went on for weeks with intermittent discussion concerning "the capabilities of the Negro, his unflagging loyalty to his country, and his patience with persecution." [14]

These efforts were never publicized and were apparently not mentioned in any trade paper. Their value is of course impossible to assess. Later the Hummerts, at War Department suggestion, provided similar droplets for Anglo-American relations, which were marred by explosions of mutual rancor. Also at War Department suggestion, the Hummerts launched *Chaplain Jim*—first as a daily serial, later as a Sunday series—to show mothers that army life was not all tough sergeants; there was one person ready to help solve problems. Chaplain Jim was a David Harum/Ma Perkins in uniform. Again it was Cowan who conveyed the War Department idea to the Hummerts. He also took it to Edgar Kobak at NBC-blue, which promptly agreed to underwrite the series.[15]

A more important and more spectacular War Department achievement under Kirby was *The Army Hour*. In a Sunday one-hour period made available by NBC-red—starting April 5, 1942—the army began to do pickups—each a soldier's eye-witness account of overseas activity—from London, Chungking, Moscow, Cairo, Pearl Harbor. The audience heard

14. *An Analysis of Negro Talent on the Columbia Broadcasting System*, p. 10.
15. Cowan, *Reminiscences*, pp. 58–60.

Brigadier-General James Doolittle describe an early bombing of Tokyo, and Brigadier-General Claire Chennault describe action of the Flying Tigers in China. "*The Army Hour*," said Secretary of War Henry Stimson, is "not a radio program but a military operation of the United States, heard and felt over the world." Its director was Wyllis Cooper, who had taught Oboler how to write *Lights Out*. NBC-red supported it with a budget of $500,000 per year.[16]

Government broadcasts to the American public were at first a chaos of diffused jurisdictions. Virtually every agency connected with the war took up program production. Among these, the radio unit organized under William B. Lewis was the most notable. It produced a four-network series titled *This Is War* with scripts by Maxwell Anderson, Stephen Vincent Benét, Philip Wylie, Norman Corwin, and others. Its purpose was "to inspire, to frighten, to inform." *Variety* praised it for "tough-talking, spade-calling, spine-walloping propaganda of pugnacity." The tone was set early:

NARRATOR: Soft music can have the evening off. No one is invited to sit down and take it easy. Later, later. There's a war on![17]

Some of it dealt with "the enemy" and was so well received that it generated "know your enemy" broadcasts throughout the country. These stirred a debate on just how much "hate" propaganda—if any—was needed. As in England, hate was apparently becoming "acceptable."[18]

In July 1942 the Lewis unit became the radio bureau of the OWI domestic branch and the main government voice at home. It suggested, and helped to set in motion, a CBS dramatic series produced by Edward R. Murrow and written and directed by Norman Corwin. It was produced from England with BBC co-operation and entitled *An American in England*.

Because recorded programs were still taboo on CBS, the original broadcasts were done live at 4 A.M. London time for simultaneous rebroadcast

16. *Broadcasting*, July 13, 1942; Cowan, *Reminiscences*, pp. 54–5; *RCA Annual Report* (1942)), p. 21.
17. *This Is War*, p. 5; *Variety*, February 18, 1942.
18. See Dryer, *Radio in Wartime*. Dryer quotes with disapproval the CBS series *The Nature of the Enemy*. In discussing General Yamamoto, the program used phrases like "his own bloody deed" . . . "a kind of slippery beast" . . . "this man's stench is not a pretty one" . . . "wrinkled and beady eyes" . . . "he is no bandy-toothed raper of women. . . ." *Ibid.* p. 126.

in the United States.[19] The entire company went by bus and taxi from downtown London through the blackout to Maida Vale. A special score by Benjamin Britten was played by a 62-piece Royal Air Force orchestra—London Philharmonic musicians in uniform.

Short-wave pickups were new in drama. To Davidson Taylor at CBS in New York, Corwin played advance tests of sound effects via short-wave telephone. They tried a door slamming. "No good," Taylor reported. "Sounds like a bomb going off." Other effects were tried, with quick evaluations by Taylor. "Good . . . bad . . . impossible . . . fair . . . mushy. . . ." Two-thirds of them were ruled out and scripts revised accordingly. The first program, because of atmospheric conditions, had to be repeated entirely. But a notable series followed.

The eight programs were a dramatized first-person account, with actor Joseph Julian in the leading role, of an American and his experiences in England. In spite of the scale of the production, it was plain-spoken.

JOE: I set out by train from Cromer one sunny September morning, leaving from a station in the East End of London. The things you notice on a train ride . . .
(*Fade in coach wheels*)
. . . in a front-line country are no different from what you notice on a train ride anywhere: small talk overheard, the beard on the man sitting opposite, the pattern of the hole punched in your ticket by the conductor . . .

CONDUCTOR: Change at Cambridge for Cromer.

JOE: Yes, I know, thank you. (*Resuming confidential manner*) The little differences in railway manners, such as etchings on the walls of the compartments, and the fact that when the steward comes through to announce lunch he doesn't yell "First call for lunch!" but says:

STEWARD: Those requiring lunch will please go forward to the dining coach.

JOE (*down*): A lot of unimportant things stick in your mind. In the smoker, for example, I overheard two officers—a Canadian and an Englishman—talking very earnestly. Do you suppose they were discussing the war? Or the commonwealth of nations? Or sports? Women? Horses? Books? Not at all. They were saying:

BRITON: What does Coca-Cola taste like? Cocoa?

CANADIAN: Well, no—it's sort of hard to describe.

BRITON: Does it taste like ginger?

CANADIAN: It's more like molasses. No, that's not right either.

19. Recordings were used for subsequent broadcasts over the BBC and stations in Australia, Canada, and Egypt.

The programs used actual names of people and places. The style suggested a fusing: the drama of Corwin, the journalism of Murrow. They were, in fact, closely related forms of expression.[20]

The OWI was meanwhile tangled in a wilderness of problems. Since Pearl Harbor every government agency had bombarded sponsors, advertising agencies, directors, and performers with requests for the insertion of announcements in popular network series. Each such announcement was represented as crucial to the war effort. Americans *must* be persuaded to save cans, buy war bonds (they were no longer "defense" bonds), learn nursing, black out windows, eat properly, avoid rumors, become air raid wardens, write letters to soldiers, curb travel. The advertising agencies requested that the government determine priorities in some organized way. OWI acquired this function. The agencies themselves set up a War Advertising Council to allocate messages to appropriate media, including sponsored series. Before long the message-distribution system was in operation.

Whatever its importance may have been to the war effort, the plan proved of momentous importance to the advertising and radio industries. It was crucial in helping them defend their wartime prosperity.

Many factors were contributing to that prosperity. The closing of foreign markets caused many advertisers to concentrate on home markets, and much of this revenue was going into radio. Newspapers and magazines could not absorb the additional business because of paper shortages; in one day in 1942, the New York *Times* is said to have rejected some fifty pages of advertising. Radio, drawing spectacular audiences, was attracting some of this advertising.

Another factor was the high excess-profits tax. To prevent war profits of the sort made in previous wars, Congress had enacted tax rates up to 90 per cent. This created a temptation for large corporations to spend on advertising what would otherwise go into taxes. A prevalent doctrine heightened this urge. Advertising agencies kept telling their clients that Piedmont cigarettes and Force cereal and other products had gone to their doom after World War I because of a failure to advertise throughout the war. Even companies that temporarily had nothing to sell to the public, it was argued, should keep their names in the public consciousness. The avalanche of advertising that came to radio from 1941 on represented many

20. "Cromer" in Corwin, *More By Corwin*, pp. 30–31.

advertisers with nothing to sell. Their message was "institutional." For radio all this was wonderful. It brought rich revenue with almost no commercials. Moreover, sponsors were now delighted with prestige programs of less than maximum audience. General Motors, with no cars to sell, decided to sponsor the NBC Symphony Orchestra under Arturo Toscanini. This was by now recognized as one of the world's great orchestras; such fame could not guarantee it a sponsor in a competitive peacetime period, but it became a marketable asset in the war situation. Similarly United States Rubber, with almost no tires to sell to the public, became interested in the New York Philharmonic. Allis Chalmers, in a similar plight, adopted the Boston Symphony Orchestra. This trend had started before Pearl Harbor and continued throughout the war, creating dizzying vistas. "Stated bluntly," said *Broadcasting* early in 1942, "business is wonderful. Now if it will only keep that way for twelve months, 1942 will smash all the business records established in 1941." [21]

But there were clouds. Economists pointed out that taxpayers were really shouldering the cost of this boom. The swollen advertising budgets, deducted in tax returns as a necessary business expense, were being absorbed in the price paid by the government for war matériel. Was it in any sense a necessary business expense? The government was curious. During 1941 Assistant Attorney-General Thurman Arnold wrote to oil companies asking why, in a rationed and war-limited market, they were spending so much on advertising.[22] Some critics went so far as to call it "waste." The air was full of pleas for conservation, but precious electronic facilities, huge funds, highly paid personnel were being poured into advertising campaigns that sold nothing and probably had an inflationary effect. Many government leaders wanted to stop it. Senator Harry S. Truman, chairman of the Senate committee to investigate the national defense program, suggested that if war contractors wanted to do all this advertising they should at least pay for it from their own pockets, and not hand the cost to the government as a necessary expense.[23]

During the early months of 1942 the issue created turmoil behind Washington doors. Many of the largest corporations felt a stake in it. For radio it was a crisis hour. If the advertising should be disallowed as a tax expense, the radio boom would be a punctured balloon.

21. *Broadcasting*, January 5, 1942.
22. The Atlantic Refining Company, for example, was sponsoring football games over 83 stations. *Broadcasting*, August 18, September 8, 1941.
23. Quoted, Rorty, "Advertising Rides the War," *Common Sense*, December 1943.

While some government groups were pressing their argument against war advertising, others were playing into the hands of the advertisers. The government units besieging sponsored radio for help with war announcements were providing it with a potent argument. Advertising began to call itself "the information industry" and to dramatize its role in the relaying of war messages. The War Advertising Council could cite the pleas of government agencies and the subsequent letters of praise and gratitude. The war, it seemed, could hardly be won without advertising. By mid-1942 the lobbying battle was over. After a conference with U. S. Treasury officials, advertising leaders announced triumphantly that agreement had been reached. Advertising, including institutional advertising, would be deductible if "reasonable." Attempts to define "reasonable" got nowhere; they generally ended by relying on the word "reasonable." But the effort was soon forgotten. Advertising, it appeared, *was* deductible—even for companies whose only customer was the United States.[24]

The result was this: although advertising had dropped during World War I, it increased steadily in World War II—especially in radio.

Meanwhile the war messages routed via the War Advertising Council were heard on countless programs, and the "information industry" proclaimed its services in brochure after brochure. Some were triumphs of tastelessness. "THIS IS AN ARMY HITLER FORGOT!" was the banner title of a promotion piece from the National Association of Broadcasters. It proclaimed:

$100,000,000 worth of talent and time pooled and contributed by—

—4 major networks
—919 U. S. radio stations
—U. S. advertisers and advertising agencies

This was followed by a picture of the "army"—fifty stars of the entertainment world—and statistics to the effect that they had contributed "9,000,000 listener impressions per week" which had "helped to persuade" 23,972 women to study nursing and "helped to increase" victory gardens by 8,000,000.[25]

The victory of the advertisers made the radio boom secure. Its programs, regular and war-effort, continued in a deluge from the major centers and countless foreign pickup points. The quantity of live program-

24. *Broadcasting*, August 31, 1942.
25. *This Is an Army Hitler Forgot!*, pp. 1–7.

ming was scarcely believable; its quality, impressive; its standing with the public, high. A government survey conducted between January and May of 1942 asked, "Do you have more confidence in the war news on the radio or the war news in the newspapers?" Forty-six per cent said, "Radio." Eighteen per cent said, "Newspapers." [26] Even intellectuals were becoming radio devotees. A Writers War Board organized by the Authors League of America persuaded numerous prominent writers to turn to radio. Stephen Vincent Benét's *They Burned the Books* (1942) and Edna St. Vincent Millay's *The Murder of Lidice* (1943)—both given lavish network productions—were among the results. The board's scripts were offered free for local use and resulted in scores of local productions. They were also made available for government short-wave broadcasts. In 1942 publishers organized a Council on Books in Wartime; one of its first moves was to offer books free to NBC for dramatization, resulting early in 1943 in the series *Words At War*.

It is difficult to realize that the period 1941–43, a time of extraordinary network productivity and co-operation with government, also witnessed one of the bitterest of struggles between networks and government. While Washington emissaries like Louis Cowan felt astonishment at the generosity and promptness of network support for their proposals, this struggle was in progress—a rumbling *obbligato* to the theme of co-operation. In a sense the two themes were incompatible; yet they were related. Network leaders, responding to the war crisis, had one more incentive to make the response spectacular: a crisis in their relations with government.

CHAIN BREAK

The chain broadcasting investigation—or "monopoly" probe, as it was often called—begun by the Federal Communications Commission in 1938, finally ended in 1941, when the FCC's conclusions were issued and circulated. They made reform proposals which were angrily attacked by broadcasters. The FCC then made some amendments and, by a five to two vote, ordered the reforms put into effect the following year.[1]

NBC and CBS were outraged. (MBS approved.) Niles Trammell, succeeding Lenox Lohr as NBC president, said the FCC plan would bring

26. Dryer, *Radio in Wartime*, pp. 142–3.
1. *Report on Chain Broadcasting*. Commissioners T. A. M. Craven and Norman S. Case dissented.

"chaos." William Paley, speaking for CBS, called it a "wrecking operation" that would make broadcasters "impotent vassals" of government. That fall both NBC and CBS filed suit to halt the "sudden death" orders. CBS would fight "all the way," said Edward Klauber. *Broadcasting* echoed the network stand and referred to the FCC's five-man majority as "the five men who voted for the destruction of the existing system of broadcasting." The NAB resolved to fight the FCC to the finish. Free enterprise itself was declared at stake. As the nation mobilized for global war, measures also took shape to negate the FCC moves through congressional and other action. A stormy struggle lay ahead.[2]

During the monopoly study the FCC had acquired a new chairman, James Lawrence Fly. He succeeded Frank R. McNinch, an elderly gentleman who, over-reacting to complaints, periodically created a to-do over specific broadcasts such as the Mae West and Martian invasion programs. He would write letters expressing shock and demanding explanations; then he would solemnly admonish. He projected an image of the FCC as a watch-and-ward society, and one with only nuisance powers.[3]

Fly was determined to avoid such a role. He wanted to be an active chairman, but not through involvement in individual programs. A station once licensed, he felt, must have utmost freedom. The chief duty of the FCC, as he saw it, was to take its licensing functions seriously. It should foster competition—including competition in ideas—through diversity of licensees. In view of the anti-monopoly provisions of the Communications Act,[4] he felt that the FCC must through its licensing policies prevent concentration of ownership and control. He saw such concentration as especially dangerous in an information medium. His views were, of course, in harmony with the anti-trust emphasis of the "second New Deal."

The New Deal came late to the FCC; when it did, in the person of James Lawrence Fly, it came strongly. As general counsel for the Tennes-

2. *Broadcasting*, November 15, 1940; May 12, 19, November 3, 1941.
3. One McNinch incident involved an NBC production of O'Neill's *Beyond the Horizon*. A listener in St. Paul, Minnesota, said he had heard profanity on the local NBC outlet. The Communications Act forbids profanity. The "profanity" was found to have been of network origin. NBC received an FCC demand for an explanation, and referred it to its script chief Lewis H. Titterton. He found that a character in *Beyond the Horizon* had exclaimed, "Oh my God!" Titterton then wrote to Monsignor Cicognani, the apostolic delegate to the United States, enclosing the text and earnestly seeking guidance. Was this truly profanity or perhaps a soul in perplexity calling on the Lord for help? Monsignor Cicognani considered it the latter. His reply permitted the crisis to subside; projected hearings were canceled. Interview, Lewis H. Titterton.
4. Sections 313, 314.

see Valley Authority he had proved a battler. Warding off attacks of private-power groups on the TVA—which they considered socialistic—he had won victories in the U. S. Supreme Court. As a result Wendell Willkie considered him a dangerous man—"to have on the other side." [5] With this background Fly came to the FCC.

President Roosevelt gave him full backing. While concerned with monopoly in a general way, Roosevelt was also troubled about a special radio problem, which he hoped the FCC would tackle. Newspaper publishers had become increasingly active in radio since the mid-1930's. By 1940 more than one-third of all stations were owned or controlled by newspapers. Many of these stations had been acquired by purchase. In ninety-eight localities, the only radio station was owned by the only newspaper. Roosevelt could hardly help seeing this as a threat to New Deal reforms. The press had been overwhelmingly against him in every election, and his victories had been ascribed to the rise of radio as an alternative channel. Unified control of press and broadcasting could well produce a communication monopoly more powerful than any yet known.

Late in 1940 Fly received a one-sentence note from the President:

December 3, 1940

Memorandum for Hon. James L. Fly

Will you let me know when you propose to have a hearing on newspaper ownership of radio stations.

F. D. R.[6]

Fly was eager to tackle this issue. He was also ready to do battle on superpower, another issue that had monopoly implications. But Fly insisted on giving top priority to completion of the long-running chain broadcasting investigation. Under his vigorous direction the *Report on Chain Broadcasting* took shape.[7]

The report and its proposals gave attention to several problems. The first was NBC ownership of two networks. The report proposed *divorcement*. RCA had used NBC-blue, said the report, as buffer to suppress competition against NBC-red. The power of the combined networks, con-

---

5. Quoted, *Saturday Evening Post*, July 22, 1944.
6. Fly, *Papers*.
7. Participants in the work included FCC general counsel Telford Taylor; also Joseph Rauh, Seymour Krieger, Edward Brecher.

trolling an overwhelming majority of high-powered stations, was seen as a deterrent to new radio enterprise, and monopolistic in effect.

Because the FCC licensing power concerned stations—not networks—the divorcement was pushed in a curiously roundabout way. The order said:

> No license shall be issued to a standard broadcast station affiliated with a network organization which maintains more than one network.[8]

To hold affiliates for one of its networks, NBC would have to dispose of the other. NBC attacked this indirect style of regulation as illegal.

Another reform concerned the network *option*. CBS was still using affiliation contracts that gave it the right to take over any period in an affiliate's schedule. This surrender of control by the station was regarded in the report as a violation of the license. The option was also pictured as a discouragement to meaningful local programming and a threat to its very existence. The FCC looked more favorably on a plan developed by NBC. Since 1935 NBC had included in its affiliation contracts an option that covered only specific hours—"network optional time." Other hours remained under station control as "station time." The FCC at first wanted to abolish network options entirely but, by way of compromise, proposed an arrangement like that at NBC. The broadcast day would be divided into four segments. In each segment the option would be limited to three hours.[9]

A third major topic was *artist bureaus*. The report noted that the broadcasters, rising in power, tended to gain control over adjacent fields. They virtually controlled the phonograph field and through it the making of transcriptions. Transcribed programs were potential rivals to network programs; control could inhibit such competition. Broadcasters were also, it was noted, moving toward control of the music-publishing field through BMI.[10]

A more immediately pressing issue was seen in the network-owned artist bureaus. Artists had flocked to these talent-representation units in the

8. *Report on Chain Broadcasting*, p. 92.
9. The segments: 8 A.M. to 1 P.M.; 1 P.M. to 6 P.M.; 6 P.M. to 11 P.M.; 11 P.M. to 8 A.M.
10. In an action paralleling the FCC's chain report, the Justice Department in 1941 signed consent decrees with BMI and ASCAP. BMI, formed to combat the ASCAP control of music copyrights, was seen by some observers as the beginning of an even more powerful concentration, controlled by broadcasters. The Justice Department moved to limit the competitive practices of both BMI and ASCAP.

hope of network employment. Yet the network, being a major employer, was not a fit agent. The report explained why:

> As agent for artists, NBC is under a fiduciary duty to procure the best terms possible for the artists. As employer of artists, NBC is interested in securing the best terms from the artists. NBC's dual role necessarily prevents arm's length bargaining and constitutes a serious conflict of interest. Moreover, this dual capacity gives NBC an unfair advantage over independent artists' representatives who do not themselves control employment opportunities or have direct access to the radio audience. Many of these independent artists' representatives have complained to the Commission. . . .[11]

The FCC proposed to give this problem "continuing attention."

Further reforms were discussed. Network-affiliate relations were to be loosened further in various ways. An affiliate, in spite of the permitted network option on specific hours, was to have the right to reject network programs in favor of other programs whenever this would, in its opinion, serve the public interest. A program not accepted by a regular affiliate was to be available under certain circumstances to another station in the same community—ending rigid "exclusivity" clauses. No licensee was to have two standard broadcasting stations in a community. There was to be a limit—not yet determined—on the number of stations to be assigned throughout the country to any one licensee.

The networks, despite their invective against the *Report on Chain Broadcasting*, took its arguments more seriously than they admitted. They moved with extreme speed to divest themselves of their artist bureaus. The CBS Artist Bureau was sold to Music Corporation of America, originally an agent for musical talent only. The purchase of the CBS Artist Bureau made it overnight the representative of a great diversity of talent including performers, writers, directors, commentators. It would become known as Management Corporation of America, or MCA. The CBS-controlled Columbia Concerts Corporation was sold to a group of its own management headed by Arthur Judson. The NBC Artist Bureau became a new agency, National Concerts and Artists—NCAC. All these moves were completed during 1941.

Meanwhile the networks prepared for all-out battle on other issues. NBC's special concern was the divorcement order; CBS's, its special option clause. Curiously, each network had a history that undermined the

11. *Report on Chain Broadcasting*, p. 17.

arguments of the other. CBS said it could not live without its option clause, but NBC had done so. NBC said amputation of one network would be fatal, but CBS had always lived as a single network.

Perhaps this basic weakness diverted fire to other targets—mainly, to Fly himself. Even the network leaders aimed their attacks repeatedly at him. In this they got help from others. Fly was rapidly becoming a favorite industry bogeyman.

He was a disturbing phenomenon. No other FCC chairman had even faintly resembled him. He put a certain passion into his FCC work. To the NAB he quoted Walt Whitman: "I say there can be no safety for these States—without free tongues, and ears willing to hear the tongues." For Fly this meant that control by "special interests" was dangerous. The "public interest" had meaning for him.[12]

He was ready to back his ideas with relentless energy. He could be persuasive, resourceful, even Machiavellian. He spoke with a slight Texas drawl and wore a quizzical, humorous look, but behind it was seriousness.

His zeal was readily portrayed by his opponents as political venom. His concern over newspaper ownership was pictured as a desire to "get" publishers unfriendly to the New Deal. He was also constantly portrayed as a megalomaniac. Through Fly's genius, said a *Saturday Evening Post* article by Alva Johnson, "one modest phrase in a statute" could give a bureaucrat "more power than Ivan the Terrible or the Great Cham of Tartary." The FCC under Fly, said *Collier's*, was "public enemy number one." [13]

Fly could use language too. In May 1941 the National Association of Broadcasters invited him to a meeting to explain the *Report on Chain Broadcasting*—although the NAB had already decided to combat it through pressure on Congress. At a well-attended session Fly found himself on the platform listening to an attack on himself and his policies. He calmly made notes, assuming he would be allowed to reply. But the chairman suddenly adjourned the meeting. Fly was furious. He was told he could answer at a later session, but found this inadequate. Speaking to the press, he borrowed a phrase from John Randolph of Roanoke; the NAB, said Fly, reminded him of a "dead mackerel in the moonlight—it both shines and stinks." [14]

But Fly scarcely knew what was in store for him. Late in 1941 Repre-

12. *Broadcasting*, August 15, 1940.
13. *Broadcasting*, March 24, 1941; *Saturday Evening Post*, September 28, 1940; *Collier's*, May 25, 1940.
14. *Broadcasting*, May 19, 1941; Landry, *This Fascinating Radio Business*, pp. 225–6.

sentative Martin Dies, chairman of the House committee on un-American activities—created in 1938 during a time of alarm over camps where people were goose-stepping—began to make statements about subversives in government agencies. He said there were more than a thousand and that he was sending a list to the U. S. Attorney-General. The FCC harbored some of them, he said. New attacks came from other quarters. Early in 1942 Representative Eugene E. Cox, a member of the powerful House rules committee, began a barrage of invective against Fly—"the most dangerous man in Washington," who was turning the FCC into "a Gestapo, the equal of which has never been seen under a free government." Cox asked the House to appoint a special committee, with himself as chairman, to investigate the FCC. Meanwhile the House committee on interstate and foreign commerce began hearings on a bill to scuttle the chain reforms. Between April and June Fly made eight separate appearances—perhaps an endurance record—to denounce the bill.[15]

In the months that followed Fly was harassed as few public servants have been. He was trying to serve as FCC chairman, implement the chain rules, and do a new job as chairman of a top-level Defense Communications Board, while all the time Dies, Cox, interstate commerce and other committee hearings battered away at him. Fly stood his ground. His endurance was unbelievable; the persistence of his attackers, more so. The most extraordinary was Eugene Cox.

COALITION

Representative Eugene Cox of Georgia, who in 1942 injected himself into the broadcasting spotlight, was one of the most powerful men in Washington. That fall he became more powerful. The wartime congressional elections of that year brought a conservative tide that ousted liberal Northern Democrats, while anti-New Deal Southern Democrats rode high. Already in strategic positions on House committees, they now moved into firm control. Among them Eugene Cox was said to have a majority of votes on the rules committee "in his pocket." He now used this to block liberal legislation, while supporting administration war measures.[1]

15. H. R. 5497. *Broadcasting*, October 27, 1941; February 2, July 6, 1942.
1. The following is based on Wilson, *Congress: Corruption and Compromise,* and other sources as mentioned.

Cox, being from a state with a poll tax and race barriers, had repeatedly been sent to Congress by a handful of the adults in his district—in 1938, by 3.8 per cent. He represented an area that felt a stake in cheap labor and feared the CIO. He warned CIO president John L. Lewis "and his communistic cohorts" to stay away; the Southland, said Cox, would not tolerate a new carpetbag invasion "under the red banner of Soviet Russia." Cox made it clear in 1940 that we would prefer "a strong militaristic government of the type of Germany and Italy." Opposition to wage-and-hour legislation and other labor-supported measures was the keystone of his policies. His passions were shared by Representative Martin Dies of Texas and other Southern colleagues and also formed the basis for a working coalition with conservative Northern Republicans. This coalition dominated the politics of the period and, not unnaturally, had its impact on the broadcasting field.

Seeing communism in most liberal ideas, Cox and Dies had a special dislike for Southern liberals, who seemed traitors to their heritage. Cox regarded Supreme Court Justice Hugo Black as an anarchist; Fly, a Texan, earned similar indignation.

Cox, having served four years as a judge in Albany, Georgia, liked to be called "Judge Cox." At one time he is said to have had nine relatives on the government payroll, including a son, a brother, three nephews, two sisters, a brother-in-law, and a son-in-law.[2]

Aside from political reasons, Cox had another motive for turning on Fly. Cox had made frequent representations to the FCC on behalf of WALB, Albany, Georgia, during the time the station obtained its license. An FCC field investigator visiting WALB found that Cox had been paid to help the station get its license. A canceled $2500 check and minutes of a stockholders' meeting made this absolutely clear. Acceptance of a fee by a congressman for work before a government agency was illegal under Section 113 of the Criminal Code. The investigator took the evidence to Fly.

Shortly afterward Cox began his attacks on Fly, and demands for a probe to be headed by himself.

The FCC sent photostats of the Cox evidence to the Justice Department and to Speaker of the House Sam Rayburn, to show that Cox was hardly a proper investigator of the FCC. The Justice Department paid no attention

2. Drew Pearson in syndicated column "Washington Merry-Go-Round," August 15, 1939.

—perhaps out of respect for Cox's power. Rayburn referred the documents to the House judiciary committee which, after months of delay,
decided it did not have jurisdiction.

Meanwhile both Cox and Dies continued their attacks. The Dies committee, after calling a number of FCC employees subversive, began a concerted attack on two: Goodwin Watson, chief analyst for the Foreign
Broadcast Intelligence Service; and William E. Dodd, Jr., its assistant
news editor. Despite heavy congressional pressures, the FCC refused to
fire them. After long congressional maneuvering the House appropriations
committee, apparently impressed by Dies's ominous charges, passed a
rider to an appropriation bill, barring payment of any federal funds to
Watson and Dodd.[3] The Senate at first refused to accept this rider; a long
conference committee struggle followed.

The FCC staff was shaken by these events. The Foreign Broadcast Intelligence Service was doing specialized and challenging work. Its
achievements had been praised by many agencies. Now the impression
was given to the public that a disloyal conspiracy existed within the Service. If true, it was sickening; if untrue, and made in the interests of some
political struggle, the charge was vicious and loathsome. Did one of these
express the truth, or was there still another explanation? Among staff
members—and their families—the need to get at the truth was apparently
stronger than among committees and subcommittees threading their way
through charge and countercharge. At various homes an unrelenting effort
got under way to piece together a fantastic jigsaw puzzle of the time. "It
began," recalled Edward Brecher, staff assistant to Fly, "as an after-hours
form of debauchery." But it became deadly serious.

A charge against Goodwin Watson was that he was a member of the
board of *Consumers' Union,* an organization which the Dies committee
considered un-American and communistic. It prepared research reports on
household articles including widely advertised products. It had been
praised by many businessmen, although attacked by some whose products
were found substandard. Watson readily admitted the membership.

He also admitted that he had agreed to serve as advisor (along with ex-
President Alexander Meiklejohn of Amherst and others) to the American
Student Union, but said he had never been asked for advice.

3. The rider also barred salary payments to Robert Morss Lovett, former University
of Chicago professor who had become Governor of the Virgin Islands.

Most other Dies committee "citations" against Watson involved petitions and endorsements. These showed that he had:

supported medical aid to the Spanish loyalists
> (with Bishop Francis J. McConnell and others)

endorsed the American Youth Act
> (with Warden Lewis E. Lawes of Sing Sing and others)

supported public education
> (with Robert Millikan of the California Institute of Technology and others)

supported work camps
> (with Mrs. Franklin D. Roosevelt and others)

favored Pan American democracy
> (with Rabbi Stephen Wise and others)

attacked anti-Semitism
> (with Vice President Henry Wallace and others)

criticized the Dies committee
> (with President Emeritus Mary Woolley of Mt. Holyoke College and others)

favored a Communist party place on the ballot
> (with Professor Zechariah Chafee of Harvard and 450 other scholars, all identifying themselves as non-communists)

spoken for democracy at a forum which discussed the relative merits of democracy, fascism, and socialism

The "citations" on William E. Dodd, Jr., followed a similar pattern and to some extent duplicated those cited above. Half the Dodd citations actually represented research errors; they really referred to William E. Dodd, Sr., former ambassador to Germany. Others showed that William E. Dodd, Jr., had:

urged a change in policy toward Spain
> (with Henry L. Stimson and others)

demanded a boycott of Japanese goods
> (with Maxwell Stewart and others)

appealed for aid to China
> (with President Frank Graham of the University of North Carolina and others)

signed a statement against intolerance
> (with Thomas E. Dewey and others)[4]

4. *Dies Committee Accusations: Comments*, pp. 1–59.

In the after-hours sessions the participants became more and more interested in the many "others." Wives began to pore through newspaper
files and old letters. The search became a need. "I remember," Brecher
recalled, "my wife Ruth making a trip to New York on the trail of some
long-defunct letterhead, and I remember two other girls coming back
from New York with a treasure trove." [5]

From this the amateur researchers composed a massive document. It
showed that if the Dies committee "citations" had any validity as a guide to
action, the nation should promptly protect itself by purging:

> The Vice President
> The Secretary of War
> The Secretary of the Navy
> The Secretary of the Interior
> 3 Supreme Court Justices
> 1 Admiral
> 10 U. S. Senators
> 3 Representatives
> 8 Bishops and Archbishops
> 21 University Presidents[6]

and be on guard against such subversives as Thomas E. Dewey, Helen
Keller, Mayor Fiorello H. La Guardia, Alfred E. Smith, Grover Whalen,
Harold C. Urey, and Dorothy Thompson.

The brilliant *reductio ad absurdum* document, informally circulated,
stiffened the FCC. It voted support of Watson and Dodd and continued to
defy the Dies committee.

But the battle went on, with hearing on hearing. The House appropriations committee voted to cut the FCC budget 25 per cent. A member told
Robert Leigh of the Foreign Broadcast Intelligence Service: "Larry Fly
has been defiant of Congress for a long time . . . now his chickens have
come home to roost." Goodwin Watson, after a hearing of an appropriations subcommittee, talked to a congressman from his home state of Wisconsin. "What are you fellows trying to do? Watson asked him. The congressman reassured him; they had nothing against Watson. "They want to
get Fly." [7]

Cox kept up his end, and announced plans for the impeachment of Fly.

5. Correspondence, Edward M. Brecher.
6. Untitled mimeographed document, pp. 1–18. Brecher files.
7. Leigh, "Politicians vs Bureaucrats," *Harper's Magazine,* January 1945. Watson,
Reminiscences, p. 87.

In addressing the House, he was quoted as calling the FCC the "nastiest nest of rats" in Washington, although some thought he said "reds." With such invective Cox persuaded the House to approve his probe, with him as chairman. *Broadcasting* expressed satisfaction, considering the probe "competently manned." Cox began at once to issue subpoenas, demanding FCC files by the truckload. No time was allowed for the listing of seized documents. From individual commissioners he ordered personal financial records back to 1937. Most acquiesced. One decided to refuse.[8]

He was a new commissioner, Clifford J. Durr—from Alabama. He was a brother-in-law of Supreme Court Justice Hugo Black. Soft-spoken, modest in manner, and scholarly, Durr had been assistant general counsel for the Reconstruction Finance Corporation. Some time before that he had been a Rhodes scholar. He was outraged at what was happening. Impatient at the failure of the Justice Department and of Speaker Rayburn to take note of Cox's behavior and unfitness, Durr decided to take his own political life in his hands. With photostats he visited Eugene Meyer, editor and publisher of the Washington *Post*. On the following day—September 27, 1943—"A Public Letter to Speaker Rayburn" appeared on the front page of the *Post*.

> In the opinion of no qualified and dispassionate observer has this investigation proven anything but a mockery of basic American traditions of fair play. It has been a star chamber; it has been black with bias; it has sought to terrorize those who exposed the chairman's corrupt practices.

Meanwhile Durr had left a hundred photostats of the Cox check on the press tables at the FCC. The facts were now in the open, and at last became too much. Four days later, in a tearful farewell, Cox resigned as chairman of his probe. "Confidence in his honor," said Rayburn with a straight face, "is unshaken." [9]

Broadcasting promised that an "infinitely stronger" investigation would result. However, the final outcome, months later, was a virtual vote of confidence in the FCC.[10]

Meanwhile the Senate had reluctantly accepted, and the President had signed—with protest—the appropriation bill with its rider barring pay-

8. *Broadcasting*, January 18, 25, May 17, 1943.
9. Washington *Post*, September 27, October 1, 1943; interview, Clifford Durr.
10. *Investigation of the Federal Communications Commission: Final Report*, pp. 1–53. One member of the investigating committee filed a strong dissent. Another concurred in the report but expressed reservations.

ment to Watson and Dodd. The President signed it because the salaries of thousands of government employees were being held up by the battle. But Fly insisted that both Watson and Dodd remain on the staff long enough to lay the basis for a lawsuit—technically, to recover lost wages, but also to test the legality of the congressional rider. The suit was brought and eventually won by the employees in the U. S. Supreme Court, which commented scathingly on the unlawful "bill of attainder." [11]

Meanwhile the Supreme Court had also upheld—May 10, 1943—the FCC's actions in regard to the chain broadcasting report. NBC and CBS, described as "stunned" by the defeat, prepared to comply. NBC-blue was put up for sale.

Somehow Fly had survived a fantastic period of attack by a determined coalition. His resilience, always remarkable, was epitomized by a press conference held before the turning of the tide, at a time when the roof seemed to be falling in on him. Fly greeted the press in almost chipper fashion. The Cox committee, he said, had not yet accused the FCC of killing Cock Robin, but that could come. Then he added:

> This investigation, at this point, reminds me of that old story about the man who stopped to watch some kids playing a sandlot baseball game. A youngster told him the score was 38 to 0 in favor of the other side. "Good heavens!" said the man, "You're taking an awful beating!" "Heck no!" the boy replied, "We haven't come up to bat yet!" [12]

At one point during the Cox assault Fly received a memorandum by mistake. A reporter for Hearst's International News Service sent the Cox committee counsel some pointers on how to get maximum newspaper impact out of the Fly hearings, but a secretary—inadvertently or intentionally—put them in an envelope addressed to Fly. The first bit of advice was:

> Decide what you want the newspapers to hit hardest and then shape each hearing so that the main point becomes the vortex of the testimony. Once that vortex is reached, *adjourn.*

Another recommendation was:

> Don't ever be afraid to recess a hearing even for five minutes so that you keep the proceedings completely in control so far as creating news is concerned.[13]

11. *United States* v. *Lovett,* 328 U. S. 303 (1946).
12. Press conference, New York City, August 13, 1943. Fly, *Papers.*
13. Fly, *Papers.*

Throughout this period of struggle, broadcasting industry spokesmen had stood aside or quietly applauded the attackers. For the first time the industry was facing an FCC with a mind of its own and with exceptional integrity. The experience appeared distasteful. But Fly remained.

GULLIVER

". . . one of the most eloquent programs in radio history," was the phrase used by *Time* to describe *Open Letter on Race Hatred,* broadcast by CBS in the summer of 1943. The program had an unusual history. William N. Robson of *Columbia Workshop* wrote its dramatic portions and was producer-director. The subject was the Detroit riots of June 1943. The star was Wendell L. Willkie.

Something had happened to Willkie—a change that brought some one-time supporters close to apoplexy. After his defeat he had been invited to the White House. At President Roosevelt's invitation he undertook a mission: a journey around the world as presidential representative. He left in August 1942 in an army bomber converted for transport—the Gulliver. Hitler's armies were near Moscow and Stalingrad and held most of North Africa and the Balkans; the Japanese were in Indonesia, Malaya, Burma, and threatening Australia and India. At this juncture Willkie—accompanied by Gardner Cowles and Joseph Barnes—made his forty-nine-day tour, talked with Stalin, Chiang Kai-shek, and other world leaders, and returned to write *One World,* reporting in fascinating detail on his journeys and talks. In two months the book sold more than a million copies and gave Willkie overnight a new image and standing, confounding party lines. His words came as the war tide seemed to turn, both in Europe and the Pacific. Willkie told Americans that Soviet Russia had surprised him; it had "survival value" and could not be "by-passed in any future world." He warned his countrymen: postwar leadership would not be an exclusive prerogative for America and Britain. Not only Russia but also China and emerging nations of Asia and Africa would have to be reckoned with. This meant that Americans would share a fate with people of many tongues and many colors, and called for an end to "our racial complacency." It must be truly "one world," invigorated by justice at home and abroad.[1]

It sounded somewhat like Vice President Henry Wallace, who was considered a dreamer. But the words came from Wendell Willkie, utility mag-

1. Willkie, *One World,* pp. 53, 87, 189.

nate and Republican standard bearer, and therefore had greater impact. He became a symbol of many aspirations—including racial harmony.

When race riots in June 1943 left thirty-four dead on the streets of Detroit, with more than 700 injured and 1300 arrests, Walter White of the National Association for the Advancement of Colored People turned to Willkie and found him ready to help. Their plan was a dramatization—to be written by William Robson, and culminating in a statement by Willkie. Robson was eager to co-operate and encouraged White to propose the idea to Douglas Coulter—who had become CBS vice president in charge of programs.

The association of Willkie with the proposed "open letter" gave it a unique status. It was "advocacy"—usually poison at CBS—but with Willkie as spokesman, the project required special consideration.

The tensions surrounding the project were reflected in the tortuous steps by which it moved forward. Robson studied available riot reports, interviewed witnesses, and began work on the script. He was told that William Paley would have to hear a recording of a rehearsal before giving a final go-ahead.

> So I wrote this show, produced it fully, with complete cast, complete orchestra—everything but Wendell Willkie, who was going to come on at the end—and then went up to Paley's office. There was Paley, Doug Coulter, Paul White, myself. . . . Just the four of us. . . . We played this record and discussed it. It was a matter of "be careful here," "caution here," "you're overboard there,"—that kind of thing. (I leaned on the side of the downtrodden, you know) . . . Fine. I went back to the typewriter.

Robson rewrote, reassembled cast and orchestra, and again recorded an entire production. A similar meeting was held. Further changes were called for. For a third time Robson gathered his cast and orchestra and recorded an entire production.

Meanwhile an executive of CBS-owned station WBT, Charlotte, North Carolina, visited the network and read the script. "I wouldn't touch this thing," he told Coulter. "I know my people down there." On the same day Robson was summoned by Paley. Robson recalls Paley telling him, "I have a report from our man in Washington that the FBI had definite proof that the Negroes started the riot in Detroit. How about that? You don't say it in your script."

"I don't have that evidence. If the FBI's got it, how come your man in Washington knows it and nobody else knows it?"

"Are you certain that your facts are correct?"

"I am certain of my facts."

Paley decided on one more preliminary. The recording of the third full production was put on the network lines—not broadcast—so that all CBS affiliates in all parts of the country could hear it and decide whether to carry the broadcast. A number of Southern stations decided not to carry it. But the die was cast—the program would be scheduled. Once again the cast and orchestra were assembled, along with Wendell Willkie, for the broadcast and the West Coast repeat.

The final passage of *Open Letter on Race Hatred*, spoken by Willkie, referred to the world impact of news from America.

WILLKIE: . . . Two-thirds of the people who are our allies do not have white skins. And they have long, hurtful memories of the white man's superior attitude in his dealings with them. . . . When the necessities of war cease to make co-operation valuable to the white man, will his promises mean anything? . . .

Our whole purpose today is, with our allies, to defeat fascism. But all the forces of fascism are not with our enemies. . . . The desire to deprive some of our citizens of their rights—economic, civic, or political—has the same basic motivation as actuates the fascist mind when it seeks to dominate whole peoples and nations.

It is essential that we eliminate it at home as well as abroad.

It was a new Willkie talking.

The day of the broadcast posed problems. Between the first broadcast and the West Coast repeat the participants had to eat. Walter White of the NAACP, who had a light complexion, could be taken to any midtown restaurant, but not his wife and fourteen-year-old daughter, who were darker. Robson decided on a party at his apartment on 51st Street. With the Walter Whites came Roy Wilkins and Thurgood Marshall of the NAACP, and Wendell Willkie. Willkie sat in the big yellow chair in the living room. They had drinks. Willkie was expansive and happy. He fluffed a few lines on the West Coast repeat.[2]

The war changed some people. Willkie was one of them; another was Albert Lasker.

2. Robson, *Reminiscences*, pp. 16–20. The script of *Open Letter on Race Hatred* is in Barnouw (ed.), *Radio Drama in Action*.

Lasker was a Willkie supporter in 1940. Later, when other conservative Republicans broke with Willkie, Lasker did not. He was going through a crisis in his own life, and being psychoanalyzed. His wife had died; he had remarried, but a divorce had followed quickly. During this time his ideas began to change. He married again, and the new marriage—to Mary Lasker—furthered the process of change.

The man who had helped to mastermind the defeat of the League of Nations suddenly became a Willkie internationalist. He explained that isolationism hadn't worked, so why not try something else—even if it was the opposite?

He gave up the Lake Forest palace, where he had entertained the great of the nation. He explained that it was "the kind of place that's going to be surrounded by an angry mob some day. . . . When that happens I intend to be part of the mob."

The man who had once talked three days about the glories of advertising arrived at the Lord & Thomas office one day and asked himself, "Why am I doing this?" Unable to answer the question, he decided to liquidate the agency. He let his aides reorganize it as Foote, Cone & Belding.

Concerning his psychoanalysis, he said to publisher Richard Simon of Simon and Schuster: "I'm doing it to get rid of all the *hate* the advertising business put into me." To Robert Hutchins he wrote: "I am the most superficial man on earth, and yet I am the dean of my profession . . . there must be something wrong with the profession." Asked if he missed the old advertising life, he answered: "The Lasker of the advertising business died in 1942. I never think of him, and I'm not sure I ever knew the man."

In 1943 he gave $50,000 to Planned Parenthood and began planning other gifts. The man who had worked as hard as anyone for nationwide cigarette addiction began to give money for cancer research. He became an enthusiastic backer of Franklin D. Roosevelt. He had come full circle.

The new causes kept him busy, and he opened a new office. Over its door was an inscription from Maurice Maeterlinck:

> At every crossing on the road that leads to the future, each progressive
> spirit is opposed by a thousand men appointed to guard the past.[3]

In the broadcasting field the war changed many people. Scattered to the four winds, they could hardly come back the same.

3. Gunther, *Taken At the Flood*, pp. 257–99.

Off the Malayan coast Cecil Brown was on a British battleship that was hit from the air by Japanese bombs and began to sink.

> I was aboard the *Repulse* with hundreds of others and escaped. Then, swimming in thick oil, I saw the *Prince of Wales* lay over on her side like a tired war horse and slide beneath the waters . . .

He had jumped twenty feet into the water from the deck of the *Repulse*, and later found that his watch had been smashed at 12:35. He broadcast his account over CBS via short-wave on December 11, 1941.[4]

In North Africa in 1942 Charles Cummings Collingwood, handsome and impeccably dressed·Cornell graduate and Rhodes scholar, found himself in the thick of action as CBS reporter of the Allied invasion of Africa —the first move into Hitler-held territory. Collingwood had gone to Oxford to delve into medieval law but Armageddon seemed too close; he digressed into reporting. Hired by Murrow, he wrote his family: "This is the kind of job I like and I think I can do it." In North Africa a few months later he was broadcasting a dozen times a week. Each day in the 8 A.M. and 6:45 P.M. newscasts, Eastern time, listeners would hear two and a half minutes of vivid reporting by Collingwood in a firm, precise voice. He was finding army officers suspicious of the new breed, the radio reporter, but managed to illuminate the scene with "the illusion of uncanny insight," as *Newsweek* called it. He often suggested trends days ahead of the news columns. He remained impeccable. Actress Kay Francis, touring to entertain troops, said that Collingwood was the only man in North Africa who knew where to get a suit pressed. But he was turning into a sharp-eyed student of the current world. Reporting a military invasion, he was more concerned with a needed "invasion of ideas." [5]

In Assam in 1943 Eric Sevareid boarded a C46—a "flying coffin"—to clear the hump of the Himalayas en route to an assignment in China. When the left engine went dead en route, passenger luggage was thrown frantically from the plane, but this wasn't enough to maintain altitude and there was a sudden clutching at parachutes and men leaping into space and vanishing with a screaming whistle. The pilot stood shouting at Sevareid, who could not make out the words. Beneath him a mountain peak whisked by as the plane went into a dive. He jumped.

4. Hohenberg, *Foreign Correspondence,* pp. 311–48.
5. *Newsweek,* February 1, 1943; *Current Biography* (1943) pp. 136–8.

> The mind ceased to operate, and I have no recollection of thought. I
> do not know whether the air felt cold or warm, but instantly there was
> a terrific rush of wind.

He pulled the cord. A terrible blow seemed to strike his body. From a
green mountainside ahead of him a geyser of orange flame spurted as the
plane hit. He glimpsed a brown river. Then branches were slashing at
him.

The battered survivors found each other over a period of days, some
badly injured. One man had died. Meanwhile a score of short, naked men
with spears and knives, and chanting in unison, approached and formed a
semi-circle before them. A childhood memory caused Sevareid to step forward, raise a palm, and say, "How!" It seemed to find acceptance as a
gesture of friendship. Tribesmen came forward and rubbed parachute silk
over their faces. An American plane dropped warnings: this was an area
of Naga headhunters and the group must be on guard. A rescue party
would be organized but might take weeks. A Japanese reconnaissance
plane passed over. The group took up residence on a grassy hillside shelf,
posting a guard day and night. A radio transmitter was dropped for them
but smashed. A receiver was also dropped; it survived the fall. Huge
bags of salt were dropped, landing like bombs, for use as tokens of friendship. On the radio they picked up Bob Hope from somewhere; also a
crooner called Frank Sinatra, and Glenn Miller's band. A fellow survivor
told Sevareid, "I—uh—used to hear you on the radio from London and
Washington."

The rescue party arrived and took them over mountain and forest trails
back to India and hospitalization. They encountered a touring U. S. Senator, "Happy" Chandler of Kentucky, whom Sevareid had never met. "Eric,
my dear boy, I *prayed* for you every night! Yessirree, got right down and
prayed for you!" Months behind schedule, Sevareid was ready to start
once more for his CBS assignment in China.[6]

In Chungking announcer Jeff Sparks, who had announced for NBC and
before that for WLW and WMCA, was on duty for the Red Cross. Three
times a week he would do a program over NBC-blue, which was relayed
to America by Chinese short-wave station XGOY, Chungking. Its transmitter was under rock, and the Japanese had tried to bomb it into silence,
but it remained the one effective radio link with the United States. The
words were picked up in California by a dentist who was a short-wave

6. Sevareid, *Not So Wild a Dream*, pp. 250–301.

Paul White and H. V. Kaltenborn during Munich crisis, 1938.

Raymond Swing of MBS and BBC.

Edward R. Murrow in London, 1941.

Norman Corwin directing war-time broadcast.

CBS

WE

CBS bond-selling broadcast, from Boston. Crossing at center, director William N. Robson. A microphone, Dwight Weist. Seated with script, Eddie Albert.

April 20, 1939. David Sarnoff dedicates RCA pavilion at New York World's Fair.

RCA

May 17, 1939. First baseball telecast — Princeton vs. Columbia, from Baker Field.

NBC

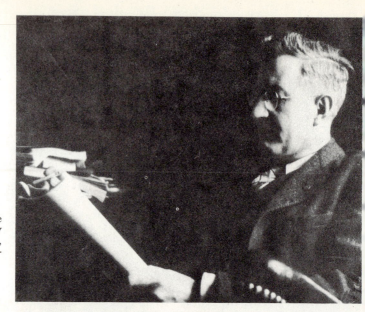

"We are going to elevate to a new level of dignity informers, stool pigeons, and gossips." Commissioner Clifford J. Durr.

"...dead mackerel in the moonlight...it both shines and stinks." Chairman James Lawrence Fly.

"THIS IS THE ARMED FORCES RADIO SERVICE."

AFRS expeditionary station in Italy, 1943.

U.S. Department of Defense

AFRS station in Guadalcanal, South Pacific, 1944.

COMMAND PERFORMANCE

Edgar Bergen and Ingrid Bergman with Charlie McCarthy's sidekick Mortimer Snerd.

An ad lib by Bing Crosby fractures Frank Sinatra at Hollywood rehearsal.

Sounds of home: Betty Hutton fries a steak, with commentary by Bob Hope.

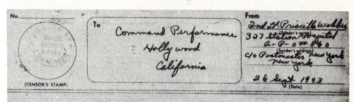

JUDY GARLAND.   19819
c/o COMMAND PERFORMANCE,
SPECIAL SERVICE DIVISION,
U.S.A.

24 JUN 1943   Write the message very plainly below this line

LT. C. SOPPET. R.A   Date   19ᵗʰ JUNE. 43
Sender's Address 25/4 81ˢᵗ HEAVY A.A. REGT. R.A.
MIDDLE EAST FORCES.

DEAR JUDY.
        AS YOU CAN SEE FROM THE ADDRESS
WE ARE STATIONED IN EGYPT AND WE CAN'T
TELL YOU HOW MUCH WE APPRECIATE YOUR
SONGS. NEXT TIME YOU ARE ON COMMAND
PERFORMANCE WHAT ABOUT LETTING US HAVE
"ME AND MY GIRL" AGAIN — WE LIKE IT
WE ALWAYS MAKE EVERY EFFORT TO LISTEN TO
COMMAND PERFORMANCE AND ONE HEARS SOME
VERY BAD LANGUAGE IF JERRY COMES OVER
AND STOPS US FROM LISTENING TO YOU. CAN
YOU LET US HAVE A PHOTOGRAPH OF
YOURSELF. WE WISH YOU ALL THE LUCK IN
THE WORLD AND WE HOPE TO HEAR YOU
AGAIN SOON.
        YOURS VERY SINCERELY.
        CLIVE SOPPET.
        (Soppet Lt. RA)

No.   To   Command Performance   From 2nd Lt. Priscilla Webber
                Hollywood   327 Station Hospital
                California   a. P. o. 860
                            c/o Postmaster New York
(CENSOR'S STAMP)   New York
                            26 Sept 1943 (Date)

Dear Sirs:
    I am writing for a group of army nurses in Iceland
to tell you how much we enjoy listening to your broadcasts.
It brings us all a laugh and is almost as good as a letter
from home.
    Our request is: Would you please have Frank Sinatra
sing "You Would Be So Nice To Come Home To" for the Old
Maids in Quarters 46 in Iceland.
    We sincerely appreciate all you on the home front are
doing to keep up our morale. Our thanks to all of you for
your time and effort you freely give to make these broadcasts
possible.
    Thanks a lot and we shall be listening for our song.
                Sincerely
                2nd Lt. Priscilla Webber n.n.c.

U.S. Department of Defense

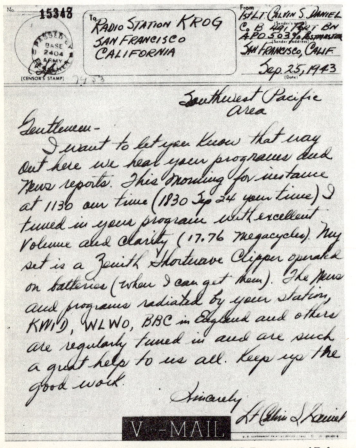

FAN MAIL FOR AFRS
from the Pacific.

No.

PASSED BY
NAVAL CENSOR

To Walter Huston
Great Music
Special Services
Los Angeles Calif.

From H. E. LEGLER, LIEUT-COMDR. U.S.N.R.
Advance Naval Base
Navy 156
F.P.O. San Francisco Calif
Nov 26, 1943.

Mrs. Huston —
I have a keen desire to hear Claude De Bussy's "Clair de Lune" on your Great Music program. Perhaps it has been presented before and I missed it. If so, please repeat it.
Just heard one of your presentations through Radio Suva, VPD2. I like the type of music you present and wish I could be fortunate to hear them regularly.

Respectfully
H. E. Legler.

No. 15343

PASSED
BASE
2404
ARMY
[CENSOR STAMP]

To RADIO STATION KROG
SAN FRANCISCO
CALIFORNIA

From 1st Lt. Calvin S. Daniel
Co. B 441 TEngr Bn
APO 503 % Postmaster
San Francisco, Calif.
Sep 25, 1943

Southwest Pacific
Area

Gentlemen —
I want to let you know that way out here we hear your programs and News reports. This morning for instance at 1136 our time (1830 Sep 24 your time) I tuned in your program with excellent volume and clarity (17.76 megacycles). My set is a Zenith Shortwave Clipper operated on batteries (when I can get them). The News and programs radiated by your station, KWID, WLWO, BBC in England and others are regularly tuned in and are such a great help to us all. Keep up the good work.

Sincerely
Lt. Calvin S. Daniel

V.-MAIL

U.S. Department of Defense

enthusiast and made it his hobby to relay such material to networks. The Chungking station, directed by Mike Peng, identified itself, "This is United Nations Radio," although the United Nations as an organization did not yet exist.[7]

Larry Lesueur, after months of visiting Soviet fighting fronts, industries transplanted to the Ural mountains and beyond, and collective farms, hospitals, and schools, returned to the United States in 1943 to publish a book about his experiences and appear as the central figure in the CBS series *An American in Russia,* written by Sylvia Berger and directed by Norman Corwin.

They were all Gullivers, opening strange worlds.

LIFESAVER

NBC-blue had to be sold, and the job was given to NBC vice president Mark Woods.

He had joined WEAF in 1922 as accountant and risen gradually to treasurer and vice president.[1] He was unspectacular but was always needed because he understood the books. For some years he had urged that, financially speaking, separation of NBC-red and NBC-blue would be beneficial for both. In 1938 he had written a detailed company memorandum to that effect. This view was not publicized because the official NBC doctrine at the time, as argued vociferously before FCC, District Court, Supreme Court, and elsewhere, was that such separation would be a mortal blow to NBC and probably to free enterprise.

During 1942-43 NBC-red and NBC-blue divided up stations, transmitters, studios, control equipment, microphones, sound effects, desks, chairs, wastebaskets, filing cabinets, and staff members. In 1943 a separate corporation under Mark Woods—the Blue Network—was put on the block. Sarnoff approved an asking price of $8,000,000.

For a time Woods thought that Edward J. Noble, the Lifesaver king, was interested; but he cooled off, considering the price too steep.

Woods began complex negotiations with the investment house Dillon, Reed & Co. They offered $7,750,000. The details of the transaction were put in writing, but Woods had trouble getting David Sarnoff on the tele-

7. After the war both Jeff Sparks and Mike Peng joined the radio staff of the United Nations in New York. Sparks, *Interview,* pp. 50–52.
1. See *A Tower in Babel,* pp. 113, 238.

phone. Finally he reached him. Woods later recalled: "I explained to Mr. Sarnoff that my new associates were in my office with me, and I would like to bring them to his office so that he could meet them."

Sarnoff answered, "There must be some mistake, Mark! I have just sold the Blue Network company to Ed Noble and James McGraw. . . . They are in my office; I would like you to meet them and we'll close the deal."

When Woods got to Sarnoff's office, he learned that Noble had finally agreed to pay $8,000,000 for the network. He told Woods he had tried to get it for $7,000,000, but Sarnoff had been unwilling to budge.

Woods saw a chance to do something for the man who was apparently destined to become his boss. Woods reminded Sarnoff that they had discussed an RCA-sponsored series over the projected independent network. Could they settle that now? Woods had specific figures in mind. For the first year, time costs should be $650,000; talent, $350,000. The total, $1,000,000.

Sarnoff said, "Is that what you want, Mark?"

"Yes!"

Sarnoff agreed. Noble, seeing he had recouped a million dollars, was pleased.[2]

The remaining problem was the FCC. The $8,000,000 cash purchase included three stations—WJZ, New York; WENR, Chicago; KGO, San Francisco. The transfer of those licenses required an FCC finding that the public interest would be served thereby.

FCC chairman James Fly had staked his career on the idea that "diversity" of station ownership would create a more vigorous forum of ideas. He was relieved that a sale had been negotiated. His concern was to make sure that "diversity" had been achieved.

The hearings brought testimony by Edward J. Noble, who would be chairman of the new network; and Mark Woods, who would be president.

Woods was questioned by Fly: "Suppose you had an opportunity to put on the *Ford Sunday Evening Hour,* would you take it—and along with it, Mr. Cameron?" "Yes," said Woods. Would he sell time, Fly asked him, to the American Federation of Labor? "No," Woods answered, explaining that time was sold "for a specific purpose only . . . the sale of goods." Fly pointed out that many sponsors had no goods to sell. Woods admitted

2. Woods, *Reminiscences*, pp. 101–11. According to Woods, RCA actually spent $1,100,000 on the program. James H. McGraw, of McGraw-Hill, withdrew. Noble became sole purchaser.

that. In wartime, he explained, it was important to them to maintain "good will," and "keep their names before the public." Suppose, asked Fly, the American Federation of Labor wanted to maintain good will and keep its name before the public, would the network then sell the time? "No, sir," said Woods, "We will not sell them time because they have a particular philosophy to preach."

Fly wondered whether Cameron might not also have "a particular philosophy" to preach. Did not Woods think so?

Woods, apparently feeling the pressure, shifted to a civil-liberties stance. "Well, we would not control or attempt to control what Mr. Cameron had to say." Besides, he added, the views would be those of Cameron, not Ford. Fly asked whether Ford didn't select Cameron. Of course, said Woods.

Now suppose, asked Fly, that it became apparent that Cameron—or any commentator—did regularly reflect the views of his sponsor, what would the network do? "Well, if it happened to be coincidence, we might permit it."

Repeatedly Woods retreated to a position he apparently considered basic. "We are in the advertising business, gentlemen, and that business is the business of selling goods to the American people."

Sometimes he cited the NAB code of recommended policies. They included a policy of not selling or giving time for membership promotion. An American Federation of Labor program would necessarily be a membership promotion, Woods felt. The network intended to live up to the NAB code.

Fly asked whether the network was not selling time to mutual life insurance companies, and did that not mean they were already promoting memberships? Woods said that was different. Fly asked, what about the American Red Cross? That was different too, Woods said.

Fly was saving his more crucial ammunition for Edward Noble. When Noble came on the stand, he was obviously ill at ease in matters of the sort Fly was pursuing. Noble was not new to radio, for he owned WMCA, New York—which he would have to sell before acquiring WJZ. But he had always stayed away from day-to-day decisions. At the new network he meant to do the same, leaving such matters to present executives, experienced men in whom he said he had utmost confidence, and who knew industry practices and the NAB code—which he apparently considered a sort of Ten Commandments.

Fly suddenly tossed his papers down. He suggested that if Noble was merely going to hide behind old formulas, play the old games, using them to justify *not* doing this and that, it would be "just no use." He decided abruptly to adjourn the hearings. He urged Noble to give policy matters very intense—and very rapid—thought and to submit a restatement. They would reconvene, Fly suggested, whenever Noble was ready.

Noble, left dangling by this sudden adjournment, did the proposed re-thinking. The FCC report for the year records that "sale of the Blue Net-work Company, Inc. (wholly owned by RCA) to American Broadcasting System, Inc. (wholly owned by Edward J. Noble)" was approved on October 12, 1943, and that Edward J. Noble had submitted a statement:

> I propose to meet each request for time with an open mind and to consider such requests strictly on their individual merits and without arbitrary discriminations.

He promised a policy whereby

> all classes and groups shall have their requests, either for sponsored or sustaining time, seriously considered . . . in accordance with true democratic principles. . . .

On this basis the transfer was found to serve "the public interest, convenience, and necessity." A new network was born, soon renamed the American Broadcasting Company—ABC. It adopted a policy of selling time to organized labor.[3]

STARS AND ATABRINE

That same year another network, global and without precedent, began to take shape. At the start of 1943 the Armed Forces Radio Service had 21 outlets; by the end of the year, 306 outlets. It was in 47 countries and growing rapidly. Each week each of its outlets received 42 hours of recorded programming by plane from the United States, plus other programs—news and such special events as baseball games—by short-wave relay. Outlets did additional programs in the field. It was the most extraordinary explosion of wartime radio, and far-reaching in effect.[1]

3. FCC Docket No. 6536, *Hearings*, pp. 10–135, 182–266; FCC *Reports* (1943–45), 214. WJZ was renamed WABC. The CBS flag station WABC was renamed WCBS. The historic call letters WJZ were reclaimed by Westinghouse and eventually used in Baltimore.

1. The following is based on De Lay, *An Historic Study of the Armed Forces Radio*

The first programs for troops had gone to them direct by short-wave. During 1942, when Colonel Thomas H. A. Lewis took charge and the Armed Forces Radio Service was born, time was also leased on foreign stations—in most cases government stations. American troops in Reykjavik, Iceland, were entertained by programs in a block of leased time on TFU, Reykjavik. Arrangements of this sort were also made in New Zealand, Australia, India, China, and elsewhere; eventually more than a hundred stations of this sort were involved.

But the real career of the Armed Forces Radio Service began with the creation of its own "American expeditionary stations."

Its first, a 1000-watt station, went up in Casablanca in March 1943. Watching its impact, General Eisenhower at once ordered additional stations. Transmitters soon went up in Oran and Tunis. As the Italian campaign got under way a station started in Sicily. Six days after the capture of Naples, an AFRS station was broadcasting there.

As troops moved forward, the system needed mobility. The result was the Fifth Army Mobile Station—a 400-watt transmitter mounted on a 1½-ton army truck with power unit in a trailer, and a second truck that housed the studio. It closely followed the armies north and kept within range of front-line troops.

Stations of lower power were needed for compact areas. AFRS designed a 50-watt station complete in five suitcases. In 1943 more than a hundred such "suitcase transmitters" were manufactured for AFRS. They went with instruction booklets to training camps in Britain and also resulted in 50-watt expeditionary stations with such exotic call letters as VUZZW, Agra, India; KJAM, Chungking, China; JCZE, Cairo, Egypt; WVTU, Nandi, Fiji.

AFRS programming also began to serve wired sound systems at airbases: the Air Transport Command base at Gander, Newfoundland; Zandery Field in Dutch Guiana. The programming was used by ships, including submarines. As troops moved forward, the network grew by leaps. An AFRS observer on a transport in the Pacific wrote:

> There was a PA system aboard . . . turntables located in the chaplain's office. . . . As more than five hundred men are listening to the PA system at one time and in two groups, this is group listening at its groupiest. . . . Some were playing cards, reading *Esquire,* writ-

Service; also *Armed Forces Radio Service: Progress Report* (1944); and other sources as noted.

ing letters, standing in line for chow, sleeping, sharpening knives, leaning over the rail, throwing up, daydreaming. . . .

The programming on the PA system included AFRS favorites—Bob Hope, André Kostelanetz, *G. I. Jive, Family Hour*—and the army phonograph records called "V-discs." The observer later wrote:

> An officer from a munitions ship told us how they pipe programs from Eniwetok, Kwajalein, and Saipan thru the ship's PA system as they near each port.

Each advance saw new AFRS expeditionary stations go up in tent or shack. The fantastic island-hopping advance in the Pacific brought strange reports to AFRS headquarters:

> You can smell the sweet odor of decaying bodies almost any place you go. . . . The boys are erecting a tent in the back to house the studios temporarily until the quonset is finished. They expect to go on the air Sunday if all goes well.[2]

By 1945 more than eight hundred outlets were getting the weekly shipments of AFRS programs. They were served by means of two hundred sets of the recordings, with each set being routed to a group of outlets. A set went from Los Angeles to Attu in the Aleutians; two weeks later to Shemya; from there to Kiska; there it was put on a transport or hospital ship. Eventually it vanished. Some groups of stations became regional chains, exchanging program material. New Guinea had its Jungle Network. A group of smaller islands had a Mosquito Network. Stations in Britain became a wire-linked American Forces Network, fiercely intent on autonomy.

Shortage of radios was a problem. At first there were weird reports of soldier ingenuity: one had invented a "fox-hole radio" in which a razor blade served as a crystal. Captured equipment began to ease the situation. On a ship in Australia 60,000 Dutch Phillips sets were found and commandeered by General Douglas MacArthur. Later German and Italian sets were captured in North Africa, and Japanese sets in the Philippines. American sets supplemented these.

The distribution of sets involved problems. A 1944 War Department order forbade issue of any receivers "to officer clubs, officer recreation rooms, or groups of officers until the enlisted men of the command had

2. Peterson, *Hitchhiker on AFRS Road to Tokyo*, reports 1, 3, 10, 18.

adequate broadcast reception facilities." But a touring AFRS staff member in Italy reported:

> Here at Caserta the entire enlisted men's billets boasted one radio while the great majority of officers' billets had radios, more than half of which were government issue sets.

Serving the whole vast sprawling network of stations was AFRS headquarters in Los Angeles, a bustling program factory at 6011 Santa Monica Boulevard peopled by a glamorous concentration of talent. Under wartime authority it controlled most of the nation's disk-pressing facilities. Because its commandant, Colonel Thomas H. A. Lewis, had been vice president of Young & Rubicam—always known as "Y&R"—the most Hollywood-oriented advertising agency, much top talent was drawn from the agency's productions. The uniformed staff, representing both army and navy, was supplemented by civilians. Some of the uniformed men had been drafted, then re-routed back to Hollywood and the "Y&Rmy." Some had been commissioned. For a time the program chief was Lt. Sylvester ("Pat") Weaver of the U. S. Navy, former Y&R director. A top program executive was Major True Boardman, former chief writer of *Silver Theater*. Writing *Mail Call*, a "letter from home" series about happenings in the United States, were Sergeants Jerome Lawrence and Robert E. Lee, who had been contributors to Y&R's *Screen Guild Theater*. The staff included writers for various leading comedians.[3]

Colonel Lewis was married to screen star Loretta Young. Socially and professionally AFRS was "in." Hollywood stars and starlets crowded its programs. One AFRS *Command Performance* production, recorded on February 15, 1945, outdid itself and assumed historic dimensions. It concerned the wedding of Dick Tracy and had the following cast:

DICK TRACY	Bing Crosby
TESS TRUEHEART	Dinah Shore
OLD JUDGE HOOPER	Harry Von Zell
POLICE CHIEF	Jerry Colonna
FLAT TOP	Bob Hope
VITAMIN FLINTHEART	Frank Morgan
SUMMERS SISTERS	Andrews Sisters

3. Sylvester Weaver later became president and chairman of the board of NBC. True Boardman became a producer-writer for screen and television, contributor to *The Virginians*. Lawrence and Lee, continuing their collaboration, later wrote *Inherit the Wind*, the stage play *Auntie Mame*, the musical *Mame*, and other stage and screen successes.

THE MOLE	Jimmy Durante
LITTLE SNOWFLAKE	Judy Garland
SHAKEY	Frank Sinatra
GRAVEL GERTIE	Cass Daley

While comedy and music ranked high at AFRS, other items did too. *Words and Music* offered poetry, read by young actresses backed by "dreamy" music. A complaint from the field read: "The gals picked to read poetry sound as though they had never come across the stuff before." The complainant offered names of male actors who might be more at home with poetry—such as Ronald Colman—but it was a naïve suggestion. The stations earmarked the series for "sack-time" use and considered it great. Many stations signed off with it.[4]

While some programs were AFRS productions, most were adapted from network series. All networks, sponsors, advertising agencies, and unions signed sweeping releases. Although the American Federation of Musicians in 1942 adopted a resolution forbidding its members to make recordings, the policy exempted government projects. AFRS engineers recorded hours of programming off network lines onto glass-based disks—aluminum was not available—and "denatured" it by eliminating commercials, references to specific dates, and allusions to home-front concerns. The process involved new techniques. Off-the-network glass disks were made in duplicate. The engineer would begin to record a new master from one of these duplicates, then jump to the other when a cut had to be made. This required technical virtuosity, since it meant dropping a playing needle into the right spot on the right groove at the right moment. Editing-on-disk, scarcely tried before the war, became a highly developed specialty at AFRS.

The master disk went to a factory for processing and the production of pressings of vinylite, a light and unbreakable material. The pressings were packed in cartons for shipment to the stations; if there was room in the carton, it was stuffed with comic books. A report from the field said: "Great idea!"

AFRS work in the field had a shaking-up effect on many participants. Improvisation was the order of the day, and many old rules seemed to fall by the wayside. Robert Smiley, who had done student announcing at WAKR, Akron, found himself production manager at the AFRS station in Florence, Italy, and never had such a time. They tried anything they felt

4. Peterson, *Hitchhiker on AFRS Road to Tokyo*, reports 3, 20.

like trying. When Arthur Treacher, celebrated for his butler roles in motion pictures, came through with a USO tour, they persuaded him to read the evening newscast, just to study the effect, which they found delightful and astonishing. Smiley decided he would have to spend the rest of his life in radio.[5] The Negro actor "Wonderful" Smith made a similar decision. He had acted stereotyped roles on the Red Skelton program in the United States, but at AFRS in Calcutta he became an announcer, presenting a program of recordings selected by himself. He could be himself—no hamming up required. Perhaps things were changing.[6]

At Hollywood headquarters, the Y&R patronage gave AFRS a glittering headstart but raised problems. The order creating AFRS described its purpose as "information, education and entertainment of armed forces overseas." It was conceded that "entertainment" should have early attention; however, the tendency at Santa Monica Boulevard was to forget entirely the priority objectives "information" and "education." When asked about achievements in these areas, AFRS officers repeatedly mentioned atabrine. "We gather them in with Bing Crosby and then sell them their atabrine," they liked to say. The atabrine campaign for malaria prevention could be seen by Y&R men in terms of advertising experience. An atabrine "spot" was developed which emulated an Alka-Seltzer commercial. "Listen to it fizz!" The use of mosquito repellent was likewise promoted via quasi-commercials. "Make yourself alluring. Be repellent." The use of such "commercials" was regarded as a morale factor, a welcome reminder of radio at home.[7]

However, the Information and Education Division of the War Department, which became responsible for AFRS, had a broader definition of "education." This called for "the type of education which the majority of our people must have if they are to be good citizens, parents and workers." Feeling that AFRS was falling short in this respect, the War Department decreed an East Coast educational unit to feed documentaries and forum programs into the weekly package.

The move was deeply resented in Hollywood, creating in AFRS a split similar to that in network broadcasting. A barrage of objections was raised, including the argument that the proposed programs would eliminate the carton space devoted to comic books, and bring howls of protest

5. Smiley, *Interview*, pp. 4–5.
6. Edmerson, *A Descriptive Study of the American Negro in United States Professional Radio 1922–1953*, pp. 36–9.
7. *AFRS Playback*, June 1, 1945.

from the field. Nevertheless the material began to enter the weekly package. Some series, such as *This Is the Story* and *Science Magazine*, remained for years and reached high ratings in AFRS popularity polls. Much of the material was selected from network productions.[8]

The documentaries precipitated a few controversies. There was a short series entitled *They Call Me Joe*, in which each program was narrated by a fictional service man telling his family history—a thread in America's melting-pot tradition. Each family chronicle began in a different land. Each program opened in a standard way: "My name is José—they call me Joe"; or "My name is Giuseppe—they call me Joe"; or "My name is Josef —they call me Joe." Thus the series dealt with "G. I. Joe and the generations behind him." It was planned as a contribution to intercultural understanding.

The series brought a summons to Major Paul Horgan of the War Department Information and Education Division, from a member of a congressional committee. What was the significance, the congressman demanded to know, of the name "Joe?" He repeated it, "Joe." Horgan was puzzled.

> It took me some moments to realize, and when I did it was with the effect of a staggering revelation, that he was trying to unite the expression "G. I. Joe" with the name of Josef Stalin.[9]

Fortunately Major-General Frederick Osborn, head of the Information and Education Division, found the episode delightfully amusing. But AFRS also received a protest over the series theme song, a selection from "Ballad for Americans," which had been featured at the Republican National Convention of 1940 but was now considered communistic.

For the educational programs the War Department specified a gauntlet of consultants. A designated sociologist was to approve—in regard to "intergroup strategy"—any program on race; the OWI was to approve any program touching international affairs; an educational consultant was to certify authenticity. Disks of programs so approved went to AFRS headquarters in Hollywood to be checked for technical quality, and were then put into mass production.

A *This Is the Story* program entitled *The Story They'll Never Print* completed the gauntlet. It had been produced by the American Negro Theater

8. *Education by Radio*, pp. 1–10.
9. Correspondence, Paul Horgan.

over WNEW, New York, and dealt with the first Negro to work in a formerly "lily-white" factory. During the war a number of factories were taking this step, often with trepidation. The script was based on case histories of the National Urban League, which was working to encourage the trend. The program depicted newspapermen "covering" the event, expecting an incident. But they reported to their newspapers that "nothing" had happened, there had been no clash. Therefore no newspaper stories appeared. The final narration, protesting this, said that something *had* happened: men had taken a step they had not considered possible before.[10]

The disk of the approved program arrived in Hollywood, and AFRS producer Samuel Newman watched over its processing. The opening and closing of *This Is the Story* were added and a master made. A day later he was summoned to the office of an AFRS lieutenant-colonel.

"Are you responsible for this?"

"Yes."

"Now get this straight and you'd better remember it! No nigger-loving shit goes out over this network!" The lieutenant-colonel raised the master disk and smashed it on the edge of his desk.[11]

DRIVE

In the spring of 1944 an unprecedented mobilization of radio talent joined the crush of humanity in Britain. The event was approaching—the drive across the English Channel into the heart of fortress Europe.

This was the test. Other moves, such as the drives into Africa and Italy, had in a sense been sideshows—demanded by Winston Churchill although deplored by General George C. Marshall, chairman of the joint chiefs of staff. President Roosevelt had accepted the Churchill arguments, and General Marshall had reluctantly gone along. "We failed to see," he said, explaining his switch and choosing his words oddly, "that the leader in a democracy has to keep the people entertained." [1]

Those entertainments were now well launched and the big show about to begin. "Everybody" was there. Colonel David Sarnoff, recalled by the Signal Corps, was flown to London on March 20 and went straight to the

---

10. The script is in Liss (ed.), *Radio's Best Plays*, pp. 199–215.
11. Interview, Samuel Newman. He later became story consultant for *Perry Mason*, and an attorney.
1. Pogue, *George C. Marshall: Ordeal and Hope*, p. 330.

Hotel Claridge. Next morning the chambermaid brought him a bundle of laundry. Sarnoff was puzzled; he had not been there long enough to make laundry. The laundry, it turned out, belonged to Colonel William Paley of Psychological Warfare, who had had that room but changed to another that was more to his liking.[2]

Preparation of equipment and procedures to broadcast the invasion news to the American people, the troops in the field, the world at large, and the enemy, went forward at fever pitch. A story in *Broadcasting* expressed the mood: "For all of us alive today, the biggest story since Creation is about to break." [3]

Psychological warfare plans were getting crucial attention. Davidson Taylor of CBS had joined William Paley in this assignment. Working closely with heads of occupied countries, they prepared recordings to be hurled at the Continent on D-Day. To the studio came, one by one, the prime ministers of the governments-in-exile of Poland, Belgium, Luxembourg, and the Netherlands; also, King Haakon of Norway; finally, General Charles de Gaulle of France, who had been kept away as long as possible because his security arrangements were considered shaky. The recordings were intended to give guidance to resistance groups in occupied lands. At the end of each day the completed recordings were locked in a vault. They would be broadcast from BBC transmitters and also from ABSIE—the American Broadcasting Station in Europe, especially created for the great drive.

ABSIE went on the air on April 30, 1944, with words by Robert E. Sherwood:

> This is the American Broadcasting Station in Europe. . . . In this historic year of 1944, the Allied radio will bring you tremendous news . . . we shall give you the signal when the hour comes for you to rise up against the enemy and strike. . . .[4]

Day by day Davidson Taylor and his colleagues reviewed the accumulating recordings. In listening to a recording made by General Dwight D. Eisenhower, Taylor noticed a passage that alarmed him. At the recording session it had not seemed to trouble anyone, but Taylor became convinced that the announcement must be re-recorded. The General's headquarters told Taylor it was impossible—the implication seemed to be, too late. Tay-

2. Kirby and Harris, *Star-Spangled Radio*, pp. 244–5.
3. *Broadcasting*, May 1, 1944.
4. Kirby and Harris, *Star-Spangled Radio*, pp. 123–4.

lor played the recording for Paley, who agreed on the need for re-doing the recording and undertook to persuade Eisenhower.

Eisenhower had recorded: "Do not needlessly endanger your lives until I give you the signal. . . ."

At six o'clock one morning Eisenhower re-recorded the announcement: "Do not needlessly endanger your lives. Wait, until I give you the signal to rise and . . ." [5]

As the assault began, correspondents took the radio spotlight. They were now armed with wire recorders. These had been tried in Italy and had been welcomed. Convenient for censorship, they also made possible a great deal of simultaneous description of action. The new device brought new names to the fore—among them, George Hicks of ABC. His modest voice, incapable of false drama, was at its best when immersed in the chaos of D-Day. He was on a navy ship nearing Normandy.

HICKS: . . . This is George Hicks speaking. . . . I can count twenty-two of the squat square-nosed landing crafts, carrying vehicles . . . as they turn and bounce in the choppy sea . . . and start in toward the beach . . . The first Allied forces are reaching the beaches of France. . . .
(*Sound of planes*)
It's planes you can hear overhead now . . . here comes a plane . . . the whole seaside is covered with tracer fire, going up . . . bombs . . . machine-gunning . . . the plane seems to be coming directly overhead . . .
(*Sound of plane, machine-gun fire, and ack-ack*)
Well, that's the first time we've shot our guns . . . directly right over our heads. . . . If you'll excuse me, I'll just take a deep breath for a moment and stop speaking. . . . Here we go again! . . . Another one is coming over! . . . something burning is falling through the sky and hurtling down . . . . it may be a hit plane!
(*Terrific noise in background*)
Here he goes . . . they got one!
(*Voices cheering*)
Great splotches of fire came down and are smoldering now just off our port side in the sea . . . smoke and flame there. . . . It was their first kill for this gun, and the boys are pretty excited about it. . . . [6]

With such present-tense reports the wire recorder began chipping away at the network taboo against recorded speech. The networks regarded it, for the moment, as a temporary concession to military need.

5. Taylor, *Reminiscences*, pp. 29–31.
6. Kirby and Harris, *Star-Spangled Radio*, pp. 178–80.

For many correspondents the months that followed were a kaleidoscope of strange vignettes. Into Normandy for NBC went W. W. Chaplin.

> Our first press camp in Normandy was a 300-year-old castle, complete with turrets, drawbridge, and a moat in which one dirty swan pushed its way through the green scum. That was in the village of Colombiers, and in an apple orchard out back of the château was the army radio truck that was our link with the world. Its call letters were JESQ or in radio language Jig Easy Sugar Queen. . . .

> To get out to Jig Easy from our castle we had to cross the moat and then feel our way at night through the orchard and a field planted thickly with heavy poles designed to wreck any incoming gliders. There was a sentry by the drawbridge and he had a reputation of being trigger-happy—shoot now and find out later.

> One night I started out, whistling my off-key version of "The Stars and Stripes Forever" to allay the sentry's jitters, when I heard his "Who is there?" I said, "Bill Chaplin of NBC, going back to the radio truck." He said, "What's the password?" I said: "Lord, I forgot to get it or somebody forgot to give it to me. What now?" He said: "Oh, go ahead. They forgot to give it to me too; I thought maybe you could fill me in." [7]

Nearby at the village of Isigny, Chaplin had his first glimpse of Charles de Gaulle. Chaplin was walking down a path made by army bulldozers through rubble that had been Isigny. People were digging for relatives and possessions. A jeep appeared, in which sat General de Gaulle, so folded that his knees touched his chin. A general and an admiral followed in other jeeps. They stopped amid the rubble, and de Gaulle unlimbered, mounted a small platform, and began a political speech. A small crowd gathered. Through the crowd came a peasant woman pushing a wheelbarrow.

> I looked into the barrow and there lay the body of a baby. The mother had found her child in the rubble and was on her way to the cemetery outside town to perform a burial. She stood briefly with her awesome cargo, looking up at the tall general. . . .

He talked on, asking the support of the villagers. The "Marseillaise" was sung and then the jeeps departed.[8]

As Allied forces pushed into any large city there was a rush to seize available transmitters and studios—if possible, intact. Through Paris

7. Brown and Bruner (eds.), *I Can Tell It Now*, pp. 82–3.
8. *Ibid.* p. 84.

streets echoing with armored vehicles and hysterical crowds Colonel David Sarnoff of the Signal Corps, with pistol on hip, dashed with a contingent to Boulevard Haussmann—to French short-wave station CTSF. In its executive office they came upon a lone man at a desk—its director, a collaborationist. A radio pioneer, he was known to Sarnoff. Now he waited, in tears and in terror. Sarnoff told him: "I am here in the name of the United States Army." Sarnoff took control and supervised the repair of damage. By the end of summer CTSF was serving the Allies as a link with the Western Hemisphere.[9]

American Forces Network, the chain of AFRS stations in Britain, was meanwhile pushing onto the Continent. It set up a station in Havre; later others in Paris, Reims, Biarritz, and elsewhere. Wire connections followed. In Paris the former residence of Emperor Napoleon III was taken over as a suitable AFN headquarters.[10]

When troops reached Luxembourg, a priceless radio asset fell into Allied hands—the most powerful station in Europe, Radio Luxembourg. Before 1940 it had aimed American-sponsored programs—including jazz and Hummert serials—at the British market. Since 1940 the Germans had used it. Retreating Germans set dynamite charges but failed to detonate them. The Luxembourg engineer had encouraged them to shoot holes in the transmitter tubes—apparently to divert them from more catastrophic sabotage. With the arrival of the Americans, he dug up from the garden a complete set of tubes he had buried there four years earlier for such a day.[11] Miraculously, Radio Luxembourg was in full operation as an American station by September 22, 1944—twelve days after the troops entered Luxembourg. The station was found to have a great collection of Guy Lombardo, Benny Goodman, Dorsey Brothers, and Glenn Miller records used by the Germans for their propaganda broadcasts to Britain. Now it became the special instrument of the psychological warfare unit of the 12th Army Group.

The psychological warfare strategists could now implement, among other plans, a "black radio" project blueprinted months earlier. Every night, from 2 to 6 A.M., the Luxembourg transmitter operated on a changed frequency—1212 kilocycles—and became a mysterious German-language station. "Hello, this is Twelve Twelve calling." Using 30,000

9. Lyons, *David Sarnoff*, pp. 259–60.
10. *The American Forces Network*, p. 2.
11. *Yank*, May 11, 1945.

watts instead of the full 120,000 watts, the station gave the impression of being an underground setup operating in the Rhine Valley, behind German lines. It was not overtly anti-Nazi but hinted that the German authorities were not infallible. It carried detailed, scrupulously accurate reports of the military situation behind German lines. It used no music or other entertainment. Only a few German voices, of correct regional quality, took part—to suggest a compact underground group. These men lived and worked in monkish isolation, so that no hint of interaction with other Radio Luxembourg programming would creep into their broadcasts. That the station was winning confidence among German listeners was soon clear: prisoners, interrogated about the situation behind German lines, began to quote "Twelve Twelve." The trust placed in "Twelve Twelve" became a fearful weapon. During the Moselle breakthrough by Allied troops, "Twelve Twelve" suddenly created chaotic confusion in western parts of Germany by flamboyant misinformation. Reporting tanks near Nuremberg and Ludwigshafen, it caused panic in those cities. This had been its task. After 127 nights on the air, "Twelve Twelve" vanished as abruptly as it had appeared.[12]

Meanwhile, using its full 120,000 watts and regular frequency, Radio Luxembourg was an avowed American voice during daytime and evening hours. It featured a daily program called *Front Post*—a title also carried on millions of leaflets showered on Germany.[13] *Front Post* was a sort of newspaper of the air, utilizing a host of propaganda devices.

During the drive through France the Allies had seized quantities of undelivered German letters, sent to and from the front. These became the basis for a daily series titled *Letters That Didn't Reach You* (*Briefe Die Sie Nicht Erreichten*), read simply by a Luxembourg girl with a warm, winning voice. Even the American staff found them deeply moving, suggesting as they did the total disruption of lives everywhere.[14]

Radio Luxembourg encouraged desertions from German armies by bringing to the microphone a procession of prisoners who said, in effect: "Hello, Ma! I'm safe—I'm a prisoner of the Americans!"

There were grimmer features. Two German soldiers in civilian clothes had been captured nearby on a spying mission. Radio Luxembourg covered the trial, then interviewed the convicted prisoners as they went for

12. *Publicity and Psychological Warfare,* pp. 197–200.
13. From August 1944 to May 1945 some 30,000,000 leaflets were dropped. *Ibid.*
14. Hanser, *Reminiscences,* p. 7.

execution to a prison courtyard. They were asked if they had had a fair trial. Yes, they said. Did they realize the penalty for what they had done was death? No, said the men, their officers had neglected to tell them that. They were then led away. The radio audience heard the click of rifle bolts, the shouted command, the volley, and the echo of rifle fire. It may have been the first on-the-air execution.[15]

Probably the most successful psychological warfare creation at Radio Luxembourg was "a sort of Central European Bob Hope"—as *Yank*, the army weekly, described him. He was Richard Hanser of New York, former city editor of the newspaper *P.M.*[16]

Hanser had studied for the ministry at Concordia Lutheran Institute of Bronxville, New York, which required every student to learn enough German to deliver a sermon. Hanser had thus achieved some fluency in German but spoke it with an unmistakable American accent. This led to his being cast as "Corporal Tom Jones," a G. I. who supposedly hailed from Green Bay, Wisconsin. The strategy behind this figure was developed by Hans Habe, a prewar Viennese editor who had fled Austria in 1939, enlisted in the French army, been captured by the Germans, escaped to the United States, and entered its army. He had already seen psychological warfare action in North Africa and Sicily. Now he devised ideas for Hanser, whose guileless, engaging manner—with its charmingly peculiar accent—soon built an enormous German audience and won a steady stream of mash notes. He was heard nightly between 8 and 8:15 as a feature of *Front Post*. Sometimes he talked about things that were seemingly irrelevant, like what he used to do in his spare time in Green Bay (Habe picked Green Bay because it sounded so American to him), but such things could suggest an extreme personal freedom, devoid of obligatory youth groups. Another Corporal Tom Jones specialty was anti-Nazi jokes he reported having heard from German prisoners. Hundreds of such jokes were in covert circulation among Germans and now became a smash-hit as a Tom Jones sign-off feature. The utterly forbidden was suddenly on the air. He relayed these stories in somewhat innocent fashion, without malice. Some represented gallows humor.

> They used to say, "No enemy aircraft over the Reich!" They still say it, but differently. Now they say, "No Reich under the enemy aircraft!"

15. *Yank*, May 11, 1945.
16. He later became an NBC television writer, co-author of *Victory At Sea* and chief writer of NBC's *Project Twenty* series.

> In the old days, it used to be that you'd go to the railway station, and the train was gone. Now you go for a train, and the station is gone.

> A man told a Gestapo agent: "I'd rather work for the Nazis than anyone else!" The pleased Gestapo agent asked: "What sort of work do you do?" "I'm a gravedigger." [17]

The reputation of "Corporal Tom Jones" spread to Green Bay—where Hanser had never been. A Green Bay newspaper asked the Associated Press to gather information about its famous son, and it sent someone to Luxembourg to see him. But Hanser's identity was kept secret.[18]

The push into Germany produced a discovery of fateful impact on radio as well as on other fields. The troops approached radio stations that were broadcasting but were found without personnel. The broadcasting was being done by a machine never seen before; the Germans called it a Magnetophon. A plastic strip, magnetically recorded, was broadcasting with a fidelity Americans had never before heard in a recording, and without surface sound. The principle of magnetic recording had long been known.[19] The wire recorder was an application of it, and a steel-tape recorder was based on the same idea. But neither of these permitted easy editing. Miraculously, the German recorder used tape that could be cut with scissors and spliced with adhesive plastic tape, all without affecting the recorded material. Crates of seized tape recorders were sent to Washington for evaluation by the Signal Corps, but privately "liberated" samples also reached the United States. The complex disk-editing processes used at AFRS were suddenly seen as obsolete. Spurred by "liberated" equipment, American imitations took shape. Before long American tape recorders began to appear—and to revolutionize radio production and programming, with repercussions in the phonograph, film, television, and numerous other fields.

There were other discoveries. In April 1945 Edward R. Murrow, broadcasting over CBS from Germany, told of things that had been only an ugly and unbelievable rumor.

MURROW: Permit me to tell you what you would have seen, and heard, had you been with me on Thursday. It will not be pleasant listening. . . . I

17. *Front Post,* December 11, 1944; April 6, 15, 1945.
18. Hanser, *Reminiscences,* pp. 7–12.
19. It apparently stems from the work of the Danish Valdemar Poulsen, who recorded speech magnetically in 1898 during telephone experimentation. He called his invention the Telegraphone.

propose to tell you of Buchenwald. It is on a small hill about four miles outside Weimar, and it was one of the largest concentration camps in Germany. . . .

And now, let me tell you this in the first person. . . . There surged around me an evil-smelling horde. Men and boys reached out to touch me; they were in rags and the remnants of uniform. Death had already marked many of them, but they were smiling with their eyes. . . .

As we walked out into the courtyard, a man fell dead. Two others—they must have been over sixty—were crawling toward the latrine. I saw it but will not describe it. . . .

He saw a former acquaintance—Peter Zenkl, onetime mayor of Prague— but could not recognize him. Men kept coming to speak to him and touch him—professors from Poland, doctors from Vienna, men from all over Europe. He also went to a sort of garage.

There were two rows of bodies stacked up like cordwood. They were thin and very white. Some of the bodies were terribly bruised, though there seemed to be little flesh to bruise . . . I tried to count them as best I could and arrived at the conclusion that all that was mortal of more than five hundred men and boys lay there in two neat piles. . . .[20]

That same month Richard C. Hottelet told over CBS of one more moment in the great eastward lunge.

HOTTELET: The American and Russian armies have met! We made contact at 1:32 Wednesday afternoon on the bank of the Elbe River northwest of Dresden. There were no brass bands, no sign of the titanic strength of both these armies. The Americans who met the Red Army were a couple of dust-covered young lieutenants and a handful of enlisted men in their jeeps on reconnaissance. . . .

General Omar Bradley, knowing the Russians were near, had held his men back for more than a week. The Russian commander had similarly held his men back. Then American patrols probed ahead and spotted the Russians.

That's just the way it was . . . just some men meeting, shaking hands, glad to see each other.[21]

The massive eastward drive that had begun in June 1944 was nearing its end. American listeners had watched it through the eyes of radio newsmen. For months it had dominated their lives—but not entirely.

20. CBS, April 15, 1945; Bliss (ed.), *In Search of Light*, pp. 91–4; Murrow, *A Reporter Remembers* (LP Album), side 4.
21. CBS, April 27, 1945; Commager (ed.), *The Pocket History of the Second World War*, pp. 549–50.

THE CHAMP

June 1944 had also launched a presidential campaign. Like other campaigns it produced radio innovations.

Late that month the Republicans chose Thomas E. Dewey and John W.
Bricker to head their slate. In July the Democrats nominated Roosevelt for
a fourth term; the chief tension was over the vice presidential nomination.
Harry S. Truman, Roosevelt's last-minute choice, proved an acceptable
compromise between party factions.

The Republican platform, echoing its 1940 ancestor, came out for a
"free" radio. *Broadcasting* chided the Democrats with ignoring this issue.
Stephen Early, presidential secretary, said they had by no means ignored
it. He pointed out that the Democratic platform said: "We reassert our
faith in competitive enterprise free from control by monopolies, cartels, or
any arbitrary private or public authority." [1]

Wendell Willkie, the 1940 standard bearer, by now world famous for his
One World, died suddenly on October 8. He had stood almost wholly
outside the campaign, repudiated by his own party. Its conservatives were
in control.

Roosevelt once again held back in his campaign. He planned to confine
his main efforts to the final two weeks, and once more this worried his
advisers. Widespread confidence in his victory held a danger. In their view
the balance of power was held by independent voters—perhaps ten million in number—who might or might not go to the polls. The problem was
to activate them. Assumptions about the outcome might keep them at
home.

The early Dewey strategy seemed designed to keep them at home. He
said little to get anyone aroused. He seldom criticized war policies. He did
not attack domestic reforms. He gave the impression that a Dewey administration would carry on with little change of direction but more efficiency
and integrity. Radiating clean, youthful vigor, he pictured the Roosevelt
administration as tired and old.

Here he had facts on his side. At an appearance at the Brereton Navy
Yard in Seattle, Roosevelt had seemed in extreme discomfort; photographs
showed it. The reason was that he was wearing his steel leg braces—which
he wore only for stand-up speeches—for the first time in many weeks.
Such episodes spurred rumors of ill health.

1. *Broadcasting,* October 16, 1944.

On the other hand, those around him found a Roosevelt full of buoy-ancy. Robert Sherwood, returning from Europe, found the President thin-ner but in fine humor. Sherwood and others hoped for a more active campaign.

While most of Dewey's utterances were unexceptionable, the campaign produced undercurrents of scandalous rumor and innuendo, which in-volved virtually every member of the large Roosevelt family. Along with a few Hearst columnists, radio stations seemed to contribute to this. It was first noted in 1944 that stations in Los Angeles, Detroit, and Cleveland regularly followed or preceded items about the Roosevelt family with items about scandal, corruption, or communism. Some felt this was a de-liberate policy. Roosevelt told Hopkins he considered the campaign the meanest in his experience. Some advisers felt he should take note of the scandal-mongering, and drafted possible statements. But in the end Roo-sevelt handled it in his own way. In a broadcast from a Teamsters Union convention, he said:

> These Republican leaders have not been content with attacks on me, or my wife, or on my sons. No, not content with that they now in-clude my little dog Fala. Well, of course, I don't resent attacks, and my family don't resent attacks, but Fala *does* resent them. You know —you know, Fala is Scotch, and being a Scottie, as soon as he learned that the Republican fiction writers in Congress and out had concocted a story that I had left him behind on the Aleutian islands and had sent a destroyer back to find him—at a cost to the tax-payers of two or three, or eight or twenty million dollars—his Scotch soul was furi-ous. He has not been the same dog since.

Thus Roosevelt, to uproarious laughter, belittled and dismissed the rumor-mongers.

The health matter was likewise handled in his own way. When he came to New York on October 20 for a major foreign-policy broadcast, the weather was vile. There was a cold, slashing rain. Plans called for an open-car motorcade through the city; Roosevelt decided to go ahead with it. He would let millions see him vigorous and laughing. It became a bizarre news event reported throughout the day by radio bulletins. Speech-writer Robert Sherwood, who followed the President's incredible ordeal via radio, found him afterward in a state of "high exhilaration," grateful to the weather for giving him a chance to score a political coup.[2]

2. Sherwood, *Roosevelt and Hopkins*, v. 2, pp. 455–60.

The dangers of apathy were tackled in a different way and resulted in a most unusual campaign broadcast.

Late that summer Paul Porter, chairman of the Democratic National Committee, got in touch with Norman Corwin to ask him to produce an election-eve program over all four networks. Corwin was astonished and protested that he was "not a politician." What was the program supposed to accomplish?

Paul Porter replied with a six-page single-spaced memorandum dated September 15, marked "personal and confidential." The purpose of the program would be to create the "sense of urgency" that would get voters to the polls. Porter wanted the emphasis not on war needs but on postwar vistas—on the need for pressing forward with reforms interrupted by war.

Corwin wrote a two-page outline. He was promised that if the President approved it, he would have a free hand. The President's only reaction, as reported to Corwin, was: "My God, can he do all this on one show?" The President approved and Corwin was given a go-ahead. He received a leave from CBS, where he was just finishing a series entitled *Columbia Presents Corwin.*

A curious problem faced him. He was a dramatist. Network policy at CBS and NBC still barred "dramatization" of political messages. But what was dramatization? Corwin would make it difficult for the networks to decide.

He proposed a program in which scores of people would take part. Each would speak as himself. It would begin with very short statements by: a soldier and a sailor returning from action; a TVA farmer; several union members; a World War I veteran who had sold apples in the Depression; a housewife; an industrialist; a small businessman; a prominent Republican for Roosevelt; an old man who had voted in fourteen elections; a young girl about to vote in her first election—who would introduce the President.

But these statements, short as they would be, would later be followed by a music-backed sequence in which the statements would be even shorter. A long succession of well-known people would come to the microphone for messages of not more than eight or ten words. This would be backed by a musical "train" motif—an orchestral effect accompanied by a chorus speaking and singing in locomotive rhythm. This would be the "Roosevelt Special" and it would have East Coast and West Coast sections.

The climactic sequence brought moments like this:

CHORUS: *All aboard for tomorrow!*
LUCILLE BALL: This is Lucille Ball. I'm on this train.
CHORUS: *Vote!*
TALLULAH: This is Tallulah Bankhead. So am I.
CHORUS: *Vote!*
JOAN BENNETT: Joan Bennett—for the champ.
CHORUS: *Vote!*
IRVING BERLIN: Irving Berlin—
MRS. BERLIN: And Mrs. Berlin.
CHORUS: *For Roosevelt!*

The cataract of names went on and on, with surprises such as:

JOHN DEWEY: Dewey—John, not Tom. Philosopher.

The program created an extraordinary bandwagon effect.

The Republicans had bought a period coast-to-coast immediately following the Democratic finale. The Democrats worried that their galaxy of names would build an audience for the Republican last word, but this problem was solved. The Democratic program ended several minutes early, and the time was filled with dreary organ music, which suggested to many people that it was time to go to bed. Among politicians this was thought to have been a brilliant Machiavellian ruse by the Democrats, but it was really something else. The truth was that a leading comedian, scheduled to perform a satiric musical number on the Corwin broadcast, had withdrawn at the last moment under sponsor pressure, leaving a gap. A Republican sponsor had caused the organ music.

Paul Porter told Corwin that some party leaders credited the Democratic finale with "a million votes." Roosevelt wrote Corwin that he had not been prepared "for the really incredible performance which you so ably organized." [3]

The popular vote was: Roosevelt, 25,602,505; Dewey, 22,006,278. The electoral vote was 432 to 99. An audience study revealed that 38 per cent of a population sample felt their votes had been influenced by radio, whereas only 23 per cent felt they had been influenced by the press. [4]

The inauguration was one of the shortest. Roosevelt, standing in leg braces, spoke less than five minutes. Then he left for a secret and distant destination—Yalta. When he returned, and reported to Congress on his

3. Letter, November 27, 1944; Corwin, *Interview*, pp. 34–7.
4. Lazarsfeld, *The People's Choice*, pp. 127, 131.

meetings with Stalin and Churchill, he made what seems to have been his one public reference to leg braces. In the hearing of the nation, he said he hoped it would be all right for him to sit, as it made it "a lot easier for me not having to carry ten pounds of steel around in the bottom of my legs."

He looked ill, but pushed on with preparations for the United Nations charter meeting, scheduled for late April in San Francisco. But on April 12 he was dead.

The events of the following days were closely covered by radio. Tributes from all parts of the world were broadcast. As Roosevelt's body was brought back to Washington, crowds stood bareheaded along the track.

In the series of programs recently completed at CBS, Norman Corwin had presented a sort of cantata about the death of Lincoln. It was *The Lonesome Train,* by Millard Lampell with music by Earl Robinson. Burl Ives was the Ballad Singer who carried the story.

BALLAD SINGER: A lonesome train on a lonesome track,
     Seven coaches painted black . . .
     A slow train, a quiet train,
     Carrying Lincoln home again. . . .

In depicting extremes of feeling toward Lincoln, *The Lonesome Train* had suggested a parallel with Roosevelt. War was another parallel.

BALLAD SINGER: The slaves were free, the war was won,
     But the fight for freedom was just begun . . .
     Freedom's a thing that has no ending,
     It needs to be cared for, it needs defending. . . .[5]

The program had already become a Decca Records album. Mrs. Roosevelt was familiar with it, and thought of it as she rode toward Washington in the car behind that which carried the President's body.

I lay in my berth all night with the window shade up . . . watching the faces of the people at stations, and even at the crossroads, who came to pay their last tribute all through the night.

The only recollection I clearly have is thinking about *The Lonesome Train,* the musical poem about Lincoln's death. I had always liked it so well—and now this was so much like it.[6]

5. *The Lonesome Train,* by Millard Lampell and Earl Robinson. Copyright © 1943 and 1945 by MCA Music, a division of MCA, Inc., New York, N. Y. Used by permission. All rights reserved.
6. Asbell, *When F. D. R. Died,* p. 161.

Stations throughout the country played the album during the following days.

Roosevelt had made nearly three hundred broadcasts in his lifetime. He once quipped: "I know what I'll do when I retire. I'll be one of these high-powered commentators." [7] When he died, he was working on a talk to be broadcast to nationwide Jefferson Day dinners. The unused script, found on his desk at Warm Springs, included these remarks:

> Today this nation which Jefferson helped so greatly to build is play-ing a tremendous part in the battle for the rights of man throughout the world. Today we are part of the vast Allied force—a force com-posed of flesh and blood and steel and spirit—which is today destroy-ing the makers of war, the breeders of hate, in Europe and in Asia. . . .

> But the mere conquest of our enemies is not enough. . . . Today we are faced with the pre-eminent fact that, if civilization is to survive, we must cultivate the science of human relationships—the ability of all peoples, of all kinds, to live together and work together, in the same world, at peace. Let me assure you that my hand is the steadier for the work that is to be done, that I move more firmly into the task, knowing that you—millions and millions of you—are joined with me in the resolve to make this work endure. . . .[8]

SUMMIT

From the moment of his four-network political broadcast, Norman Corwin was busy with summitry. Douglas Coulter at CBS felt that victory in Eu-rope was near; he wanted Corwin to prepare a one-hour commemorative script to be broadcast over CBS on the night of victory in Europe. By the time Corwin had completed a draft of *On a Note of Triumph*—with the fighting still raging—CBS asked him to go to San Francisco to produce a program for the birth of the United Nations. As he worked on *Word From The People*—Jan Masaryk and other world leaders were on it—he kept the script of *On a Note of Triumph* close at hand. During the meeting came news of the murder of Mussolini and the suicide of Hitler. From San Francisco Corwin rushed to Los Angeles, and telephoned to New York to summon Martin Gabel, whom he wanted as narrator. As Gabel left for California, a large cast and orchestra began rehearsals. In the midst of

7. *Broadcasting*, April 16, 1945.
8. Roosevelt, *Selected Speeches*, pp. 388–90.

rehearsals came a false armistice report. The broadcast was scheduled, then canceled. Finally on May 8—as hostilities ended—*On a Note of Triumph* went on the air.

Congratulations poured in. CBS in New York received a thousand phone calls; in Hollywood, 1600 calls. A Simon and Schuster book edition of 50,000 copies was sold in two weeks. A Columbia Records album sold out equally quickly. Carl Sandburg, in a letter to Corwin, called it "a vast announcement, a terrific interrogatory, and certainly one of the all-time great American poems." John Mason Brown, in a cover-featured story in the *Saturday Review*, found the script "with its Whitmanesque cadences . . . a newsreel in words of war emotions, battle reasons, and peace hopes . . . an important and stirring statement." He admired "the driving conciseness of his phrases, and the happy mixture of the colloquial and the eloquent." There were dissenters; Bernard De Voto in *Harper's Magazine* found it pretentious and compared it with Pare Lorentz's film *The River*, which he likewise despised. But praise predominated. Corwin had caught the mood of many people.

At times the script was flat in statement:

NARRATOR: Peace is never granted outright: it is lent and leased.

In reviewing history it could be mordant:

> Next week, umbrella dance at Munich—Salome bearing the head of John, the Czech.

It could draw on colloquial maxim—like a phrase in cockney:

> The duration's goin' to be a lot longer than the war, guv'nor.

In a roundup of voices it could turn brusquely political:

FRENCHMAN: We've learned that nations that don't know what they want will get what they don't want.
(*Music: stroke*)
NEW YORKER: We've learned that a newspaper with a big circulation right at home can lie with a straight face seven days a week and be as filthy and fascist as a handout in Berlin.
(*Music: stroke*)
SENATOR: We've learned that those most concerned with saving the world from communism usually turn up making it safe for fascism.
(*Music: stroke*)
VERMONTER: We've learned that freedom . . . must be exercised, like a healthy muscle.

At the end it could stick its neck out with risky eloquence—that brought many to tears. Martin Gabel gave it a quality that was both Old Testament and Broadway:

NARRATOR: Lord God of fresh bread and tranquil mornings . . .
Deliver notice to the fallen young men
That tokens of orange juice and whole egg appear now before the
hungry children;
That night again falls cooling on the earth as quietly as when it leaves
your hand . . .

Lord God of the topcoat and the living wage . . .
Do bring sweet influences to bear upon the assembly line:
Accept the smoke of the milltown among the accredited clouds of the
sky
Fend from the wind with a house and a hedge, him whom you made
in your image . . .

Lord God of test-tube and blueprint . . .
Appear now among the parliament of conquerors and give instruction
to their schemes:
Measure out new liberties so none shall suffer for his father's color or
the credo of his choice:
Post proofs that brotherhood is not so wild a dream as those who profit
by postponing it pretend. . . .[1]

A few months later Corwin was again called on to commemorate a moment. Scarcely anyone expected World War II to end as quickly as it did when atom bombs fell on Hiroshima and Nagasaki. The script entitled *14 August* was broadcast within hours of the Japanese surrender. It was a moment filled with horror as well as relief, and called for a statement akin to prayer. In expanded form—as *God and Uranium*—it was repeated the following Sunday, a day set aside by President Harry S. Truman as a day of prayer. On both occasions the main voice was that of Orson Welles, who had narrated *The Fall of the City* eight years earlier.

The renascence that had come to radio in those years had touched a high-water mark. It had been a remarkable movement. Corwin had become one of its symbols. He had opened and closed a war, dedicated a parliament of nations, and provided an ode to lay Presidents to rest. In introducing a Corwin anthology, Carl Van Doren called him radio's

1. Corwin, *On a Note of Triumph;* see also Corwin, *Untitled and Other Radio Dramas*, pp. 439–545. Eric Sevareid adopted the phrase "not so wild a dream" as the title of his memoirs.

Christopher Marlowe.[2] The phrase suggested that Van Doren foresaw a golden age of radio in the postwar years.

But there were already signs that the renascence, though not finished, was reaching a stage of decline. Much of its most spectacular flowering had been in unsold time. That frontier desert was vanishing rapidly. Before the war approximately one-third of network time had been commercially sponsored; by the end of the war, it was two-thirds. The motivation of this programming was also changing. Almost all network sponsors were beginning to think about postwar times when they—and their competitors —would have consumer goods for sale. Throughout network schedules there was a jockeying for high ratings. The idea that cultural and public-affairs programs could be sponsored was in rapid decline. Such programs were being edged into fringe network periods—and dropped. At the local level they were falling aside for recorded programs. Throughout 1944–45, as executives by the score headed back from Washington, the competitive fever mounted.

There was another note, chilling to some who heard it. In the final days of the war in Europe, five leaders of wartime radio drama were taken on a War Department European junket. They were William N. Robson of *Open Letter on Race Hatred,* who was currently producing and directing *The Man Behind the Gun;* Robert Lewis Shayon, who was directing the war series *The Commandos;* Earle McGill, a frequent *Columbia Workshop* director; Anton Leader of *Words At War;* and Frank Telford, a Young & Rubicam director. In their war productions they had relied on their imaginations but now received a front-line tour, complete with high-echelon briefings. During the tour they met with other radio figures like Edward R. Murrow, Davidson Taylor, Brewster Morgan, Charles Collingwood. All were exhilarated by wartime achievements of broadcasting. "We thought," Shayon recalls, "that what we had been allowed to do in war would inevitably and without question be carried over into the postwar period." They saw endless social problems to be illuminated—via radio, and perhaps via television. But the tour also produced talk they had not expected. They heard it first from military leaders. Once the Germans and Japanese were beaten, they were told, it would be necessary to deal with the Russians.[3] They heard it in Italy from religious leaders. There

2. Preface, Corwin, *Thirteen by Corwin,* p. vii.
3. Shayon, *Reminiscences,* pp. 10–22.

was no chance, they were told, of a *modus vivendi* with atheistic communism. This was identified as the next problem.

Far away in Chungking, Eric Sevareid had heard similar talk. He had tried to tell America—but wartime censors had not permitted it—that arms sent to Chiang Kai-shek were not used against the Japanese but held for another struggle. He had found Chiang Kai-shek—and some Americans who supported him—wholly intent on a coming crusade against communists.[4] Before the war had even ended, another had begun in the minds of many men.

Thus peace brought a confusion of imminent changes—from armaments to consumer goods—live to recorded programming—radio to television —emergency concerns to profit margins—hot to cold war—seller's market to buyer's market—scarcity to luxury—idealism to cynicism. The winds of change—sometimes merging, sometimes conflicting—whistled around the broadcaster. It was called peace, but was more like the eye of a hurricane.

4. Sevareid, *Not So Wild a Dream,* pp. 323–4.

4 / PEACE

We are a nation of word killers: *hero,*
   veteran, tragedy—
Watch the great words go down.
EDNA ST. VINCENT MILLAY

The back-to-business tide, already well started, became a mounting force
as the fighting ended. Within days after the Japanese surrender, President
Truman approved the manufacture of radio receivers for home use, and
RCA was retooling for television set manufacture.

NBC was featuring "welcome home" auditions. The War Department
was broadcasting the series *Assignment Home,* written by young Sergeant
Arthur Laurents, dealing with the adjustment problems of returning soldiers.[1]

Broadcasters had little trouble adjusting. Because of war work and war
rationing, many people had money to spend—waiting in war bonds, war
stamps, savings accounts. Sponsors, agencies, networks, and stations expected to help activate it. Quite aside from this, many broadcasters were
already making profits they had not previously known. In Depression days
the networks and large stations had been profitable. Now even small stations were sharing in the boom. Only a handful of small stations—NBC
president Niles Trammell called them "coffee pots"—had failed to make a
profit in 1944.

In local programming the new prosperity involved a rising phenomenon
—the DJ. These initials no longer suggested "Department of Justice" but
"disk-jockey."

The origin of this figure is not clear. In a sense he had begun with the

1. He later wrote *Home of the Brave, Anna Lucasta, West Side Story,* and many
other plays.
216

Christmas Eve broadcast by Reginald Fessenden in 1906.[2] A shift in focus from the records to their introducer had taken place during the 1930's. But at that time programs based on phonograph records had involved many hazards.

One stemmed from FCC rules. Recordings had to be identified as such —so frequently as to stigmatize them. In 1940 the FCC eased this problem by changing its requirements: announcement every half hour became sufficient, and wording would be optional.

Another hazard had been a legal one. For many years Bing Crosby, Fred Waring and other performers had placed on their phonograph records the warning: "NOT LICENSED FOR RADIO BROADCAST." They had backed this warning with lawsuits. The purpose was to prevent phonograph records from undermining their network contracts, which usually called for exclusive services. But in 1940 the litigation came to a debacle in a suit involving Paul Whiteman records. The court ruled that a broadcaster, having purchased a phonograph record, could broadcast it without further obligation, regardless of the wishes of artists or manufacturers. The warning on the label was held to have no legal significance. The U. S. Supreme Court declined to review the case.[3] The ruling put the disk-jockey for the first time on a secure legal footing.

Meanwhile spectacular demonstrations of his potentialities were available. By 1941 Martin Block's *Make Believe Ballroom*—the WNEW series launched as a filler during the Lindbergh kidnap trial—was reported to be getting 12,000 letters per month, and it had twenty-three sponsors and a waiting list. One month as participating sponsor on *Make Believe Ballroom* was said to have won for Purity Bakers a sales increase of 432,000 doughnuts per week.[4] WNEW, which had been founded by advertising executive Milton H. Biow, became the first station to operate on a twenty-four-hour-a-day basis when it installed *Milkman's Matinee,* an all-night disk-jockey show presided over by Stan Shaw, and later by Art Ford. It became another WNEW bonanza. Stations and sponsors throughout the country took note of all this. Phonograph companies were meanwhile doing an about-face in attitude. Programs like *Make Believe Ballroom* and

2. See *A Tower in Babel,* p. 20.

3. *RCA* v. *Whiteman* et al., 114 Fed. (2nd) 86; 311 U. S. 712 (1940). The court recognized that the performing artist had a common-law copyright in his rendition but this "ended with the sale of records." Copyright law provided no statutory copyright for phonograph records.

4. *Broadcasting,* February 3, 1941.

Milkman's Matinee seemed to create phonograph record hits as well as doughnut successes. Disk-jockeys began to be wooed and cultivated, and became the chief promotion channel for the reviving phonograph record industry.

For local programmers the trend was delightful. Martin Block, who had come to WNEW in mid-Depression "with holes in his shoes," [5] was becoming wealthy, but the station was also reaping a rich harvest. Such programming seemed to require a minimum investment. The "talent" consisted of a disk-jockey on a commission basis. In quest of commissions he himself tended to spearhead new-business efforts. He also helped "merchandise" his program with appearances at department stores and supermarkets. He might be an "entertainer" but was also a supersalesman; this became his main economic role.

During the war the outlook for disk-jockeys was temporarily clouded by industry disputes with ASCAP and the American Federation of Musicians. In 1941 ASCAP music was temporarily off the air as broadcasters successfully defied ASCAP's demands for higher royalties and relied on BMI and public domain music. (During this period listeners were driven almost frantic by endless repetitions of Stephen Foster's "Jeannie With the Light Brown Hair.") In 1942 the American Federation of Musicians decided— by unanimous vote at its convention—to halt the making of recordings. Its president James C. Petrillo said that five hundred radio stations were no longer employing any musicians—the disk-jockey was one of the reasons— and that jukeboxes and sound films had likewise thrown countless musicians "on the human scrapheap." [6] His peace terms, accepted by Decca in 1943 and by RCA-Victor and Columbia in 1944, called for a welfare fund to which employers of musicians would make payments—a not unreasonable approach to a serious problem, although generally pictured by the broadcasting trade press as an act of gangsterism. As this dispute came to an end, and as vinylite and shellac once more became available for civilian use, the stage was finally set for the golden age of the disk-jockey. An upsurge of transcribed programs also became possible.[7]

Many a radio station entered the postwar era with a new look. It no longer resembled a theatrical stock company. Its economic base was the

5. Biow, *Butting In*, p. 135.
6. White, *The American Radio*, p. 50.
7. A "transcribed program" or "transcription" was merely a recorded program, generally in the form of a 16-inch disk, recorded at 33⅓ revolutions per minute. The terms had been introduced to avoid the stigma attached to recorded programs.

disk-jockey. It might need a writer for announcements or promotion mate-rial. Commercials tended to be taken care of ad lib by the disk-jockeys themselves with the help of material provided by the sponsors. The station scarcely needed a studio. News programs called for an AP or UP or INS news ticker. All of these now provided material written especially for radio. A "rip-and-read" operation could provide a news service. Such news programs were replacing commentators at scores of stations. Engineers and salesmen were the main need. To accountants the trend was a delight. Low overhead, few headaches. Sponsors waited in line. It was a matter of how many sponsors could be squeezed in. Specialized disk-jockeys ap-peared on the scene—rock-and-roll, easy-listening, and hillbilly specialists. These could deliver specific portions of the market.

The NAB code of 1939, proclaiming a new day, had given the impres-sion of doing something about the length and frequency of commercials. But it had included the proviso:

> The above limitations do not apply to participation programs, an-nouncement programs, "musical clocks," shoppers' guides and local programs falling within these general classifications.[8]

This apparently meant that disk-jockeys with twenty-three sponsors were safely within the NAB code and that the new era had a green light.

Among those who headed back from war duties in 1944 was J. Harold Ryan, who had been radio chief of the Office of Censorship. He became the new president of the NAB. In 1945 American broadcasting was cele-brating its twenty-fifth anniversary, and Ryan in his new role felt a key-note utterance was needed. Catching the warm glow of the hour, he told broadcasters:

> American radio is the product of American business! It is just as much that kind of product as the vacuum cleaner, the washing machine, the automobile and the airplane. . . . If the legend still persists that a radio station is some kind of art center, a technical museum, or a little piece of Hollywood transplanted strangely to your home town, then the first official act of the second quarter century should be to list it along with the local dairies, laundries, banks, restaurants, and filling stations.[9]

To many, NAB president Ryan was the hero of the day.

8. *Radio Annual* (1940), pp. 156–8.
9. Quoted, Siepmann, *Radio's Second Chance*, pp. 186–7.

THE GROUPS

J. Harold Ryan represented a rising force in the radio industry. With his brother-in-law, George Storer, he ran a number of stations generally known as "the Storer stations." Ryan had for years been their general manager. The stations were not wire-connected; they were operated separately. As station operation became more lucrative, the Storer stations became enormously prosperous. But station operation was not the sole or main interest of the Storer partners. They were constantly selling and buying stations, strengthening their line-up. Profits from the sale of stations were taxed at the low capital-gains rate, whereas profits from station operation were taxed at a higher rate. The buying and selling of stations could therefore be a quicker path to riches. The Storer group seemed to think of its stations as "properties" to be nursed for profitable sale.[1]

It was no accident that Ryan linked radio stations with filling stations. The Storer company had begun as a group of filling stations and gradually transferred its investment to radio. It also had other interests, including at various times the Standard Tube Company, which made welded tubing; the Miami Beach Publishing Company; the Empire Coil Company; and eventually, Northeast Airlines. The Storer stations were considered a power in the radio industry, but were not renowned for programming. Their program philosophy seems to have been summed up by Ryan in his 1945 keynote speech.

The Storer stations and similar station groups confronted the FCC with several issues. Was it in the public interest for stations to be owned by a conglomerate corporation with interests in numerous other fields? Was a station likely to be a pawn in larger business operations? Did not an operation of this sort inevitably involve absentee ownership? Was this in the public interest? Would it be preferable to favor license applicants with a personal interest in the community?

It seemed to some members of the FCC that the commission by quick

1. Radio stations acquired and later sold by the Storer group (with time periods held) have included WGHP, later renamed WXYZ, Detroit (1929–30); CKLW, Windsor (1930–31); WWVA, Wheeling (1931–62); WMMN, Fairmont (1935–53); WBLY, renamed WLOK, Lima (1938–51); WALR, renamed WHIZ, Zanesville (1939–47); WAGA, Atlanta (1940–59); WSAI, Cincinnati (1951–53); KABC, renamed KGBS, San Antonio (1953–54). After station ownership quotas were set by the FCC, the group usually held the permitted quota, selling and buying to improve its holdings. It sold WWVA to buy WHN, New York. Storer, *The Storer Story*, pp. 1–11; Ryan, *Reminiscences*, pp. 1–7.

approvals of station sales had lost control and failed in its responsibilities. Most stations on the air at the end of World War II had obtained their licenses via purchase—*not* as a result of the weighing of competing applicants by the FCC. Trafficking in licenses was on the increase, with prices rising. Each new buyer, with a larger investment to recoup, seemed all the more inclined to pursue an aggressively commercial policy. Among the most commercial were the multiple-station owners.

Under the chairmanship of James Fly the FCC had taken the step of limiting a licensee to six AM stations, with not more than one in any one community. This had forced some multiple-station owners—including Storer—to sell or exchange stations. But most of the multiple-station issues had not been faced.

Late in 1944 James Fly retired to private law practice and was succeeded as FCC chairman by Paul Porter, formerly of the Democratic National Committee. He inherited the unsolved problems.

The multiple-station owners or "group owners" had risen to power with little public notice. Their rise had contrasted sharply with that of the networks, which were always in the public spotlight. FCC members could hardly help having some knowledge of what the national networks were broadcasting: evidence was available on their Washington outlets. Most of the group owners had no Washington outlets; the FCC had little direct knowledge of what some of them were up to. This helps explain the rise of power aggregates like the Storer stations, and of other groups representing more appalling problems.

The group known as "the Richards stations" was not as numerous as the Storer stations, but more powerful. It consisted of three 50,000-watt stations, each in a major metropolis: WJR, Detroit, which Richards had purchased in 1926; WGAR, Cleveland, acquired in 1930; and KMPC, Hollywood, acquired in 1937. Their potential influence was enormous.

Like Storer, Richards had other business interests. He had started as an automobile dealer. He became owner of the Detroit Lions football team.

After acquiring KMPC he spent much time at a Beverly Hills home and a Palm Springs ranch. Various Hollywood figures held shares in KMPC, "The Station of the Stars."

It was at WJR, "The Good Will Station," in Detroit, that Father Coughlin had his radio start. While Coughlin was accused of anti-Semitic overtones, George Richards, the WJR licensee, was overtly anti-Semitic. He was obsessed with a personal crusade to get "the Jews" out of government.

He repeatedly told his news staffs that Jews were communists and communists were Jews; the patriotic mission of the Richards stations, expressed in innumerable memoranda as well as staff meetings, was to drive them out of positions of influence. He sometimes used "Arab" as a euphemism for Jew. The Arabs were taking over Washington.

While Richards's extremist views were a subject of discussion for some time, the extent to which they shaped news policies at three powerful stations was only gradually made clear and documented.[2]

His main target for many years was President Roosevelt, a "Jew-lover" who was out to communize the nation. "We have got to get rid of that bastard in the White House." Richards gave his news staffs orders to carry no items favorable to Roosevelt. Several newsmen testified to orders by Richards to "tie in" items about Roosevelt with items about communists or criminals, so that they would seem related. After the death of Roosevelt the policies remained in effect for all members of his family. Concerning Mrs. Roosevelt he told staff members to "give her hell" whenever possible—"the old bitch." When she had an automobile accident in 1946, he called Robert Horn at KMPC to ask if he couldn't report the news in a way that would give the impression she was drunk. Horn felt this would be difficult.

Richards often ordered the use of specific expletives. Henry Wallace was to be called "pig boy" or "tumbleweed." Harry Truman was to be "pipsqueak." When Democratic party publicist Charles Michelson died, Richards instructed that the obituary should refer to him as "the smear artist of the Roosevelt regime." News writers sometimes found ways of carrying out such instructions while softening the effect. On this occasion KMPC news director Clete Roberts wrote: "Michelson, considered by some as the smear artist of the Roosevelt regime, died today at the age of 78." Richards insisted on obedience and made constant checks. Writers suspected of disloyalty to him were promptly fired.

When David Lilienthal, former TVA director, was nominated for the Atomic Energy Commission, Richards went to great lengths to head off his confirmation. "He is a Jew and a communist," he told the KMPC staff. "We don't want him in the government." He ordered Lilienthal's foreign

2. The following details are based on FCC investigations of 1948–51, Docket Nos. 9405 (WGAR), 9468 (KMPC), 9469 (WJR). The thousands of pages of testimony and hundreds of exhibits dealt mainly with the years 1943–47. See also *Proposed Findings of Fact and Conclusions of Law of General Counsel of the Federal Communications Commission*, pp. 1–340.

birth to be emphasized. He ordered a staff writer to write an anti-Lilien-thal speech and arranged for actor Adolphe Menjou to broadcast it, urging listeners to write letters opposing confirmation. He wrote to Clete Roberts:

> We should learn to beat the New Dealers with their attacks on busi-ness and other issues. . . . Beat them to the punch—accuse them of everything under the sun. Put them on the defensive instead of allow-ing them to be on the offensive. . . . Keep fighting, Clete. Our coun-try is worth it.[3]

Other favorite targets were Melvyn Douglas—"We have got to get these kike actors out of Hollywood"—and his wife Helen Gahagan Douglas, who was constantly attacked over KMPC during her successful 1946 cam-paign to represent the district in Congress.

In 1944 and again in 1948, Richards made determined attempts to influ-ence the presidential election. For this purpose he started in 1944 the WJR series *Victory F. O. B.,* which featured on each program—after a drama-tized introduction—a businessman discussing "postwar problems." Richards wrote to Leo Fitzpatrick, WJR manager, that this was the station's chance do its part in the election. "This New Deal must be ousted or we all can call it a day. . . . Get *F. O. B.* going great guns." CBS, of which WJR was an affiliate, agreed to carry the series. When Leo Fitzpatrick pointed out some weeks later that only Republicans had been used and that this might cause trouble with the FCC—presumably because of the Mayflower doc-trine—Richards wrote: "The FCC can't ruin us with Dewey in." He wrote to Paro Thomas, WJR treasurer: "If Fitz won't help I want to know it as soon as possible." When CBS demurred over the lack of balance on *Victory F. O. B.,* Richards waved the objections aside, replying that "Americanism is not controversial." He wrote WJR that he was willing to have some labor leaders on the series—the right ones—but "CIO & Com-munists & Arabs, never." The NAB code was apparently never mentioned in these discussions.

David Anderson, a journalist who had served as foreign correspondent for the New York *Times* and subsequently as a radio news writer for sev-eral stations including KMPC, later said:

> I have worked in newsrooms in many parts of the world . . . and I have worked under both political and military censorship . . . I have never in all my radio experience encountered an atmosphere as de-

3. *Ibid.* FCC Exhibit 246.

pressing, as morally depressing, as professionally depressing, as was the newsroom at KMPC.

Some awareness of the Richards policies must have reached FCC commissioners, though not perhaps in a form that could serve in a legal record. An *Atlantic Monthly* article by Dixon Wecter in June 1945 carried a veiled reference to Richards, mentioning his anti-Semitism and the information that he had fired seven news editors in three years. But meanwhile Richards was considered a radio tycoon. His financial standing was unassailable. His WJR was "one of the three or four most prosperous stations in the United States." [4] Eddie Rickenbacker, president of Eastern Air Lines, was his friend and had been best man at his wedding. Another friend was baseball hero Ty Cobb; whenever he came to Detroit, a Richards limousine was at his disposal. Richards was said to be an admirer—even a friend —of J. Edgar Hoover, and to send him long letters about the communist conspiracy.

The Du Pont company gave Richards its 1945 public service award for *Victory F. O. B.* and other series.[5]

The Richards licenses were thus regularly renewed.[6] Richards, chagrined over the Republican defeat of 1944, began to make plans for 1948. He soon knew what he wanted. This time he was sure he would succeed. He usually explained his determination in patriotic terms. But sometimes it was simply: "This is my station and I'll do what I want with it."

There were other multiple-station owners with a similarly independent attitude. One was Powel Crosley, Jr. In 1945 Crosley bought WINS, New York, for $1,700,000 from another group, the Hearst stations. The FCC was planning hearings on this transfer when Powel Crosley suddenly confronted it with a new request.

In one spectacular package, Crosley presented to the FCC all the issues of multiple-station ownership and license-trafficking. If the FCC wished to face these issues, its chance had come.

4. Landry, *This Fascinating Radio Business*, p. 100.
5. *Broadcasting*, March 12, 1945.
6. In 1944 the FCC began issuing licenses for three-year periods, the maximum permitted by the Communications Act of 1934.

A LOW-COST AUTOMOBILE

From his start with patriotic radiator caps Crosley had gone on to radios, refrigerators, and other products, promoted both nationally and internationally through his radio stations, but his heart was still in automobiles. Before World War II he had planned a low-priced car and now wanted to take the plunge. For capital needs and to free himself from distractions, he now decided to put his other properties—except the Cincinnati Reds—on the block.

The Aviation Corporation—AVCO—was interested. Already involved in the making of airplane engines, ships, boilers, heaters, kitchen sinks, bombers, jeep bodies, it saw Crosley radios and refrigerators as logical additions. When Crosley said that his radio stations must "for tax reasons" be included in the package, AVCO was willing. Besides its manufacturing interests it already operated airlines, oil fields, a stock brokerage firm, and a public utility.

AVCO agreed to a $22,000,000 price for the Crosley package. Twenty-three radio licenses—AM, FM, facsimile, short-wave—were involved. The FCC was asked to approve their transfer. It scheduled hearings for July 10, 1945. The sale was to take effect by mid-August.

Some commissioners favored prompt approval. Concerning themselves chiefly with financial qualifications and technical standards, they saw no possible objection to AVCO.

However, when AVCO officials testified at the hearing, Commissioner Clifford J. Durr asked questions. These brought out clearly that AVCO had originally had no thought of buying the stations and only did so to get the "package." This seemed to show the stations in the role of pawns. To be sure, AVCO chairman Victor Emanuel said the directors had become "tremendously interested and enthused," but he admitted he knew very little about broadcasting and "nothing at all" about international broadcasting. He had not read the Communications Act. He admitted he knew virtually nothing about WLW programming. No AVCO director lived in the WLW listening area. Asked what would be the best time for a sustaining program, Emanuel thought "late at night . . . around midnight." He felt a station could give satisfactory service if 100 per cent sponsored. He had no idea what part of the $22,000,000 price was for factories and what part for broadcasting stations. He felt he could easily justify AVCO's sudden interest in broadcasting. Many of AVCO's businesses were, he said, "romance" businesses. Broadcasting seemed to him also a "romance" business.[1]

Three of the commissioners—Durr, Walker, and Wakefield—opposed the transfer. One reason was the nature of AVCO—a holding company. Durr and Walker stated:

> This is a type of corporate structure which has long been a matter of concern to the people of this country and to Congress itself because of its effectiveness as a device by which small groups of individuals, through the use of other people's money, are enabled to dominate large segments of our national economy. . . . If to this concentration of economic power there is added the tremendous power of influencing public opinion which goes with the operation of major broadcasting facilities, domestic and international, the result is the creation of a repository of power able to challenge the sovereignty of government itself.

They also saw the case as a flagrant example of "trafficking in licenses." On the matter of programming, and of AVCO's total ignorance of it, they remarked:

> We do feel that any reasonably prudent business man entering a new line of business should be expected to inform himself about the nature of that business before embarking on it.[2]

Among the four commissioners who wished to approve the transfer, some saw validity in these objections. But they felt that disapproval would be precedent-shattering and create chaos. Right or wrong, they wanted to be consistent. They were willing for future procedure to depart from dubious precedent, but only with advance notice of a new policy.

Thus approval of the $22,000,000 package was followed by a new rule—the "AVCO rule." [3] In any future transfer, said the FCC, there would be opportunity for others to apply to the FCC for the channel to be vacated. Regardless of bids made to the departing licensee—who theoretically had no property right in the channel—the question would be decided in the "public interest."

The announcement caused consternation among many licensees. If the FCC stuck to its AVCO rule, station sales prices would drop to a fraction

1. FCC Docket No. 6767.
2. *FCC Reports* (1945–47), pp. 3–44; Siepmann, *Radio's Second Chance*, pp. 167–83.
3. The AVCO rule was the rule *not* followed in the AVCO case, just as the Mayflower rule was the rule *not* followed in the Mayflower case. In each case dissenting commissioners, facing defeat, settled for a proclamation.

of current market prices. *Broadcasting* called it "an assault upon time-honored concepts of the rights of property owners." Its inequity, said the editorial apocalyptically, would be "visited upon this and future generations." *Broadcasting* was beginning to look on Commissioner Durr as a favorite target, replacing Fly. It invented a new term of scorn—"Durrmocracy." [4]

There would soon be new examples of Durrmocracy at work.

BLUE BOOK

The FCC had drifted into the habit of renewing batches of licenses solely on the basis of engineering reports, with no scrutiny of past programming. If engineering reports found "no violations," twenty licenses might be renewed with one rap of the gavel.

In a sense this was a heritage of the Fly regime. He had devoted the full energies of the FCC to battling for diversity of ownership. Program review had tended to disappear. The policy had seemed justified: most observers felt that programming had improved in the war years.

The view that 1945–46 had seen a catastrophic decline, particularly in local programming, was also prevalent. But the mass-renewals continued.

The procedure disturbed Commissioner Durr, and he began to refrain from voting for license renewals when he felt there was no basis for judgment. He began to ask for detailed information on stations about to be renewed.

Curiously, it was an engineering report that first directed attention to WBAL, Baltimore—one of the Hearst group of stations. An FCC engineer was troubled because a five-minute sales talk had run through the time when the station was supposed to identify itself. This was put down as a technical violation of the rule on call letters. But Durr was curious about the five-minute commercial and asked for more information about WBAL.

WBAL was a 50,000-watt station, an NBC affiliate. Once known for live classical music, it had been acquired by the Hearst group in 1935. Since that time its programming had changed. In a sample week in 1944 the hours 2–10 P.M., Monday through Friday, included not a single sustaining program. WBAL carried NBC's sponsored programs but ignored almost all its public-affairs programs, such as *University of Chicago Round Table* and *Words at War*. Many of these periods were used for recordings with

4. *Broadcasting*, June 4, 1945; January 7, 1946.

spot announcements. One forty-five-minute period included sixteen spot announcements—one every 2.8 minutes. The sample week included almost ten hours of "religious" programming, but almost all of it had been sold to religious groups at commercial rates. The station managed to jam 507 spot announcements into its station-time periods during one week.

Durr's staff, digging into the records instead of relying on Engineering Department summaries, discovered that such cases were not unique. The logs of KIEV, Glendale, California—not a network affiliate—showed that 88 per cent of its time in a sample week was devoted to phonograph records and transcribed music, interspersed with 1034 commercial spot announcements and eight public-service announcements. But the champion was KMAC, San Antonio, Texas, which broadcast 2215 commercial spot announcements during 133 hours of a sample week in 1945—an average of 16.7 spots an hour.

In renewing licenses "it is the manifest duty of the licensing authority" to consider past programming, said the National Association of Broadcasters at 1934 hearings on the Communications Act.[1] Most commissioners also held to this view, in spite of the practical difficulties of implementing it.

Chairman Paul Porter, in his first speech to the NAB in March 1945, outlined a new approach to the problem of deteriorating programming. For some years license applicants had been asked to outline their program plans. Chairman Porter suggested that it might be time to start comparing promise and performance. It seemed a mild suggestion.

By April Durr and his staff had amassed promise-and-performance data on a number of stations scheduled for renewal. The results were so startling that instead of renewing for the full three-year period, the FCC put all twenty-two stations on "temporary" licenses. Later it put many additional stations in this category.

How long could stations be kept in this state of uncertainty, and to what effect?

Chairman Porter suggested the speedy preparation of a report. He proposed that renewals be kept "temporary" while the report was being prepared. The report would describe the state of the industry and make clear the FCC's reasons for concern. It would outline future standards of public interest.

The plan called for rapid work. FCC staff member Edward Brecher,

1. *Hearings: on H. R. 8301* (April 10, 1934), p. 117.

who had taken part in the promise-and-performance research for Durr, was asked to complete a report within a month. He started late in June. At Durr's suggestion he phoned Charles Siepmann at the latter's summer home in Newfane, Vermont, to enlist his help.

Siepmann had been a lecturer on radio at Harvard, where he had done research on the social impact of broadcasting. Early in the war he had become consultant to the U. S. Office of Facts and Figures under Archibald MacLeish, had made a study of wartime propaganda, and attracted attention with a valuable booklet titled *Radio in Wartime.* He was an American citizen of British birth. During July Siepmann served as an FCC consultant for twenty-one days, assisting Brecher with the report and receiving $839.67 in salary and travel expenses.

With this help and the aid of FCC statistician Dallas Smythe, Brecher completed the report on schedule, delivered it to chairman Porter, and went to New York to recuperate. Later he phoned the FCC to see if there were messages. He found that Porter had left a message for him. "Tell Ed—I know now how Truman felt when they told him he had an atom bomb." [2]

After checking and revision, the report was printed and ready for release by March 1946. Its title, suggested by general counsel Rosel Hyde, was *Public Service Responsibility of Broadcast Licensees.* The cover stock, selected by assistant general counsel Harry Plotkin, was blue. The only alternative cover stock available at the printing department was red. The booklet soon became known as "the blue book." [3]

The blue book was one of the most enlightening of FCC documents. Whereas the *Report on Chain Broadcasting* had analyzed network affairs, the blue book put the spotlight on local broadcasting, and provided a vivid picture of its characteristics at the end of the war. Along with case histories such as those of WBAL, KMAC, KIEV, and other stations, it offered revealing economic data, such as:

> For every three writers employed by 834 broadcast stations in October 1944, there were four salesmen employed. For every dollar paid to the average writer, the average salesman was paid $2.39. . . . The average local station employed less than ⅓ of a full-time musician and less than ⅙ of a full-time actor.[4]

2. Interview, Edward M. Brecher.
3. Interview, Harry Plotkin.
4. *Public Service Responsibility of Broadcast Licensees,* p. 39.

That all this was not a result of financial pressures was clear. In 1944 the industry as a whole had earned a profit of 222.6 per cent (before federal income taxes) on the depreciated cost of its tangible property. The comparable figure for 1939 had been 67.1 per cent.

Research for the blue book had included the recording of a full day's programming on all six Washington stations, including two network-owned stations. All were found to exceed NAB "self-regulation" code standards.

Contrasts between promise and performance were, in some cases, spectacular. WTOL, Toledo, originally a daytime station, had applied for full-time operation in 1938 on the ground that it needed time to carry the Toledo civic opera and serve the needs of the local Council of Churches, YMCA, American Legion, and Boy Scouts of America. It expected to devote 84 per cent of its nighttime hours to local live programming. In contrast to these representations, the schedule for a sample week in 1944 was 91.8 per cent commercial. The nighttime hours for the week included only twenty minutes of local sustaining programs—ten minutes of bowling scores and ten minutes of other sports news—and nothing for the YMCA, American Legion, Boy Scouts of America, or any other local organization.[5]

During the dinner hour the WTOL log showed spot announcements apparently uninterrupted by distractions of programming:

6:39:30	Transcribed spot announcement
6:40:00	Live spot announcement
6:41:00	Transcribed spot announcement
6:42:00	" " "
6:43:00	" " "
6:44:00	" " "

The FCC felt, with justice, that its own negligence had contributed to the trend. The blue book was reporting, to an extent, on its own failures. The FCC took occasion to pay tribute to valuable programming on a number of stations.

The blue book offered revealing data on the fate of network public-affairs features. During the war NBC had begun to give time to organized labor and won praise for it. The *Labor for Victory* series, scheduled Sunday afternoons, was presented alternately by the AFL and CIO. However, a sample *Labor for Victory* was found to have been carried by only 35 NBC affiliates and ignored by 104. Similarly *Lands of the Free*, a Sunday

5. *Ibid.* pp. 43–9.

afternoon drama series of the NBC *University of the Air* dealing with Latin American history, and movingly written by Morton Wishengrad[6]— previously of the education department of the International Ladies Garment Workers Union—was carried by only 24 NBC affiliates, ignored by all others. In many cases, recordings and spot announcements replaced the series locally.[7]

In trying to arrive at a future policy on renewals, the blue book looked to industry leaders for applicable standards. It quoted NBC president Niles Trammell, CBS president William Paley, and others. They had made eloquent statements about commercial excesses and about the important role of sustaining programs in (1) providing balance; (2) dealing with subjects unsuitable for sponsorship; (3) serving minority interests; (4) serving needs of non-profit groups; (5) experimenting with new techniques.

On the basis of standards derived from these industry leaders, the FCC proposed in the future to examine for renewal purposes the time devoted to *sustaining programs,* to *local live programs,* to *discussion of public issues,* and to the station's ability to resist *advertising excesses.*

The first reactions to the blue book included applause from a number of sources.[8] *Variety* said: "The FCC recommendations as such could well stand as a primer for the operation of a good radio station." The St. Louis *Post-Dispatch* found the blue book deserving of praise from "millions of radio listeners." The Hartford *Courant* said: "FCC to the rescue! . . . Hats off to the FCC!" Most broadcasters, said *Broadcasting* in an early comment, considered the book "nothing to get alarmed about."

But these reactions were followed by something quite different. Justin Miller, who had succeeded J. Harold Ryan as NAB president, apparently felt that broadcasters should never—tacitly or otherwise—have conceded to the FCC the right to interest itself in programming—even past programming. Any FCC decisions based on programming were in his view "censorship," violating the freedom of speech guarantees in the Communications Act and the Constitution. He apparently considered it a life-or-death matter for the industry to discredit and defeat the blue book. As a result, a torrent of vitriol assailed the FCC.

The idea that the people owned the air—although fundamental to the

6. See Wishengrad, "The Last Inca," in Liss (ed.), *Radio's Best Plays,* pp. 222–30.
7. *Public Service Responsibility of Broadcast Licensees,* pp. 19–36.
8. The following is based on Meyer, "Reaction to the Blue Book," *Journal of Broadcasting,* Fall 1962; other sources as noted.

Communications Act—was to Miller "hooey and nonsense." He looked on the FCC as "that type of government . . . from which our forefathers struggled to escape." *Broadcasting* began to echo the Miller doctrine:

> Have we forgotten so soon the fanatical Pied Pipers of destruction who led the German and Italian people down a dismal road by the sweet sound of their treacherous voices on a radio which they programmed? . . . There is more at stake than the ultimate pattern of American broadcasting. There is at stake the pattern of American life, and you can find that truth in the charred ruins of a chancellory in Berlin.[9]

Such attacks continued in *Broadcasting* for months on a weekly basis, with occasional slight shifts of focus. The discovery that Charles Siepmann had been a consultant in the preparation of the blue book was welcomed like manna from heaven. Before coming to the United States, Siepmann had been with the British Broadcasting Corporation as director of talks and director of program planning. To the blue book opponents this apparently meant "socialism" and almost any other available horror. Siepmann found himself called "radio's Cassius." The members of the FCC were "stooges for the communists." They were grabbing power like Goering. The Hearst press alerted the citizenry that the FCC had "brushed off the Bill of Rights and the memory of the Minute Men of Concord." Congressmen entered the battle. "Seven bureaucrats," said Representative B. Carroll Reece of Tennessee, chairman of the Republican National Committee, were threatening that freedom of the air which the Republicans had pledged to defend. It would be a major issue, he said, in the coming congressional elections. FCC commissioners began to get anxious inquiries from congressmen. What was going on down there?

Sometimes the attack shifted to Commissioner Durr, who was sarcastically depicted as the FCC's knight errant riding forth "from the commission's castle on the Potomac to protect the people" against horrors of radio.

> He enters the jousts in righteous splendor, garbed in an academic grey suit and gripping tightly in one hand—the blue book. And the banner he bears high—is it the white of purity, or is there a tint of pink? [10]

In mid-1946 the outcome of the shrill battle of words—and of pressures and maneuvers behind it—was not yet clear. Just before the appearance

9. *Broadcasting*, March 18, 1946.
10. *Ibid.* May 13, 1946.

of the blue book Paul Porter had been transferred by President Truman from the chairmanship of the FCC to the directorship of the Office of Price Administration. Inflation was a serious threat and the transfer reflected confidence in Porter, but removed from the FCC a man who seemed ready for battle. His successor, Charles R. Denny—perhaps the handsomest of FCC chairmen—also gave the impression of being ready for battle. He said of the blue book: "We do not intend to bleach it."

The members of the FCC felt dazed by the bitterness their document had stirred up. Words hurled at them seemed to have no relation to the blue book or its contents, and this increased their bafflement. They were soon confronted with moments offering a choice between advance and retreat. One came in the summer of 1946. Station WBAL, the Hearst station in Baltimore—a major exhibit of horrors in the blue book—applied for a Baltimore television channel. The FCC decided to grant it, without even a hearing.

That fall brought still another moment, again involving WBAL. A group headed by Drew Pearson and Robert S. Allen, newspaper columnists and radio newsmen, applied for the radio channel occupied by WBAL. Nothing in the Communications Act barred such a competing application. The applicants, calling themselves Public Service Radio Corporation, emphasized that as licensees they would run the station—there would be no absentee ownership. They pointed out that the granting of their application would avert the concentration of power which the FCC had often deplored; Hearst, in addition to radio station WBAL, had a Baltimore newspaper and a television license. They also pointed out, by citing the blue book, that Hearst Radio, Inc., had proved unable to operate WBAL in the public interest. Many oft-proclaimed principles of the FCC seemed at stake in this challenge. The FCC, keeping WBAL on a temporary license, scheduled hearings. Long delays and maneuvers followed. Eventually a one-man hearing was decreed, to be chaired by Rosel Hyde. He heard testimony and solemnly toted up the score. "We have found that both of the applicants are legally, technically, and financially qualified," he declared. He felt it was a close decision, but that he had to give the edge to Hearst Radio "on the basis of its demonstrated competence." [11] His ruling was eventually upheld by the FCC by a three to two vote, with two commissioners abstaining. The Hearst group kept its lucrative license.

11. *FCC Reports* (1950–51), pp. 1149–89.

By then the FCC's hesitations and delays had signaled the outcome of the battle. It was clear by the end of 1946 that the blue book had indeed been bleached. It might remain as a statement of principle, of mysterious status, but would not be a guide to action. It had been a bold effort to give meaning to "public interest" but it had failed. Broadcasters knew it and were soon proceeding as if it did not exist.

A statement by FCC chairman Charles R. Denny, who had presided over the bleaching, encouraged this trend. In discussing programming, he said:

> This matter is principally in the hands of the licensees of the thousands of stations throughout the country. They are the ones to whom listeners should give credit for fine service; and they are the ones whom listeners should hold responsible for service that is not good.[12]

He seemed to say the FCC had washed its hands of all that. He began to be regarded by the industry as a statesmanlike chairman. The drift continued. Protests sounded increasingly like cries of despair.

Lee de Forest, a claimant to the title of "father of radio," expressed himself in a letter to the 1946 fall meeting of the NAB in Chicago. He addressed the broadcasters through the "letters to the Editor" column of the Chicago *Tribune:*

> What have you gentlemen done with my child? . . . You have sent him out in the streets in rags of ragtime, tatters of jive and boogie woogie, to collect money from all and sundry for hubba hubba and audio jitterbug. You have made of him a laughing stock to intelligence, surely a stench in the nostrils of the gods of the ionosphere; you have cut time into tiny segments called spots (more rightly stains) wherewith the occasional fine program is periodically smeared with impudent insistence to buy and try.[13]

The blue book had weaknesses that contributed to its failure. The emphasis it placed on sustaining programs was, in a sense, obsolete. With the rise of the disk-jockey style of programming, the term "sustaining" was beginning to lose meaning. Before the blue book a Chicago station regularly scheduled:

> phonograph record
> commercial
> phonograph record

12. New York *Times,* January 2, 1947.
13. Chicago *Tribune,* October 28, 1946.

commercial
phonograph record
commercial
phonograph record
commercial
phonograph record
etc.

After the blue book appeared, the station revised its scheduling:

commercial
commercial
commercial
phonograph record
phonograph record
phonograph record
commercial
commercial
commercial
etc.

Each group of three phonograph records was logged for the FCC as a "sustaining program." The commercials were "between programs." [14]

A more fundamental weakness, inherent in reliance on report forms, was that the categories assured nothing. A local "discussion of public issues" could be as one-sided as Richards's *Victory F.O.B.* A local "live program" was not necessarily an expression of local culture; the magnetic recorder, just beginning its career, might prove a more apt revealer of truth than "live" programming.

But these flaws were probably unimportant. The contents of the blue book were never at issue. Scarcely anyone rose to defend WBAL, KIEV, WTOL, KMAC. No one argued with what the blue book *said*. The crime was that the FCC had said it. In showing an interest in programming, it had done something that required, in the view of NAB president Justin Miller, instant and total retaliation.

In the blue book saga, the role of the radio press—particularly *Broadcasting*—was of interest. The weekly issues of *Broadcasting* were providing the fullest available account of events in the industry, with emphasis on business aspects. The magazine was indispensable to any student of broadcasting. It was considered the unofficial voice of the NAB and was read by most station managers. It carried transcripts of hearings, often

14. Brecher, "Whose Radio," *Atlantic Monthly*, August 1946.

with admirable completeness. A station manager working his way through these could get a liberal education. But if he relied on the editorials in shaping his views, he could be strangely misled. These dedicated themselves persistently to the task of countering FCC regulatory moves and keeping the commissioners off-balance. This involved much juvenile rhetoric, which perhaps gave pleasure to many an uneasy licensee.

Variety, which addressed itself to the entertainment world rather than the station manager, frequently offered a very different interpretation of events. "Obviously," said *Variety* in commenting on the blue book, "the industry has brought upon itself the FCC proposals by its abuses. . . ." [15]

The increasingly close ties of the industry with Congress also played a part in the blue book saga. Many congressmen had acquired a financial interest in radio stations. In addition, many were getting free time on home stations for regular reports to their constituents. Since 1935 the House Office Building had been equipped with a Congressional Radio Room, where engineer Robert Coar could assist congressmen in making radio transcriptions for use back home. Begun as a private concession, the Congressional Radio Room acquired official status after World War II, when Coar went on the government payroll. More and more congressmen made regular trips to the studio to address their constituents. The congressman paid a modest fee for the recording service. Coar prepared the disks for mailing, and the congressman's office mailed them. Radio stations were increasingly eager to give time for such recordings—free time except during campaigns. Some Senators sent out dozens of copies of each disk, for statewide coverage. All this meant that a regular relationship was established between congressmen and radio stations. The radio station manager—the benefactor—had ready access to the congressman.[16]

In this situation a "power move" by the FCC—such as the chain report or the blue book—promptly produced "power moves" in Congress: speeches of protest; demands for investigations; resolutions; proposed amendments to the Communications Act. This had become a ritual cycle. In the blue book saga it was enacted in classic form.

15. *Variety*, March 13, 1946.
16. *Ibid.* June 25, 1952.

MEANWHILE BACK AT THE NETWORKS

The return of Edward R. Murrow from Europe in 1946 marked the beginning of a new setup at CBS. Paley appointed him vice president in charge of news and public affairs, and Davidson Taylor vice president in charge of other programming. The appointments were widely welcomed. People who felt that local broadcasting was skidding saw little reason to fear such a decline at the networks, particularly at CBS. Murrow held a world reputation. Taylor, as assistant to both Lewis and Coulter, had supervised many of the most celebrated CBS series—the New York Philharmonic, *Columbia Workshop, Mercury Theater on the Air, Pursuit of Happiness,* and others. The two men had seen much of each other in London and respected each other.

Frank Stanton, who held a Ph.D. in sociology and had risen in the CBS ranks as research specialist, became CBS president in 1946. He was assuming the role of buffer between Paley and the world—a role long occupied by Klauber, who had retired. Paley became chairman of the board.

The new team began its work with idealism and spirit. Just before leaving England Murrow, addressing the British people, had broadcast these words:

> I am persuaded that the most important thing that happened in Britain was that this nation chose to win or lose this war under the established rules of parliamentary procedure. It feared nazism but did not choose to imitate it. . . . Representative government, equality before the law survived. Future generations who bother to read the official record of proceedings in the House of Commons will discover that British armies retreated from many places but that there was no retreat from the principles for which your ancestors fought. . . . I have been privileged to see an entire people give the reply to tyranny that their history demanded of them.[1]

He left an England scarred with ruins and came to a prosperous America. Here he had no less the feeling that history makes its demands. In September 1946 he launched the CBS Documentary Unit to tackle major issues, national and international, "and involving extraordinary research and preparation." A few months later he began a phonograph album on the war years, *I Can Hear It Now,* in collaboration with a young writer from Providence, Rhode Island, Fred Friendly, who had suggested the

1. Murrow, *A Reporter Remembers* (LP album), side 4.

idea. It later developed into a documentary radio series, *Hear It Now.*

Under Taylor other challenging projects took shape, including the series *CBS Was There,* later retitled *You Are There.* Directed by Robert Lewis Shayon, it pretended to place a CBS news team at historic events. The fantasy formula, which might find newsman John Daly interviewing Louis XVI at Versailles, followed by other newsmen interviewing members of the mob outside the Bastille, allowed drama to go to the heart of many historic events. It was punctiliously researched.

One of the most arresting postwar projects, also organized in 1946, was *One World Flight.* In honor of Wendell Willkie a One World Award had been established, and its first recipient was Norman Corwin. He was to fly around the world as Willkie had done, and talk with world leaders and ordinary citizens. He decided to take a General Electric wire recorder— American tape recorders were not yet ready—and amass material for a CBS series. Engineer Lee Bland traveled with Corwin. Guy Della Cioppa became associate director.

The flight, which took four months and touched thirty-seven countries, was made at a time of rising tension between the United States and the Soviet Union. This polarization seemed to touch almost every interview, in every land. The magnetic recorder began to show its unique capacities as a barometer.

A young Filipino girl, while rejoicing that the fighting had ended, rec-ommended that President Truman should "finish up Russia, because if he does that right now, we have no further worry about her in the future." An Australian, after rejoicing that fascism was dead, expressed the view that the greatest remaining threat to peace now lay in the colored races and the notion of educating them. They would become, he said, "a Frankenstein monster."

Jawaharlal Nehru, about to lead his nation into independence, said: "But if you think of freedom for One World, then all this racialism, and one nation or one country being fundamentally superior to another—that has to be given up."

Philip Noel-Baker, British Minister of State, deplored the tendency of manipulators of public opinion—"publicity magnates," he called them—to consider only disputes to be newsworthy. He said relations between coun-tries were being exacerbated by the way reporters handled them. The novelist J. B. Priestly, who had become a celebrated BBC broadcaster during the war, noted that a common enemy had held the Allies together;

now, with the enemy beaten, the victors apparently had to *"invent* enemies, almost."

In Czechoslovakia, questions reflected currents of thought behind what Churchill had just given the name "the iron curtain."

INTERPRETER: Dr. Yerka would like to know if America has the right information about this country. . . .

INTERPRETER: Dr. Naumann would like to know if from the American economic system there will not develop a new economic imperialism in the world.

INTERPRETER: Dr. Shaffanik would like to know what truth there is in the rumor that the Americans in the American zone of Germany prefer the Germans to other people.

In Russia there were endless toasts to American-Russian friendship. It seemed as though the headline disputes were discounted there. Asked what he wanted to see, Corwin submitted a list of thirty items; twenty-seven were accommodated. The others were not denied, but not arranged. (They were meetings with Stalin, Shostakovitch, and the chairman of the Soviet committee on religions.) He was allowed to record interviews freely on streets and in parks; no attempt was made to censor the recordings. On the other hand, this was the only country in which he saw no high government official.

Editor Michael Borodin of *The Moscow News* told him: "There are people who would start a world conflagration—as our great Gorky said—in order to warm their hands over the fire."

China was the most startling experience. The minister of information in the Chiang Kai-shek government welcomed Corwin to Peiping: "I am very happy that you arrived at our capital on the birthday of Confucius, who is the forerunner of the One World idea." The team did its recording at Executive Headquarters, recently established by General George C. Marshall, who had been sent by President Truman to attempt mediation between the nationalist government of Chiang Kai-shek, which controlled more than half of China, and the communists under Mao Tse-tung, who controlled the remainder, with headquarters at Yenan. At first the mediation seemed to succeed. The recording arrangements were an instance of it. By agreement, interviews were recorded at Executive Headquarters with the American commissioner, the nationalist commissioner, and the communist commissioner. According to the agreement, approval by all three would be needed for the release of any of the material. But the mediation was under strain and appeared to collapse before the CBS microphones. The communists were charging that American planes had flown surplus United States war matériel to nationalist troops facing the communists. The communist commissioner, General Yeh Chien-ying, recorded these comments—in Chinese, translated by an interpreter:

GENERAL YEH: Such one-sided help [will] cost the failure of General Marshall's mission. Now the American government is at the crossroads. Either withdraw its one-sided support . . . or drop its position as mediator.

The American commissioner Walter Robertson, who was present, protested. He told General Yeh that if he wanted to propagandize he should "issue that statement from Yenan, but it can't come from here." According to Corwin's recollection, Yeh looked at Robertson silently, then continued recording:

GENERAL YEH: We hope the American government will change its present double-edged policy . . . so that the Chinese people will have a chance to exert their own pressure to bring about peace. This will enable the American representatives to restore their position as fair and just mediators. . . .

By the ground rules of Executive Headquarters, both the Chinese nationalist commissioner and the American commissioner had the right to veto use of such material. But by the time the CBS team had reached the United States the civil war had been resumed in force. Since the mediation had been abandoned, CBS included, in its broadcast of March 11, 1947, a full spectrum of the views expressed in China.[2]

One World Flight marked a moment of transition. On February 11, 1946, *Broadcasting* carried the headline: CHINA IS RIPE FOR U. S. ADVERTISING. This shiny mirage faded quickly. The Chinese struggle, while tearing China apart, also put pressure on other world relationships. The polarization of attitudes continued.

In October 1946 Soviet Russia decided that Russian short-wave facilities would no longer be available to American broadcasters. In February 1947 the United States began propaganda broadcasts to the Russian people.

One World Flight marked still another transition. The wire recorder, for all its value, had proved in some ways a "dreadful instrument." Splicing

2. Corwin, *Interview*, pp. 38–41. Quotations from *One World Flight* are from programs broadcast over CBS January 14, 21; February 11, 18; March 11, 1947.

was almost impossible. "You had to tie a knot in the wire and then fuse it with the lit end of a cigarette," Corwin recalls. "And the quality was miserable." By the time the CBS team completed its trip, tape recorders were on the American market and wire recorders doomed. *One World Flight* material was re-recorded onto tape for editing.[3] The tape recorder began its career as the supreme instrument of documentary production—the basis of the Murrow-Friendly *Hear It Now* and many subsequent series.

Like most Corwin series, *One World Flight* was broadcast opposite Bob Hope, in a period CBS still found unsalable but which could, nevertheless, provide an audience of millions. After the series Corwin left for Hollywood for a screen writing assignment. A few months later, on an eastward journey on *The Chief*, he found William Paley on the same train. They had a meal together.

CBS was at this moment under attack over a matter involving William L. Shirer. The Shirer broadcasts had been moved by CBS to a time period he considered inferior, and he resigned. To admirers of Shirer it seemed CBS was trying to muffle a notable wartime voice; his liberal views were said to be responsible. The dispute coincided with charges by Oliver Bryce, in the *New Republic*, that two dozen left-of-center commentators had been dropped from the four networks—by sponsor or network action —since the war.[4] Paley was disturbed over the Shirer dispute and told Corwin he had had no intention of penalizing Shirer. Paley was getting congratulations from some quarters for having disposed of Shirer, and said he was not happy about this. He foresaw a "wave of reaction."

They talked about Corwin's future. Corwin later carried away a recollection of Paley picking at a salad. "Well, you know, you've done epic things that are appreciated by us and by a special audience, but couldn't you write for a broader public? That's what we're going to need, more and more. We've simply got to face up to the fact that we're in a commercial business." Paley described the situation as highly competitive, and getting tougher. If the network did not reach as many people as possible, "why then we're not really making the best use of our talent, our time and our equipment." [5]

Paley seemed to have misgivings about the trend but did not regard the future as entirely dark. He mentioned that Jack Benny might be coming to CBS.

3. At first paper tape was used but was soon replaced by plastic tape.
4. *New Republic*, January 13, 1947.
5. Corwin, *Interview*, pp. 45–51.

Some months later Corwin received a new contract from CBS. It was like previous contracts except in one respect. CBS had added a clause by which it would receive 50 per cent of Corwin's earnings from subsidiary uses, such as anthologies or screen versions of plays written for CBS. The contract seemed to Corwin impossible to accept, and perhaps it was meant to be. He continued with screen work and took the post of Chief of Special Projects for United Nations Radio, where he produced several programs on the scale of his wartime projects. For *Document A/777*, on the Universal Declaration of Human Rights, Aaron Copland composed a setting for the preamble, and Laurence Olivier flew from London especially to read its text—a three-minute stint—backed by the Boston Symphony Orchestra under Leonard Bernstein. However, only MBS carried the program. CBS, NBC, ABC, were busy with other matters.

TAX-WISE

The postwar years, as Paley had predicted, brought relentless competition. Among major networks it was now an NBC-CBS-ABC struggle. All had substantial radio earnings, but the specters of television, FM, and other developments loomed over them. No network dared ignore their beckoning, but no one knew where they might lead. Would they perhaps take radio to its doom? Some thought so—but rushed on.

RCA was forcing the pace, determined to move full speed ahead with television. It constantly urged its affiliates to apply for television licenses at the first chance.

In 1945 the FCC, in reviewing spectrum allocations, made a crucial decision. It decided, after all, to move FM "upstairs" to another part of the spectrum. The move was desperately protested by Edwin Armstrong and the FM forces. The letters "FM" had become a rallying cry for many who felt disenchanted with the drift of radio. FM, at a propitious time, seemed to offer redemption. This was the theme of Charles Siepmann's book *Radio's Second Chance*, a stirring manifesto for the new medium, which appeared in 1946. But the FCC decision suddenly made all prewar FM sets worthless, erasing the audience already won. FM proponents said it would also saddle their industry with $75,000,000 in conversion costs and set the medium back for years.

The RCA-NBC forces, however, rejoiced. The new development tended to protect the status quo in radio while providing spectrum space for the expansion of television. RCA promised television sets by mid-1946. A new take-off for television was coming into view.

The FCC began issuing new licenses. The pace of television activity suddenly quickened. Returning servicemen with radar experience were grabbed by many stations; their knowledge was convertible to television.[1] Advertising agencies were clearly ready for a television boom. A 1944 survey of leading agencies had shown that half already had television departments. During the war some had experimented with commercials and programming.[2]

CBS was taken aback by the rush of events. It had expected a slower pace of development and had advised its affiliates to hold off on television and secure FM licenses. Some CBS stations had actually given up television channel assignments.

A reason for the CBS misjudgment was the unresolved issue of color television. CBS was urging a color method it had developed, and demonstrated to great acclaim. It involved a rotating wheel, and its pictures could not be seen on the existing black-and-white system. The CBS system gave brilliant and stable colors, and CBS considered it sufficient reason to hold off the freezing of television standards, until the color issue could be resolved.

RCA was scornful of the CBS color method. In six months, Sarnoff promised the FCC, RCA engineers would demonstrate an electronic color system "compatible" with black-and-white sets. Asked how he knew they would have it ready, Sarnoff answered: "I told them to."[3]

In the summer of 1946 RCA got its black-and-white sets on the market. That fall it demonstrated an electronic color system—crude and unstable but "compatible." In March 1947 the FCC shunted the CBS system aside and decreed a go-ahead under the existing system. RCA was exuberant. CBS had suffered a major defeat.

In October of that year FCC chairman Charles Denny, who had presided over these pro-RCA decisions, resigned from the FCC to become NBC vice president and general counsel.[4]

1. Love, *Reminiscences*, p. 13.
2. *Broadcasting*, April 17, 1944. In an experimental 1944 Lowell Thomas television newscast, Hugh Downs had delivered a commercial at a desk piled high with cans of Blue Sunoco. *Broadcasting* considered it a "novel" commercial.
3. Interview, Harry Plotkin.
4. The move, like earlier metamorphoses of this sort, caused a hue and cry. When had the subject of a network executive berth first been hinted? Such protests brought an amendment to the Communications Act, adopted in 1952, barring any commis-

Television fever was spreading rapidly. Both studio and receiving equipment had been improved since the prewar debut of television, and the results were evident. In June 1946 an NBC telecast of the Joe Louis–Billy Conn heavyweight championship prizefight caused the Washington *Post* to comment: "Television looks good for a 1000-year run." By July the FCC had issued twenty-four new licenses. As sets appeared, taverns rushed to acquire them. Sports events proved an especially powerful attraction. In every television city, groups clustered around tavern sets. The program repertoire expanded. In January 1947 the opening of Congress was televised for the first time. In February a "blue baby" operation was televised by NBC at Johns Hopkins and witnessed on television sets by several hundred doctors and nurses. In May the *Kraft Theater* television drama series made its NBC debut. That summer the Zoomar lens got into action in a CBS telecast of a baseball game between the Brooklyn Dodgers and the Cincinnati Reds. Its ability to leap from a full-field long shot to a close-up of the pitcher working his wad of chewing tobacco caused a stir.

Most of the program advances were associated with NBC. CBS and ABC faced a desperate problem of catching up.

The general strategy at the networks was to try to make radio profits pay the television development bill. An NBC research department memorandum of June 18, 1946, foresaw an $8,000,000 loss from television operation over a four-year period. It felt that radio could and should be made to finance it. The memo said:

> By deducting telecasting losses from sound broadcasting profits, it is estimated that during 1946–1949 some $3.5 million could be saved on federal income taxes . . . compared with what would have to be paid if the two activities were incorporated separately.[5]

This meant that radio, provider of funds, had to be kept going at maximum profit and minimum expense. Many sustaining features fell by the wayside. The NBC *University of the Air* vanished. At NBC James Rowland Angell, former president of Yale, was still listed as Public Service Counselor but began to feel he was "window dressing." [6] It was said that even the world-famed NBC Symphony Orchestra under Toscanini might

---

sioner from representing a client before the commission for a full year after resigning. *Communications Act,* Title I, Sec. 4 (b) as amended.
5. *Prospects for NBC Telecasting 1946–50.* Hedges, *Papers.*
6. Miller, *Interview,* p. 24.

in time have to go—unless television sponsors proved interested. At CBS the *American School of the Air* was moved to make room for sponsored daytime serials, and was then dropped. Other sustaining features suffered a similar fate.

Profitable programs became a focus of inter-network struggles. Bing Crosby was a bone of contention. In 1946 renewal negotiations he asked for the right to tape-record his Kraft radio series, scheduled on NBC. This would allow him to edit, to experiment, and to record only when in good voice. NBC resisted the plan, fearing it would doom network broadcasting. But ABC quickly welcomed Crosby and the tape recorder, and began to lure other talent with the same privilege. By doing repeat broadcasts via tape, ABC also began to save overtime costs. By 1947 ABC welcomed the disk-jockey to network programming. Before long the other networks followed suit.

Meanwhile CBS scored a more startling competitive coup. During the war radio comedians, who still led network radio ratings, had paid the high income taxes associated with upper brackets. In conversations between CBS and MCA—which represented many comedians—a tax suggestion developed. It was pointed out that "the Jack Benny program" and "the Edgar Bergen-Charlie McCarthy program" and "the *Amos 'n' Andy* program" and others—all scheduled on NBC—could be considered properties which, if sold, would involve taxation at the low capital-gains rate. CBS was willing to make capital investments of this sort. The comedians would enjoy a bonanza at low tax rates and could also continue to receive regular salaries for acting on the CBS-owned series. In 1948 Jack Benny stepped over to CBS, followed by Edgar Bergen and Charlie McCarthy, *Amos 'n' Andy*, Red Skelton, Burns and Allen. The move was a blockbuster. CBS had bought NBC's Sunday night and gained control of important talent for the television age. No one called it statesmanlike, but it was considered shrewd.

CBS and RCA became antagonists in another realm. In 1948 Columbia Records came out with the 33⅓ rpm long-playing microgroove phonograph record, RCA-Victor with the 45 rpm record. They battled hard for sovereignty of the disk-jockey world.

Meanwhile license applications of all sorts—television and radio—poured in on the FCC, and precipitated another kind of struggle. Economic dog-fights began to have an element of international political tension.

OR AFFILIATED SYMPATHETICALLY WITH . . .

While considering license applicants the FCC began getting unsolicited memoranda from J. Edgar Hoover, director of the Federal Bureau of Investigation. Concerning a group applying for a California license, Hoover wrote:

> I thought you would be interested in knowing that an examination of this list reflects that the majority of these individuals are members of the Communist Party or have affiliated themselves sympathetically with the activities of the communist movement.

The FCC asked Hoover for more specific information. It pointed out that rejected applicants were by law entitled to a public hearing. Could the FBI supply information that could be presented as evidence? Hoover said this would be impossible, because its sources had to be kept confidential.

The FCC, where Charles Denny was still chairman, dispatched its own investigator to California. He reported that it was impossible to determine who was a communist and who was not, but that the people referred to were, on the whole, well regarded. Their main political activity had revolved around efforts to re-elect President Roosevelt. The FCC, having no basis for unfavorable action that could be defended in court, simply refrained from acting. The applicants knew nothing of charges made against them; they only knew there was delay. But the result, Durr felt, was "to deny the application by not acting on it." He was disturbed over this and referred to it at a meeting of educational broadcasters in Chicago. This resulted in a Washington *Post* column by Marquis Childs—which brought the problem into the open.[1]

FBI director Hoover was furious. In a statement to the press he said the FBI was only being helpful, doing its job. It passed along information and did not "evaluate this information," he said, although most observers felt his memorandum had been an evaluation.

Hoover asked the FCC whether he should assume they were not interested in FBI data.

On December 1, 1947, the FCC met in crisis atmosphere to decide on a reply. Durr summarized what he considered the contribution of the FBI data-gathering. He felt it to be

> of little help to the commission to be informed that an applicant was, in 1944, at the height of the war, reported by an unidentified source

1. Washington *Post*, November 19, 1947; *Nation*, November 21, 1953.

as being in contact with another unidentified individual "who was *suspected* of *possible* pro-Russian activity"; or that the applicant was reported by an unidentified informant to have been a visitor in the residence of another individual who was reported by another unidentified source to have been identified by still another unidentified source with communistic activities . . . or that "according to an unknown outside source" the name of the applicant "appears" as a member of a committee of an organization of artists and professional people which was active in support of the Democratic presidential nominee in the 1944 presidential elections; or that another unidentified source has described such organization "as a communist infiltrated and/or influenced organization" . . . or that a local Democratic committee has been reported by an unidentified informant "to be under the influence of the communist element"; or that according to a newspaper account of a speech delivered by vice-presidential candidate Bricker in the 1944 campaign, the speaker charged that the Democratic party had become the "Hillman-Browder communistic party" and that the applicant had left his job with the government to support the campaign of President Roosevelt, the founder of this "communistic party"; or that the applicant has been reported by an unidentified source to have been a member of the committee to greet the late president of a large labor union. . . .

But the FCC decided to send FBI director Hoover a conciliatory letter, assuring him it welcomed continued advice. The action was, in effect, a repudiation of Durr.[2]

The tide was against Durr. The year 1947 was dominated by a monomania. The concern of the nation was a search for traitors, who might be anyone, including your neighbor—probably your neighbor. Almost every government agency was said to be crawling with "them." They might be people with communistic ideas or people who had associated sympathetically with them or been seen in restaurants with them or reading questionable magazines. Denouncing them became the business of the hour. It was time to stand up and be counted—*for* what, was not clear; *against* what, was not quite clear either. But time was pressing. The oratory of the day was typified by that of Senator Homer Capehart of Indiana, who charged that "evidence unfolds daily that in our own government household, communists and their New Deal fellow travelers are being harbored in key positions where they can sabotage our nation's policies."

Few Presidents have been so badgered by a hostile legislature as was

2. Minutes, Federal Communications Commission, December 1, 1947; quoted, Cook, *The FBI Nobody Knows*, pp. 393–5.

Harry S. Truman by the 80th Congress. The anti-liberal coalition of Southern Democrats and Northern Republicans handcuffed his programs, ignored his appointments, and talked about treachery. Truman was a scrapper, but wanted to get on with his program, so he announced Executive Order No. 9835—a loyalty-security program under which, at a cost of many millions of dollars, 2,500,000 federal employees would be checked by loyalty review boards. Derogatory information from the FBI and other sources would be carefully and discreetly weighed. As a guide, Attorney General Tom Clark prepared a list of organizations he considered subversive.

Among those who spoke out against this mass-hunt was Commissioner Durr. Addressing the annual meeting of the American Political Science Association in December 1947, he said:

> We are going to elevate to a new level of dignity informers, stool pigeons and gossips, a class which since the days of Leviticus we have been taught to regard with suspicion and scorn. We are going to fight communism by employing the methods upon which we profess to base our abhorrence of communism.[3]

Earlier he had told a group of churchmen:

> Can we safely vest in our secret police jurisdiction over the "association" and "sympathetic affiliation" and thoughts of men, and be sure that we are safe? Can men be fairly tried when their right to face their accusers, and to be fully advised of the nature and cause of the charge against them, depends upon the "discretion" of those who accuse them?

Durr emphasized that the loyalty-security program applied to government employees only, but asked:

> . . . will the example of government stop with government itself? Once it has been established and accepted, can its influence be kept from spreading to industry, to the press, to our schools and universities, and even to our churches? [4]

The questions were answered almost before he asked them. Late in October 1947 the House committee on un-American activities, by then headed by Representative J. Parnell Thomas of New Jersey, opened public hearings on communism in the film industry. It was a show in which star witnesses from Hollywood would repeat testimony already given behind

---

3. *Broadcasting*, January 5, 1948.
4. Cook, *The FBI Nobody Knows*, p. 391.

closed doors while others—summoned by subpoena—would face unre-
hearsed confrontations before camera and microphone.

The show started on October 20, 1947, in a caucus room of the House
office building in Washington.[5] NBC, CBS, and ABC microphones were
there. Eleven newsreel and television cameras were in operation. Flood-
lights hung among crystal chandeliers. Scores of news-gathering agencies
were there to speed the word to all continents. In spectator seats sat screen
notables, many in dark glasses. Crowds hung in corridors and around the
building. Special police were on hand. Behind a long table, facing the
witness chair, sat a subcommittee of the House committee on un-American
activities: John McDowell of Pennsylvania, Richard M. Nixon of California, J. Parnell Thomas of New Jersey (chairman), Richard B. Vail of Illinois, and John S. Wood of Georgia.[6]

Chairman Thomas in his opening statement spoke of the propaganda
power of film and the need for studying infiltration by those "whose loyalty
is pledged in word and deed to the interests of a foreign power."[7]

After this ominous opening with its hint of treason, the hearings seemed
determined for a time to descend into farce. The first witness, Jack L.
Warner, had said things behind closed doors that had whetted committee
appetites, and its members were eager to get these items into circulation.
He had said the wartime film *Mission to Moscow*, based on a book by
U. S. Ambassador Joseph E. Davies and reflecting a sympathetic attitude
toward the Soviet Union, had been undertaken by Warner Brothers under
pressure from the White House. The subcommittee wanted him to get into
that matter in detail. But Jack Warner had meanwhile refreshed his recollection and found it wasn't so. The truth was, his brother Harry Warner
had on his own initiative contacted Mr. Davies to get the film rights. The
committee was dismayed over this about-face, and tried at least to get him
to admit the film was an outrage. This made Warner uncomfortable; it
was his film. In embarrassment he described it as a sort of "intellectual
lend-lease." But he tried to oblige in other ways. He would be glad to

---

5. The following is based on Suber, *The 1947 Hearings of the House Committee on
Un-American Activities into Communism in the Hollywood Motion Picture Industry*;
other sources as noted.
6. Other members of the House committee, not on the subcommittee, were Herbert C.
Bonner of North Carolina, F. Edward Hebert of Louisiana, Karl E. Mundt of South
Dakota, J. Hardin Peterson of Florida, John E. Rankin of Mississippi.
7. Quotations are from *Hearings: Before Committee on Un-American Activities on
Communist Infiltration of Hollywood Motion Picture Industry*, pp. 1–61; 101–2; 168–
70; 232–3; 282–4; 366–7; 459–82.

subscribe, he said, to a "pest-removal fund" to ship American communists to Russia.

Warming to his role, he said communist writers had many ways of injecting propaganda into films. They included "poking fun at our political system" and picking on rich men. There was also "the routine of the Indians and the colored folks. That is always their setup."

Producer Sam Wood likewise felt that communist writers worked by portraying bankers and senators as "heavies." Adolphe Menjou, who described himself as a close friend of J. Edgar Hoover, was asked whether a communist actor could inject propaganda into a scene, and answered: "Under the proper circumstances, by a look, by an inflection, by a change in the voice, I think it could easily be done." He added: "I have never seen it done, but I think it could be done." Mrs. Lela Rogers, mother of Ginger Rogers, identified *None But the Lonely Heart* as communistic; to prove her point she quoted *Hollywood Reporter,* which had found the picture "pitched in a low key . . . moody and somber throughout, in the Russian manner." Walt Disney spoke of his struggles against communists, and said he had been pressed by the League of Women Voters, a "communist front," to accept the Screen Cartoonists Guild, but had resisted. (Deluged with protests, he later sent a telegram saying it was not the League of Women Voters.)

All this was great comedy, and pointed up a difficulty of the hearings. Subversive propaganda was an alleged reason for the hearings, and some effort had to be made to find it. Chairman Thomas said he would produce a list of communistic films, but never did. A few films—including Warner's *Mission to Moscow* and MGM's *Song of Russia*—were mentioned several times but with inconclusive results. Louis B. Mayer of MGM fervently maintained that *Song of Russia* was not communistic; if he had to meet his God, he would still say so. However, all this was merely preliminary.

The real heart of the show was a trial of sorts. A number of screen writers under subpoena were confronted with evidence—photostats of documents said to be membership cards—that they were or had been members of the Communist party. Most refused to confirm or deny memberships of any sort—including membership in the Screen Writers Guild. They used various formulas to do this.

EDWARD DMYTRYK: What organizations I belong to, what I think, and what I
    say cannot be questioned by this committee. . . .

ALBERT MALTZ: Next you are going to ask me what religious group I belong to. . . .

DALTON TRUMBO: You must have some reason for asking this question?

RING LARDNER, JR.:   I could answer that . . . but I would hate myself in the morning. . . .

Some, like John Howard Lawson, answered with indignant invective. He was dragged shouting from the witness stand. Many were unnerved by the spectacle.

Most of the subpoenaed witnesses were forbidden to read statements. "It's against our policy," Chairman Thomas told them. But a few were given permission. Albert Maltz read this:

> Whatever I am, America has made me. And I, in turn, possess no loyalty as great as the one I have to this land, to the economic and social welfare of its people, to the perpetuation and development of its democratic way of life.

Maltz declared his own views were not fixed and unchanging, but he would insist on his right to think and speak freely, to publish what he wished, and to criticize public officials including members of the House committee on un-American activities. He made clear that he considered some of them contemptible, including the chairman and especially John Rankin of Mississippi, who sometimes embroidered his congressional addresses with allusions to "kikes" and "nigras."

The first result of the hearings seemed to be a closing of ranks in Hollywood. Eric Johnston, president of the Motion Picture Association of America, and others asserted that the industry would never accept dictation on hiring or editorial policies. Of the ten writers who had been "unfriendly" witnesses, five were under contract at the time. The contract of Ring Lardner, Jr., expired two weeks after the hearing but was promptly renewed. Edward Dmytryk was assured by his boss at RKO, Dore Schary, that his job was secure. Speeches and resolutions against the House committee were numerous. But suddenly the show of courage collapsed. On November 24, 1947, a group of top film executives met at the Waldorf-Astoria in New York and decided that, for the safety of the industry, the "unfriendly" writers had to be cleaned out. Because of legal barriers to firing employees on political grounds, they were "suspended without pay."

On the same day they were cited in Washington for contempt of Congress.

Membership in the Communist party, although clouded by the Smith Act of 1940, was not illegal; this was repeatedly emphasized at the hearings. Presumably any illegal acts could be prosecuted and punished through normal processes of justice. The absence of illegal acts had apparently called for a novel trial of this sort—the show trial of October 1947. The writers who had chosen not to answer the "$64 question," as chairman Thomas repeatedly called it—doing honor to a radio quiz program—felt confident their right to do so would be upheld. Their confidence proved ill-founded. All went to prison for contempt of Congress—two of them to the same prison as chairman J. Parnell Thomas, who had meanwhile been convicted of conspiracy to defraud the government with mythical names on his payroll and other fraudulent practices, in which he was found to have engaged continuously from 1940 to 1948.

Hollywood entered a period of fear. No one knew when the axe might fall and, if it fell, what reasons might lie behind the action, or who had made charges. "It was like a small Terror," recalled director John Cromwell, "with a small-town Robespierre and a Committee dealing out the future of a great many people." [8] Political discussion tended to vanish, but silence itself could seem suspicious. The patrioteering speech was much in evidence.

In Washington Clifford Durr, who had warned that the terror would spread, reached the end of his FCC term in 1948. President Truman asked him to accept reappointment, but Durr said he would not, because of his aversion to the loyalty-security program. Truman urged Durr to understand that he, the President, had had to adopt such a program to avert something far worse. Truman asked Supreme Court Justice Black, brother-in-law to Durr, to persuade the commissioner to stay.[9] But Durr still declined and returned to private law practice in Alabama, where he would be heard from again in connection with civil rights cases. The time would come when he would receive an award from the New York Civil Liberties Union—a Lasker award.[10]

Durr had been right. Once established and accepted, the idea was bound to spread. Radio and television were next.

8. Cromwell, *Reminiscences*, p. 30.
9. Letter from Hugo Black, *Congressional Record*, v. 112, appendix, pp. 2309–10.
10. The Florina Lasker civil liberties award, established by a sister of Albert Lasker.

5 / PURGE

O Liberty, how many liberties
are taken in thy name!
            OGDEN NASH

Let us pry!
            JAMES JOYCE, *Finnegans Wake*

Among the thousands of new and temporary employees of the Federal
Bureau of Investigation during World War II were Kenneth M. Bierly,
John G. Keenan, and Theodore C. Kirkpatrick. Working together in the
New York office of the FBI, they saw a good deal of each other and talked
about what they might do after the war.

In 1945 Kirkpatrick stepped from the FBI into a job as assistant to the
protection manager of the Bloomingdale department store, but was restless. "It seemed to me small, petty. It was concerned with shoplifting
when the communists were taking over the country." [1]

Bierly was still with the FBI, and Keenan was practicing law, but they
kept in touch. Early in 1946 they found their opening. With the help of
Alfred Kohlberg, an importer who was an ardent Chiang Kai-shek supporter and a backer of various anti-communist projects, they rented space
at 240 Madison Avenue. This was reached by freight elevator, but Kirkpatrick considered it "fine for our purpose because we did not want com-
mies snooping, and we had no reason for dealing with the public." The
space was intended mainly for research files. The idea was to accumulate
information on the communist movement, start a newsletter, and do "special investigations."

They launched two corporations. One was John Quincy Adams Associates, a nonprofit organization which they hoped would attract tax-free

1. The following is based on Miller, *The Judges and the Judged;* and Cogley, *Report
on Blacklisting* (v. 1): *Radio-television;* other sources as noted.

253

gifts toward their research. An unfavorable ruling from the U. S. Treasury —which apparently considered it political propaganda rather than education—ended this plan. Then they formed—April 1947—American Business Consultants, Inc., and borrowed the John Quincy Adams Associates funds to get it started. About $15,000—almost all derived originally from Kohlberg—seems to have launched the new enterprise.

At 240 Madison Avenue they amassed bound volumes of the New York *Times* as well as the *Daily Worker,* the *New Masses* and other magazines, and voluminous pamphlets, clippings, fund-raising appeals, programs of rallies and benefit performances, letterheads, and miscellaneous other documents. They also collected reports of the House committee on un-American activities, including the mysterious Appendix IX, which is said to have listed 100,000 Americans and their "front" connections but was withdrawn by the House committee after publication. They also collected reports of the California legislative committee on un-American activities.

Bierly had by now left the FBI, and in May 1947 the partners started their four-page weekly newsletter *Counterattack: The Newsletter of Facts on Communism.* Editorial and research help was hired. Subscribers were solicited by mail and also by floor-to-floor canvassing of New York City office buildings. Most subscribers were business firms, but government offices also took subscriptions. Kirkpatrick told Merle Miller, "I have been amazed at how many! Scarcely a week passes that we don't get a government check of one type or another." Broadcasting stations also took subscriptions. George A. Richards instructed his stations to quote *Counterattack* whenever possible. From the start the newsletter was a financial success. The company was soon said to be grossing $100,000 a year from this part of its business.

Counterattack hammered endlessly at dangers of communist "infiltration" and scolded businessmen for laxness and stupidity. The publishers did not originally intend to concentrate on broadcasting; this emphasis came gradually, as it bore rich fruit. The visibility of the broadcasting industry, and the economic and political tensions surrounding it, made it an apt target.

Counterattack, following the example of Representative Martin Dies, listed celebrities with "citations" of their "front" activities. It stated: "Proof is available for every statement made in *Counterattack*." This meant less than it seemed to. A *Counterattack* citation might say that the *Daily Worker* had reported Actor X as attending a meeting of Organization Y, considered subversive. In such a case *Counterattack* might have proof of just one thing: that the *Daily Worker* had so reported. *Had* he actually attended? *Was* the organization subversive? *Counterattack* felt it could not be concerned with such subsidiary problems. A New York *Daily News* reporter asked Kirkpatrick:

> . . . I have been reading in *Counterattack* that communists cannot be trusted, that they are devious, that they are full of intrigue and so forth. And yet you can sit there and tell us that you take things out of the *Daily Worker* and do not check them—and print them?

This question often confronted Kirkpatrick. On a radio program he gave this answer, as reported by Merle Miller:

> When names are printed in the *Daily Worker*, it's presumed that those names are checked before they're printed; otherwise, that person has recourse to the *Daily Worker*.

Counterattack "citations" went far beyond the Attorney General's list of subversive groups. Early in 1948 the newsletter gave a list of 192 organizations it considered "fronts," only 73 of which were on the Attorney General's list.

Counterattack was sweeping in philosophy and definitions. Its articles used terms like "dupes," "stooges," "fifth columnists," "quislings," "appeasers," "fronters," "innocents," but its listings did not distinguish among them. They all "helped communism" and were therefore considered part of "communism." All had to be treated alike. *Counterattack* was clear about what should be done with all these people. In September 1947 it stated:

> Most important thing of all is to base your whole policy on a firmly moral foundation. Space should not be rented to the Communist Party or to any communist front. Supplies should not be sold to them. They should not be allowed to participate in meetings . . . Communist actors, announcers, directors, writers, producers, etc., whether in radio, theater, or movies, should all be barred to the extent permissible by law and union contracts.

In October it added:

> The way to treat communists is to ostracize them. How would you act towards men who had been convicted of treason? Would you befriend them, invite them, listen to them? Or would you treat them as outcasts?

Citing an artist's "record," *Counterattack* with increasing frequency urged readers to demand action from network, sponsor, or agency. At first such demands were often sloughed off. Joseph H. McConnell, who succeeded Niles Trammell as NBC president in 1949, suggested to a group of protesting letter writers that they should send any "pertinent information" to the FBI. *Counterattack* was outraged by this. "He implies that they should stop bothering him. . . . This policy is one of DOING NOTHING!"

Many executives—at networks, sponsors, and agencies—appear to have taken a prompt dislike to *Counterattack*—and then done business with it. The reasons were not subtle.

In addition to issuing a newsletter, the publishers did "special investigations" for a fee. This might range from $5 to check a name in its files to thousands of dollars for large loyalty appraisals—as of a whole staff. This investigative work was done from an office in 42d Street with a picture of J. Edgar Hoover on the wall. The service was constantly promoted through solicitations.

On one occasion a representative of the firm called on the Hutchins advertising agency and said that one of its programs, sponsored by Philco, was using a "commie" actress. He offered the firm's "research facilities" to study the loyalty of the program talent, suggesting a fee of $1,000. The agency declined. Three weeks later the newsletter carried an article attacking Philco for hiring an actress who was a "fellow traveler." To Merle Miller, Kirkpatrick admitted this sequence of events but said it was a coincidence.

Sponsor magazine seemed to feel otherwise, and suggested that *Counterattack* was hanging "a double-edged sword" over the advertiser and his agent.[2] These men were likely to be prudent people, and *Counterattack* acquired an impressive array of clients—General Motors, Du Pont, F. W. Woolworth, Metropolitan Life Insurance Company, R. J. Reynolds Tobacco Company, Bendix Aviation. CBS at one time commissioned a study of program talent by American Business Consultants. It was a grubby business, but beginning to feel its power.

It was so obviously a fertile field for enterprise that others were pushing into it. Some had financial ambitions, but others seemed to seek only a sense of achievement.

Again with help from the importer Alfred Kohlberg, an American Jewish League Against Communism was organized in 1948, directed by Rabbi

2. *Sponsor,* October 22, 1951.

Benjamin Schultz. Many Jewish organizations dissociated themselves from it, and it apparently had only a thin scattering of members in New York, Dallas, and Los Angeles, but it launched sporadic attacks against Albert Einstein, Paul Robeson, Mrs. Franklin D. Roosevelt, and others. At about the same time an Americanism commission of the American Legion started a newsletter entitled *Summary of Trends and Developments Exposing the Communist Conspiracy.* It advised its readers:

> Organize a letter-writing group of six to ten relatives and friends to make the sentiments of Americans heard on the important issues of the day. Phone, telegraph, or write to radio and television sponsors employing entertainers with known front records. . . . DON'T LET THE SPONSORS PASS THE BUCK BACK TO YOU BY DEMANDING "PROOF" OF COMMUNIST FRONTING BY SOME CHARACTER ABOUT WHOM YOU HAVE COMPLAINED. YOU DON'T HAVE TO PROVE ANYTHING. . . . YOU SIMPLY DO NOT LIKE SO-AND-SO ON THEIR PROGRAMS.[3]

To learn what broadcasters to attack, the *Summary* recommended *Counterattack* and other lists. According to Merle Miller, the *Summary* was largely a one-man job.

The various compilers of lists constantly quoted each other, reinforced each other—and tried to outdo each other. Clearly in the lead was American Business Consultants with its *Counterattack* newsletter and investigative service. Within two years it appeared to be earning about $200,000 per year from its two operations.

The broadcasting industry in 1948 was deriving $616,500,000 from the sale of time. The $20,000 company with the office on 42d Street was finding it could exert a lot of leverage on the $616,500,000 industry. How much, it was only beginning to learn.

GIVE 'EM HELL

Harry S. Truman at the start of 1948 seemed a lonely figure about to be overwhelmed by a rising tide of hostile forces. But he felt he had a chance.

The Republican and Democratic parties both chose Philadelphia for their 1948 conventions and for the same reason—television. It was on the co-axial cable linking New York and Washington, which by mid-summer was expected to reach fourteen Eastern stations with audiences in thirteen states—having an electoral vote of 168. Both parties were told by Roger

3. Quoted, Miller, *The Judges and the Judged,* pp. 159–60.

W. Clipp of WFIL and WFIL-TV, Philadelphia, that the television audience would run in the millions. Late in 1947 each party made its decision, and the factions began straining toward a Philadelphia climax.[1]

Preparatory moves for the decisive hour included a series of intensive meetings in January 1948 in Los Angeles. Here George A. Richards—of WJR, Detroit; WGAR, Cleveland; KMPC, Los Angeles—assembled leading personnel of his three stations for strategy sessions and instructions. A letter of welcome stated his purpose:

> I place in importance, over and above all these various individual problems, the all-important one of a new administration in Washington. . . . We need new vigorous, honest, Christian leadership.[2]

On January 26, 1948 they all dined together at Perino's restaurant. The date was significant: it was the birthday of General Douglas MacArthur. This would launch a campaign by the Richards stations to nominate and elect MacArthur.

To prepare for this, Richards had sent KMPC news director Clete Roberts—a Purple Heart winner under MacArthur in World War II—to Tokyo to tape interviews with MacArthur. Roberts had returned with his tapes and added his own word pictures of MacArthur. Richards had reviewed this highly laudatory material and given instructions about it.

During the dinner at Perino's restaurant a radio was brought in. The assembled executives would hear the MacArthur program together, as it was broadcast from KMPC. It proved a climactic moment in the life of George A. Richards.

He had told Clete Roberts to omit any hint of MacArthur's age—he was sixty-eight—but Roberts had not done so. The Roberts commentary as heard at Perino's restaurant mentioned a tremor in MacArthur's hand as he lifted his pipe to his mouth. When Richards heard the offending passage, he turned on Roberts in livid anger. When the item was later quoted in a network program by Walter Winchell—who had the highest-rating series on the ABC network—Richards's fury mounted. Roberts was fired.

When Roberts told his story at the Radio News Club of Southern California—of which Chet Huntley was president—it started a movement. The club was by now well populated by people who had written for Rich-

1. *Broadcasting*, November 2, 1947.
2. FCC Exhibit 6; quoted, *Proposed Findings of Fact and Conclusions of Law*, p. 224.

ards. Early in March 1948 the FCC received from the Radio News Club a package containing affidavits from numerous radio newsmen about instructions to slant, distort, and falsify news.

Ironically, all this material arrived at the FCC as it was holding hearings on a proposal to amend the Mayflower decision—the doctrine that a licensee "cannot be an advocate."

It also arrived in the same week as WGAR's application for a renewal of its license.

The FCC after a preliminary investigation decided to schedule hearings on the renewal of the Richards licenses. Richards began to make clear that he would spend millions to save them. He removed himself to the chairmanship of the board and persuaded Frank Mullen, executive vice president of the National Broadcasting Company, to leave the network for the presidency of the Richards stations, under a five-year contract that would virtually make Mullen a millionaire.[3] A fantastic struggle developed, involving batteries of high-priced counsel, unnumbered legal stratagems and delays, 280 witnesses, more than 1000 exhibits, and 18,265 pages of testimony.

Thus the Richards plans for the 1948 election campaign were interrupted.

Meanwhile Harry S. Truman had become the first President to sit in the White House and watch the nomination of his rival on television. Truman saw the Republicans nominate Thomas E. Dewey and Earl Warren. The Democrats nominated Truman and Alben Barkley.

Two splinter candidates also entered the field: Strom Thurmond for the States' Rights Democrats, who hated Truman for his interest in civil rights; and Henry Wallace for the Progressives, who accused Truman of fomenting the cold war.

Truman made the unusual decision to de-emphasize radio in his campaign. He felt that radio, along with the press, was working against him. "As far as I was concerned," he writes in his memoirs, "they had sold out to the special interests, and that is why I referred to them in my campaign speeches as the 'kept press and paid radio.' "[4]

He decided on a Herculean barnstorming drive. In the final thirty-five

3. *Broadcasting*, May 17, 1948.
4. Quotations and statistics are from Truman, *Memoirs: Years of Trial and Hope*, pp. 167, 211–21.

days of the campaign he traveled 31,700 miles and made 356 "off the cuff" speeches—an average of more than ten a day. The arguments were never complex.

> I simply told the people in my own language that they had better wake up to the fact that it was their fight. If they did not get out and help me win this fight, I emphasized, the Republicans would soon be giving the farmers and the workers the little end of the stick again . . . if they were fools enough to accept the little end again, they deserved it.

It was not the kind of thing presidential candidates said in radio addresses, and perhaps for that reason drew crowds. Politicians were amazed at the swarms Truman attracted. He began to enjoy himself. "Give 'em hell, Harry!" the people shouted. Harry said that was just what he meant to do. He often excoriated radio and the press. On the air Thomas E. Dewey was making dignified speeches. His advertising agency, Batten, Barton, Durstine & Osborn, recommended a barrage of spot announcements, but Dewey vetoed the idea, and stuck to somewhat lofty addresses. As entertainment the radio campaign of 1948 was an outstanding failure. But almost all polls agreed that Dewey would win. Many people said they were "undecided."

On election night an exhausted Truman slipped away to the Elms Hotel at Excelsior Springs, Missouri, had a Turkish bath, and retired to his room at 6:30 P.M. After a ham sandwich and a glass of milk he went to sleep. He awoke at midnight, turned on the radio and found H. V. Kaltenborn explaining that Truman was ahead by 1,200,000 votes but that it did not mean anything. He slept again until 4 A.M., when he again heard Kaltenborn explain that Truman was ahead—this time by 2,000,000—but that it meant nothing; he could not win.

Next day President Truman imitated H. V. Kaltenborn for the reporters. It was a smash hit. The vote ran: Truman, 24,105,812; Dewey, 21,970,065. The electoral vote was 303 to 189, with 39 electoral votes for Thurmond.

PEACE MEETING

Throughout the campaign Truman was denounced by the Republicans as an appeaser of communists and by the Wallace forces as a warmonger.

Truman was trying to walk a line that appeared clear to him. He was determined to react with force to any communist take-over by force; this determination was shown by prompt military aid to Greece and Turkey to combat insurrections receiving aid from iron-curtain countries.

At the same time he was trying to maintain lines of communication with Soviet leaders. In this he was less successful; they were increasingly suspicious and hostile. The campaign oratory of 1948 probably contributed to this. The atom bomb, sole possession of the United States, was also an invisible presence at any attempted negotiation.

During the 1948 campaign Truman asked Chief Justice Frederick M. Vinson if he would go to the Soviet Union to see Stalin, to persuade him of America's peaceful purposes. "I had a feeling that Stalin might get over some of his inhibitions if he were to talk with our own Chief Justice." Truman told Vinson that "all manner of approaches" to the Russians had been tried but that all had dissolved in suspicion and intransigence.

The idea of the Vinson mission leaked out and was so violently attacked in the press and on the air that it was abandoned. But Truman kept his determination to ease tensions through "all manner of approaches." In a speech at an American Legion convention in Miami, in October 1948, he referred to the aborted Vinson mission and then added:

> . . . I want to make it perfectly clear that I have not departed one step from my determination to utilize every opportunity to work for peace. . . .[1]

After the election a plan took shape for a meeting at the Waldorf-Astoria to be attended by representatives of the arts and professions from both sides of the iron curtain, to discuss co-operation for peace. Among those attending from the Soviet Union would be the composer Dmitri Shostakovitch. Yugoslav delegates were expected. The U. S. Department of State raised no objections.

The writer Arthur Miller, whose scripts had been heard on the Du Pont *Cavalcade of America*—no fire-arms permitted—and on the postwar series *Theater Guild on the Air* sponsored by U. S. Steel, had become a successful Broadway playwright with *All My Sons*. It had won the 1948 Drama Critics' Circle Award and was getting productions abroad. As a rising young playwright, he was invited to participate in the Waldorf peace conference.

When *Counterattack* called the meeting a communist-front plot, Miller was advised that for public-relations reasons it would be unwise to attend.

1. Truman, *Memoirs: Years of Trial and Hope*, pp. 212–18.

This annoyed him. If the State Department could give visas to Shostako-vitch and others, and they came halfway around the world to talk to Americans in a midtown hotel, the thought of staying away for public-relations reasons repelled him. "I just felt that having been invited, if I turned it down I would be turning myself down, so I went."

It was an experience not to be believed or forgotten. "There were nuns on their knees around the Waldorf-Astoria praying for the souls of those within, and enormous loud and violent picket lines. . . ." The meeting became a "citation" in the dossiers of scores of Americans.

Arthur Miller later remarked, "The amazing kind of spaghetti that was being cooked here—you couldn't follow one thread more than two inches." [2]

WHAT WE ALL WANT

Among television series launched in 1948 was *Toast of the Town*, a CBS variety program with Ed Sullivan as producer and master of ceremonies. It later became known as *The Ed Sullivan Show.*

Inasmuch as Kate Smith's variety series had enjoyed a fifteen-year radio run and *Vallee Varieties* a sixteen-year run, and the Bing Crosby series was going strong in its seventeenth year, the variety formula was promis-ing. Sullivan, a New York *Daily News* columnist, had advantages as a program entrepreneur. He could and did give performers extra rewards with column items. He went after the biggest names and assembled im-pressive aggregations. Though he himself was kidded for his unsmiling face and awkwardly dangling arms, his program gathered momentum and soon reached the top in television ratings in several cities.[1] It acquired the Ford Motor Company as sponsor and began to look like big business. As Sullivan prospered, even his performing deficiencies became assets. He became a man mimicked on amateur hours: in short, one of the great.

Late in 1949 Sullivan booked dancer Paul Draper for a *Toast of the Town* appearance in January 1950. This was, to an extent, a courageous act. An appearance by Draper and harmonica player Larry Adler in Greenwich, Connecticut, had recently called forth a campaign of virulent

2. Miller, *Reminiscences,* pp. 21–39.

1. *Pulse* surveys, making local reports in a number of cities, showed Sullivan in first place in New York and Philadelphia. *Broadcasting,* October 18, 1948.

letter-writing led by a Mrs. Hester McCullough of Greenwich, wife of a *Time* picture editor—abetted by Hearst columnist Igor Cassini, who wrote as "Cholly Knickerbocker." Mrs. McCullough had for some time been interested in the hunt for subversives—"I guess you might say I was always on the lookout for them" [2]—and demanded that the Greenwich appearance be canceled. She called Draper and Adler "pro-communist in sympathy" and said that any such person "should be treated as a traitor." Draper and Adler issued a statement, carried by the Associated Press, that they were not and never had been communists, members of the Communist party, pro-communists, or traitors, and that they owed and gave allegiance "solely to the United States under the Constitution." They filed suit against Mrs. McCullough. The Greenwich appearance proceeded without incident. Draper and Adler seemed to have weathered the storm.[3]

Under these circumstances Sullivan booked Draper for *Talk of the Town*. It appeared a further vindication.

But "Cholly Knickerbocker," along with other Hearst columnists—George Sokolsky and Westbrook Pegler—and various newsletters, took up the battle again and demanded that the Ford Motor Company cancel the television booking.

The advertising agency for Ford was Kenyon & Eckhardt, where William B. Lewis, former CBS vice president for programs, was president. After conferences, sponsor and agency decided to go ahead with the Draper appearance. (The possibility of a lawsuit was a factor in the decision.)

The columnists and newsletters, continuing their protests, managed to call forth on the Ford Motor Company a barrage of 1294 angry letters and telegrams in response to the telecast. As in many such campaigns, there were duplicates. Clusters came from the same post office. Most letters echoed published attacks. Eight per cent said that "leftists" and "pinks" should be sent back to Stalin. Thirteen per cent said that communism threatened Western civilization. The mail caused enough anguish to produce further meetings between sponsor and agency, in which it was de-

2. Miller, *The Judges and the Judged*, p. 151.
3. Kahn, "The Greenwich Tea Party," *New Yorker*, April 15, 1950. Draper and Adler, like many performing artists, had been in demand for wartime benefit performances. Draper had danced at fund-raising events for an Anti-Fascist Refugee Committee and for Russian War Relief, which also received free time from CBS. Another "citation" was that he had supported Henry Wallace for President.

cided that Ed Sullivan should send William B. Lewis a letter, which was drafted for the purpose by public-relations counsel, and which would also serve as a press release.

January 25, 1950

Dear Bill:

I am deeply distressed to find out that some people were offended by the appearance, on Sunday's *Toast of the Town* television show, of a performer whose political beliefs are a matter of controversy. That is most unfortunate. You know how bitterly opposed I am to communism and all it stands for. You also know how strongly I would oppose having the program used as a political forum, directly or indirectly.

After all, the whole point of the *Toast of the Town* is to entertain people, not offend them. . . . If anybody has taken offense, it is the last thing I wanted or anticipated, and I am sorry.

I just want *Toast of the Town* to be the best show on television. I know that's what you and the sponsor want, too. Tell everybody to tune in again next Sunday night, and if I can get in a plug, it will be a great show—better than ever.

Sincerely,
Ed Sullivan

After a detailed study of the mail, Kenyon & Eckhardt assured their sponsor that the incident had not damaged the Ford Motor Company but that every step was being taken "to diminish the chances of a recurrence." [4]

Paul Draper found he could no longer earn a living in the United States and went to live in Europe. [5]

Ed Sullivan, apparently as anxious as Kenyon & Eckhardt to "diminish the chances of a recurrence," turned to Theodore Kirkpatrick of *Counterattack* for guidance. According to Merle Miller, liaison between Sullivan and Kirkpatrick became "extremely close." [6]

In case of doubt about any artist, Sullivan now checked with Kirkpatrick. If the entertainer seemed to have "explaining to do," and Sullivan still wanted to use him, he would get Kirkpatrick and the artist together to see

4. *A Report on the Results of Paul Draper's Appearance,* pp. 1–16; also appendix.
5. The suit against Mrs. McCullough resulted in a hung jury.
6. Miller, *The Judges and the Judged,* p. 174.

if things could be ironed out. Sullivan seemed anxious to proclaim this closeness. He told column readers:

> Kirkpatrick has sat in my living room on several occasions and listened attentively to performers eager to secure a certification of loyalty. On some occasions, after interviewing them, he has given them the green light; on other occasions, he has told them: "Veterans' organizations will insist on further proof."

Sullivan felt that *Counterattack* was doing "a magnificent American job." [7] In this same column he gave readers some advance inside information: a "bombshell" was about to be dropped into the offices of networks, advertising agencies, and sponsors. It would be a book exposing a conspiracy.

It appeared the following day.

DESK COPY

On the paper cover of the 215-page *Red Channels: The Report of Communist Influence in Radio and Television* was a red hand closing on a microphone. The title page reported the work to be "by American Business Consultants, publishers of *Counterattack, the Newsletter of Facts To Combat Communism*, 55 West 42 Street, New York. . . ."

The introduction said: ". . . the Cominform and the Communist Party USA now rely more on radio and TV than on the press and motion pictures as 'belts' to transmit pro-Sovietism to the American public." The book was offered as a portrait of the infiltration carried out for this purpose—by order, it was implied, from abroad.

An unidentified "former head of a Soviet espionage ring" was quoted as saying:

> What American businessmen and the American public do not seem to realize is that these people are playing for keeps, with no holds barred. They don't lose time just making resolutions or having meetings. They're *activists!* Until we Americans learn to take prompt, effective action, too, they'll win every round!

This was followed by a quotation from *Broadcasting*:

> Where there's red smoke there's usually communist fire.

Setting the stage with such words, *Red Channels* listed 151 people—alphabetically arranged for easy reference—with "citations."

7. New York *Daily News*, June 21, 1950.

The list was enough to bring gasps. Advance hints from *Counterattack* and columnists had made the industry expect revelations of insidious underground activity. What they received was a list of 151 of the most talented and admired people in the industry—mostly writers, directors, performers.

They were people who had helped to make radio an honored medium, had played a prominent role in its wartime use, and had been articulators of American war aims.

In short, it was a roll of honor.[1]

To many observers the list seemed a preposterous hoax. The "citations" strengthened this impression. They gave a summary of what these men and women—with countless others—had been concerned with over the years. They had opposed Franco, Hitler, and Mussolini, tried to help war refugees, combated race discrimination, campaigned against poll taxes and other voting barriers, opposed censorship, criticized the House committee on un-American activities, hoped for peace, and favored efforts toward better U. S.-Soviet relations. Most had been New Deal supporters. Some

---

1. The total list: Larry Adler, Luther Adler, Stella Adler, Edith Atwater, Howard Bay, Ralph Bell, Leonard Bernstein, Walter Bernstein, Michael Blankfort, Marc Blitzstein, True Boardman, Millen Brand, Oscar Brand, J. Edward Bromberg, Himan Brown, John Brown, Abe Burrows, Morris Carnovsky, Vera Caspary, Edward Chodorov, Jerome Chodorov, Mady Christians, Lee J. Cobb, Marc Connelly, Aaron Copland, Norman Corwin, Howard Da Silva, Roger De Koven, Dean Dixon, Olin Downes, Alfred Drake, Paul Draper, Howard Duff, Clifford J. Durr, Richard Dyer-Bennett, José Ferrer, Louise Fitch, Martin Gabel, Arthur Gaeth, William S. Gailmor, John Garfield, Will Geer, Jack Gilford, Tom Glazer, Ruth Gordon, Lloyd Gough, Morton Gould, Shirley Graham, Ben Grauer, Mitchell Grayson, Horace Grenell, Uta Hagen, Dashiell Hammett, E. Y. Harburg, Robert P. Heller, Lillian Hellman, Nat Hiken, Rose Hobart, Judy Holliday, Roderick B. Holmgren, Lena Horne, Langston Hughes, Marsha Hunt, Leo Hurwitz, Charles Irving, Burl Ives, Sam Jaffe, Leon Janney, Joe Julian, Garson Kanin, George Keane, Donna Keath, Pert Kelton, Alexander Kendrick, Adelaide Klein, Felix Knight, Howard Koch, Tony Kraber, Millard Lampell, John Latouche, Arthur Laurents, Gypsy Rose Lee, Madeline Lee, Ray Lev, Philip Loeb, Ella Logan, Alan Lomax, Avon Long, Joseph Losey, Peter Lyon, Aline MacMahon, Paul Mann, Margo, Myron McCormick, Paul McGrath, Burgess Meredith, Arthur Miller, Henry Morgan, Zero Mostel, Jean Muir, Meg Mundy, Lynn Murray, Ben Myers, Dorothy Parker, Arnold Perl, Minerva Pious, Samson Raphaelson, Bernard Reis, Anne Revere, Kenneth Roberts, Earl Robinson, Edward G. Robinson, William N. Robson, Harold Rome, Norman Rosten, Selena Royle, Coby Ruskin, Robert St. John, Hazel Scott, Pete Seeger, Lisa Sergio, Artie Shaw, Irwin Shaw, Robert Lewis Shayon, Ann Shepherd, William L. Shirer, Allan Sloane, Howard K. Smith, Gale Sondergaard, Hester Sondergaard, Lionel Stander, Johannes Steel, Paul Stewart, Elliot Sullivan, William Sweets, Helen Tamiris, Betty Todd, Louis Untermeyer, Hilda Vaughn, J. Raymond Walsh, Sam Wanamaker, Theodore Ward, Fredi Washington, Margaret Webster, Orson Welles, Josh White, Ireene Wicker, Betty Winkler, Martin Wolfson, Lesley Woods, Richard Yaffe.

had favored Henry Wallace. They had backed lost causes. They had used the neglected right of petition. Many had perhaps been naïve. But to relate their thoroughly public activities to "infiltration," "conspiracy," and "espionage" was clearly absurd. The compilation could be seen as a move to pillory the liberal impulses of two decades as traitorous.

But calm appraisal was not easy in a time that thrived on the preposterous. *Red Channels* came on the heels of speeches that had suddenly propelled Senator Joseph R. McCarthy into the spotlight. The junior Senator from Wisconsin had told an audience of ladies in Wheeling, West Virginia, on February 9, 1950:

> While I cannot take the time to name all of the men in the State Department who have been named as members of the Communist Party and members of a spy ring, I have here in my hand a list of two hundred and five that were known to the Secretary of State as being members of the Communist Party and who nevertheless are still working and shaping the policy of the State Department.[2]

The statement had caused such a stir that McCarthy was suddenly in wide demand. In the following months he kept changing the numbers: in Salt Lake City and Reno he mentioned 57 "card-carrying" communists in the State Department, then switched in later appearances to 81, 10, 116, 121, and 106. The zig-zags were perhaps a diabolical new technique: he had half the nation disputing over precisely how many communists there *were* in the State Department.

The McCarthy mushroom grew like a monstrous thing, feeding on various matters that had prepared the soil. During a few preceding months the Soviet Union had detonated an atom bomb, the Chinese communists had won control of mainland China, eleven Communist party leaders had been sentenced to jail, and former Assistant Secretary of State Alger Hiss had been convicted of perjury—after denying the passing of government documents to Whittaker Chambers. If such things were possible, was *Red Channels* strange?

Within days after *Red Channels* the Korean war broke out. Broadcasting executives were suddenly thumbing the pages of *Red Channels* against a background not of peace but of war.

The unbelievable nature of the *Red Channels* list multiplied its impact. Every *Counterattack* subscriber received a copy; a few others went on sale in stores at $1 a copy. Most copies disappeared quickly into the drawers of

2. Wheeling *Intelligencer;* quoted, Rovere, *Senator Joe McCarthy*, p. 125.

executive desks at networks, advertising agencies, and sponsors. Few people discussed its contents openly. If they spoke of it, they seldom mentioned who was listed. Artists, even those listed, seldom saw a copy. Many
of those listed did not know about it for weeks. Some artists began to
guess it from the changed behavior of friends, or from the fact that producers no longer accepted their phone calls.

Millard Lampell, writer of dozens of scripts, including *The Lonesome
Train,* experienced a sudden end of job offers. One day his agent called
him in. Shutting the door, she whispered nervously that he was apparently
"on the list." She had not seen it, had not even been told so, definitely.
There had only been a hint that he was "in a little trouble." Later a producer with too many martinis confirmed it. "Pal, you're dead. I submitted
your name for a show and they told me I couldn't touch you with a barge
pole." He later added: "Don't quote me . . . I'll deny I said it." Lampell
sold his car, moved his wife and children to a small apartment in a cheap
neighborhood, and began a long siege. He started writing under pseudo-
nyms for various media. Long-time acquaintances passed him on the
street without sign of recognition. Once a "rock-ribbed" conservative actor
sent him an envelope with a $500 check and a note. "I have a feeling that
life is going to get pretty rough in the days ahead. This is a gift, to use
when you need to catch your breath and get back your perspective." [3]

For others, especially actors, results were more overt and sudden. They
could not work anonymously.

The Aldrich Family after eleven seasons on radio was scheduled to start
a television version on NBC in the summer of 1950. The Young & Rubicam
advertising agency held auditions, chose screen star Jean Muir for the role
of the mother, and announced it in a press release three days before the
scheduled premiere—Sunday, August 27. When Theodore Kirkpatrick of
Counterattack learned about it on Saturday morning, he at once made
phone calls. He did not phone network or sponsor—instead, he called
other people to get *them* to make phone calls. One person he phoned was
Mrs. Hester McCullough of Greenwich, who had been so active in the
Draper-Adler matter. She at once got busy on the phone. "I knew this was
a fight that had to be won," she later told an interviewer. While getting
others started, she herself called the National Broadcasting Company to
protest and found it was already getting other calls of protest. She also
called a Young & Rubicam executive living in Greenwich. He listened and

3. New York *Times,* August 21, 1966. Lampell says he did not use the check.

said: "But Mrs. McCullough, she's just an actress. What harm can she possibly do?" He seemed reluctant to talk, explaining that a relative had died a few hours before, "but I insisted on his listening to me and told him that in times like these, personal matters don't count." [4]

General Foods executives were likewise getting phone calls at their homes. Many of the callers claimed to speak for large groups.[5] The executives began nervously to get in touch with each other. The total number of protesting phone calls received by General Foods was variously reported. One account mentioned two hundred calls, but an executive confided to Merle Miller that it was closer to twenty.

Jean Muir got her first inkling of all this when she was notified that the opening telecast had been postponed a week. Later she was told her contract was being canceled: a cash settlement was offered. Her husband, an attorney, insisted she accept. The firing had been decided at the highest echelons of General Foods. It was headlined throughout the country.

Jean Muir flatly denied association with four of the nine organizations listed in her *Red Channels* entry. She dimly remembered wartime appearances at two others. Three "citations" she admitted and avowed. One was the signing of a cable of congratulations to the Moscow Art Theater on its fiftieth anniversary. A student of the Stanislavski acting method, she had rejoiced in the opportunity to join in this message. But such matters were not an issue. General Foods made no investigations, asked no explanations, claimed no disloyalty on her part. It merely asserted the need to avoid "controversial" people on programs it sponsored.

Jean Muir found her career virtually finished. She descended for a time into a spiral of alcoholism.[6]

Shortly after the Jean Muir episode a newly launched television version of *The Goldbergs*, sponsored on CBS by Sanka—another General Foods product—was subjected to protests over another *Red Channels* listee, Philip Loeb, who played Jake. A stand by Mrs. Berg—author, star, and owner of the series—for a time prevented a firing, but the sponsor dropped the series "for economic reasons" a few months later. After an interval the series reappeared on NBC under another sponsor and without Loeb. He was reported to have received a settlement. Mrs. Berg told the New York *Times*: "Philip Loeb has stated categorically that he is not and

4. Miller, *The Judges and the Judged*, pp. 36–8.
5. *Sponsor*, October 8, 1951.
6. Lamparski (ed.), *Whatever Became Of . . .* , radio interview with Jean Muir, WBAI, 1965.

never has been a communist. I believe him. There is no dispute between Philip Loeb and myself." The Loeb case was widely reported. His radio and television work ceased. His theater appearances were harassed. He eventually took an overdose of sleeping pills.[7]

After the Muir and Loeb cases, dismissals were handled more quietly, avoiding headlines. But the cases went on. Scarcely anyone listed in *Red Channels* remained unaffected. For those not under contract it meant a sudden drop in engagements. A number of listees went to Europe. Some, like Joseph Losey, became important in the European film world, along with Hollywood blacklist exiles.

A justification sometimes advanced for *Red Channels* was that anti-communist actors and writers were systematically blacklisted by "communist" producers and directors. Miller and Cogley were not able to find organized activity of this sort.

While *Red Channels* spread its influence, it was constantly criticized. Some who used it also criticized it—usually for wrong inclusions. A Batten, Barton, Durstine & Osborn executive, after studying the list, expressed horror. "I've known Abe Burrows for years. He's no subversive!" This protest led to an inquiry and a decision that Abe Burrows *could* be hired at BBD&O. Those involved felt they were "fighting the blacklist." They scarcely considered that *ad hoc* chipping at the list really conceded the principle—that those whom one did not know well should be expelled to outer darkness, once listed.

The situation favored some who, like Abe Burrows, were articulate. It worked against many who had seldom expressed themselves—especially those who kept an open mind and were willing to listen to all sides. Attendance at long-ago meetings was a frequent citation. "Ears willing to hear" were on the blacklist.

Red Channels itself did not specifically accuse anyone of anything—so its publishers insisted. It merely culled information from "public sources" —about petitions signed, meetings attended, organizations sponsored. The original sources sometimes proved wrong but the culling had been carefully done. The editors conceded that they did not know the political affiliation of most listees, and that "fellow travelers" and "dupes" and others had been lumped together. They admitted that the list might even include "anti-communists." The editors defended all this. One wrote: "It is suffi-

7. Cogley, *Report On Blacklisting: Radio-television*, pp. 35–8.

cient if they advance communist objectives with complete unconscious-
ness." [8]

The "cited" activities were said to "help communism" on the authority
of the Attorney General's list or of a legislative committee report or of
testimony at a hearing or, in some cases, the opinion of the publishers
themselves. Thus a "citation" against Philip Loeb was that he had been a
sponsor of an "End Jim Crow in Baseball Committee," which "helped
communism" on the sole authority of *Red Channels* itself.

Keenan was willing to concede that some listees should not have been
listed. But he said the "innocent" could always come forward and "clear"
themselves. Many artists seem to have visited the offices of *Counterattack*
for such clearance. One editor told a *Sponsor* reporter: "You should hear
the big act some of them put on in this office. It's a panic to hear them." [9]

Ireene Wicker, whose *Singing Lady* program had been entertaining children for years and had been sponsored by Kellogg, was dropped by the
sponsor after *Red Channels.* Her sole citation said she had sponsored a
petition for the re-election of Benjamin J. Davis to Congress in 1945. The
citation was based on an item in the *Daily Worker,* which supported
Davis. Ireene Wicker said she had never heard of Benjamin J. Davis. Also,
she had not been in New York when the petition was circulated. She told
this to Kirkpatrick. The rest of their discussion was described by her to
John Cogley, whose account is in his *Report on Blacklisting.*

> He shifted the conversation then to a discussion of what Miss Wicker
> had done to express her opposition to communism. She cited several
> patriotic activities—she conducted an "I'm glad I am an American
> because—" contest for children, she recorded a series based on Amer-
> ican history entitled "Sing a Song of History," etc. But Kirkpatrick
> was not impressed. Then the actress mentioned that she had allowed
> her only son to enlist in the Royal Canadian Air Force before he was
> 18. The boy, who was shot down in Europe, joined up in 1940 during
> the Hitler-Stalin pact, a time when American communists were en-
> gaged in their "Yanks Are Not Coming" campaign. But even that was
> not enough. Miss Wicker left the *Counterattack* office without con-
> vincing Kirkpatrick.

She later obtained a court order so that her lawyer could examine all
30,000 names on the nominating petitions for Benjamin Davis. Her name

8. *Red Channels*, Introduction, pp. 5–6.
9. *Sponsor*, October 22, 1951.

was not on the list. Ireene Wicker was "cleared" but her agent still found that sponsors "wouldn't touch her." She had become "controversial." [10]

Most artists did not wish to plead for "clearance." One said: "I don't want to have anything to do with pigmies playing God."

Much of the discussion about *Red Channels*, centering as it did on alleged listing errors, sidestepped more basic issues. Raymond Swing, when invited to debate Kirkpatrick before the Radio Executives Club of New York, took a more long-range view. Many people were saying the Founding Fathers would turn in their graves over *Red Channels*. Swing doubted it.

> I don't believe the Founding Fathers would be in the least astonished, not about *Red Channels* or its author. There were some pretty feverish libelers and defamers in their time, and they threw their filth and disseminated their odors most widely and injuriously. A free society is free also to the unworthy, something the Founding Fathers understood quite well. . . . Democracy is a free market. . . . But Democracy is, among other things, a belief that in this free market the unworthy will ruin themselves and truth in time—yes, only in time—will triumph.

Swing then discussed dangers facing our society. He did not see the *Red Channels* approach solving any of them. On the other hand, he did not see blacklisters themselves as the real danger. The real danger, said Swing,

> would come from those who, having been given responsibility for one of America's most vital institutions, unwittingly, or carelessly, or timidly, yield some of their authority to people who are not entitled to it. . . .

> If, by some bleak and dreadful tragedy, American radio should come under the control of persons intent on producing a single conformity of thinking in America, it will not be the pressure groups or the blacklisters who will be to blame, but those now in charge of radio. *They* have it in their keeping, and what *happens* to it will be *their* doing and only their doing.[11]

The executives are said to have applauded loudly.

One result of the speech was that Swing, who was not in *Red Channels*, began to get attention from *Counterattack*. He had become chief commentator for the Voice of America—a logical choice, since he was known

10. Cogley, *Report on Blacklisting: Radio-television*, pp. 32–4.
11. Swing, *Good Evening!*, pp. 256–62.

throughout the globe and knew many world leaders. The range of his career gave *Counterattack* oceans to fish in; the newsletter suggested that his background showed a dangerous internationalism. This apparently aroused the interest of Senator McCarthy, already intent on discrediting the State Department. As the Senator's harassments began to center on the Voice of America, they began to include Swing.

Meanwhile, in spite of the applause of the Radio Executives Club, *Red Channels* extended its sway. There was a new reason for this, to be found not among networks and agencies but in another world, only slightly removed from it—the supermarket.

SUPERMARKET

Mrs. Eleanor Johnson Buchanan of Syracuse, New York, whose father owned four supermarkets, was a crusader like Hester McCullough. She was a student of *Counterattack* and *Red Channels*. When her husband went to Korea with the marines, she busied herself with angry letters and speeches against "red sympathizers on radio and television . . . and those do-nothing patriotic citizens who discuss the wrongs of the world over a dinner table" while her husband—"my quiet, unassuming Jack"—ate C-rations on a battlefield amid flies "from the dead Gook twenty feet away." [1]

Her father, Laurence A. Johnson, the supermarket owner, helped her with mimeographing, mailing, and contacts, and became increasingly involved. His position as a supermarket executive became a key factor. Gradually he took over leadership in the work.

In June 1951 father and daughter had a talk with members of an American Legion Post in Syracuse. Afterward she wrote the legionnaires:

> Dad and I were pleased that you agree manufacturers can be persuaded to remove communist sympathizers from their advertising programs on radio and television. As you gentlemen pointed out in our meeting last Friday, the task is too great for me alone. I am grateful for your aid. . . .

A few weeks later the local Legion group created its own Americanism committee, and began issuing a newsletter, often taking material from *Counterattack*. With the help of this local group, Laurence Johnson and

---

1. The following is based on Cogley, *Report on Blacklisting: Radio-television*, pp. 56–109; other sources as noted.

his daughter became a force felt throughout the radio and television world.

At first the team seemed only a Syracuse phenomenon—efficient but local. A sponsor described its mode of operation to John Cogley:

> At one o'clock I got a telegram signed Larry Johnson. At two o'clock a telegram arrived signed by the Syracuse American Legion Post. At three o'clock there was a wire from the veterans' action committee of Syracuse supermarkets.

This committee was headed by Francis W. Neuser, fruit and vegetable buyer for Laurence Johnson.

But Johnson, in addition to owning supermarkets, was elected to office in the National Association of Supermarkets, and this enabled him to give the impression—few wanted to test it—that he had influence over thousands of outlets throughout the country. Similarly pronouncements of the local Legion group were often accepted as national Legion pronouncements.

Laurence Johnson was an elderly man of imposing presence, gracious in manner, who slipped easily into patriotic talk. Many people considered him naïve, but he was a canny operator. He devised a diabolical technique for bringing pressure on sponsors.

One of the most successful early television drama series was *Danger*, launched by CBS in 1950. It acquired as sponsor the Block Drug Company, maker of Amm-i-dent, a chlorophyll toothpaste. When Johnson learned that *Danger* used actors listed by *Counterattack*, he wrote a long letter to Mr. Block the sponsor, calling attention to the casting and making an offer.

He would display Amm-i-dent and its chlorophyll competitor Chlorodent side by side at his supermarkets. In front of each display would be a sign.

The Chlorodent sign would say that its manufacturer, Lever Brothers, was using only pro-American artists and shunning "Stalin's little creatures."

The Amm-i-dent sign, to be written by the Block Drug Company itself, would explain why its programs chose communist fronters.

Johnson's letter asked: "Would not the results of such a test be of the utmost value to the thousands of supermarkets throughout America . . . ?"

As a final touch Johnson added: "This letter will be held awaiting your answer for a few days. Then copies will be sent to the following. . . ." Here he added a list that included the United States Chamber of Commerce, the Sons of the American Revolution, the Catholic War Veterans, the Super Market Institute in Chicago and other organizations—a list raising a specter of national obloquy.

From the veterans' action committee of the Syracuse supermarkets a letter also went to CBS president Frank Stanton—an audience-research specialist—offering to set up a poll at the supermarkets. Boxes marked *Yes* and *No* would allow customers to vote on the question: "Do you want any part of your purchase price of any products advertised on the Columbia Broadcasting System to be used to hire communist fronters?" [2]

The offers of such "polls" and the phrase "Stalin's little creatures" became trademarks of Johnson campaigns. His letters were reinforced by phone calls and frequent visits to sponsors and advertising agencies. That these made an impression is suggested by various testimonial letters that Johnson was soon able to exhibit, all praising his patriotic achievements.[3] An assistant vice president of the Borden Milk Company wrote him:

> I want to tell you again how grateful I am for the time and help you gave me on Tuesday. It is no exaggeration to say that my eyes have been opened as a result of your cooperation. The same goes for Francis Neuser and his group. He mentioned the fact that they are unpopular, but I know he isn't right. No one could meet them without being impressed by the honesty and zeal with which they are pursuing a fine course, and with their obvious determination to be fair.

A Kraft Foods vice president wrote him:

> It is indeed heartening to know that you are continuing your crusade. . . . I sincerely hope you keep up the good work.

The president of the General Ice Cream Corporation wrote:

> I think it is wonderful that you have taken this interest in ferreting communists out of our entertainment industry. I wish there were more people like you.

When he started on his zealous campaigns, Johnson felt he needed help from an inside-information expert. He hired Harvey Matusow, a former

2. These and other letters became evidence in a lawsuit filed in 1956 by John Henry Faulk against Laurence Johnson and others. Nizer, *The Jury Returns*, pp. 324–5.
3. The following are quoted in Cogley, *Report on Blacklisting: Radio-television*, pp. 56, 102.

Communist party member whose 1949 testimony as paid government witness had helped convict Communist party leaders under the Smith Act. When Matusow later admitted he had invented parts of his testimony and was jailed for perjury, Laurence Johnson turned to a rising star in the blacklist field—Vincent Hartnett.

Hartnett had written the introduction to *Red Channels*. Not a member of the Kirkpatrick group, he had done this task on a freelance basis and received a royalty from *Red Channels* sales. He had earned B.A. and M.A. degrees with honors from Notre Dame, and during World War II had served as intelligence officer in the Navy. Afterward he joined the Phillips H. Lord production company and worked on the *Gangbusters* series, but digressed into work as a consultant on subversive activities. Building up his own files on the affiliations of artists, he offered his services to sponsors, agencies, and networks. He charged $20 for checking a name. A large number of names brought the price down to $5 per head; for rechecking, to $2. As clients he obtained the Borden company, Lever Brothers, the Young & Rubicam agency, the Kudner agency, and the ABC network.[4] Meanwhile his connection with *Red Channels* added to his standing. He often referred to the book as "my *Red Channels*." He also began preparing a more comprehensive directory entitled *File 13*, to sell at $5. *Red Channels*, he said in an advertisement, was a "piker" and had only scratched the surface.[5] He also planned an encyclopedia on American communists, which was to list several thousand names and sell at $500.00. He advertised himself as "the nation's top authority on communism and communications." His connection with Laurence Johnson augmented the power of both. Johnson kept recommending Hartnett to food and drug companies to keep them out of difficulties. Hartnett watched casting announcements and fed Johnson up-to-date information on suitable targets, while Johnson marshaled the Syracuse forces.

Not every Johnson sortie met with success. In 1951 the important documentary television series *See It Now*, a collaboration of Edward R. Murrow and Fred W. Friendly, had its CBS debut under the sponsorship of Alcoa. It was an outgrowth of the radio series *Hear It Now*, which had developed from the LP album *I Can Hear It Now*. Murrow and Friendly at once tackled a variety of controversial topics, which stirred up a Syracuse campaign against *See It Now*. It apparently had no effect on the

4. Nizer, *The Jury Returns*, pp. 357–8.
5. Miller, *The Judges and the Judged*, p. 120.

sponsor—perhaps because the fate of aluminum did not depend on super-markets.

Another failure or partial failure concerned the singing group the Weavers, one of the first targets of the Syracuse Legion unit. Learning that the group included Pete Seeger, a *Red Channels* listee, the unit began telling local radio stations, music stores, and juke box operators that they should boycott recordings of the Weavers. Representatives of the Syra-cuse University radio-television center and the six Syracuse stations met to discuss this—and refused. That ended the matter within Syracuse broad-casting circles. A Syracuse executive later told John Cogley: "I don't know what's the matter with those people in New York. Maybe they're so big they have to be stupid."

In 1950, foods, drugs, cleaning products and toiletries—items sold through supermarkets—accounted for over 60 per cent of the revenue of the broadcasting industry. This was the force in the Laurence Johnson whipsaw operation. To sponsors, agencies, networks, Laurence Johnson became a bane and a salvation. He was their justification. They loathed and needed him. Executives who felt foolish knuckling under to a silly woman from Greenwich found in Johnson a certified demonstration in economic—i.e. respectable—terms. He was *proof* that what they were doing was stark necessity and that the alternative was ruin. "I don't have to be ashamed of what I'm doing!" an advertising agency executive told researcher Marie Jahoda, perhaps because of a shamed feeling. "I am just here to protect the interests of our clients. Controversial people are bad for their business." An American Tobacco Company executive, however, said he had to protect the interests of his 80,000 shareholders. In any case Laurence Johnson was exhibits A, B, C, and D.[6]

Broadcasting itself was a sort of supermarket, with programs from many producers and distributors clawing for precious shelf space. Here the voice from the supermarket was readily understood.

Only one further step was needed to complete the blacklist structure. Networks and agencies grew weary of being attacked and decided to take charge of the whole business themselves. Blacklist administration became part of the built-in machinery of the industry.

CBS, which in 1950 established a sort of loyalty oath, followed this in 1951 with the appointment of an executive specializing in security. Some

6. Jahoda, "Anti-Communism and Employment Policies in Radio and Television," in Cogley, *Report on Blacklisting: Radio-television*, pp. 252–3.

artists called him the "vice president in charge of treason." At NBC the legal department assumed similar duties. Large advertising agencies acquired special security officers under various titles. Some agencies continued to employ Kirkpatrick, Hartnett, and others, but during the early 1950's the kingpins of the structure became the hush-hush officials at networks and large agencies.

Mysterious protocol was devised to veil their work. Producers had to submit to superiors the names of writers, actors, and directors being considered. A copy was routed to the security chief. A phone call later conveyed approvals or disapprovals. Memoranda and face-to-face meetings were avoided. The voice at the other end would go down the list of proposed names with "Yes," "No," "Yes," "Yes," "No." Questions were not to be asked. Rituals were prescribed for staff producers and independent producers alike. David Susskind, who plunged into television early as a "packager"—producing *Armstrong Circle Theater, Philco Television Playhouse, Appointment for Adventure, Justice,* and many subsequent series— testified on one occasion about his relations with Young & Rubicam. For one series he made "ten or fifteen" phone calls daily to the agency to check names. About five thousand name checks were made during a year. A third of the names, "perhaps a little higher," were rejected. He had to agree never to tell an actor why he could not be used. If a reason was needed, it must be "not tall enough," or "the leading man is too short." Each time an actor was used, he had to be checked again. Even children had to be checked. An eight-year-old daughter of a controversial father was banned; Susskind had to find "another child whose father was all right."[7]

There was wide use of semantic disguises. The word "blacklist" was taboo because it suggested concerted action—a conspiracy to deny employment. Such action was denied; the point was, each company was by now developing its own list or lists. In approval or disapproval of names, novel terminology took root. The banned actor was said to be "not available." Misuse of language perhaps protected the self-image.

The installation of staff security officers did not halt outside pressures; if anything, it encouraged them. Competition among investigators and newsletters was strenuous. None wanted to be outdone in zeal or success. Lists kept getting longer. *Red Channels* was a starting point for many but was soon obsolete.

7. Nizer, *The Jury Returns,* pp. 288–90.

Programs of all types were affected. "The first thing I knew," Mary Margaret McBride revealed later, "was when the advertising manager of one of the companies phoned." He had just seen a delegation of women with a list of allegedly suspect people who had been on her program.

> And lo, Eleanor Roosevelt led all the rest! Then came Pearl Buck, Carl Van Doren, Fannie Hurst, and many more of my best friends. . . . I confess it shamefacedly. . . . I finally yielded to pressure and turned down several who were on the committee's lists. . . . It is the blackest memory of my radio life.

Unhappily, her economic instincts reasserted themselves even in these recollections. She added this footnote to her black memory: "We lost only one sponsor that I know of as a result of the witch hunt, and that place was filled at once." [8]

All talent unions experienced vicious schisms as a result of the blacklists. Efforts to clear away the aura of disloyalty produced "non-communist" slates in several union elections. These were deeply resented because they seemed to impugn other slates as "communist." The "non-communist" slates combined strange bedfellows: they included ardent proponents of blacklists and others who—emulating the American Civil Liberties Union —felt that non-communists could more effectively combat blacklists. The internal dissensions seem to have given comfort to anti-union executives at networks, sponsors, and agencies; they hampered effective union action.

John Cogley found that two companies, the Columbia Broadcasting System and Batten, Barton, Durstine & Osborn, were especially zealous in institutionalizing blacklisting. Artists have generally concurred with this conclusion. There was an irony in the finding, for these companies had been especially noted for the vigor and range of their programming; the new development seemed, in fact, a by-product of the very policies that had won high regard for their work.

BBD&O was responsible for *Cavalcade of America* which, for Du Pont reasons, had stressed peace and social values during the 1930's, and had attracted writers concerned with such issues. It also had the *The March of Time,* which under *Time* supervision had attracted similar writers. It had *Theater Guild on the Air,* sponsored by U.S. Steel, which had given the celebrated Theater Guild maximum freedom during the era of product shortage and institutional advertising. All these series had drawn on artists

8. McBride, *Out of the Air,* p. 146.

able to cope with ideas and complex issues. Such artists had especially roused the suspicions of blacklisters. The blacklist era was thus sharply felt at BBD&O and led to an upheaval in hiring.

At CBS the renascence of the 1930's had developed around the drama of ideas. At a time when NBC dominated the air with vaudeville comedians and singers, CBS had welcomed the ferment of the Depression and thereby made its mark—and also made itself a happy hunting ground for blacklisters. CBS, reacting, had become purge headquarters—at precisely the time when it was taking over the NBC comedians. The networks were switching roles.

Among several who suddenly disappeared from CBS was William N. Robson. He had been assistant director for *The Fall of the City,* become chief director of *Columbia Workshop,* brought honor to CBS with the *Open Letter on Race Hatred* starring Wendell Willkie, directed the superb wartime series *The Man Behind the Gun,* and gone on to commercial success as director of *Big Town.* Both writer and director, he had been one of the handful of radio people selected for a War Department tour of battle areas during the closing weeks of the war in Europe.

In 1950, while working at CBS in Los Angeles, he learned he was listed in *Red Channels.* The listing was at first treated lightly by his CBS superiors. According to Robson's recollection, his supervisor said jokingly, "You dirty communist!" Robson urged him not to say such things, even in jest. Shortly afterward he was sent to New York and assigned to a new CBS television series, *Sure as Fate*—a mystery series. It had its debut in the summer of 1950. After a time, without explanation, he was relieved of his duties, although his contract fee for the series—$600 per week—arrived regularly. He was told another assignment would be made, but many weeks passed. One day, in desperation, he tried to telephone chairman of the board William S. Paley, who was out of town. He asked for—and received—an immediate appointment with president Frank Stanton. Within an hour he was telling Stanton of his situation, mentioning the *Red Channels* listing. According to Robson's recollection, Stanton expressed shocked surprise. "Are you in *Red Channels?* . . . But you're not a communist."

"No, I'm not. I'll give you any statement you require to that effect."

"Will you give me a statement to that effect?"

"Certainly."

Stanton expressed concern, and reassured him. Robson said: "Look, you're losing a lot of money on me." Stanton answered that that was not the important thing." [9]

Robson went back to Los Angeles but heard nothing further. The *Sure as Fate* contract expired and payments stopped. On a freelance basis he directed some programs for the CBS radio series *Escape,* and wrote a few scripts for the CBS television series *Suspense,* using a pseudonym. Then he was told that orders from CBS headquarters in New York had forbidden further assignments to him.

The *Red Channels* listing for William N. Robson contained four items. It said that (1) in 1942 he had been sponsor of an Artists Front To Win the War organized at a meeting in Carnegie Hall; (2) in December 1946 he had made a speech in Los Angeles, protesting encroachments on freedom of expression ;(3) in 1948 he had signed with other artists a "We are for Wallace" advertisement in the New York *Times;* (4) he was listed as an "associate" on the masthead of the *Hollywood Quarterly,* a scholarly journal of film, radio, and television published by the University of California Press.[10]

Robson could scarcely believe that those *Red Channels* citations had doomed his career. Did executives at CBS, a network long known for liberalism, seriously regard him as a threat—and on the basis of those items? He was out of work for about two years, and for a time went to Europe.[11]

The blacklist era scarred many who clung to jobs along with those who could not. An interest in race relations, an artist told Marie Jahoda, now had to be avoided; it caused suspicion. Another actor said he would not risk walking into an advertising agency with a copy of the New York *Post* —a usually Democratic newspaper. An address in Greenwich Village had become professionally risky. An actor said:

> My wife had a copy of Karl Marx that she got when she was 16 or 17 years old. One night we were having a producer and his wife over for dinner and we didn't want him to see this book, so we removed it from the shelf.[12]

9. Robson, *Reminiscences,* pp. 22–4.
10. *Red Channels,* pp. 123–4. The *Hollywood Quarterly* became the *Quarterly of Film, Radio, and Television* and later *Film Quarterly.*
11. He felt the effects throughout the 1950's. A decisive change came when Edward R. Murrow took over the direction of the Voice of America under President John F. Kennedy, and invited Robson to join that sensitive agency. Apparently no obstacle was found to his security clearance, which came promptly, and he began a long tenure with the Voice. Robson, *Reminiscences,* pp. 24–7.
12. Jahoda, "Anti-Communism and Employment Policies in Radio and Television," in Cogley, *Report on Blacklisting: Radio-television,* pp. 248–9.

Drama plots were affected. In mystery stories bankers or businessmen were no longer useful characters because they could not be suspects. In history plays the word "peace" made people uneasy: it sounded communist. In Hollywood a story about Hiawatha, with an important peace-pipe scene, was actually abandoned for this reason. It was too reminiscent of the Waldorf-Astoria peace meeting.[13]

Pearl Buck, who had written many radio documentaries during World War II—some were short-waved to Asia in Chinese by the OWI overseas branch—later formed an East and West Association with a radio department to arrange guest broadcasts by prominent Asians. Finding that the activity was considered suspect, she ended it late in 1950. She wrote:

> Today it is dangerous even to declare belief in the brotherhood of peoples, in the equality of the races, in the necessity for human understanding, in the common sense of peace—all those beliefs in which I have been reared. . . .

She was dismayed over "the strange atmosphere that has pervaded my country since 1946. . . ."[14] Many people were dismayed.

Raymond Swing had spoken of the responsibility of "those now in charge of radio." Who were they? Who *was* in charge?

The FCC? Its powers were limited.

The stations licensed by the FCC? Theoretically the system was built on their sovereignty, but they had surrendered it to the time-brokerage firms called networks.

The networks? They had relinquished much of their time, and the choice of content, to advertising agencies.

The agencies? They took orders from sponsors.

The sponsors? They spoke of their responsibility to stockholders. . . .

Network spokesmen publicly defended what was happening, but many were also aghast. The dispersal of authority seemed to some of them a fatal error of the radio era. Among these was William Paley, who was determined that broadcasters must regain the control surrendered to agencies and sponsors at the dawn of network radio. Another was Sylvester L. ("Pat") Weaver, who in 1949 had joined NBC as vice president in charge of television. Aside from wartime service with the U. S. Navy—this had included a tour of duty at the Armed Forces Radio Service—and with the Coordinator of Inter-American Affairs, he had had a career with

13. *The Reporter Political Yearbook* (1951), p. 29.
14. Buck, *My Several Worlds*, pp. 434–5.

POLITICS

Republican candidate
Thomas E. Dewey.

The 1944 "Roosevelt Special." Left line: Tallulah Bankhead, Irving Berlin, Virginia Bruce, Claudette Colbert, Linda Darnell, Paulette Goddard (obscured), John Garfield (obscured), Walter Huston, Groucho Marx, Jane Wyman. Right line: Joan Bennett, Mrs. Irving Berlin, Harry Carey, Joseph Cotton (obscured), Rita Hayworth, Rex Ingram, Danny Kaye, Paul Muni, others.

1946: Norman Corwin interviews Eduard Beneš in Prague for *One World Flight*. In foreground, wire recorder.

1950: NBC-TV covers a session of the United Nations.

RADIO TODAY

WAAT.. 970	WEAF.. 660	WJZ 770	WOR 710
WABC.. 880	WEVD..1330	WLIB...1190	WWRL..1600
WBBR..1330	WHN...1050	WMCA.. 570	WOV ...1280
WBNX..1430	WHOM..1480	WNEW..1130	WPAT.... 930
WBYN..1430	WINS...1010	WNYC.. 830	WQXR...1560

THURSDAY, NOV. 11, 1943

Armistice Day Ceremonies, Tomb of the Unknown Soldier—WEAF, WMCA, 10:58-11:04 A. M.
Eternal Light Ceremonies: Mayor La Guardia, Newbold Morris, at Madison Square Park—WNYC, 11 A. M.-12 M.
Armistice Day Message, Arlington National Cemetery; Warren H. Atherton, Legion Commander, and Others—WJZ, 11:45 A. M.-12 M.
Armistice Day: Mrs. A. C. Kane, President, Women's Auxiliary, V. F. W.—WJZ, 1:45-2.
Debate, N. Y. U.-Columbia: "Two-Thirds Vote of Senate on Treaties Is an Obstacle to A Durable Peace"—WNYC, 4:30-5:30.
Attorney General Biddle, Speaking at Jewish Theological Seminary Annual Dinner—WABC, 6:30-6:45.
Bob Burns, Variety; Spike Jones and Others—WEAF, 7:30-8.
Variety: Fanny Brice, Frank Morgan, Hanley Stafford—WEAF, 8-8:30.
Variety: Mary Astor, Charles Ruggles, Mischa Auer—WABC, 8-8:30.
Armistice Day Drama—WNYC, 8-8:30.
Play: "The Aldrich Family," With Dickie Jones—WEAF, 8:30-9.
Human Adventure: "Story of Dr. Ignaz Semmelweis"—WOR, 8:30-9.
Town Meeting of the Air: "Are America's and Britain's Economic Aims Incompatible?"—Senator Brewster of Maine, Dr. Harry Gideonse and Others—WJZ, 8:30-9:30.
Music Hall: Bob Crosby; Lum and Abner, Guests—WEAF, 9-9:30.
Amateur Program: Major Bowes, Director—WABC, 9-9:30.
Variety: Joan Davis, Jack Haley; Edward Everett Horton, Guest—WEAF, 9:30-10.
Dinah Shore Show: Cornelia Otis Skinner, Roland Young; Donald O'Conner, Guest—WABC, 9:30-10.
Abbott and Costello, Comedy; Akim Tamiroff, Guest—WEAF, 10-10:30.
Former Governor Lehman and Others, From United Nations Conference, Atlantic City—WABC, 10-10:30.
March of Time: Interviews With Wounded Servicemen at Walter Reed Hospital; Lieut-Gen. Thomas Holcomb, Speaker—WEAF 10:30-11.

Where there is no listing for a station the preceding program is on the air

MORNING

5:30-WABC—Reveille Sweetheart Music
　WNEW—News; Recorded Music
5:45-WOR—Farmers' Digest
6:00-WHN—Radio Newsreel
6:30-WEAF—Farm News
　WOR—News, Farmers' Digest
　WABC—Arthur Godfrey, Talk; Music
　WNEW—News; Recorded Music
6:45-WMCA—Early Bird Music
　WNEW—Morning Meditations
6:55-WEAF—News; Arthur Godfrey; Music
7:00-WEAF—News; Pat Barnes, Music
　WOR—News; Musical Clock
　WJZ-Ed East Variety Show
　WNYC—Sunrise Symphony
　WHN—Recorded Music
　WEVD—News; Recorded Music
　WQXR—Headlines and Harmonies
7:15-WMCA—News; Bing Crosby Records
　WHN—News; Recorded Music
7:25-WQXR—News; Music
7:30-WEAF—Songs of the Plain
　WNEW—News; Recorded Music
　WIN in Yiddish
7:45-WJZ, WABC—News Reports
　WABC—Help Wanted—Ads
　WEVD—Morning Melodies
7:55-WQXR—News; Music
8:00-WEAF—News Reports
　WOR—News; Aunt Jenny's Stories
　WJZ—Kibitzers; Music; Comedy
　WABC—News; Music; Comedy
　WMCA—N. Y. Times News Bulletins
　WNYC—News; Recorded Music
　WEVD—Romantic Serenader
8:03-WMCA—Horace Heidt Orchestra
8:15-WEAF—Minute Men—Ralph Dumke
　WMCA—Unity Viewpoint—Talk
　WNYC—Want Ads; Song
　WEVD—Good Morning, Madam
8:25-WNYC—Consumers Talk: Mrs. Frances F. Gannon
8:30-WEAF—News—Radcliff Hall
　WOR—Shopping—Peggen Fitzgerald
　WJZ—Nancy Craig—Talk
　WABC—Missus Goes A-Shopping
　WMCA—News; Recorded Music
　WNYC—Food—Margaret Conner
　WNEW—News; Recorded Music
　WEVD—Song Vendor
8:55-WNYC—Morning Serenade
8:45-WEAF—Definition—Quiz; Music
　WABC—Margaret Arlen—Talk
　WNYC—News; City Guide
　WHN—News Reports
　WEVD—Folk Singer
8:55-WOR, WQXR—News Reports
9:00-WEAF—Everything Goes, Variety
　WOR—Food—Victor H. Lindlahr
　WJZ—Breakfast Club—Variety
　WABC—News Reports
　WMCA—N. Y. Times News Bulletins

WNYC—Masterworks Hour
WHN Gloom Dodgers– Variety (To 1)
WNEW—Dick Brown, Songs
WEVD—News in Yiddish
9:03-WMCA—Alice Hughes, Comments
9:15-WOR—Talks and Music
　WABC—School of the Air
　WMCA—Guy Lombardo Records
　WEVD—Women in the News; Music
　WQXR—American Melodies
9:30-WEAF—Adelaide Hawley, News
　WOR-Food—Alfred W. McCann
　WMCA—Funny Money Man
　WNEW—News; Western Songs
　WQXR—Pop Concert
9:45-WEAF—Robert St. John, News
　WABC—The Market Basket—Isabel Manning Hewson
　WMCA—Glen Gray Records
　WEVD—News in Yiddish
9:55-WQXR—News Reports
10:00-WEAF—Lora Lawton—Sketch
　WOR—News—Henry Gladstone
　WJZ—Bingo
　WABC—Valiant Lady—Sketch
　WMCA—N. Y. Times News Bulletins
　WNYC—Women in War—Helen Brockman
　WNEW—Make Believe Ballroom
　WQXR—Popular Music
10:05-WMCA—Recorded Music
10:15-WEAF—The Open Door—Sketch
　WOR—Bessie Beatty Program
　WJZ—Roy Porter, News
　WABC—Kitty Foyle—Sketch
　WQXR—Tremendous Trifles
10:30-WEAF—Help Mate—Sketch
　WJZ—The Baby Institute: Elizabeth Hawes, Guest
　WABC—Honeymoon Hill—Sketch
　WMCA—News; Recorded Music
　WNEW—News; Recorded Music
　WOR-Gilbert-Sullivan Music
10:45-WEAF—First Piano Quartet
　WJZ—Sweet River—Sketch
　WABC—Bachelor's Children—Sketch
　WNYC—Our Navy—Sketch
10:55-WQXR—News Reports
10:58-WEAF—Armistice Ceremonies, Tomb of Unknown Soldier (also WMCA)
11:00-WOR—News—Tro Harper; Music
　WJZ—Breakfast With Breneman
　WABC—Cooking—Mary Lee Taylor
　WMCA—N. Y. Times News Bulletins
　WNYC—Armistice Day Ceremonies at Eternal Light, Madison Square Park; Mayor La Guardia and Newbold Morris, Speakers
　WQXR—Other People's Business—

NEWS BROADCASTS

Every hour on the hour
from 8 A. M. through 11 P. M.
NEW YORK TIMES *news bulletins*
over WMCA—570

Morning

6:00-WHN
6:30-WEAF, WOR,
　WNEW
6:55-WABC
7:00-WEAF, WOR,
　WNYC, WEVD,
　WQXR
7:15-WMCA, WHN
7:25-WQXR
7:30-WEAF, WNEW
7:45-WJZ, WABC
7:55-WQXR
8:00-WEAF, WOR,
　WABC, WMCA,
　WNYC

8:30-WEAF, WMCA,
　WNEW
8:45-WNYC, WHN
8:55-WOR, WQXR
9:00-WABC, WMCA
9:30-WEAF
9:55-WEAF
10:00-WOR, WMCA
10:15-WJZ
10:30-WEAF, WNEW
11:00-WOR, WMCA,
　WNYC
11:30-WJZ, WMCA,
　WNEW
11:55-WQXR

Afternoon

12:00-WEAF WOR,
　WABC, WMCA
12:25-WJZ
12:30-WOR, WNEW
12:35-WQXR
1:00-WOR, WMCA
1:30-WMCA; WNEW
1:45-WEAF
1:55-WQXR
2:00-WMCA, WNYC
2:30-WOR, WNEW
2:35-WQXR
3:00-WMCA

3:15-WABC
3:30-WMCA, WNEW
3:45-WNYC
3:55-WQXR
4:00-WABC
4:25-WABC
4:30-WJZ, WMCA, WNEW
4:55-WQXR
5:00-WMCA
5:15-WQXR
5:25-WQXR, WHN
5:30-WMCA, WNEW

Evening

6:00-WOR, WJZ,
　WABC, WMCA
6:15-WEAF
6:25-WQXR
6:30-WOR, WNEW,
　WMCA
6:45-WJZ, WMCA,
　WNYC
7:00-WOR, WMCA,
　WHN, WQXR
7:15-WEAF
7:25-WQXR
7:30-WOR, WMCA,
　WNEW
7:45-WHN
8:00-WJZ, WMCA
8:30-WNEW
8:45-WHN, WEVD
9:00-WOR, WMCA,
　WQXR
9:30-WMCA, WNEW

9:55-WQXR
10:00-WOR, WJZ,
　WMCA
10:15-WJZ, WHN
10:30-WOR, WMCA,
　WNEW
10:50-WQXR
11:00-WEAF WJZ,
　WQXR
11:15-WEAF
11:25-WHN
11:30-WNEW
12:00-WEAF, WJZ,
　WABC, WMCA,
　WQXR
12:55-WHN
1:00-WJZ, WABC,
　WMCA
1:45-WHN
2:00-WNEW

BY SHORT WAVE

Time, Eastern War—Megacycles

LONDON
9:00, 11:00 A. M., 12 Noon—15.30
3:45-6:45, P. M.—11.68, 9.58
9:05 P. M.—9.53, 6.11
10:45 P. M., 12:30 A. M.—9.00, 9.58, 7.15,

MOSCOW
7:40 A. M.—15.75
6:48 P. M.—15.23, 15.11

MELBOURNE
8:00 A. M.—9.54

BERNE
10:00 P. M.—6.165

STOCKHOLM
11:00 A. M.—15.158

FROM ENEMY SOURCES

BERLIN
7:30, 9:30 A. M.—15.11
7:00, 9:00, 11:00 P. M.—7.24.

TOKYO
6:15, 7:15 P. M.—15.105, 15.16, 11.725

Lina Dettinger
11:03-WMCA—Recorded Music
11:04-WEAF—Road to Life—Sketch
11:15-WEAF—Vic and Sade—Sketch
　WABC—Bright Horizon—Sketch
11:30-WEAF—Brava Tomorrow—Sketch
　WJZ—Gilbert Martyn, News
　WMCA—News; T. Dorsey Records
　WNEW—News; Recorded Music
　WQXR—Concert Music
11:45-WEAF—David Harum—Sketch
　WOR—Topics
　WJZ—Armistice Day Message: Warren H. Atherton, Commander American Legion; Mrs. Lawrence Smith, Pres., Legion Auxiliary from Arlington National Cemetery
11:55-WQXR—News; Luncheon Concert

On this and following page—a 1943 program listing. Note proliferation of news programs. Serials dominate daytime on CBS and NBC-red. Comedy and variety still rule ratings at night. All network programs are still live except for items on MBS (WOR). Disk-jockeys are on the rise in local programming. All-night schedules have begun on several stations. New York *Times*, Thursday, November 11, 1943. For comparison, see following 1952 listings.

AFTERNOON

A 1943 radio program listing—continued. On facing page, see comparable 1952 listing.

ON THE RADIO

WAAT .... 970.	WINS 1010	WNBC 660	WOV 1280
WBNX 1380	WJZ 770	WNEW 1130	WPAT 930
WCBS 880	WLIB 1190	WNJR 1430	WQXR 1560
WEVD 1330	WMCA 570	WNYC 830	WVNJ 620
WHOM 1480	WMGM 1050	WOR 710	WWRL 1600

FM PROGRAMS

WFUV 90.7	WJZ-FM 95.5	WABF 95.5	
WNYE 91.5	WQXR-FM .. 96.3	WMGM-FM . 100.3	
KE2XCC ... 93.1	WNBC-FM .. 97.1	WCBS-FM .. 101.1	
WNYC-FM .. 93.9	WOR-FM ... 98.7	WNYC-FM .. 107.5	

DUPLICATING AM PROGRAMS

6:01 A. M. to 1:30 A. M.—WQXR-FM
6:30 A. H. to 1:30 A. M.—WNBC-FM
6:00 A. M. to 9:00 P. M.—WQXR-FM
6:30-A. M. to 1:30 A. M.—WQXR-FM
8:30 A. M. to 1:30 A. M.—WEVD-FM
9:00 A. M. to 12:00 P. M.—WJZ-FM
9:00 A. M. to 12:00 P. M.—WOR-FM
3:00 P. M. to 9:00 P. M.—WMGM-FM

FM ONLY

7:40-WGHF—American Bible Society
8:00-WGFH—Music and News (To 6)
10:00-WFUV—Blue Chapel Mass
10:00-WFUV—News; Airmail
10:30-WFUV—Poetry of Music
11:00-WFUV—Paris Star Time
WNYC—Famous Artists
11:30-WFUV—French Lesson
11:45-WFUV—Sacred Heart Program
12:00-WFUV—Noon Concert
WNYC—Midday Symphony
1:00-WFUV—News; Industrial Relations
1:15-WFUV—Speak Up, Americans
1:30-WFUV—News (Sign Off)

(Program schedule continues in multiple columns — A.M., DAYTIME, EVENING)

A. M.

1—U. N. General Assembly (Also 3-6)—WNYC.
:30—Adventures of Casanova: With Errol Flynn—WOR.
:30—The Top Guy: With J. Scott Smart—WJZ.
:30—Meet Millie: With Audrey Totter—WCBS.
5-9—Symphony Hall: Featuring Rachmaninoff's Symphony No. 2 in E Minor—WQXR.
0-9—Father Knows Best: With Robert Young—WNBC.
0-9—Hardy Family: Mickey Rooney, Lewis Stone—WOR.
0-9—Junior Miss: With Margaret Whiting—WCBS.
0-8:55—Chicago Round Table: "Corruption in Government"—Sen. Paul H. Douglas, Prof. Donald Meiklejohn, John Nuveen (Recorded)—WNYC.
0—Pro-Basketball Doubleheader: Knicks-Minneapolis Lakers; Rochester Royals-Milwaukee Hawks—WMGM.
:30—Escape With Me: Kathi Norris, Narrator—WJZ.
30-10—Eddie Cantor Show—WNBC.
30-10—Michael Shayne: With Robert Sterling—WJZ.
30-10—Bing Crosby: With Dinah Shore and Joe Venuti, Guests—WCBS.
30-10—The Challenge: "Should We Arm Western Europe to Meet the Threat of Soviet Aggression?"—WMCA.
35-10:30—Autumn in New York: Jimmy Carroll—WCBS.
35-11—Through the Years: With Jane Pickens, Frank Black Orchestra—WNBC (Première).

The New York Times

NEWS BULLETINS

every hour on the hour
7 A. M. to midnight over
WQXR
(1560 on your dial)
WQXR—FM
96.3 mc. (on FM sets)

A 1952 radio program listing — New York *Times*, Thursday, November 13, 1952. See reverse for television listing of same date.

ON TELEVISION

Channel 2 ..... WCBS—TV	Channel 7 ..... WJZ—TV
Channel 4 .... WNBT	Channel 9 ..... WOR—TV
Channel 5 .... WABD	Channel 11 .... WPIX
Channel 13 .... WATV	

11 A. M.—U. N. General Assembly—(4) 4:30—(2).
5-5:15—Calling All Women—(11) (Premiere).
7-7:15—Advancing Human Frontiers: "Life After 50," With Robert M. Goldenson, Narrator—(4).
8-8:30—George Burns and Gracie Allen Show—(2).
8-8:30—Groucho Marx: "You Bet Your Life"—(4).
8:30-9—Amos 'n' Andy Show—(2).
8:30-9—Treasury Men in Action: "The Undercut Lace," With Walter Greaza and Others—(4).
8:30-9—Chance of a Lifetime: Margaret Phelan, Guest—(7).
9-9:30—Biff Baker, U.S.A.: With Alan Hale Jr.—(2).
9-9:30—Gangbusters: "Tri-State Gang," Part 1—(4).
9-9:30—Perspective: "The U. N. and Korea"—Lester Pearson, President of the General Assembly; Dean Rusk, Bethuel M. Webster—(7) (Premiere).
9—Pro Basketball: New York Knickerbocker vs. Minneapolis Lakers, Madison Square Garden—(11).
9:30-10—Big Town: With Patrick McVey, Jane Nigh—(2).
9:30-10—Play: "Protect Her Honor," With Jane Wyatt, Lloyd Nolan and Others—(4).
9:30-10—What's the Story?—News Quiz, With Walter Kiernan, Moderator—(5).
10-10:30—Author Meets the Critics: "Report on the American Communist"—Morris Ernst, Leo Cherne, Louis Budenz, Virgilia Peterson, Moderator—(5).
10:30-11—I've Got a Secret: With Garry Moore; Chester Morris, Henry Morgan, Kitty Carlisle, Guests—(2).
10:30-11—Foreign Intrigue: With Jerome Thor—(4).

DAYTIME

6:55-(4)—Sermonette
7:00-(4)—Today, With Dave Garroway
8:50-(2)—News; Previews
9:00-(2)—Film: Woman of Dolwyn, Edith Evans, Part II
   (4)—Music, With Morey Amsterdam
9:45-(2)—News and Comments
10:00-(2)—Arthur Godfrey Time
   (4)—Film: Secrets of a Sorority Girl, With Mary Ware
10:30-(4)—Josephine McCarthy
11:00-(2)—There's One in Every Family
   (4)—U. N. General Assembly
   (5)—Morning Chapel
   (7)—Second Cup of Coffee
11:15-(5)—News Reports
   (7)—Kitchen Kapers
11:30-(2)—Strike It Rich
11:45-(5)—One Man's Experience
12:00-(2)—Bride and Groom
   (4)—Herb Sheldon
   (5)—Take the Break—Don Russell
   (7)—Film: Border Patrolman
12:15-(2)—Love of Life
12:30-(2)—Search for Tomorrow
   (5)—Broadway Matinee
12:45-(2)—Ernie Kovacs Show
   (5)—News Reports
1:00-(4)—Feature Film
   (5)—Ladies Date
   (7)—Claire Mann
1:15-(11)—Music and Newsreel
1:30-(2)—Garry Moore Show
   (5)—Film: Never Too Late to Mend
   Tod Slaughter
   (7)—Domestically Yours
   (11)—New York Cooks
   (13)—TV Pastor: Health Aids
1:45-(13)—Feature Film; News
1:55-(4)—Jack Barry
2:00-(7)—Everywhere I Go
   (4)—Jim McCrary

(11)—Film Shorts
2:30-(13)—The Guiding Light
   (4)—Here's Looking at You
   (5)—Susan Adams—Kitchen Fare
   (7)—Nancy Craig Time
   (9)—TV Town Topics
   (11)—Ted Steele
2:45-(2)—Linkletter's House Party
3:00-(4)—The Big Pay-Off
   (5)—Paul Dixon Show
   (7)—Letter to Lee Graham
   (9)—Food for Thought
   (13)—Shop, Cook—Ruth Bean
3:15-(2)—Mike and Buff: John Crosby, Faye Emerson, guests
   (7)—The Fitzgeralds
3:30-(4)—Welcome Travelers
   (7)—Homemaker's Jamboree
   (9)—Film: Manhattan Shakedown
   (13)—A Woman's Work
4:00-(2)—Margaret Arlen
   (4)—Kate Smith Hour
   (5)—Film: Conway
   (7)—Films: Escape to Paradise, O'Malley of the Mounted
   (13)—Western Round-Up
4:30-(7)—U. N. in Action
   (9)—Sally Smart's Kitchen
5:00-(2)—Film: Flirting With Fate, With Joe E. Brown
   (4)—Hawkins Falls, Pop. 6,200
   (9)—Western Playhouse
   (11)—Calling All Women (Premiere)
   (13)—Junior Frolics—Uncle Fred
5:15-(4)—Gabby Hayes
   (11)—Film Shorts
5:30-(4)—Howdy Doody—Bob Smith
   (11)—Six-Gun Playhouse
   (13)—Feature Film
5:45-(5)—Sports Varieties
5:50-(7)—News Reports

EVENING

6:00-(2)—News Reports
   (4)—Rootie Kazootie
   (5)—News Reports
   (7)—Film: Life of Jack London, with Susan Hayward, Michael O'Shea
   (9)—Mailman—Ray Heatherton
   (11)—Boys' Railroad Club
6:10-(7)—Sports—Jim McKay
6:15-(2)—Film: Song of the Open Road, with Jane Powell, W. C. Fields, Edgar Bergen, Charlie McCarthy
   (4)—Ask the Camera—Quiz
   (5)—Weather Report
   (11)—Kids' Movie
6:20-(5)—Western Film
6:30-(4)—Stitch Henderson
   (5)—Serial—Wolf Dog
   (9)—TV Dinner Date
   (11)—Telepix; Weather
   (13)—Sports Highlights
6:35-(13)—Weather Report
6:45-(4)—News Reports
   (11)—Sports—Jimmy Powers
   (13)—Picture News
6:50-(4)—Sports Show
6:55-(4)—Weather by Wethbee
7:00-(4)—Advancing Human Frontiers: Life After 50—Dr. Robert M. Goldenson
   (5)—Captain Video
   (11)—News Reports
   (13)—Western Prairie Theatre
7:15-(4)—Short Short Dramas: Meet Me at the Library, With Henry Jones
   (7)—Sports—Tommy Henrich
   (11)—Movie Quiz
7:25-(2)—Weather Report
7:30-(7)—News Reports
   (4)—Dinah Shore
   (5)—Play: Comes the Day
   (7)—Lone Ranger
   (9)—Broadway TV Theatre: Seven Keys to Baldpate, With Buddy Ebsen
   (11)—First Show: The Admiral Was a Lady, With Wanda Hendrix
7:45-(2)—Heaven for Betsy, With Jack Lemmon, Cynthia Stone
   (4)—News Reports
8:00-(2)—Burns and Allen
   (4)—Groucho Marx—You Bet Your Life
   (5)—Football This Week, With Norman Sper
   (7)—All-Star News, Comments
   (13)—Film: Sins of Children
8:15-(5)—Newsreel
8:30-(2)—Amos 'n' Andy
   (4)—Treasury Men in Action: The Undercut Lace, With Walter

Greaza
   (5)—Broadway to Hollywood
   (7)—Chance of a Lifetime—Dennis James, Margaret Phelan
9:00-(2)—Biff Baker—U. S. A.: With Alan Hale Jr., Randy Stuart
   (4)—Gangbusters: Tri-State Gang, Part 1
   (5)—Trash or Treasure?
   (7)—Perspective: Lester Pearson, President, General Assembly, U. N.; Others (Premiere)
   (9)—News Reports
   (11)—Basketball: Knicks-Lakers, From Madison Square Garden
9:10-(9)—Boxing, Sunnyside
9:15-(13)—Vic Mansilio
9:30-(2)—Big Town, With Patrick McVey, Jane Nigh
   (4)—Play: Protect Her Honor, With Jane Wyatt, Lloyd Nolan
   (5)—What's the Story?—Quiz
   (7)—Maggi McNellis Show
   (13)—Rate the Record
10:00-(2)—Racket Squad, With Reed Hadley
   (4)—Martin Kane—Lee Tracy
   (5)—Author Meets the Critics: Report on the American Communist—Morris Ernst, Louis Budenz, Leo Cherne, Virgilia Peterson, Moderator
   (7)—Pro Football Highlights
   (13)—Western Film
10:30-(2)—I've Got a Secret
   (4)—Foreign Intrigue, With Jerome Thor
   (5)—Madison Square Garden Highlights
   (7)—Phil and Ruth Alampi
   (11)—Telepix; Weather
10:45-(11)—Giant Jottings; News
11:00-(2, 4)—News Reports
   (5)—Walter Raney, Comments
   (7)—Valentino Variety
   (9)—News; Fred Robbins
   (11)—Film: Mystic Circle
   (13)—Film: Vanity Fair, With Myrna Loy
11:10-(7)—Sports—Jim McKay
   (4)—Sports Report
11:15-(2)—Film: Argyle Secrets, With William Gargan
   (4)—Weather Report
   (5)—Weather Report
   (7)—News Reports
11:20-(4)—Film: I Met My Love Again, With Joan Bennett, Henry Fonda
   (5)—Bill Silbert Show
12:15-(13)—Picture News
12:20-(4)—Sermonette
12:30-(11)—News Reports

A 1952 television program listing. Radio is still getting major attention—for the moment. New York *Times*, Thursday, November 13, 1952.

TRADEMARKS: TV 1949-53

The Milton Berle
Program—brashness

Kukla, Fran, and
Ollie—whimsy

The Faye Emerson Show
—plunging neckline

The Garroway *Today*
series—visual aide

NBC

In upper right, broadcasting booths.

NBC

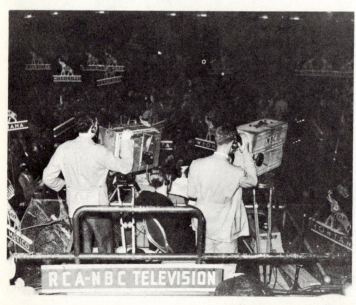

NBC-TV cameramen at Republican convention: Chicago, July 1952.

NBC

Young & Rubicam and had been advertising manager for American Tobacco Company, where he worked under George Washington Hill in the
environment portrayed in the novel *The Hucksters*. But, like a politician
elevated to the Supreme Court, he showed signs of liberation from past
pressures. The network, he said, must regain control.

The television era, many were saying, would have to be different.

HIGH PLACES

Edwin Armstrong felt outmaneuvered. FM had been hamstrung by its
move in the spectrum. It had received another blow when the FCC
approved duplication of programming on AM-FM combination stations.
The incentive to purchase FM sets had been lessened.

He had another problem. Although RCA had used FM in its TV as well
as FM sets, it had never paid a cent of royalty. FM royalties had been
paid to Armstrong by General Electric, Stromberg-Carlson, Westinghouse,
Zenith, and others. RCA had paid nothing.

RCA had at times offered to negotiate a settlement—a million dollars
had been mentioned. But this raised a question of fairness to those who
had always paid royalties based on sales. Zenith had paid more than a
million.

In 1948 Armstrong made his decision. He brought suit against the mammoth RCA. He had spent most of his royalty earnings on the battle for
FM. This added to his determination to press the lawsuit.

RCA had a policy of cash settlements in preference to royalty payments.
It did not pay royalties; it collected them. Perhaps Armstrong was encouraged by the one exception it had made—for Philo Farnsworth. RCA had
so badly needed the Farnsworth television patents that it had settled with
him on a royalty basis. The RCA patent attorney, Otto Schairer, is said to
have had tears in his eyes as he signed the contract.[1]

RCA as defendant had the right to examine Armstrong in pre-trial hear-
ings. These began in February 1949 in the lower Manhattan law offices of
Cravath, Swaine & Moore. RCA attorneys began questioning the inventor.
They kept it going for a full year.

Q. You are the plaintiff in the present action?
A. Yes.
Q. What is your occupation?

1. Everson, *The Story of Television: The Life of Philo T. Farnsworth*, p. 246.

A.   I am an electrical engineer.
Q.   Do you have any other occupation?
A.   I am a professor of electrical engineering at Columbia University.
Q.   Do you have any other occupation?
A.   I occasionally make inventions.

Armstrong, normally patient, became a man possessed. All his energies came to be centered on the suit. Three o'clock in the morning would find him poring over transcripts. At all hours he called attorneys to discuss tactics.

The RCA position gradually emerged. RCA, Sarnoff said, had done more than anyone to develop FM. Early discussions with Armstrong were even cited in support of this. The claim stirred Armstrong to a cold fury.

His expenses mounted. His wife and friends pleaded with him to accept a settlement. But now victory had become a terrible need. The meaning of his life was at stake. In 1953 he fell ill; for a time it was thought he had had a stroke. A broken man, at odds with family and friends, he finally authorized a settlement.

He had always had an obsession about high places. As a boy he had frightened Yonkers neighbors, swaying in the wind on a huge antenna pole. As a successful young inventor he had done a spectacular, jaunty balancing act on a globe atop RCA headquarters in mid-Manhattan. Later he had climbed around his fantastic Alpine FM tower to supervise every detail of construction.

One day, neatly dressed, he stepped out of a window of his thirteenth-floor East Side apartment. He was found on a third-floor extension. Shortly afterward RCA made a million-dollar settlement on the estate.[2]

SIC TRANSIT

At mid-century radio network sales were holding firm:[1]

1948	$198,966,000
1949	187,800,000
1950	183,069,000

Could anything change all this?

Just as impressive as the figures was the granite permanence of much programming. The year 1950 bore a startling resemblance to the 1930's.

2. Lessing, Man of High Fidelity, pp. 277–99.
1. Broadcasting Yearbook (1952), p. 14.

Network schedules in 1950 contained 108 different series that had been on the air a decade or more. Twelve series had been on for two decades and were almost as old as network broadcasting.[2]

Topping the polls, as in the 1930's, were comedians from vaudeville and musical comedy. Most were now film-radio stars. The highest rating went to Jack Benny, an eighteen-year network veteran. Of like vintage, and close behind in rating, were Edgar Bergen and Charlie McCarthy, Bob Hope, Burns and Allen, and others. Bing Crosby, nineteen-year veteran, led the variety hours. The amateur-hour tradition was holding firm, led by veteran Arthur Godfrey.

Leading the drama ratings was *Lux Radio Theater,* with sixteen network years. It was one of forty-four drama series that had been on the network air at least a decade. These included twenty-three serials.

Amos 'n' Andy, grandfather of serials, with twenty-one network years, had become a once-a-week comedy series. It remained among the top ten programs in ratings.

The Romance of Helen Trent, with sixteen years, and *Ma Perkins,* with eighteen years, were rivals for the daytime rating lead.

The chief missing items were sustaining drama series, which had almost vanished.

While radio had a look of permanence, an artificial factor was at work. Late in 1948 the FCC, having issued approximately a hundred television licenses, called a sudden halt. Interference problems had to be studied. A television "freeze" was declared. The Korean War became a reason for keeping the freeze, which lasted three and a half years.

Thus 1948–52 was a strange twilight period. It saw 108 television stations in action. But only twenty-four cities had two or more stations; most cities had only one station, or none. Coverage was spotty.

New York and Los Angeles each saw seven stations reach the air; here television seemed in full swing.

But major cities like Houston, Kansas City, Milwaukee, Pittsburgh, St. Louis, had only one station each. Cities without any televison included Austin, Denver, Little Rock, Portland, Maine, and Portland, Oregon.

2. *Amos 'n' Andy,* Betty Crocker, *Catholic Hour,* H. V. Kaltenborn, *National Farm and Home Hour, National Radio Pulpit, National Vespers,* New York Philharmonic, Salt Lake City Tabernacle Choir, *Southernaires,* Lowell Thomas, *Voice of Firestone.* Statistics in this section are based on the compilation of Harrison B. Summers, *A Thirty-Year History of Programs Carried on National Radio Networks in the United States 1926–1956.*

Even cities with only one television station saw signs of economic earth-
quake and drastic changes of habit. In 1951 almost all television cities
reported a 20 to 40 per cent drop in movie attendance. In non-television
cities, movie attendance was holding firm or rising.

Areas well saturated with television were reporting movie theater closings in waves: 70 closings in eastern Pennsylvania, 134 in southern California, 61 in Massachusetts, 64 in the Chicago area, 55 in metropolitan
New York. The rise of outdoor drive-in theaters was a factor in this, but
television was considered the main cause.

A drastic decline at sports events was seen in most television cities,
although wrestling, a prominent feature in early television, was doing
well. Effective handling of television rights was clearly a life-or-death matter for professional sports. Minor leagues faced an uncertain future.

Restaurants and night clubs felt the impact. When Sid Caesar was on
the air Saturday nights, said a Hartford, Connecticut, restaurateur, people
ate early and rushed home. Television sets had briefly drawn people to
taverns, but now home sets kept them at home. Many cities saw a drop in
taxicab receipts, and it was blamed on television. Jukebox receipts were
down. Some public libraries, including the New York Public Library, were
reporting a drop in book circulation, and many book stores reported a sales
drop.[3]

Radio listening was dropping sharply in all television cities. But the
sponsor wanting national coverage could not yet get it in television. In one-
station cities all networks and their sponsors and advertising agencies
were competing, pleading, cajoling, and bargaining for even fringe periods. In the non-television areas they could not even get that.

The tendency for national sponsors was therefore to hang onto a coast-
to-coast radio network program while getting a foothold in television. It
was a time for straddling. Soon—after the freeze—they would make the
big jump.

Thus network radio, with a sense of doom, had a final fling.

Many programs sounded the same. But as audiences shrank, battles for
the remnants grew fierce.

In the midst of such a battle was the beguiling Fred Allen. Most urbane
of comedians, leading the ratings as late as 1948, he had seemed inde-
structible. In the late 1940's he had been amusing the industry with jibes
at vice presidents who tried to interfere with his programs. An agency

3. New York *Times,* June 24, 1951.

vice president, he said, was a "molehill man." Each morning at 9 A.M. there would be a molehill on his desk.

> He has until 5 P.M. to make this molehill into a mountain. An accomplished molehill man will often have his mountain finished even before lunch.[4]

At the height of his career, Allen came up against something more formidable than a molehill man. As competition on ABC he faced a new series that was in many ways a mirror of its time: *Stop the Music!*

It was launched by Louis G. Cowan, creator of *The Quiz Kids.* After his varied wartime activities, which he ended as head of the OWI overseas branch, he resumed independent production. He tried to promote a rich diversity of ideas and succeeded in many, but his first runaway success was *Stop the Music!* The idea, brought to him by orchestra leader Harry Salter, was simplicity itself. Salter's orchestra played popular songs but was periodically interrupted by announcer Bert Parks shouting, "Stop the music!" A phone call would be placed to a number anywhere in the United States. If its owner was at home and could identify the interrupted tune, he got an avalanche of gifts: a new car, television set, boat, refrigerator, fur coat for his wife, set of perfumes, trip to Florida. The gifts might add up—in retail value—to twenty or thirty thousand dollars. All this the producers got free in exchange for mention of product and brand name.

The producers and the ABC network thought the idea novel but scarcely anticipated what would happen. Arriving on the air in 1948, *Stop the Music!* came after two decades of austerity—Depression austerity and wartime austerity. A consumer-goods era was at last dawning, and even to hear the product names rattled off on the air seemed an hypnotic experience.[5]

On the NBC network Fred Allen plummeted from his 28.7 rating in January 1948 to 11.2 in January 1949.

Opposing him on the ABC network, *Stop the Music!* went from nowhere to a 20.0 rating in January 1949.

Fred Allen, in desperation, persuaded an insurance company to underwrite any listener who, by listening to Fred Allen, lost merchandise offered on a competing program. The move proved futile. Fred Allen's sponsor, the Ford Motor Company, decided to drop him. By 1950 he was

4. Allen, *Treadmill to Oblivion,* p. 27.
5. Cowan, *Reminiscences,* p. 135.

gone from the scene. The *Stop the Music!* success meanwhile built a mania for series in which money or merchandise was the attraction: *Hit the Jackpot* (1948), *Go for the House* (1948), *Chance of a Lifetime* (1949), *Shoot the Moon* (1950). Like buzzards on carrion, said Fred Allen, the giveaway shows were "descending on the carcass of radio." [6]

It didn't last long—not in radio. From its 20.0 rating in 1949, *Stop the Music!* dropped to 8.3 in 1951. The give-away shows began to move into television—or oblivion.

Even comedians saw transitions of this sort. Bob Hope radio ratings tell the story. His January ratings for three years:

1949	23.8
1951	12.7
1953	5.4

In its death agony, radio had spurts of boldness and creativity, at both network and local station. With attention turning to television, radio became freer. Vice presidents interfered less. Ad-libbing was permitted, even encouraged. Taboos fell. Venereal disease, long a forbidden subject, was suddenly discussed on scores of programs. Comedy was also liberated. The situation permitted the emergence of such carefree spirits as Bob and Ray—Bob Elliot and Ray Goulding—whose wildness would scarcely have been possible in earlier years.

In 1951 Bob and Ray were solemnly offering "without obligation" a Bob and Ray Burglar Kit including jimmies, glass cutters, files, etc., and the Bob and Ray Burglar Book. "When the postman brings your package, in a plain wrapper marked only 'Burglar Kit,' take $3.98 from him." The book was said to include useful aliases "such as Benjamin Franklin, or Mary Queen of Scots." It had such chapter headings as "Forging Ahead" and "Casing a Joint." Bob and Ray also offered a Home Surgery Kit. "How many times have you said to yourself, 'Golly, I wish I could take out my tonsils.'" [7] Parodying the serial *Backstage Wife* and its heroine Mary Noble, Bob and Ray offered installments of *Mary Backstage, Noble Wife*, which outlived the series it lampooned.

This period of desperation also produced *Conversation*, a Louis G. Cowan production in which a small group of celebrated conversationalists were simply encouraged to talk, without inhibition of any sort. It led

6. Allen, *Treadmill to Oblivion*, p. 217.
7. Quoted by John Crosby in syndicated column "Radio and Television," July 30, 1951.

Lyman Bryson to wonder whether radio, in its extremity, might become the medium of the intellectual.

Stations in many cities, emulating WQXR, New York, were finding audiences for classical music and folk music. The classical-music disk-jockey was on the rise.

The period produced a strange flowering in sportscasting: the "re-created" baseball game. It built a short-lived chain, the Liberty Network. Saving the expense of pickups from baseball parks, entrepreneur Gordon McLendon staged hair-raising play-by-play descriptions in a Dallas studio from information on a news-agency ticker while an engineer, like an organist selecting stops, faded sound-effects records in and out: quiet crowds, restless crowds, hysterical crowds. His selections stimulated the announcer, who invented reasons for any sudden crowd excitement: a fan had made an unbelievable one-hand catch of a foul, or a peanut vender had fallen downstairs. McLendon was scholarly too: he had tape recordings of "The Star-Spangled Banner" as played at each ball park. The McLendon broadcasts were often more exciting than the ball games. The Liberty Network syndicated them to several hundred stations during the television freeze. With the spread of televised sports, the business collapsed.[8]

Amid intimations of death, radio began to interest itself in the Negro. Magazines like *Ebony* were attracting advertising because they were found to reach a buying public not touched by "white" media. The years 1948–52 saw an eruption of "Negro radio stations" aiming at the same "market," mainly through "rhythm and blues" music. Most of these stations, while using Negro talent and seeking a Negro audience, were white-owned; but there were exceptions. WSOK, Nashville, had several Negro shareholders. WERD, Atlanta, was wholly Negro-owned—apparently the only such station in 1951. It had been bought for $50,000 by a Negro certified public accountant and his son. To their surprise, many white job applicants came forward. In 1951 the twenty-two-member staff included six white men. The station found that 20 per cent of its listeners were white. In some communities the Negro-oriented stations were not so well received. In Birmingham the WEDR antenna tower was at one point destroyed by a white posse. WDIA, Memphis, had angry phone calls when it opened in 1948, but the protests subsided.

8. Nelson and Hirshberg, "A Stadium Inside a Studio," *Sports Illustrated*, March 28, 1966.

Stations in many parts of the country began in the late 1940's to sched-ule Negro disk-jockeys, some of whom became commercially successful. In 1951 Joe Adams at KOWL, Santa Monica, was said to have several dozen sponsors.[9]

At the networks, too, the crisis hour brought increased attention to the Negro. But here the results were discouraging. Jackie Robinson began a series of broadcasts in January 1950 over the ABC network; lack of spon-sorship is said to have brought it to an end. CBS scheduled gospel singer Mahalia Jackson for a number of months—a Louis Cowan package—and offered her for sponsorship; no sponsor appeared and the series ended.

In one of its most desperate—but forlorn—efforts to hold big audiences to radio, NBC in 1950 threw quantities of wit and sophistication into a ninety-minute Tallulah Bankhead variety series with Goodman Ace as chief writer and music by Meredith Willson. It was a high point in radio history but too late. After two seasons it died.

Mostly there was corner-cutting and combining. Comedians whose status no longer justified orchestras and batteries of writers became hosts of quiz programs. With Groucho Marx presiding over *You Bet Your Life,* Eddie Cantor took on *Take It or Leave It,* and Herb Shriner *Two for the Money.* The great became disk-jockeys: in 1950, Frank Sinatra and Paul Whiteman; in 1951, Eddie Cantor; in 1952, Tennessee Ernie Ford. And disk-jockeys became newscasters.

None of it seemed enough. In 1952 death seemed imminent for network radio. The FCC promised an early end to the television freeze. The big sponsors were ready for the switch. As Fred Allen put it, they were ready to abandon radio, like the bones at a barbecue.

PANICSVILLE

If radio was fearful, the film world was Panicsville. An unprecedented sequence of blows had set it spinning. On the heels of the House un-Amer-ican activities hearings, the scattered explosions of television had Holly-wood shaking. In the midst came an atom bomb: the U. S. Supreme Court decision in *United States* v. *Paramount et al.*[1]

The defendants were the eight companies that had long controlled the

9. Edmerson, *A Descriptive Study of the American Negro in United States Profes-sional Radio 1922–1953,* pp. 325–50.
1. *U. S.* v. *Paramount et al.,* 334 U. S. 131 (1948).

industry: Paramount, Loew's (including Metro-Goldwyn-Mayer), RKO, Twentieth Century-Fox, Warner Brothers, Columbia Pictures, Universal, United Artists. The Supreme Court—climaxing years of litigation—agreed with lower courts that the defendants had kept out foreign products and prevented domestic competition by control over theaters. The court now ordered an end to block booking and demanded "divorcement" of theater holdings from production and distribution; it left it to lower courts to work out details. This ushered in a series of consent decrees that—unbelievably—wrote *fade out* to the story of the Big Studios—those self-contained grand duchies that had been a way of life and had symbolized Hollywood. That old Hollywood was suddenly dead—deader than a dropped option.

Convulsions shook the town. Fearing it could not unload 400 to 500 films per year on theaters no longer controlled, the major companies began to slash production schedules and cancel long-term contracts with actors, producers, directors, writers, technicians. On the heels of the blacklist terror came a new reign of fear. No job seemed safe. Every day brought gruesome television news and the rolling of heads. Screen writer Robert Ardrey has written of a lunch hour at Warner Brothers when Jack Warner came screaming into the Green Room, jabbing at his contract artists as they ate their lunches. "I can do without you! And you! And you! I can do without you!" He came to Jerry Wald, who was producing at least half of all Warner films. Warner shouted at him: "I can almost do without you!" [2] The effects would be felt for years as a different Hollywood took shape.

The splitting of the big companies began almost at once. Loew-MGM delayed longest, whistling in the dark. Betty Comden and Adolph Green, having written MGM's *It's Always Fair Weather*, were at its 1950 release ceremonies. Sticking to the classic style, MGM held a huge lunch to which everyone was summoned. It culminated in ice cream in the form of lions. "We watched them melt before our eyes, and it seemed so symbolic. . . ." [3]

Paramount promptly split into two companies—Paramount Pictures Corporation and United Paramount Theaters. By 1951 United Paramount Theaters, set adrift, negotiated a merger with the ABC network, which had itself been set adrift by the chain broadcasting report of the FCC,

2. Ardrey, "Hollywood: The Toll of the Frenzied Forties," *Reporter,* March 21, 1957.
3. Comden and Green, *Reminiscences,* p. 866.

under James Lawrence Fly. To the merger, Paramount could bring working capital—and a business of doubtful future; ABC could bring scanty working capital—and a glowing future.

Among those urging FCC approval of the proposed merger was James Lawrence Fly, who was still looking for more vigorous competition among the networks.

But the merger meant more. The television world was waiting for the starting signal for its gold rush. Never was a quest for gold anticipated with more confidence. Television, even while waiting, found power edging into its hands.

THE MARGIN OF DOUBT

Periodic confrontations of public power and private power appear to have become characteristic of our social system. In such struggles—as between FCC and commercial broadcasters—each side has power but does not know its full extent. The law is ambiguous. Neither side presses hard for clarification, for clarification involves risks. Each contents itself with manipulating what Professor Louis L. Jaffe of Harvard has called "the margin of doubt." This shifty, shadowy kind of relationship characterizes all manner of government-industry dealings. Personnel changes, political shifts, bring an ebb and flow of effective influence.[1]

In the final Truman years the dominant forces of the broadcasting industry manipulated the margin of doubt with almost constant success. In addition to de-fusing the blue book, they—

—persuaded the FCC (1949) to reverse the Mayflower decision and allow licensees to editorialize, with due regard for the right of the public to hear a balanced presentation.

—persuaded the FCC (1949) to rescind the AVCO rule calling for competitive bids in transfer cases.

—persuaded Congress (1952) to go further, and to forbid the FCC to consider applicants other than the proposed transferee.

The last two steps tended to make a channel private property, in spite of the clear denial of such property rights by the Communications Act.

In 1951 the FCC added an extraordinary footnote to this developing—though extra-legal—property right in radio licenses.

1. Jaffe, "The Role of Government," in Coons (ed.), *Freedom and Responsibility in Broadcasting*, p. 44.

Hearings on renewal of the Richards stations began in 1950 and continued for more than a year. Scores of witnesses testified to instructions by George A. Richards to slant and falsify news. Memoranda and letters substantiated the testimony. The examiner recommended that the licenses not be renewed. At the climax of these proceedings George A. Richards dropped dead.

His death occasioned new arguments, petitions, delays, and pressures. Lawyers and lobbyists worked overtime. Pleas were heard on behalf of the bereaved. Finally, on written assurance from the widow of George Richards that there would be no more news-slanting, the licenses were renewed.

The $2,000,000 said to have been spent to save the licenses could have provided for the family. Meanwhile the FCC had apparently come to believe, in spite of the law, that there was a property right in radio channels, and one that extended even beyond death.

The renewal of the Richards stations, while involving high stakes, was a scarcely noticed incident as the industry strained toward a day to come—the television freeze-lifting. To prepare for it, the FCC ceaselessly reviewed arguments over the spectrum, while the industry nagged for action. Amid these pressures, a commissioner began to manipulate a margin of doubt.

Commissioner Frieda B. Hennock had been appointed in 1948 by President Truman. At a time when he obtained from Congress almost nothing he requested, it seemed miraculous to observers that she won approval. The case involved sly politics by Truman. In nominating Frieda Hennock, he was inviting Senators to go on record as anti-feminist or anti-Semitic. They risked neither and confirmed her quickly.

Commissioner Hennock soon adopted as her hobby-horse the idea of reserving television channels for educational use. The licensing pause provided by the freeze was giving educators a chance to push for this notion. In 1950 a Joint Committee (later renamed "Council") on Educational Television was formed with backing from the National Association of Educational Broadcasters (NAEB), the American Council on Education, and others. Much of the impetus came from educational radio veterans[2]—political amateurs, but with the zeal that occasionally can make such

2. Among them: I. Keith Tyler, Ohio State University; Robert B. Hudson, University of Illinois; Richard B. Hull, Iowa State University; George Probst, University of Chicago; Seymour Siegel, New York City Municipal Broadcasting System.

efforts effective. They were fortunate to secure Telford Taylor, former FCC general counsel, to press their case. Commissioner Hennock made herself the champion of the campaigners. Commissioner Paul Walker showed early interest; other commissioners seemed at first lukewarm or cool.

Industry spokesmen scoffed at the campaign. *Broadcasting* considered the idea "illogical, if not illegal." [3] Many broadcasters thought such ideas had been scotched with the defeat of the Wagner-Hatfield amendment of 1934. Some FM channels had been set aside by the FCC for education, but that had seemed of little significance. Television channels were something else.

A device that helped the educators build impetus for their drive was a series of "monitoring studies" conducted by the NAEB with financial backing from the Fund for Adult Education of the Ford Foundation. In several cities, starting in January 1951, groups of viewers tabulated information about commercial television offerings. The finding that New York viewers could in one week witness 2,970 "acts or threats" of violence—more than seventeen "acts or threats" per hour during children's viewing periods—had an impact on many people. [4]

Commissioner Hennock, with wide-ranging speeches and conferences, helped put on pressure. Northeastern states showed only scattered interest. Groups in other areas were more responsive—for diverse reasons of their own. Western and Midwestern land-grant colleges saw channel reservations as a parallel to their own historic beginnings in land grants after the Civil War. These colleges, too, had helped to keep the flame of educational radio alive. Southern states saw additional values. Troubled by a serious educational vacuum in many areas, they saw in television a possible solution—and one that did not appear to imperil the segregated classroom.

With commercial television straining for a go-ahead, the campaign spearheaded by Commissioner Hennock began to have nuisance value. The FCC, encouraged by staff members, began to feel it had nothing to lose and much to gain from the reserved-channel idea. If educators failed to use the channels—as many industry leaders predicted—the FCC would at least have offered the chance. If educators seized the opportunity, the FCC would have led the way.

3. *Broadcasting*, November 10, 1952.
4. Smythe, *New York Television January 4-10, 1951*, 1952, p. 45.

The FCC's Sixth Report and Order, which took shape early in 1952 under the chairmanship of Wayne Coy, was an omnibus television package with items to please various groups. Channels 2 to 13 in the already established VHF (very high frequency) band were to be supplemented by seventy new channels in the UHF (ultra high frequency) band. Expansion room for commercial television seemed to be assured. Both in VHF and UHF, a number of channels were reserved for education. In all, provision was made for 242 educational stations; the number was later increased.

The channel reservations, snatching victory from old defeats, occasioned a good deal of oratory. Some saw the mounting problems of education—teacher shortages, pockets of the disadvantaged, demands of new technology—somehow solved by a miraculous dispensation of Providence.

There were also more hard-headed views. It was pointed out that the new blueprint, unlike the long-ago Wagner-Hatfield proposal, involved no plan for financing the use of the channels. It was pointed out that boards of education faced desperate financial problems. Would educational television be one more demand on them, diverting funds from needed schoolrooms, equipment, salary increases?

It seemed to some that educators had won special channels in which to go about with a tin cup in search of funds. But others said, one problem at a time. The channels first, financial problems later. Let the channels be saved. If not saved now, they would be gone forever.

So education, too, had a stake in the lifting of the freeze.

The FCC plan was officially proclaimed in April 1952. In July the "processing" of channel applications began. Stations on the air still numbered only 108, but 700 applicants were asking for channels. Almost all were commercial applicants. Would the television gold rush at last get under way?

"If elected," said General Dwight D. Eisenhower, "I shall go to Korea." The words electrified the nation; they could only mean that peace was on its way. For television applicants the words had special meaning. Television hopes became deeply entangled in the election of 1952.

1952

At the start of 1952—election year—television viewers watching fifteen million television sets in sixty-four cities were already addicted to:

Texaco Star Theater with the brash Milton Berle, sometimes called "Mr. Television."

I Love Lucy with Lucille Ball, comedy series just started and leaping into leadership.

Your Show of Shows, variety program with imaginative satiric sketches featuring Sid Caesar and Imogene Coca.

Toast of the Town, Ed Sullivan variety hour, holding strong.

Arthur Godfrey's Friends and *Talent Scouts,* two series headed by Godfrey.

Kukla, Fran and Ollie, puppet show specializing in whimsy.

Garroway at Large, variety series with an informal tone—the "Chicago style."

The Faye Emerson Show, interview series with sophisticated talk and necklines.

Philco Playhouse and *Goodyear Playhouse,* alternating Sunday drama series produced by Fred Coe and deeply impressing the theater world.

Most were live, but the runaway success of the filmed *I Love Lucy* made it clear that films would play a role in the new age. The prospect of profitable re-use of films, not only in the United States but also abroad, was a factor edging some producers away from "live" production toward production on film. The filmed *Fireside Theater* series, a venture of Bing Crosby Enterprises, exemplified the trend.

Viewers had already experienced a cycle of gore, which gave scope for technical experimentation and included *Lights Out, Suspense, Danger, The Clock, The Web,* and *Tales of the Black Cat.* Evil was also rampant on *The Front Page, Man Against Crime, The Big Story, Big Town, Cisco Kid,* and several series of westerns.

Viewers had learned that Senate committee hearings could be spellbinding, when Senator Estes Kefauver of Tennessee admitted television cameras to an inquiry into organized crime. Besides making Kefauver famous, the telecasts produced a memorable moment when Frank Costello, reputed underworld leader, objected to being televised. The producers, continuing with the dialogue of the hearings, turned the cameras into a close-up of his hands. Viewers watched—and searched for meaning in—the twitching and groping of Costello's fingers.

At Christmas they had been almost as gripped by an opera written for the NBC television network by Gian-Carlo Minotti—*Amahl and the Night Visitors*.

Viewers had seen television debuts of familiar comedy series including *The Goldbergs, The Aldrich Family,* and *Amos 'n' Andy*. The last-mentioned had caused something of a furor. In *Amos 'n' Andy* CBS was bringing Negroes to television—but Negroes trained by Freeman Gosden and Charles Correll in the nuances of the stereotype. When the National Association for the Advancement of Colored People at its 1951 convention condemned *Amos 'n' Andy* as an insult, many people were astonished. But the protest was only a beginning, a symptom of a fury making its way to the surface.

Radio had been close to lily-white, but implicitly. Television was explicitly and glaringly white. A seeming mirror of the world, it told the Negro continually that he did not exist—except in "insults" like *Amos 'n' Andy*. The long-range psychic impact was not easy for white people to comprehend. The educator John Henry Martin has told of a fourth-grade class of Negro children near New York who were asked to draw self-portraits. Not one child drew a black face. Accepting the world's verdict, they denied themselves. But the denial covered something that was heading for an explosion. It is perhaps not a coincidence that the beginnings of the Negro revolt—the rise of the "invisible man"—coincided with the spread and penetration of television.[1]

While much of television was derived from radio, there were innovations—among them *Today*, a daily two-hour early morning program devised by NBC vice president Sylvester Weaver. Its purpose had been projected in numerous NBC memoranda but was still not clear. Part news program and part variety program, it did not seem likely to succeed as either. At first, critics derided it and advertisers shunned it. But a turning point came during the first year with the arrival of J. Fred Muggs, a baby chimpanzee owned by two former NBC pages. A *Today* staff member saw him waiting for an elevator while sucking formula from a plastic bottle. Everybody kept saying television should be visual, and Muggs seemed to be that; he was not verbal. Producer Gerald Green has described what happened after Muggs became a *Today* regular.

1. See *Publishers Weekly*, May 10, 1965. The phrase "the invisible man" was given currency by the Ralph Ellison novel *Invisible Man*, the story of "a desperate man's search for his identity," which won the 1952 National Book Award.

Women proposed to him; advertisers fought for the right to use his photo in their supermarket flyers; Chambers of Commerce sought his good offices; actresses posed with him; officers of newly-commissioned naval vessels demanded that he christen them.

In Florida he got a room in a restricted hotel. He appeared as guest of honor in Central Park in New York at an I Am an American Day rally, although really a native of Cameroon.[2]

But the big show of 1952 was the election.

Although radio still commanded a larger audience than television, television for the first time received the main attention of the campaigners.

Each of the networks found a sponsor for its broadcasts of the party conventions and of the election returns. NBC combined them into a $3.5 million package sponsored by Westinghouse, in which Betty Furness became famous demonstrating refrigerators in the live commercials. She opened and closed refrigerator doors hundreds of times before the issues were settled.

The Republicans nominated Dwight D. Eisenhower and Richard M. Nixon; the Democrats, Adlai Stevenson and John Sparkman.

Listening at a Colorado ranch to Stevenson's acceptance speech, George Allen said to Eisenhower: "He's too accomplished an orator; he'll be easy to beat." [3]

Stevenson was verbal. His speeches were eloquent, witty, polished. On television he never used a teleprompter because he always polished his speeches until the final moment, and there was never time to put them on a teleprompter. At the end of a program, the viewer's final glimpse was usually Stevenson still reading, turning a page, hurrying because he hadn't finished, but not hurrying enough. Again and again he ran over. It was the despair of his advisers.

While many responded to Stevenson's verbal brilliance, it also became a target of anti-intellectuals, who scorned his "teacup words." His brilliance became in itself an object of suspicion.[4]

While Stevenson was putting faith in words, Eisenhower was conducting a very different campaign. In charge was Batten, Barton, Durstine & Osborn, and it decided from the start that an Eisenhower speech for a half-

2. Green, "What Does the Monkey Do," in Barrett (ed.), *Journalists in Action,* pp. 275–6.
3. Eisenhower, *The White House Years: Mandate for Change,* p. 50.
4. Hofstadter, *Anti-Intellectualism in American Life,* p. 227.

hour program must be twenty minutes long—no more. The broadcast was planned in three acts: (1) arrival of a hero; (2) speech; (3) departure of the hero. The middle part, the speech, was easy and could be left to speech writers. The other parts required experts, who would begin with study of the hall, and decisions on the use and placement of cameras. The drama was conceived in shots: Ike coming through the door at *back* of auditorium; Ike greeting crowd; people in gallery going wild, craning necks; Ike, escorted, making his way down the aisle; Mamie Eisenhower in box; Ike mounting platform; crowd going wild; Ike at rostrum, waving; Ike looking over toward Mamie; Mamie in box, smiling; on cue, Ike holding up arms as if to stop applause; crowd going wild. The final portion, the departure, was as carefully planned.

But BBD&O did not rely solely on pageantry. The kind of spot barrage proposed to Dewey in 1948, and rejected, was carried out for Eisenhower in 1952. The spots were all written by a volunteer from the Ted Bates advertising agency—Rosser Reeves. The basic formula called for a question and an answer in twenty seconds. All spots had the same four-word introduction.

ANNOUNCER: Eisenhower answers the nation!
CITIZEN: What about the cost of living, General?
IKE: My wife, Mamie, worries about the same thing. I tell her it's our job to change that on November fourth!

The "citizens" were shot in various locales. Eisenhower filmed the answers for all fifty spots in one day in a mid-Manhattan film studio specializing in commercials—the Transfilm studio. Reading from huge prompt cards, he occasionally expressed amazement "that an old soldier should come to this," but went along with the experts. The answers were subsequently spliced to the questions. The spots were scheduled for a saturation coverage during the last two weeks of the campaign at an expense of $1,500,-000.[5]

Stevenson and his close advisers—Senators J. William Fulbright of Arkansas and Russell B. Long of Louisiana, and others—heard about the spot plan at breakfast one morning from campaign volunteer Louis G. Cowan, who had learned the details from network personnel. The advisers all felt that Stevenson should *not* emulate the plan, and the candidate himself said he had no wish to be merchandised "like a breakfast food."

5. Mayer, *Madison Avenue, U. S. A.*, pp. 298–301.

The decision probably did not affect the outcome, for Eisenhower was the more merchandisable product.[6]

A climactic feature of the campaign was the Nixon "Checkers" speech, so-named after the family dog. There had been rumors about Nixon's finances—they related to a fund put together by California supporters after his election to Congress. At one point Thomas Dewey, polling various Republican leaders, found a majority of the opinion that Nixon should withdraw from the race because of the charges, but the Republican National Committee decided to invest in a half-hour period on a sixty-four-station television hookup—plus several hundred radio stations—for a reply by Nixon. Several advertisers offered to sponsor the broadcast, but it was considered unwise to accept.[7] Nixon went into seclusion to work on his broadcast.

Eisenhower, who emphasized that the Republican crusade needed a candidate "as clean as a hound's tooth," arranged to watch the program on a television set in the manager's office of the Cleveland auditorium, where an Eisenhower speech was scheduled. Nixon spoke from a Los Angeles studio.

On television the program opened with a close-up of Nixon's calling card, then went to Nixon sitting at a desk. Mrs. Nixon—"Pat"—sat to one side, watching him. Occasionally during the program he turned to her; at these moments the camera would move to her. Nixon spoke about the fund:

> Not one cent of the $18,000 or any other money of that type ever went to me for my personal use. Every penny of it was used to pay for political expenses that I did not think should be charged to the taxpayers of the United States. . . .

That was about all that was said about the fund, but Nixon added a "confession." It was inspired by a recollection of how successfully President Franklin D. Roosevelt had used a dog story. Nixon said:

> One other thing I should probably tell you, because if I don't they'll probably be saying this about me too, we did get something—a gift—after the election. A man down in Texas heard Pat on the radio mention the fact that our two daughters would like to have a dog. And, believe it or not, the day before we left on this campaign trip we got a

6. Cowan, *Reminiscences*, p. 149. Four years later the Stevenson campaign did utilize spot announcements.
7. Nixon, *Six Crises*, p. 98.

message from Union Station in Baltimore saying they had a package for us. We went down to get it. You know what it was? It was a little cocker spaniel dog in a crate that he sent all the way from Texas. Black and white spotted. And our little girl—Tricia, the six-year-old—named it Checkers. And you know the kids love that dog and I just want to say this right now, that regardless of what they say about it, we're going to keep it!

In conclusion he asked listeners to wire or write the Republican National Committee to help them decide whether he should stay on the ticket or "get off." He would leave it up to the committee. But whatever the outcome, he promised to campaign for the Republican ticket "up and down America until we drive the crooks and communists and those that defend them out of Washington. And remember, folks, Eisenhower is a great man, believe me. He is a great man. . . ."

Even before the deluge of supporting telephone calls and telegrams and letters began, it seemed clear that Nixon had survived his crisis. At the Cleveland auditorium office the group around Eisenhower had watched "seemingly without drawing breath." Mrs. Eisenhower and several of the men were seen to dab at their eyes with handkerchiefs. Immediately after the broadcast Eisenhower turned to Republican chairman Arthur Summerfield: "Well, Arthur, you surely got your $75,000 worth." [8]

The 1952 campaign came after twenty years of Democratic party rule. Those years had been dominated by world struggles, which had settled a number of things and left others unsettled. The American presence was felt on every continent, not only through military bases but also through its widely distributed words, sounds, and images. Its broadcasts were ceaselessly in the air, not only through the governmental Voice of America and the Armed Forces Radio Service, but also through such developments as Radio Free Europe and Radio Liberation. [9] The direction to be taken by American power would be felt everywhere.

Meanwhile several war machines had been destroyed and with them, words. Such terms as "fascist" and "nazi" were no longer serviceable as terms of abuse, although emotions and ideas associated with them were in evidence in many places.

8. Mazo, *Richard Nixon*, pp. 111–19. In Eisenhower's own account the wording was: "Well, Arthur, you sure got your money's worth." Eisenhower, *The White House Years: Mandate for Change*, p. 68.
9. These involved financial support from the Central Intelligence Agency, a fact known to few at the time.

To Stevenson the twenty years had been a time of humanitarian achievement. To another figure in the campaign, Senator Joseph McCarthy, they had been mainly "twenty years of treason." He took pleasure in referring to the Democratic candidate as "Alger—I mean Adlai—Stevenson." McCarthy depicted General George C. Marshall's attempted mediation in China as a treasonable venture. Eisenhower, an admirer of Marshall—his wartime chief—was infuriated by McCarthy's attacks on Marshall, but a number of Republican leaders felt that McCarthy was winning votes, and they sought to prevent an open break. When Eisenhower on his campaign headed for McCarthy's state—Wisconsin—a resolution of the tension was expected. Eisenhower planned, as an indirect rebuke to McCarthy, to praise Marshall in his Wisconsin speech. At the eleventh hour his aides persuaded him to delete the affronting eulogy. McCarthy boarded the campaign train and was photographed, smiling, with General Eisenhower.

The twenty years of Democratic rule had also been the years that had made network broadcasting a force in American life. The effects of that force, often discussed, were a matter of conjecture. One conclusion widely accepted was that it had created a national in place of a regional or local consciousness. Another conclusion was that it had strengthened the executive at the expense of other elements in the body politic. Such an effect had been noted also in other major nations. Franklin D. Roosevelt in the United States, Hitler in Germany, Churchill in England, had all consolidated their power through the use of radio hookups. All had been able to address and influence a widespread public directly through radio. Some observers felt that this had brought a universal dislocation of the patterns of power, which had made it easier for executives to manipulate whole populations toward action. Some felt that onslaughts such as those of Hitler in Europe and of the Japanese militarists in Asia had for this reason coincided with the growth of electronic communication.[10]

Albert Speer, armaments minister to Hitler during the war, gave force to this view when he said at the Nuremberg trials:

> The telephone, the teleprinter and the wireless made it possible for orders from the highest levels to be given direct to the lowest levels where, on account of the absolute authority behind them, they were carried out uncritically. . . . Former dictatorships needed collaborators of high quality even in the lower levels of leadership, men who

10. Innis, *Empire and Communications*, pp. 209–11.

can think and act independently. In the era of modern technique an authoritarian system can do without this.[11]

If this element of "modern technique" helped the Axis nations assemble an onslaught of incredible might, it also helped their opponents to assemble comparable—and, as it turned out, superior—might.

Hitler and his allies were defeated, but the power of the executive remained a factor. In the United States during the twenty years it had generally been at odds with the power of big business, but the war emergency had tended to bring them together, and suggested the power inherent in such a combination, backed by the complex web of communication in which network radio had become a central element.

In this web of influence, now destined to have international as well as national significance, a new and mysterious addition was being felt—the luminous television screen.

In front of television cameras Stevenson was waging a campaign of the radio age, but the radio age was waning. The word was grappling with the image, without knowing its strength.

The vote ran: Eisenhower, 33,936,252; Stevenson, 27,314,992. The electoral vote was 442 to 89. The twenty years were over.

Broadcasting magazine speculated that there would be a big cleanout at the FCC and that Senator Joseph McCarthy might well conduct a probe of its affairs.

In December Eisenhower flew to Korea and back. The *Today* television series, scoring a scoop, was the first to report that he had been to Korea and returned. The machinery toward peace was in motion.

Restrictions on war materials were already being lifted. Hundreds of new television stations were rushing to reach the air. As Eisenhower was inaugurated President of the United States, the greatest of all broadcasting booms was on its way.

11. Quoted, Schacht, *Account Settled*, p. 240.

APPENDIX A / CHRONOLOGY

1933   Franklin D. Roosevelt inauguration broadcast worldwide.
Radio "fireside chats" play important crisis role.
Armstrong demonstrates FM for RCA executives.
Radio City dedicated.

1934   Press-Radio Bureau begins operation.
Radio industry assails Tugwell bill.
Proposal to reserve 25 per cent of channels for education (Wagner-Hatfield bill) defeated.
Communications Act is passed.
WLW begins use of superpower—500,000 watts.
Father Coughlin a rising force in radio.
Mutual Broadcasting System is formed.

1935   Hauptman trial verdict broadcast from Flemington, New Jersey.
CBS "bans" laxatives.
Radio "pied pipers" Huey Long and Father Coughlin move toward coalition.
Huey Long is assassinated.
Audimeter appears as radio research tool.
Armstrong demonstrates FM for press.
Federal Radio Education Committee formed.

1936   Lenox Lohr becomes NBC president.
Republican Party produces *Liberty at the Crossroads* drama series.
RCA launches $1,000,000 television field tests.
Columbia Workshop begins.
Kaltenborn describes the battle of Irun.
Literary Digest presidential poll scores a fiasco.
New York-Philadelphia coaxial cable ready for use.

1937   NBC Symphony formed with Toscanini as conductor.
"Fall of the City" broadcast on *Columbia Workshop*.
Frank McNinch becomes FCC chairman.
American Bar Association adopts Canon 35.
"Adam and Eve" broadcast stars Mae West.
NBC television mobile unit in action in New York City.

1938   Murrow describes annexation of Austria.
World news roundup programs begin.
Munich crisis broadcasts by Kaltenborn.
Orson Welles broadcast of "War of the Worlds" on *Mercury Theater on the Air*.
FCC starts chain broadcasting study.
CBS buys Columbia Records.

1939   Armstrong completes FM station at Alpine, New Jersey.
RCA television demonstration at New York World's Fair.
Television on limited-commercial basis.
NAB establishes BMI as rival to ASCAP.
NAB adopts new code.
Fly becomes FCC chairman.
Intercollegiate Broadcasting System formed.
"Ballad for Americans," sung by Paul Robeson, scores success on CBS.
FCC ends WLW superpower.
United Fruit becomes first sponsor of commercial short-wave broadcasts.
Radar production begins.

1940   Isolationism is focus of radio debates.
FCC decides television will have FM sound.
Shirer describes French surrender at Compiègne.
Republican and Democratic conventions telecast.
Niles Trammell becomes NBC president.
FDR campaign refrain: "Martin, Barton, and Fish."
Defense Communications Board formed with Fly as chairman.
Election returns telecast first time.
Murrow describes the London blitz.

1941   Mayflower decision bars editorializing by licensees.
MacLeish heads Office of Facts and Figures.
Foreign Broadcast Intelligence Service formed.
Report on Chain Broadcasting released.
Networks sell artist bureaus.
Television goes on commercial basis.
Dies committee attacks FCC.
Roosevelt speech after Pearl Harbor heard by 79 per cent of American homes.
Amateur stations closed.
We Hold These Truths broadcast on all networks.

1942 Voluntary censorship system established.
Manufacture of receivers halted.
Manufacture of recordings curtailed.
AFM halts recording by musicians.
Television schedules curtailed.
Command Performance and *The Army Hour* launched.
Office of War Information formed, headed by Elmer Davis.
Robert Sherwood heads OWI overseas branch.
United States takes over short-wave stations.
Albert Lasker dissolves Lord & Thomas.
Armed Forces Radio Service formed.
Advertising costs ruled tax-deductible.
Collingwood broadcasts from North Africa.

1943 Cox probe of FCC.
U. S. Supreme Court upholds chain rules.
CBS broadcasts *Open Letter on Race Hatred*, with Wendell Willkie.
Noble buys Blue Network.
Sevareid bails out on India-China flight.
Cox resigns from probe after exposure by Durr.
Wire recorders in use on Italian front.

1944 ABSIE opened in London.
Hicks and others describe Normandy landings via wire recorders.
FDR's Fala speech.
FDR makes campaign tour in driving rain.
U. S. uses Radio Luxembourg for psychological warfare.
Paul Porter becomes FCC chairman.
Rise of disk-jockey programming.

1945 Broadcast of FDR report to Congress on Yalta meetings.
Murrow broadcasts a description of Buchenwald.
Hottelet describes juncture of American and Russian troops.
German tape recorders captured.
Radio tributes on death of FDR.
FCC moves FM "upstairs" in radio spectrum.
United Nations charter meeting widely covered by radio.
Broadcasts of *On a Note of Triumph* and *14 August* written and directed by Norman Corwin.
Set manufacture approved as war ends.
FCC adopts AVCO rule.

1946 The "blue book" is published.
Stanton becomes CBS president.
Murrow, new CBS vice-president, starts documentary unit.
Television sets go on sale.
Opening of United Nations Security Council televised.
Charles Denny becomes FCC chairman.

Color television demonstrations by CBS and NBC.

Corwin receives Willkie One World Award and produces *One World Flight*.

Tape recorders bring changes in programming and production.

1947   Congress opening televised for first time.

Blue baby operation televised.

Kraft Television Theater series begins.

Broadcasts to Russian people begun by State Department.

FCC denies CBS color-television petition.

Durr questions value of undocumented FBI data.

Counterattack newsletter launched.

HUAC hearings on Hollywood.

Coy becomes FCC chairman.

1948   Radio News Club of Southern California accuses Richards.

Frieda Hennock becomes first FCC woman commissioner.

33⅓ and 45 RPM records appear.

Philadelphia becomes convention site because of television cable.

Truman stresses barnstorming tour instead of radio.

CBS talent raids on NBC based on capital-gains tax rate.

Armstrong sues RCA over FM patent infringement.

U. S. v. *Paramount et al.* won by government.

FCC starts "freeze" on television licenses.

Beginnings of Negro radio stations.

1949   Inauguration telecast for first time.

Stop the Music! starts jackpot-program cycle.

Joseph McConnell becomes NBC president.

Mayflower decision amended by FCC.

AVCO rule rescinded by FCC.

I Can Hear It Now LP album appears.

1950   Paul Draper appearance on *Toast of the Town* attacked.

Red Channels appears.

Cases of Jean Muir, Ireene Wicker, Philip Loeb, and many others.

Laurence Johnson of Syracuse enters the blacklist field.

CBS institutes a loyalty oath.

Hear It Now radio series launched by Murrow.

1951   Movie attendance dropping sharply in television cities.

Wave of movie theater closings.

ABC-Paramount Theaters merger negotiated.

Richards licenses renewed by FCC after death of Richards.

NBC launches *Today* television series.

CBS starts Murrow-Friendly *See It Now* television series.

Blacklisting institutionalized at networks and agencies.

1952   FCC reserves television channels for education.

Amendments to Communications Act.

FCC lifts "freeze" and processes license applications.

Nixon "Checkers" speech.

Eisenhower 20-second spot campaign.

Hundreds of television stations rush to reach air.

1953 Widespread telecasts of inauguration of Dwight D. Eisenhower.

APPENDIX B / LAW

Communications Act of 1934[1]

Public Law No. 416, June 19, 1934, 73d Congress. An Act to provide for the regulation of interstate and foreign communication by wire or radio, and for other purposes.

Be it enacted by the Senate and House of Representatives of the United States of America in Congress assembled,

TITLE I—GENERAL PROVISIONS

PURPOSES OF ACT; CREATION OF FEDERAL COMMUNICATIONS COMMISSION

SEC. 1. For the purpose of regulating interstate and foreign commerce in communication by wire and radio so as to make available, so far as possible, to all the people of the United States a rapid, efficient, Nation-wide, and world-wide wire and radio communication service with adequate facilities at reasonable charges, for the purpose of the national defense, and for the purpose of securing a more effective execution of this policy by centralizing authority heretofore granted by law to several agencies and by granting additional authority with respect to interstate and foreign commerce in wire and radio communication, there is hereby created a commission to be known as the "Federal Communications Commission", which shall be constituted as hereinafter provided, and which shall execute and enforce the provisions of this Act.

APPLICATION OF ACT

SEC. 2. (a) The provisions of this Act shall apply to all interstate and foreign communication by wire or radio and all interstate and foreign transmission of

1. Given here in its original form. Amendments mentioned in the preceding text are indicated in footnotes.

energy by radio, which originates and/or is received within the United States, and to all persons engaged within the United States in such communication or such transmission of energy by radio, and to the licensing and regulating of all radio stations as hereinafter provided; but it shall not apply to persons engaged in wire or radio communication or transmission in the Philippine Islands or the Canal Zone, or to wire or radio communication or transmission wholly within the Philippine Islands or the Canal Zone.

(b) Subject to the provisions of section 301, nothing in this Act shall be construed to apply or to give the Commission jurisdiction with respect to (1) charges, classifications, practices, services, facilities, or regulations for or in connection with intrastate communication service of any carrier, or (2) any carrier engaged in interstate or foreign communication solely through physical connection with the facilities of another carrier not directly or indirectly controlling or controlled by, or under direct or indirect common control with, such carrier; except that sections 201 to 205 of this Act, both inclusive, shall, except as otherwise provided therein, apply to carriers described in clause (2).

DEFINITIONS

SEC. 3. For the purposes of this Act, unless the context otherwise requires—

(a) "Wire communication" or "communication by wire" means the transmission of writing, signs, signals, pictures, and sounds of all kinds by aid of wire, cable, or other like connection between the points of origin and reception of such transmission, including all instrumentalities, facilities, apparatus, and services (among other things, the receipt, forwarding, and delivery of communications) incidental to such transmission.

(b) "Radio communication" or "communication by radio" means the transmission by radio of writing, signs, signals, pictures, and sounds of all kinds, including all instrumentalities, facilities, apparatus, and services (among other things, the receipt, forwarding, and delivery of communications) incidental to such transmission.

(c) "Licensee" means the holder of a radio station license granted or continued in force under authority of this Act.

(d) "Transmission of energy by radio" or "radio transmission of energy" includes both such transmission and all instrumentalities, facilities, and services incidental to such transmission.

(e) "Interstate communication" or "interstate transmission" means communication or transmission (1) from any State, Territory, or possession of the United States (other than the Philippine Islands and the Canal Zone), or the District of Columbia, to any other State, Territory, or possession of the United States (other than the Philippine Islands and the Canal Zone), or the District of Columbia, (2) from or to the United States to or from the Philippine Islands or the Canal Zone, insofar as such communication or transmission takes place within the United States, or (3) between points within the United States but through a foreign country; but shall not include wire communication between points within the same State, Territory, or possession of the United States, or the District of Columbia, through any place outside thereof, if such communication is regulated by a State commission.

(f) "Foreign communication" or "foreign transmission" means communication or transmission from or to any place in the United States to or from a foreign country, or between a station in the United States and a mobile station located outside the United States.

(g) "United States" means the several States and Territories, the District of Columbia, and the possessions of the United States, but does not include the Philippine Islands or the Canal Zone.

(h) "Common carrier" or "carrier" means any person engaged as a common carrier for hire, in interstate or foreign communication by wire or radio or in interstate or foreign radio transmission of energy, except where reference is made to common carriers not subject to this Act; but a person engaged in radio broadcasting shall not, insofar as such person is so engaged, be deemed a common carrier.

(i) "Person" includes an individual, partnership, association, joint-stock company, trust, or corporation.

(j) "Corporation" includes any corporation, joint-stock company, or association.

(k) "Radio station" or "station" means a station equipped to engage in radio communication or radio transmission of energy.

(1) "Mobile station" means a radio-communication station capable of being moved and which ordinarily does move.

(m) "Land station" means a station, other than a mobile station, used for radio communication with mobile stations.

(n) "Mobile service" means the radio-communication service carried on between mobile stations and land stations, and by mobile stations communicating among themselves.

(o) "Broadcasting" means the dissemination of radio communications intended to be received by the public, directly or by the intermediary of relay stations.

(p) "Chain broadcasting" means simultaneous broadcasting of an identical program by two or more connected stations.

(q) "Amateur station" means a radio station operated by a duly authorized person interested in radio technique solely with a personal aim and without pecuniary interest.

(r) "Telephone exchange service" means service within a telephone exchange, or within a connected system of telephone exchanges within the same exchange area operated to furnish to subscribers intercommunicating service of the character ordinarily furnished by a single exchange, and which is covered by the exchange service charge.

(s) "Telephone toll service" means telephone service between stations in different exchange areas for which there is made a separate charge not included in contracts with subscribers for exchange service.

(t) "State commission" means the commission, board, or official (by whatever name designated) which under the laws of any State has regulatory jurisdiction with respect to intrastate operations of carriers.

(u) "Connecting carrier" means a carrier described in clause (2) of section 2(b).

(v) "State" includes the District of Columbia and the Territories and possessions.

PROVISIONS RELATING TO THE COMMISSION

SEC. 4 (a) The Federal Communications Commission (in this Act referred to as the "Commission") shall be composed of seven commissioners appointed by the President, by and with the advice and consent of the Senate, one of whom the President shall designate as chairman.

(b) Each member of the Commission shall be a citizen of the United States. No member of the Commission or person in its employ shall be financially interested in the manufacture or sale of radio apparatus or of apparatus for wire or radio communication; in communication by wire or radio or in radio transmission of energy; in any company furnishing services or such apparatus to any company engaged in communication by wire or radio or to any company manufacturing or selling apparatus used for communication by wire or radio; or in any company owning stocks, bonds, or other securities of any such company; nor be in the employ of or hold any official relation to any person subject to any of the provisions of this Act, nor own stocks, bonds, or other securities of any corporation subject to any of the provisions of this Act. Such commissioners shall not engage in any other business, vocation, or employment.[2] Not more than four commissioners shall be members of the same political party.

(c) The commissioners first appointed under this Act shall continue in office for the terms of one, two, three, four, five, six, and seven years, respectively, from the date of the taking effect of this Act, the term of each to be designated by the President, but their successors shall be appointed for terms of seven years; except that any person chosen to fill a vacancy shall be appointed only for the unexpired term of the commissioner whom he succeeds. No vacancy in the Commission shall impair the right of the remaining commissioners to exercise all the powers of the Commission.

2. A 1952 amendment (Public Law No. 554, July 16, 1952, 82nd Congress) struck out the preceding sentence and inserted: "Such commissioners shall not engage in any other business, vocation, profession, or employment; but this shall not apply to the presentation or delivery of publications or papers for which a reasonable honorarium or compensation may be accepted. Any such commissioner serving as such after one year from the date of enactment of the Communications Act Amendments, 1952, shall not for a period of one year following the termination of his services as a commissioner represent any person before the Commission in a professional capacity, except that this restriction shall not apply to any commissioner who has served the full term for which he was appointed."

(d) Each commissioner shall receive an annual salary of $10,000, payable in monthly installments.

(e) The principal office of the Commission shall be in the District of Columbia, where its general sessions shall be held; but whenever the convenience of the public or of the parties may be promoted or delay or expense prevented thereby, the Commission may hold special sessions in any part of the United States.

(f) Without regard to the civil-service laws or the Classification Act of 1923, as amended, (1) the Commission may appoint and prescribe the duties and fix the salaries of a secretary, a director for each division, a chief engineer and not more than three assistants, a general counsel and not more than three assistants, and temporary counsel designated by the Commission for the performance of special services, and (2) each commissioner may appoint and prescribe the duties of a secretary at an annual salary not to exceed $4,000. The general counsel and the chief engineer shall each receive an annual salary of not to exceed $9,000; the secretary shall receive an annual salary of not to exceed $7,500; the director of each division shall receive an annual salary of not to exceed $7,500; and no assistant shall receive an annual salary in excess of $7,500. The Commission shall have authority, subject to the provisions of the civil-service laws and the Classification Act of 1923, as amended, to appoint such other officers, engineers, inspectors, attorneys, examiners, and other employees as are necessary in the execution of its functions.

(g) The Commission may make such expenditures (including expenditures for rent and personal services at the seat of government and elsewhere, for office supplies, law books, periodicals, and books of reference, and for printing and binding) as may be necessary for the execution of the functions vested in the Commission and as from time to time may be appropriated for by Congress. All expenditures of the Commission, including all necessary expenses for transportation incurred by the commissioners or by their employees, under their orders, in making any investigation or upon any official business in any other places than in the city of Washington, shall be allowed and paid on the presentation of itemized vouchers therefor approved by the chairman of the Commission or by such other member or officer thereof as may be designated by the Commission for that purpose.

(h) Four members of the Commission shall constitute a quorum thereof. The Commission shall have an official seal which shall be judicially noticed.

(i) The Commission may perform any and all acts, make such rules and regulations, and issue such orders, not inconsistent with this Act, as may be necessary in the execution of its functions.

(j) The Commission may conduct its proceedings in such manner as will best conduce to the proper dispatch of business and to the ends of justice. No commissioner shall participate in any hearing or proceeding in which he has a pecuniary interest. Any party may appear before the Commission and be heard in person or by attorney. Every vote and official act of the Commission shall be entered of record, and its proceedings shall be public upon the request of any party interested. The Commission is authorized to withhold publication of records or proceedings containing secret information affecting the national defense.

(k) The Commission shall make an annual report to Congress, copies of which shall be distributed as are other reports transmitted to Congress. Such report shall contain such information and data collected by the Commission as may be considered of value in the determination of questions connected with the regulation of interstate and foreign wire and radio communication and radio transmission of energy, together with such recommendations as to additional legislation relating thereto as the Commission may deem necessary: *Provided,* That the Commission shall make a special report not later than February 1, 1935, recommending such amendments to this Act as it deems desirable in the public interest.

(l) All reports of investigations made by the Commission shall be entered of record, and a copy thereof shall be furnished to the party who may have complained, and to any common carrier or licensee that may have been complained of.

(m) The Commission shall provide for the publication of its reports and decisions in such form and manner as may be best adapted for public information and use, and such authorized publications shall be competent evidence of the reports and decisions of the Commission therein contained in all courts of the United States and of the several States without any further proof or authentication thereof.

(n) Rates of compensation of persons appointed under this section shall be subject to the reduction applicable to officers and employees of the Federal Government generally.

DIVISIONS OF THE COMMISSION

SEC. 5. (a) The Commission is hereby authorized by its order to divide the members thereof into not more than three divisions, each to consist of not less than three members. Any commissioner may be assigned to and may serve upon such division or divisions as the Commission may direct, and each division shall choose its own chairman. In case of a vacancy in any division, or of absence or inability to serve thereon of any commissioner thereto assigned, the chairman of the Commission or any commissioner designated by him for that purpose may temporarily serve on said division until the Commission shall otherwise order.

(b) The Commission may by order direct that any of its work, business, or functions arising under this Act, or under any other Act of Congress, or in respect of any matter which has been or may be referred to the Commission by Congress or by either branch thereof, be assigned or referred to any of said divisions, for action thereon, and may by order at any time amend, modify, supplement, or rescind any such direction. All such orders shall take effect forthwith and remain in effect until otherwise ordered by the Commission.

(c) In conformity with and subject to the order or orders of the Commission in the premises, each division so constituted shall have power and authority by a majority thereof to hear and determine, order, certify, report, or otherwise act as to any of said work, business, or functions so assigned or referred to it for action by the Commission, and in respect thereof the division shall have all the jurisdiction and powers now or then conferred by law upon the Commission, and be subject to the same duties and obligations. Any order, decision, or report made or other action taken by any of said divisions in respect of any matters so assigned or referred to it shall have the same force and effect, and may be made, evidenced, and enforced in the same manner as if made, or taken by the Commission, subject to rehearing by the Commission as provided in section 405 of this Act for rehearing cases decided by the Commission. The secretary and seal of the Commission shall be the secretary and seal of each division thereof.

(d) Nothing in this section contained, or done pursuant thereto, shall be deemed to divest the Commission of any of its powers.

(e) The Commission is hereby authorized by its order to assign or refer any portion of its work, business, or functions arising under this or any other Act of Congress or referred to it by Congress, or either branch thereof, to an individual commissioner, or to a board composed of an employee or employees of the Commission, to be designated by such order, for action thereon, and by its order at any time to amend, modify, supplement, or rescind any such assignment or reference: *Provided, however,* That this authority shall not extend to investigations instituted upon the Commission's own motion or, without the consent of the parties thereto, to contested proceedings involving the taking of testimony at public hearings, or to investigations specifically required by this Act. All such orders shall take effect forthwith and remain in effect until otherwise ordered by the Commission. In case of the absence or inability for any other reason to act of any such individual commissioner or employee designated to serve upon any such board, the chairman of the Commission may designate another commissioner or employee, as the case may be, to serve temporarily until the Commission shall otherwise order. In conformity with and subject to the order or orders of the Commission in the premises, any such individual commissioner, or board acting by a majority thereof, shall have power and authority to hear and determine, order, certify, report, or otherwise act as to any of said work, business, or functions so assigned or referred to him or it for action by the Commission and in respect thereof shall have all the jurisdiction and powers now or then conferred by law upon the Commission and be subject to the same duties and obligations. Any order, decision, or report made or other action taken by any such individual commissioner or board in respect of any matters so assigned or referred shall have the same force and effect, and may be made, evidenced, and enforced in the same manner as if made or taken by the Commission. Any party affected by any order, decision, or report of any such individual commissioner or board may file a petition for rehearing by the Commission or a division thereof and every such petition shall be passed upon by the Commission or a division thereof. Any action by a division upon such a petition shall itself be subject to rehearing by the Commission, as provided in section 405 of this Act and in subsection (c). The Commission may make and amend rules for the conduct of proceedings before such individual commissioner or board and for the rehearing of such action before a division of the Commission or the Commission. The secretary and seal of the Commission shall be the secretary and seal of such individual commissioner or board.

(TITLE II, dealing with common carriers, is here omitted.)

TITLE III—SPECIAL PROVISIONS RELATING TO RADIO
LICENSE FOR RADIO COMMUNICATION OR TRANSMISSION OF ENERGY

SEC. 301. It is the purpose of this Act, among other things, to maintain the control of the United States over all the channels of interstate and foreign radio transmission; and to provide for the use of such channels, but not the ownership thereof, by persons for limited periods of time, under licenses granted by Federal authority, and no such license shall be construed to create any right, beyond the terms, conditions, and periods of the license. No person shall use or operate any apparatus for the transmission of energy or communications or signals by radio (a) from one place in any Territory or possession of the United States or in the District of Columbia to another place in the same Territory, possession, or District; or (b) from any State, Territory, or possession of the United States, or from the District of Columbia to any other State, Territory, or possession of the United States; or (c) from any place in any State, Territory, or possession of the United States, or in the District of Columbia, to any place in any foreign country or to any vessel; or (d) within any State when the effects of such use extend beyond the borders of said State, or when interference is caused by such use or operation with the transmission of such energy, communications, or signals from within said State to any place beyond its borders, or from any place beyond its borders to any place within said State, or with the transmission or reception of such energy, communications, or signals from and/or to places beyond the borders of said State; or (e) upon any vessel or aircraft of the United States; or (f) upon any other mobile stations within the jurisdiction of the United States, except under and in accordance with this Act and with a license in that behalf granted under the provisions of this Act.

ZONES

SEC. 302. (a) For the purposes of this title the United States is divided into five zones, as follows: The first zone shall embrace the States of Maine, New Hampshire, Vermont, Massachusetts, Connecticut, Rhode Island, New York, New Jersey, Delaware, Maryland, and the District of Columbia; the second zone shall embrace the States of Pennsylvania, Virginia, West Virginia, Ohio, Michigan, and Kentucky; the third zone shall embrace the States of North Carolina, South Carolina, Georgia, Florida, Alabama, Tennessee, Mississippi, Arkan-

sas, Louisiana, Texas, and Oklahoma; the fourth zone shall embrace the States
of Indiana, Illinois, Wisconsin, Minnesota, North Dakota, South Dakota, Iowa,
Nebraska, Kansas, and Missouri; and the fifth zone shall embrace the States of
Montana, Idaho, Wyoming, Colorado, New Mexico, Arizona, Utah, Nevada,
Washington, Oregon, and California.

(b) The Virgin Islands, Puerto Rico, Alaska, Guam, American Samoa, and
the Territory of Hawaii are expressly excluded from the zones herein established.

GENERAL POWERS OF COMMISSION

SEC. 303. Except as otherwise provided in this Act, the Commission from time
to time, as public convenience, interest, or necessity requires, shall—

(a) Classify radio stations;

(b) Prescribe the nature of the service to be rendered by each class of
licensed stations and each station within any class;

(c) Assign bands of frequencies to the various classes of stations, and assign
frequencies for each individual station and determine the power which each
station shall use and the time during which it may operate;

(d) Determine the location of classes of stations or individual stations;

(e) Regulate the kind of apparatus to be used with respect to its external
effects and the purity and sharpness of the emissions from each station and from
the apparatus therein;

(f) Make such regulations not inconsistent with law as it may deem necessary to prevent interference between stations and to carry out the provisions of
this Act: *Provided, however,* That changes in the frequencies, authorized
power, or in the times of operation of any station, shall not be made without the
consent of the station licensee unless, after a public hearing, the Commission
shall determine that such changes will promote public convenience or interest or
will serve public necessity, or the provisions of this Act will be more fully complied with;

(g) Study new uses for radio, provide for experimental uses of frequencies,
and generally encourage the larger and more effective use of radio in the public
interest;

(h) Have authority to establish areas or zones to be served by any station;

(i) Have authority to make special regulations applicable to radio stations
engaged in chain broadcasting;

(j) Have authority to make general rules and regulations requiring stations
to keep such records of programs, transmissions of energy, communications, or
signals as it may deem desirable;

(k) Have authority to exclude from the requirements of any regulations in
whole or in part any radio station upon railroad rolling stock, or to modify
such regulations in its discretion;

(l) Have authority to prescribe the qualifications of station operators, to
classify them according to the duties to be performed, to fix the forms of such

licenses, and to issue them to such citizens of the United States as the Commission finds qualified;

(m) Have authority to suspend the license of any operator for a period not exceeding two years upon proof sufficient to satisfy the Commission that the licensee (1) has violated any provision of any Act or treaty binding on the United States which the Commission is authorized by this Act to administer or any regulation made by the Commission under any such Act or treaty; or (2) has failed to carry out the lawful orders of the master of the vessel on which he is employed; or (3) has willfully damaged or permitted radio apparatus to be damaged; (4) has transmitted superfluous radio communications or signals or radio communications containing profane or obscene words or language; or (5) has willfully or maliciously interfered with any other radio communications or signals;

(n) Have authority to inspect all transmitting apparatus to ascertain whether in construction and operation it conforms to the requirements of this Act, the rules and regulations of the Commission, and the license under which it is constructed or operated;

(o) Have authority to designate call letters of all stations;

(p) Have authority to cause to be published such call letters and such other announcements and data as in the judgment of the Commission may be required for the efficient operation of radio stations subject to the jurisdiction of the United States and for the proper enforcement of this Act;

(q) Have authority to require the painting and/or illumination of radio towers if and when in its judgment such towers constitute, or there is a reasonable possibility that they may constitute, a menace to air navigation.

WAIVER BY LICENSEE

SEC. 304. No station license shall be granted by the Commission until the applicant therefor shall have signed a waiver of any claim to the use of any particular frequency or of the ether as against the regulatory power of the United States because of the previous use of the same, whether by license or otherwise.

GOVERNMENT-OWNED STATIONS

SEC. 305. (a) Radio stations belonging to and operated by the United States shall not be subject to the provisions of sections 301 and 303 of this Act. All such Government stations shall use such frequencies as shall be assigned to each or to each class by the President. All such stations, except stations on board naval and other Government vessels while at sea or beyond the limits of the continental United States, when transmitting any radio communication or signal other than a communication or signal relating to Government business, shall conform to such rules and regulations designed to prevent interference with other radio stations and the rights of others as the Commission may prescribe.

(b) Radio stations on board vessels of the United States Shipping Board Bureau or the United States Shipping Board Merchant Fleet Corporation or the Inland and Coastwise Waterways Service shall be subject to the provisions of this title.

(c) All stations owned and operated by the United States, except mobile stations of the Army of the United States, and all other stations on land and sea, shall have special call letters designated by the Commission.

FOREIGN SHIPS

SEC. 306. Section 301 of this Act shall not apply to any person sending radio communications or signals on a foreign ship while the same is within the jurisdiction of the United States, but such communications or signals shall be transmitted only in accordance with such regulations designed to prevent interference as may be promulgated under the authority of this Act.

ALLOCATION OF FACILITIES; TERM OF LICENSES

SEC. 307. (a) The Commission, if public convenience, interest, or necessity will be served thereby, subject to the limitations of this Act, shall grant to any applicant therefor a station license provided for by this Act.

(b) It is hereby declared that the people of all the zones established by this title are entitled to equality of radio broadcasting service, both of transmission and of reception, and in order to provide said equality the Commission shall as nearly as possible make and maintain an equal allocation of broadcasting licenses, of bands of frequency, of periods of time for operation, and of station power, to each of said zones when and insofar as there are applications therefor; and shall make a fair and equitable allocation of licenses, frequencies, time for operation, and station power to each of the States and the District of Columbia, within each zone, according to population. The Commission shall carry into effect the equality of broadcasting service hereinbefore directed, whenever necessary or proper, by granting or refusing licenses or renewals of licenses, by changing periods of time for operation, and by increasing or decreasing station power, when applications are made for licenses or renewals of licenses: *Provided,* That if and when there is a lack of applications from any zone for the proportionate share of licenses, frequencies, time of operation, or station power to which such zone is entitled, the Commission may issue licenses for the balance of the proportion not applied for from any zone, to applicants from other zones for a temporary period of ninety days each, and shall specifically designate that said apportionment is only for said temporary period. Allocations shall be charged to the State or District wherein the studio of the station is located and not where the transmitter is located: *Provided further,* That the Commission may also grant applications for additional licenses for stations not exceeding one hundred watts of power if the Commission finds that such stations will serve the public convenience, interest, or necessity, and that their operation will not interfere with the fair and efficient radio service of stations licensed under the provisions of this section.

(c) The Commission shall study the proposal that Congress by statute allocate fixed percentages of radio broadcasting facilities to particular types or kinds of non-profit radio programs or to persons identified with particular types or kinds of non-profit activities, and shall report to Congress, not later than February 1, 1935, its recommendations together with the reasons for the same.

(d) No license granted for the operation of a broadcasting station shall be for a longer term than three years and no license so granted for any other class of station shall be for a longer term than five years, and any license granted may be revoked as hereinafter provided. Upon the expiration of any license, upon application therefor, a renewal of such license may be granted from time to time for a term of not to exceed three years in the case of broadcasting licenses and not to exceed five years in the case of other licenses, but action of the Commission with reference to the granting of such application for the renewal of a license shall be limited to and governed by the same considerations and practice which affect the granting of original applications.

(e) No renewal of an existing station license shall be granted more than thirty days prior to the expiration of the original license.

APPLICATIONS FOR LICENSES; CONDITIONS IN LICENSE FOR FOREIGN COMMUNICATION

SEC. 308. (a) The Commission may grant licenses, renewal of licenses, and modification of licenses only upon written application therefor received by it: *Provided, however,* That in cases of emergency found by the Commission, licenses, renewals of licenses, and modifications of licenses, for stations on vessels or aircraft of the United States, may be issued under such conditions as the Commission may impose, without such formal application. Such licenses, however, shall in no case be for a longer term than three months: *Provided further,* That the Commission may issue by cable, telegraph, or radio a permit for the operation of a station on a vessel of the United States at sea, effective in lieu of a license until said vessel shall return to a port of the continental United States.

(b) All such applications shall set forth such facts as the Commission by regulation may prescribe as to the citizenship, character, and financial, technical, and other qualifications of the applicant to operate the station; the ownership and location of the proposed station and of the stations, if any, with which it is proposed to communicate; the frequencies and the power desired to be used; the hours of the day or other periods of time during which it is proposed to operate the station; the purposes for which the station is to be used; and such other information as it may require. The Commission, at any time after the filing of such original application and during the term of any such license, may require from an applicant or licensee further written statements of fact to enable it to determine whether such original application should be granted or denied or such license revoked. Such application and/or such statement of fact shall be signed by the applicant and/or licensee under oath or affirmation.

(c) The Commission in granting any license for a station intended or used for commerical communication between the United States or any Territory or possession, continental or insular, subject to the jurisdiction of the United States, and any foreign country, may impose any terms, conditions, or restrictions authorized to be imposed with respect to submarine-cable licenses by section 2 of an Act entitled "An Act relating to the landing and the operation of submarine cables in the United States", approved May 24, 1921.

HEARINGS ON APPLICATIONS FOR LICENSES; FORM OF LICENSES; CONDITIONS ATTACHED TO LICENSES

SEC. 309. (a) If upon examination of any application for a station license or for the renewal or modification of a station license the Commission shall determine that public interest, convenience, or necessity would be served by the granting thereof, it shall authorize the issuance, renewal, or modification thereof in accordance with said finding. In the event the Commission upon examination of any such application does not reach such decision with respect thereto, it shall notify the applicant thereof, shall fix and give notice of a time and place for hearing thereon, and shall afford such applicant an opportunity to be heard under such rules and regulations as it may prescribe.

(b) Such station licenses as the Commission may grant shall be in such general form as it may prescribe, but each license shall contain, in addition to other provisions, a statement of the following conditions to which such license shall be subject:

(1) The station license shall not vest in the licensee any right to operate the station nor any right in the use of the frequencies designated in the license beyond the term thereof nor in any other manner than authorized therein.

(2) Neither the license nor the right granted thereunder shall be assigned or otherwise transferred in violation of this Act.

(3) Every license issued under this Act shall be subject in terms to the right of use or control conferred by section 606 hereof.

LIMITATION ON HOLDING AND TRANSFER OF LICENSES

SEC. 310. (a) The station license required hereby shall not be granted to or held by—

(1) Any alien or the representative of any alien;

(2) Any foreign government or the representative thereof;

(3) Any corporation organized under the laws of any foreign government;

(4) Any corporation of which any officer or director is an alien or of which more than one-fifth of the capital stock is owned of record or voted by aliens or their representatives or by a foreign government or representative thereof, or by any corporation organized under the laws of a foreign country;

(5) Any corporation directly or indirectly controlled by any other corporation of which any officer or more than one-fourth of the directors are aliens, or of which more than one-fourth of the capital stock is owned of record or voted, after June 1, 1935, by aliens, their representatives, or by a foreign government or representative thereof, or by any corporation organized under the laws of a foreign country, if the Commission finds that the public interest will be served by the refusal or the revocation of such license.

Nothing in this subsection shall prevent the licensing of radio apparatus on board any vessel, aircraft, or other mobile station of the United States when the installation and use of such apparatus is required by Act of Congress or any treaty to which the United States is a party.

(b) The station license required hereby, the frequencies authorized to be used by the licensee, and the rights therein granted shall not be transferred, assigned, or in any manner either voluntarily or involuntarily disposed of, or indirectly by transfer of control of any corporation holding such license, to any person, unless the Commission shall, after securing full information, decide that said transfer is in the public interest, and shall give its consent in writing.[3]

REFUSAL OF LICENSES AND PERMITS IN CERTAIN CASES

SEC. 311.   The Commission is hereby directed to refuse a station license and/ or the permit hereinafter required for the construction of a station to any person (or to any person directly or indirectly controlled by such person) whose license has been revoked by a court under section 313, and is hereby authorized to refuse such station license and/or permit to any other person (or to any person directly or indirectly controlled by such person) which has been finally adjudged guilty by a Federal court of unlawfully monopolizing or attempting unlawfully to monopolize, radio communication, directly or indirectly, through the control of the manufacture or sale of radio apparatus, through exclusive traffic arrangements, or by any other means, or to have been using unfair methods of competition. The granting of a license shall not estop the United States or any person aggrieved from proceeding against such person for violating the law against unfair methods of competition or for a violation of the law against unlawful restraints and monopolies and/or combinations, contracts, or agreements

3. A 1952 amendment (Public Law No. 554, July 16, 1952, 82nd Congress) revised this section (b) to read: "No construction permit or station license, or any rights thereunder, shall be transferred, assigned, or disposed of in any manner, voluntarily or involuntarily, directly or indirectly, or by transfer of control of any corporation holding such permit or license, to any person except upon application to the Commission and upon finding by the Commission that the public interest, convenience, and necessity will be served thereby. Any such application shall be disposed of as if the proposed transferee or assignee were making application under section 308 for the permit or license in question; but in acting thereon the Commission may not consider whether the public interest, convenience, and necessity might be served by the transfer, assignment, or disposal of the permit or license to a person other than the proposed transferee or assignee."

in restraint of trade, or from instituting proceedings for the dissolution of such corporation.

REVOCATION OF LICENSES

SEC. 312. (a) Any station license may be revoked for false statements either in the application or in the statement of fact which may be required by section 308 hereof, or because of conditions revealed by such statements of fact as may be required from time to time which would warrant the Commission in refusing to grant a license on an original application, or for failure to operate substantially as set forth in the license, or for violation of or failure to observe any of the restrictions and conditions of this Act or of any regulation of the Commission authorized by this Act or by a treaty ratified by the United States: *Provided, however,* That no such order of revocation shall take effect until fifteen days' notice in writing thereof, stating the cause for the proposed revocation, has been given to the licensee. Such licensee may make written application to the Commission at any time within said fifteen days for a hearing upon such order, and upon the filing of such written application said order of revocation shall stand suspended until the conclusion of the hearing conducted under such rules as the Commission may prescribe. Upon the conclusion of said hearing the Commission may affirm, modify, or revoke said order of revocation.

(b) Any station license hereafter granted under the provisions of this Act or the construction permit required hereby and hereafter issued, may be modified by the Commission either for a limited time or for the duration of the term thereof, if in the judgment of the Commission such action will promote the public interest, convenience, and necessity, or the provisions of this Act or of any treaty ratified by the United States will be more fully complied with: *Provided, however,* That no such order of modification shall become final until the holder of such outstanding license or permit shall have been notified in writing of the proposed action and the grounds or reasons therefor and shall have been given reasonable opportunity to show cause why such an order of modification should not issue.

APPLICATION OF ANTITRUST LAWS

SEC. 313. All laws of the United States relating to unlawful restraints and monopolies and to combinations, contracts, or agreements in restraint of trade are hereby declared to be applicable to the manufacture and sale of and to trade in radio apparatus and devices entering into or affecting interstate or foreign commerce and to interstate or foreign radio communications. Whenever in any suit, action, or proceeding, civil or criminal, brought under the provisions of any of said laws or in any proceedings brought to enforce or to review findings and orders of the Federal Trade Commission or other governmental agency in respect of any matters as to which said Commission or other governmental agency is by law authorized to act, any licensee shall be found guilty of the violation of the provisions of such laws or any of them, the court, in addition to the penalties imposed by said laws, may adjudge, order, and/or decree that the license of such licensee shall, as of the date the decree or judgment becomes finally effective or as of such other date as the said decree shall fix, be revoked and that all rights under such license shall thereupon cease: *Provided, however,* That such licensee shall have the same right of appeal or review as is provided by law in respect of other decrees and judgments of said court.

PRESERVATION OF COMPETITION IN COMMERCE

SEC. 314. After the effective date of this Act no person engaged directly, or indirectly through any person directly or indirectly controlling or controlled by, or under direct or indirect common control with, such person, or through an agent, or otherwise, in the business of transmitting and/or receiving for hire energy, communications, or signals by radio in accordance with the terms of the license issued under this Act, shall by purchase, lease, construction, or otherwise, directly or indirectly, acquire, own, control, or operate any cable or wire telegraph or telephone line or system between any place in any State, Territory, or possession of the United States or in the District of Columbia, and any place in any foreign country, or shall acquire, own, or control any part of the stock or other capital share or any interest in the physical property and/or other assets of any such cable, wire, telegraph, or telephone line or system, if in either case the purpose is and/or the effect thereof may be to substantially lessen competition or to restrain commerce between any place in any State, Territory, or possession of the United States, or in the District of Columbia, and any place in any foreign country, or unlawfully to create monopoly in any line of commerce; nor shall any person engaged directly, or indirectly through any person directly or indirectly controlling or controlled by, or under direct or indirect common control with, such person, or through an agent, or otherwise, in the business of transmitting and/or receiving for hire messages by any cable, wire, telegraph, or telephone line or system (a) between any place in any State, Territory, or possession of the United States, or in the District of Columbia, and any place in any other State, Territory, or possession of the United States; or (b) between any place in any State, Territory, or possession of the United States, or in the District of Columbia, and any place in any foreign country, by purchase, lease, construction, or otherwise, directly or indirectly acquire, own, control, or operate any station or the apparatus therein, or any system for transmitting and/or receiving radio communications or signals between any place in any State, Territory, or possession of the United States, or in the District of Columbia, and any place in any foreign country, or shall acquire, own, or control any part of the stock or other capital share or any interest in the physical property and/or other assets of any such radio station, apparatus, or system, if in either case the purpose is and/or the effect thereof may be to substantially lessen competition or to restrain commerce between any place in any State, Territory, or possession of the United States, or in the District of Columbia, and any place in any foreign country, or unlawfully to create monopoly in any line of commerce.

FACILITIES FOR CANDIDATES FOR PUBLIC OFFICE

SEC. 315. If any licensee shall permit any person who is a legally qualified candidate for any public office to use a broadcasting station, he shall afford equal opportunities to all other such candidates for that office in the use of such broadcasting station, and the Commission shall make rules and regulations to carry this provision into effect: *Provided*, That such licensee shall have no power of censorship over the material broadcast under the provisions of this section. No obligation is hereby imposed upon any licensee to allow the use of its station by any such candidate.

LOTTERIES AND OTHER SIMILAR SCHEMES

SEC. 316. No person shall broadcast by means of any radio station for which a license is required by any law of the United States, and no person operating any such station shall knowingly permit the broadcasting of, any advertisement of or information concerning any lottery, gift enterprise, or similar scheme, offering prizes dependent in whole or in part upon lot or chance, or any list of the prizes drawn or awarded by means of any such lottery, gift enterprise, or scheme, whether said list contains any part or all of such prizes. Any person violating any provision of this section shall, upon conviction thereof, be fined not more than $1,000 or imprisoned not more than one year, or both, for each and every day during which such offense occurs.

ANNOUNCEMENT THAT MATTER IS PAID FOR

SEC. 317. All matter broadcast by any radio station for which service, money, or any other valuable consideration is directly or indirectly paid, or promised to or charged or accepted by, the station so broadcasting, from any person, shall, at the time the same is so broadcast, be announced as paid for or furnished, as the case may be, by such person.

OPERATION OF TRANSMITTING APPARATUS

SEC. 318. The actual operation of all transmitting apparatus in any radio station for which a station license is required by this Act shall be carried on only by a person holding an operator's license issued hereunder. No person shall operate any such apparatus in such station except under and in accordance with an operator's license issued to him by the Commission.

CONSTRUCTION PERMITS

SEC. 319. (a) No license shall be issued under the authority of this Act for the operation of any station the construction of which is begun or is continued after this Act takes effect, unless a permit for its construction has been granted by the Commission upon written application therefor. The Commission may grant such permit if public convenience, interest, or necessity will be served by the construction of the station. This application shall set forth such facts as the Commission by regulation may prescribe as to the citizenship, character, and the financial, technical, and other ability or the applicant to construct and operate the station, the ownership and location of the proposed station and of the station or stations with which it is proposed to communicate, the frequencies desired to be used, the hours of the day or other periods of time during which it is proposed to operate the station, the purpose for which the station is to be used, the type of transmitting apparatus to be used, the power to be used, the date upon which the station is expected to be completed and in operation, and such other information as the Commission may require. Such application shall be signed by the applicant under oath or affirmation.

(b) Such permit for construction shall show specifically the earliest and latest dates between which the actual operation of such station is expected to begin, and shall provide that said permit will be automatically forfeited if the station is not ready for operation within the time specified or within such further time as the Commission may allow, unless prevented by causes not under the control of the grantee. The rights under any such permit shall not be assigned or otherwise transferred to any person without the approval of the Commission. A permit for construction shall not be required for Government stations, amateur stations, or stations upon mobile vessels, railroad rolling stock, or aircraft. Upon the completion of any station for the construction or continued construction of which a permit has been granted, and upon it being made to appear to the Commission that all the terms, conditions, and obligations set forth in the application and permit have been fully met, and that no cause or circumstance arising or first coming to the knowledge of the Commission since the granting of the permit would, in the judgment of the Commission, make the operation of such station against the public interest, the Commission shall issue a license to the lawful holder of said permit for the operation of said station. Said license shall conform generally to the terms of said permit.

DESIGNATION OF STATIONS LIABLE TO INTERFERE
WITH DISTRESS SIGNALS

SEC. 320. The Commission is authorized to designate from time to time radio stations the communications or signals of which, in its opinion, are liable to interfere with the transmission or reception of distress signals of ships. Such stations are required to keep a licensed radio operator listening in on the frequencies designated for signals of distress and radio communications relating thereto during the entire period the transmitter of such station is in operation.

DISTRESS SIGNALS AND COMMUNICATIONS

SEC. 321. (a) Every radio station on shipboard shall be equipped to transmit radio communications or signals of distress on the frequency specified by the Commission, with apparatus capable of transmitting and receiving messages over a distance of at least one hundred miles by day or night. When sending radio communications or signals of distress and radio communications relating thereto the transmitting set may be adjusted in such a manner as to produce a maximum of radiation irrespective of the amount of interference which may thus be caused.

(b) All radio stations, including Government stations and stations on board foreign vessels when within the territorial waters of the United States, shall give absolute priority to radio communications or signals relating to ships in distress; shall cease all sending on frequencies which will interfere with hearing a radio communication or signal of distress, and, except when engaged in answering or aiding the ship in distress, shall refrain from sending any radio communications or signals until there is assurance that no interference will be caused with the radio communications or signals relating thereto, and shall assist the vessel in distress, so far as possible, by complying with its instructions.

INTERCOMMUNICATION IN MOBILE SERVICE

SEC. 322. Every land station open to general public service between the coast and vessels at sea shall be bound to exchange radio communications or signals with any ship station without distinction as to radio systems or instruments adopted by such stations, respectively, and each station on shipboard shall be bound to exchange radio communications or signals with any other station on shipboard without distinction as to radio systems or instruments adopted by each station.

INTERFERENCE BETWEEN GOVERNMENT AND COMMERCIAL STATIONS

SEC. 323. (a) At all places where Government and private or commercial radio stations on land operate in such close proximity that interference with the work of Government stations cannot be avoided when they are operating simultaneously, such private or commerical stations as do interfere with the transmission or reception of radio communications or signals by the Government stations concerned shall not use their transmitters during the first fifteen minutes of each hour, local standard time.

(b) The Government stations for which the above-mentioned division of time is established shall transmit radio communications or signals only during the first fifteen minutes of each hour, local standard time, except in case of signals or radio communications relating to vessels in distress and vessel requests for information as to course, location, or compass direction.

USE OF MINIMUM POWER

SEC. 324. In all circumstances, except in case of radio communications or signals relating to vessels in distress, all radio stations, including those owned and operated by the United States, shall use the minimum amount of power necessary to carry out the communication desired.

FALSE DISTRESS SIGNALS; REBROADCASTING; STUDIOS OF FOREIGN STATIONS

SEC. 325. (a) No person within the jurisdiction of the United States shall knowingly utter or transmit, or cause to be uttered or transmitted, any false or fraudulent signal of distress, or communication relating thereto, nor shall any broadcasting station rebroadcast the program or any part thereof of another broadcasting station without the express authority of the originating station.

(b) No person shall be permitted to locate, use, or maintain a radio broadcast studio or other place or apparatus from which or whereby sound waves are converted into electrical energy, or mechanical or physical reproduction of sound waves produced, and caused to be transmitted or delivered to a radio station in a foreign country for the purpose of being broadcast from any radio station there having a power output of sufficient intensity and/or being so located geographically that its emissions may be received consistently in the United States, without first obtaining a permit from the Commission upon proper application therefor.

(c) Such application shall contain such information as the Commission may by regulation prescribe, and the granting or refusal thereof shall be subject to the requirements of section 309 hereof with respect to applications for station licenses or renewal or modification thereof, and the license or permission so granted shall be revocable for false statements in the application so required or when the Commission, after hearings, shall find its continuation no longer in the public interest.

CENSORSHIP; INDECENT LANGUAGE

SEC. 326. Nothing in this Act shall be understood or construed to give the Commission the power of censorship over the radio communications or signals transmitted by any radio station, and no regulation or condition shall be promulgated or fixed by the Commission which shall interfere with the right of free speech by means of radio communication. No person within the jurisdiction of the United States shall utter any obscene, indecent, or profane language by means of radio communication.

USE OF NAVAL STATIONS FOR COMMERCIAL MESSAGES

SEC. 327. The Secretary of the Navy is hereby authorized, unless restrained by international agreement, under the terms and conditions and at rates prescribed by him, which rates shall be just and reasonable, and which, upon complaint, shall be subject to review and revision by the Commission, to use all radio stations and apparatus, wherever located, owned by the United States and under the control of the Navy Department, (a) for the reception and transmission of press messages offered by any newspaper published in the United States, its Territories or possessions, or published by citizens of the United States in foreign countries, or by any press association of the United States, and (b) for the reception and transmission of private commercial messages between ships, between ship and shore, between localities in Alaska and between Alaska and the continental United States: *Provided,* That the rates fixed for the reception and transmission of all such messages, other than press messages between the Pacific coast of the United States, Hawaii, Alaska, Guam, American Samoa, the Philippine Islands, and the Orient, and between the United States and the Virgin Islands, shall not be less than the rates charged by privately owned and operated stations for like messages and service; *Provided further,* That the right to use such stations for any of the purposes named in this section shall terminate and cease as between any countries or localities or between any locality and privately operated ships whenever privately owned and operated stations are capable of meeting the normal communication requirements between such countries or localities or between any locality and privately operated ships, and the Commission shall have notified the Secretary of the Navy thereof.

SPECIAL PROVISION AS TO PHILIPPINE ISLANDS AND CANAL ZONE

SEC. 328. This title shall not apply to the Philippine Islands or to the Canal Zone. In international radio matters the Philippine Islands and the Canal Zone shall be represented by the Secretary of State.

ADMINISTRATION OF RADIO LAWS IN TERRITORIES AND POSSESSIONS

SEC. 329. The Commission is authorized to designate any officer or employee of any other department of the Government on duty in any Territory or possession of the United States other than the Philippine Islands and the Canal Zone, to render therein such services in connection with the administration of the radio laws of the United States as the Commission may prescribe: *Provided,* That such designation shall be approved by the head of the department in which such person is employed.

TITLE IV—PROCEDURAL AND ADMINISTRATIVE PROVISIONS
JURISDICTION TO ENFORCE ACT AND ORDERS OF COMMISSION

SEC. 401. (a) The district courts of the United States shall have jurisdiction, upon application of the Attorney General of the United States at the request of the Commission, alleging a failure to comply with or a violation of any of the provisions of this Act by any person, to issue a writ or writs of mandamus commanding such person to comply with the provisions of this Act.

(b) If any person fails or neglects to obey any order of the Commission other than for the payment of money, while the same is in effect, the Commission or any party injured thereby, or the United States, by its Attorney General, may apply to the appropriate district court of the United States for the enforcement of such order. If, after hearing, that court determines that the order was regularly made and duly served, and that the person is in disobedience of the same, the court shall enforce obedience to such order by a writ of injunction or other proper process, mandatory or otherwise, to restrain such person or the officers, agents, or representatives of such person, from further disobedience of such order, or to enjoin upon it or them obedience to the same.

(c) Upon the request of the Commission it shall be the duty of any district attorney of the United States to whom the Commission may apply to institute in the proper court and to prosecute under the direction of the Attorney General of the United States all necessary proceedings for the enforcement of the provisions of this Act and for the punishment of all violations thereof, and the costs and expenses of such prosecutions shall be paid out of the appropriations for the expenses of the courts of the United States.

(d) The provisions of the Expediting Act, approved February 11, 1903, as amended, and of section 238 (1) of the Judicial Code, as amended, shall be held to apply to any suit in equity arising under Title II of this Act, wherein the United States is complainant.

PROCEEDINGS TO ENFORCE OR SET ASIDE THE COMMISSION'S ORDERS—
APPEAL IN CERTAIN CASES

SEC. 402. (a) The provisions of the Act of October 22, 1913 (38 Stat. 219), relating to the enforcing or setting aside of the orders of the Interstate Commerce Commission, are hereby made applicable to suits to enforce, enjoin, set aside, annul, or suspend any order of the Commission under this Act (except any order of the Commission granting or refusing an application for a construction permit for a radio station, or for a radio station license, or for renewal of an existing radio station license, or for modification of an existing radio station license), and such suits are hereby authorized to be brought as provided in that Act.

(b) An appeal may be taken, in the manner hereinafter provided, from decisions of the Commission to the Court of Appeals of the District of Columbia in any of the following cases:

(1) By any applicant for a construction permit for a radio station, or for a radio station license, or for renewal of an existing radio station license, or for modification of an existing radio station license, whose application is refused by the Commission.

(2) By any other person aggrieved or whose interests are adversely affected by any decision of the Commission granting or refusing any such application.

(c) Such appeal shall be taken by filing with said court within twenty days after the decision complained of is effective, notice in writing of said appeal and a statement of the reasons therefor, together with proof of service of a true copy of said notice and statement upon the Commission. Unless a later date is specified by the Commission as part of its decision, the decision complained of shall be considered to be effective as of the date on which public announcement of the decision is made at the office of the Commission in the city of Washington. The Commission shall thereupon immediately, and in any event not later than five days from the date of such service upon it, mail or otherwise deliver a copy of said notice of appeal to each person shown by the records of the Commission to be interested in such appeal and to have a right to intervene therein under the provisions of this section, and shall at all times thereafter permit any such person to inspect and make copies of the appellant's statement of reasons for said appeal at the office of the Commission in the city of Washington. Within thirty days after the filing of said appeal the Commission shall file with the court the originals or certified copies of all papers and evidence presented to it upon the application involved, and also a like copy of its decision thereon, and shall within thirty days thereafter file a full statement in writing of the facts and grounds for its decision as found and given by it, and a list of all interested persons to whom it has mailed or otherwise delivered a copy of said notice of appeal.

(d) Within thirty days after the filing of said appeal any interested person may intervene and participate in the proceedings had upon said appeal by filing with the court a notice of intention to intervene and a verified statement showing the nature of the interest of such party, together with proof of service of true copies of said notice and statement, both upon appellant and upon the Commission. Any person who would be aggrieved or whose interests would be adversely affected by a reversal or modification of the decision of the Commission complained of shall be considered an interested party.

(e) At the earliest convenient time the court shall hear and determine the appeal upon the record before it, and shall have power, upon such record, to enter a judgment affirming or reversing the decision of the Commission, and in event the court shall render a decision and enter an order reversing the decision of the Commission, it shall remand the case to the Commission to carry out the judgment of the court: *Provided, however,* That the review by the court shall be limited to questions of law and that findings of fact by the Commission, if supported by substantial evidence, shall be conclusive unless it shall clearly appear that the findings of the Commission are arbitrary or capricious. The Court's judgment shall be final, subject, however, to review by the Supreme

Court of the United States upon writ of certiorari on petition therefor under section 240 of the Judicial Code, as amended, by appellant, by the Commission, or by any interested party intervening in the appeal.

(f) The court may, in its discretion, enter judgment for costs in favor of or against an appellant, and/or other interested parties intervening in said appeal, but not against the Commission, depending upon the nature of the issues involved upon said appeal and the outcome thereof.

INQUIRY BY COMMISSION ON ITS OWN MOTION

SEC. 403. The Commission shall have full authority and power at any time to institute an inquiry, on its own motion, in any case and as to any matter or thing concerning which complaint is authorized to be made. to or before the Commission by any provision of this Act, or concerning which any question may arise under any of the provisions of this Act, or relating to the enforcement of any of the provisions of this Act. The Commission shall have the same powers and authority to proceed with any inquiry instituted on its own motion as though it had been appealed to by complaint or petition under any of the provisions of this Act, including the power to make and enforce any order or orders in the case, or relating to the matter or thing concerning which the inquiry is had, excepting orders for the payment of money.

REPORTS OF INVESTIGATIONS

SEC. 404. Whenever an investigation shall be made by the Commission it shall be its duty to make a report in writing in respect thereto, which shall state the conclusions of the Commission, together with its decision, order, or requirement in the premises; and in case damages are awarded such report shall include the findings of fact on which the award is made.

REHEARING BEFORE COMMISSION

SEC. 405. After a decision, order, or requirement has been made by the Commission in any proceeding, any party thereto may at any time make application for rehearing of the same, or any matter determined therein, and it shall be lawful for the Commission in its discretion to grant such a rehearing if sufficient reason therefor be made to appear: *Provided, however,* That in the case of a decision, order, or requirement made under Title III, the time within which application for rehearing may be made shall be limited to twenty days after the effective date thereof, and such application may be made by any party or any person aggrieved or whose interests are adversely affected thereby. Applications for rehearing shall be governed by such general rules as the Commission may establish. No such application shall excuse any person from complying with or obeying any decision, order, or requirement of the Commission, or operate in any manner to stay or postpone the enforcement thereof, without the special order of the Commission. In case a rehearing is granted, the proceedings thereupon shall conform as nearly as may be to the proceedings in an original hearing, except as the Commission may otherwise direct; and if, in its judgment, after such rehearing and the consideration of all facts, including those arising since the former hearing, it shall appear that the original decision, order, or requirement is in any respect unjust or unwarranted, the Commission may reverse, change, or modify the same accordingly. Any decision, order, or requirement made after such rehearing, reversing, changing, or modifying the original determination, shall be subject to the same provisions as an original order.

MANDAMUS TO COMPEL FURNISHING OF FACILITIES

SEC. 406. The district courts of the United States shall have jurisdiction upon the relation of any person alleging any violation, by a carrier subject to this Act, of any of the provisions of this Act which prevent the relator from receiving service in interstate or foreign communication by wire or radio, or in interstate or foreign transmission of energy by radio, from said carrier at the same charges, or upon terms or conditions as favorable as those given by said carrier for like communication or transmission under similar conditions to any other person, to issue a writ or writs of mandamus against said carrier commanding such carrier to furnish facilities for such communication or transmission to the party applying for the writ: *Provided,* That if any question of fact as to the proper compensation to the carrier for the service to be enforced by the writ is raised by the pleadings, the writ of peremptory mandamus may issue, notwithstanding such question of fact is undetermined, upon such terms as to security, payment of money into the court, or otherwise, as the court may think proper pending the determination of the question of fact: *Provided further,* That the remedy hereby given by writ of mandamus shall be cumulative and shall not be held to exclude or interfere with other remedies provided by this Act.

PETITION FOR ENFORCEMENT OF ORDER FOR PAYMENT OF MONEY

SEC. 407. If a carrier does not comply with an order for the payment of money within the time limit in such order, the complainant, or any person for whose benefit such order was made, may file in the district court of the United States for the district in which he resides or in which is located the principal operating office of the carrier, or through which the line of the carrier runs, or in any State court of general jurisdiction having jurisdiction of the parties, a petition setting forth briefly the causes for which he claims damages, and the order of the Commission in the premises. Such suit in the district court of the United States shall proceed in all respects like other civil suits for damages, except that on the trial of such suits the findings and order of the Commission shall be prima facie evidence of the facts therein stated, except that the petitioner shall not be liable for costs in the district court nor for costs at any subsequent stage of the proceedings unless they accrue upon his appeal. If the petitioner shall finally prevail, he shall be allowed a reasonable attorney's fee, to be taxed and collected as a part of the costs of the suit.

ORDERS NOT FOR PAYMENT OF MONEY—WHEN EFFECTIVE

SEC. 408. Except as otherwise provided in this Act, all orders of the Commission, other than orders for the payment of money, shall take effect within such reasonable time, not less than thirty days after service of the order, and shall continue in force until its further order, or for a specified period of time, according as shall be prescribed in the order, unless the same shall be suspended or modified or set aside by the Commission, or be suspended or set aside by a court of competent jurisdiction.

GENERAL PROVISIONS RELATING TO PROCEEDINGS— WITNESSES AND DEPOSITIONS

SEC. 409. (a) Any member or examiner of the Commission, or the director of any division, when duly designated by the Commission for such purpose, may hold hearings, sign and issue subpoenas, administer oaths, examine witnesses, and receive evidence at any place in the United States designated by the Commission; except that in the administration of Title III an examiner may not be authorized to exercise such powers with respect to a matter involving (1) a change of policy by the Commission, (2) the revocation of a station license, (3) new devices or developments in radio, or (4) a new kind of use of frequencies. In all cases heard by an examiner the Commission shall hear oral arguments on request of either party.

(b) For the purposes of this Act the Commission shall have the power to require by subpoena the attendance and testimony of witnesses and the production of all books, papers, schedules of charges, contracts, agreements, and documents relating to any matter under investigation. Witnesses summoned before the Commission shall be paid the same fees and mileage that are paid witnesses in the courts of the United States.

(c) Such attendance of witnesses, and the production of such documentary evidence, may be required from any place in the United States, at any designated place of hearing. And in case of disobedience to a subpoena to the Commission, or any party to a proceeding before the Commission, may invoke the aid of any court of the United States in requiring the attendance and testimony of witnesses and the production of books, papers, and documents under the provisions of this section.

(d) Any of the district courts of the United States within the jurisdiction of which such inquiry is carried on may, in case of contumacy or refusal to obey a subpoena issued to any common carrier or licensee or other person, issue an order requiring such common carrier, licensee, or other person to appear before the Commission (and produce books and papers if so ordered) and give evidence touching the matter in question; and any failure to obey such order of the court may be punished by such court as a contempt thereof.

(e) The testimony of any witness may be taken, at the instance of a party, in any proceeding or investigation pending before the Commission, by deposition, at any time after a cause or proceeding is at issue on petition and answer. The Commission may also order testimony to be taken by deposition in any proceeding or investigation pending before it, at any stage of such proceeding or investigation. Such depositions may be taken before any judge of any court of the United States, or any United States commissioner, or any clerk of a district court, or any chancellor, justice, or judge of a supreme or superior court, mayor, or chief magistrate of a city, judge of a county court, or court of common pleas of any of the United States, or any notary public, not being of counsel or attorney to either of the parties, nor interested in the event of the proceeding or investigation. Reasonable notice must first be given in writing by the party or his attorney proposing to take such deposition to the opposite party or his attorney of record, as either may be nearest, which notice shall state the name of the witness and the time and place of the taking of his deposition. Any person may be compelled to appear and depose, and to produce documentary evidence, in the same manner as witnesses may be compelled to appear and testify and produce documentary evidence before the Commission, as hereinbefore provided.

(f) Every person deposing as herein provided shall be cautioned and sworn (or affirm, if he so request) to testify the whole truth, and shall be carefully examined. His testimony shall be reduced to writing by the magistrate taking the deposition, or under his direction, and shall, after it has been reduced to writing, be subscribed by the deponent.

(g) If a witness whose testimony may be desired to be taken by deposition be in a foreign country, the deposition may be taken before an officer or person designated by the Commission, or agreed upon by the parties by stipulation in writing to be filed with the Commission. All depositions must be promptly filed with the Commission.

(h) Witnesses whose depositions are taken as authorized in this Act, and the magistrate or other officer taking the same, shall severally be entitled to the same fees as are paid for like services in the courts of the United States.

(i) No person shall be excused from attending and testifying or from producing books, papers, schedules of charges, contracts, agreements, and documents before the Commission, or in obedience to the subpoena of the Commission, whether such subpoena be signed or issued by one or more commissioners, or in any cause or proceeding, criminal or otherwise, based upon or growing out of any alleged violation of this Act, or of any amendments thereto, on the ground or for the reason that the testimony or evidence, documentary or otherwise, required of him may tend to incriminate him or subject him to a penalty or forfeiture; but no individual shall be prosecuted or subjected to any penalty or forfeiture for or on account of any transaction, matter, or thing concerning which he is compelled, after having claimed his privilege against self-incrimination, to testify or produce evidence, documentary or otherwise, except that any individual so testifying shall not be exempt from prosecution and punishment for perjury committed in so testifying.

(j) Any person who shall neglect or refuse to attend and testify, or to answer any lawful inquiry, or to produce books, papers, schedules of charges, contracts, agreements, and documents, if in his power to do so, in obedience to the subpoena or lawful requirement of the Commission, shall be guilty of a misdemeanor and upon conviction thereof by a court of competent jurisdiction shall be punished by a fine of not less than $100 nor more than $5,000, or by imprisonment for not more than one year, or by both such fine and imprisonment.

USE OF JOINT BOARDS—COOPERATION WITH STATE COMMISSIONS

SEC. 410. (a) The Commission may refer any matter arising in the administration of this Act to a joint board to be composed of a member, or of an equal number of members, as determined by the Commission, from each of the States in which the wire or radio communication affected by or involved in the proceeding takes place or is proposed, and any such board shall be vested with the same powers and be subject to the same duties and liabilities as in the case of a member of the Commission when designated by the Commission to hold a hearing as hereinbefore authorized. The action of a joint board shall have such force and effect and its proceedings shall be conducted in such manner as the Commission shall by regulations prescribe. The joint board member or members for each State shall be nominated by the State commission of the State or by the Governor if there is no State commission, and appointed by the Federal Communications Commission. The Commission shall have discretion to reject any nominee. Joint board members shall receive such allowances for expenses as the Commission shall provide.

(b) The Commission may confer with any State commission having regulatory jurisdiction with respect to carriers, regarding the relationship between rate structures, accounts, charges, practices, classifications, and regulations of carriers subject to the jurisdiction of such State commission and of the Commission; and the Commission is authorized under such rules and regulations as it shall prescribe to hold joint hearings with any State commission in connection with any matter with respect to which the Commission is authorized to act. The Commission is authorized in the administration of this Act to avail itself of such cooperation, services, records, and facilities as may be afforded by any State commission.

JOINDER OF PARTIES

SEC. 411. (a) In any proceeding for the enforcement of the provisions of this Act, whether such proceeding be instituted before the Commission or be begun originally in any district court of the United States, it shall be lawful to include as parties, in addition to the carrier, all persons interested in or affected by the charge, regulation, or practice under consideration, and inquiries, investigations, orders, and decrees may be made with reference to and against such additional parties in the same manner, to the same extent, and subject to the same provisions as are or shall be authorized by law with respect to carriers.

(b) In any suit for the enforcement of an order for the payment of money all parties in whose favor the Commission may have made an award for damages by a single order may be joined as plaintiffs, and all of the carriers parties to such order awarding such damages may be joined as defendants, and such suit may be maintained by such joint plaintiffs and against such joint defendants in any district where any one of such joint plaintiffs could maintain such suit against any one of such joint defendants; and service of process against any one of such defendants as may not be found in the district where the suit is brought may be made in any district where such defendant carrier has its principal operating office. In case of such joint suit, the recovery, if any, may be by judgment in favor of any one of such plaintiffs, against the defendant found to be liable to such plaintiff.

DOCUMENTS FILED TO BE PUBLIC RECORDS—USE IN PROCEEDINGS

SEC. 412. The copies of schedules of charges, classifications, and of all contracts, agreements, and arrangements between common carriers filed with the Commission as herein provided, and the statistics, tables, and figures contained in the annual or other reports of carriers and other persons made to the Commission as required under the provisions of this Act shall be preserved as public records in the custody of the secretary of the Commission, and shall be received as prima facie evidence of what they purport to be for the purpose of investigations by the Commission and in all judicial proceedings; and copies of and extracts from any of said schedules, classifications, contracts, agreements, arrangements, or reports, made public records as aforesaid, certified by the secretary, under the Commission's seal, shall be received in evidence with like effect as the originals: *Provided,* That the Commission may, if the public interest will be served thereby, keep confidential any contract, agreement, or arrangement relating to foreign wire or radio communication when the publication of such contract, agreement, or arrangement would place American communication companies at a disadvantage in meeting the competition of foreign communication companies.

DESIGNATION OF AGENT FOR SERVICE

SEC. 413. It shall be the duty of every carrier subject to this Act, within sixty days after the taking effect of this Act, to designate in writing an agent in the District of Columbia, upon whom service of all notices and process and all orders, decisions, and requirements of the Commission may be made for and on behalf of said carrier in any proceeding or suit pending before the Commission, and to file such designation in the office of the secretary of the Commission, which designation may from time to time be changed by like writing similarly filed; and thereupon service of all notices and process and orders, decisions, and requirements of the Commission may be made upon such carrier by leaving a copy thereof with such designated agent at his office or usual place of residence in the District of Columbia, with like effect as if made personally upon such carrier, and in default of such designation of such agent, service of any notice or other process in any proceeding before said Commission, or of any order, decision, or requirement of the Commission, may be made by posting such notice, process, order, requirement, or decision in the office of the secretary of the Commission.

REMEDIES IN THIS ACT NOT EXCLUSIVE

SEC. 414. Nothing in this Act contained shall in any way abridge or alter the remedies now existing at common law or by statute, but the provisions of this Act are in addition to such remedies.

LIMITATIONS AS TO ACTIONS

SEC. 415. (a) All actions at law by carriers for recovery of their lawful charges, or any part thereof, shall be begun within one year from the time the cause of action accrues, and not after.

(b) All complaints against carriers for the recovery of damages not based on overcharges shall be filed with the Commission within one year from the time the cause of action accrues, and not after, subject to subsection (d) of this section.

(c) For recovery of overcharges action at law shall be begun or complaint filed with the Commission against carriers within one year from the time the cause of action accrues, and not after, subject to subsection (d) of this section, except that if claim for the overcharge has been presented in writing to the carrier within the one-year period of limitation said period shall be extended to include one year from the time notice in writing is given by the carrier to the claimant of disallowance of the claim, or any part or parts thereof, specified in the notice.

(d) If on or before expiration of the period of limitation in subsection (b) or (c) a carrier begins action under subsection (a) for recovery of lawful charges in respect of the same service, or, without beginning action, collects charges in respect of that service, said period of limitation shall be extended to include ninety days from the time such action is begun or such charges are collected by the carrier.

(e) The cause of action in respect of the transmission of a message shall, for the purposes of this section, be deemed to accrue upon delivery or tender of delivery thereof by the carrier, and not after.

(f) A petition for the enforcement of an order of the Commission for the payment of money shall be filed in the district court or the State court within one year from the date of the order, and not after.

(g) The term "overcharges" as used in this section shall be deemed to mean charges for services in excess of those applicable thereto under the schedules of charges lawfully on file with the Commission.

PROVISIONS RELATING TO ORDERS

SEC. 416. (a) Every order of the Commission shall be forthwith served upon the designated agent of the carrier in the city of Washington or in such other manner as may be provided by law.

(b) Except as otherwise provided in this Act, the Commission is hereby authorized to suspend or modify its orders upon such notice and in such manner as it shall deem proper.

(c) It shall be the duty of every person, its agents and employees, and any receiver or trustee thereof, to observe and comply with such orders so long as the same shall remain in effect.

TITLE V—PENAL PROVISIONS—FORFEITURES
GENERAL PENALTY

SEC. 501. Any person who willfully and knowingly does or causes or suffers to be done any act, matter, or thing, in this Act prohibited or declared to be unlawful, or who willfully and knowingly omits or fails to do any act, matter, or thing in this Act required to be done, or willfully and knowingly causes or suffers such omission or failure, shall, upon conviction thereof, be punished for such offense, for which no penalty (other than a forfeiture) is provided herein, by a fine of not more than $10,000 or by imprisonment for a term of not more than two years, or both.

VIOLATIONS OF RULES, REGULATIONS, AND SO FORTH

SEC. 502. Any person who willfully and knowingly violates any rule, regulation, restriction, or condition made or imposed by the Commission under authority of this Act, or any rule, regulation, restriction, or condition made or imposed by any international radio or wire communications treaty or convention, or regulations annexed thereto, to which the United States is or may hereafter become a party, shall, in addition to any other penalties provided by law, be punished, upon conviction thereof, by a fine of not more than $500 for each and every day during which such offense occurs.

FORFEITURE IN CASES OF REBATES AND OFFSETS

SEC. 503. Any person who shall deliver messages for interstate or foreign transmission to any carrier, or for whom as sender or receiver, any such carrier shall transmit any interstate or foreign wire or radio communication, who shall knowingly by employee, agent, officer, or otherwise, directly or indirectly, by or through any means or device whatsoever, receive or accept from such common carrier any sum of money or any other valuable consideration as a rebate or offset against the regular charges for transmission of such messages as fixed by the schedules of charges provided for in this Act, shall in addition to any other penalty provided by this Act forfeit to the United States a sum of money three times the amount of money so received or accepted and three times the value of any other consideration so received or accepted, to be ascertained by the trial court; and in the trial of said action all such rebates or other considerations so received or accepted for a period of six years prior to the commencement of the action, may be included therein, and the amount recovered shall be three times the total amount of money, or three times the total value of such consideration, so received or accepted, or both, as the case may be.

PROVISIONS RELATING TO FORFEITURES

SEC. 504. The forfeitures provided for in this Act shall be payable into the Treasury of the United States, and shall be recoverable in a civil suit in the name of the United States, brought in the district where the person or carrier has its principal operating office, or in any district through which the line or system of the carrier runs. Such forfeitures shall be in addition to any other general or specific penalties herein provided. It shall be the duty of the various district attorneys, under the direction of the Attorney General of the United States, to prosecute for the recovery of forfeitures under this Act. The costs and expenses of such prosecutions shall be paid from the appropriation for the expenses of the courts of the United States.

VENUE OF OFFENSES

SEC. 505. The trial of any offense under this Act shall be in the district in which it is committed; or if the offense is committed upon the high seas, or out of the jurisdiction of any particular State or district, the trial shall be in the district where the offender may be found or into which he shall be first brought. Whenever the offense is begun in one jurisdiction and completed in another it may be dealt with, inquired of, tried, determined, and punished in either jurisdiction in the same manner as if the offense had been actually and wholly committed therein.

TITLE VI—MISCELLANEOUS PROVISIONS
TRANSFER TO COMMISSION OF DUTIES, POWERS, AND FUNCTIONS UNDER EXISTING LAW

SEC. 601. (a) All duties, powers, and functions of the Interstate Commerce Commission under the Act of August 7, 1888 (25 Stat. 382), relating to operation of telegraph lines by railroad and telegraph companies granted Government aid in the construction of their lines, are hereby imposed upon and vested in the Commission: *Provided,* That such transfer of duties, powers, and functions shall not be construed to affect the duties, powers, functions, or jurisdiction of the Interstate Commerce Commission under, or to interfere with or prevent the enforcement of, the Interstate Commerce Act and all Acts amendatory thereof or supplemental thereto.

(b) All duties, powers, and functions of the Postmaster General with respect to telegraph companies and telegraph lines under any existing provision of law are hereby imposed upon and vested in the Commission.

REPEALS AND AMENDMENTS

SEC. 602. (a) The Radio Act of 1927, as amended, is hereby repealed.

(b) The provisions of the Interstate Commerce Act, as amended, insofar as they relate to communication by wire or wireless, or to telegraph, telephone, or cable companies operating by wire or wireless, except the last proviso of section 1 (5) and the provisions of section 1 (7), are hereby repealed.

(c) The last sentence of section 2 of the Act entitled "An Act relating to the landing and operation of submarine cables in the United States", approved May 27, 1921, is amended to read as follows: "Nothing herein contained shall be construed to limit the power and jurisdiction of the Federal Communications Commission with respect to the transmission of messages."

(d) The first paragraph of section 11 of the Act entitled "An Act to supplement existing laws against unlawful restraints and monopolies, and for other purposes", approved October 15, 1914, is amended to read as follows:

"Sec. 11. That authority to enforce compliance with sections 2, 3, 7, and 8 of this Act by the persons respectively subject thereto is hereby vested: In the Interstate Commerce Commission where applicable to common carriers subject to the Interstate Commerce Act, as amended; in the Federal Communications Commission where applicable to common carriers engaged in wire or radio communication or radio transmission of energy; in the Federal Reserve Board where applicable to banks, banking associations, and trust companies; and in the Federal Trade Commission where applicable to all other character of commerce, to be exercised as follows:".

TRANSFER OF EMPLOYEES, RECORDS, PROPERTY, AND APPROPRIATIONS

SEC. 603. (a) All officers and employees of the Federal Radio Commission (except the members thereof, whose offices are hereby abolished) whose services in the judgment of the Commission are necessary to the efficient operation of the Commission are hereby transferred to the Commission, without change in classification or compensation; except that the Commission may provide for the adjustment of such classification or compensation to conform to the duties to which such officers and employees may be assigned.

(b) There are hereby transferred to the jurisdiction and control of the Commission (1) all records and property (including office furniture and equipment, and including monitoring radio stations) under the jurisdiction of the Federal Radio Commission, and (2) all records under the jurisdiction of the Interstate Commerce Commission and of the Postmaster General relating to the duties, powers, and functions imposed upon and vested in the Commission by this Act.

(c) All appropriations and unexpended balances of appropriations available for expenditure by the Federal Radio Commission shall be available for expenditure by the Commission for any and all objects of expenditure authorized by this Act in the discretion of the Commission, without regard to the requirement of apportionment under the Antideficiency Act of February 27, 1906.

EFFECT OF TRANSFERS, REPEALS, AND AMENDMENTS

SEC. 604 (a) All orders, determinations, rules, regulations, permits, contracts, licenses, and privileges which have been issued, made, or granted by the Interstate Commerce Commission, the Federal Radio Commission, or the Postmaster General, under any provision of law repealed or amended by this Act or in the exercise of duties, powers, or functions transferred to the Commission by this Act, and which are in effect at the time this section takes effect, shall continue in effect until modified, terminated, superseded, or repealed by the Commission or by operation of law.

(b) Any proceeding, hearing, or investigation commenced or pending before the Federal Radio Commission, the Interstate Commerce Commission, or the Postmaster General, at the time of the organization of the Commission, shall be continued by the Commission in the same manner as though originally commenced before the Commission, if such proceeding, hearing, or investigation (1) involves the administration of duties, powers, and functions transferred to the Commission by this Act, or (2) involves the exercise of jurisdiction similar to that granted to the Commission under the provisions of this Act.

(c) All records transferred to the Commission under this Act shall be available for use by the Commission to the same extent as if such records were originally records of the Commission. All final valuations and determinations of depreciation charges by the Interstate Commerce Commission with respect to common carriers engaged in radio or wire communication, and all orders of the Interstate Commerce Commission with respect to such valuations and determinations, shall have the same force and effect as though made by the Commission under this Act.

(d) The provisions of this Act shall not affect suits commenced prior to the date of the organization of the Commission; and all such suits shall be continued, proceedings therein had, appeals therein taken and judgments therein rendered, in the same manner and with the same effect as if this Act had not been passed. No suit, action, or other proceeding lawfully commenced by or against any agency or officer of the United States, in relation to the discharge of official duties, shall abate by reason of any transfer of authority, power, and duties from such agency or officer to the Commission under the provisions of this Act, but the court, upon motion or supplemental petition filed at any time within twelve months after such transfer, showing the necessity for a survival of such suit, action, or other proceeding to obtain a settlement of the questions involved, may allow the same to be maintained by or against the Commission.

UNAUTHORIZED PUBLICATION OF COMMUNICATIONS

SEC. 605. No person receiving or assisting in receiving, or transmitting, or assisting in transmitting, any interstate or foreign communication by wire or radio shall divulge or publish the existence, contents, substance, purport, effect, or meaning thereof, except through authorized channels of transmission or reception, to any person other than the addressee, his agent, or attorney, or to a person employed or authorized to forward such communication to its destination, or to proper accounting or distributing officers of the various communicating centers over which the communication may be passed, or to the master of a ship under whom he is serving, or in response to a subpoena issued by a court of competent jurisdiction, or on demand of other lawful authority; and no person not being authorized by the sender shall intercept any communication and divulge or publish the existence, contents, substance, purport, effect, or meaning of such intercepted communication to any person; and no person not being entitled thereto shall receive or assist in receiving any interstate or foreign communication by wire or radio and use the same or any information therein contained for his own benefit or for the benefit of another not entitled thereto; and no person having received such intercepted communication or having become acquainted with the contents, substance, purport, effect, or meaning of the same or any part thereof, knowing that such information was so obtained, shall divulge or publish the existence, contents, substance, purport, effect, or meaning of the same or any part thereof, or use the same or any information therein contained for his own benefit or for the benefit of another not entitled thereto: *Provided,* That this section shall not apply to the receiving, divulging, publishing, or utilizing the contents of any radio communication broadcast, or transmitted by amateurs or others for the use of the general public, or relating to ships in distress.

WAR EMERGENCY—POWERS OF PRESIDENT

SEC. 606. (a) During the continuance of a war in which the United States is engaged, the President is authorized, if he finds it necessary for the national defense and security, to direct that such communications as in his judgment may be essential to the national defense and security shall have preference or priority with any carrier subject to this Act. He may give these directions at and for such times as he may determine, and may modify, change, suspend, or annul them and for any such purpose he is hereby authorized to issue orders directly, or through such person or persons as he designates for the purpose, or through the Commission. Any carrier complying with any such order or direction for preference or priority herein authorized shall be exempt from any and all provisions in existing law imposing civil or criminal penalties, obligations, or liabilities upon carriers by reason of giving preference or priority in compliance with such order or direction.

(b) It shall be unlawful for any person during any war in which the United States is engaged to knowingly or willfully, by physical force or intimidation by threats of physical force, obstruct or retard or aid in obstructing or retarding interstate or foreign communication by radio or wire. The President is hereby authorized, whenever in his judgment the public interest requires, to employ the armed forces of the United States to prevent any such obstruction or retardation of communication: *Provided,* That nothing in this section shall be construed to repeal, modify, or affect either section 6 or section 20 of an Act entitled "An Act to supplement existing laws against unlawful restraints and monopolies, and for other purposes", approved October 15, 1914.

(c) Upon proclamation by the President that there exists war or a threat of war or a state of public peril or disaster or other national emergency, or in order to preserve the neutrality of the United States, the President may suspend or amend, for such time as he may see fit, the rules and regulations applicable to any or all stations within the jurisdiction of the United States as prescribed by the Commission, and may cause the closing of any station for radio communication and the removal therefrom of its apparatus and equipment, or he may authorize the use or control of any such station and/or its apparatus and equipment by any department of the Government under such regulations as he may prescribe, upon just compensation to the owners.

(d) The President shall ascertain the just compensation for such use or control and certify the amount ascertained to Congress for appropriation and payment to the person entitled thereto. If the amount so certified is unsatisfactory to the person entitled thereto, such person shall be paid only 75 per centum of the amount and shall be entitled to sue the United States to recover such further sum as added to such payment of 75 per centum will make such amount as will be just compensation for the use and control. Such suit shall be brought in the manner provided by paragraph 20 of section 24, or by section 145, of the Judicial Code, as amended.

EFFECTIVE DATE OF ACT

SEC. 607. This Act shall take effect upon the organization of the Commission, except that this section and sections 1 and 4 shall take effect July 1, 1934. The Commission shall be deemed to be organized upon such date as four members of the Commission have taken office.

SEPARABILITY CLAUSE

SEC. 608. If any provision of this Act or the application thereof to any person or circumstance is held invalid, the remainder of the Act and the application of such provision to other persons or circumstances shall not be affected thereby.

SHORT TITLE

SEC. 609. This Act may be cited as the "Communications Act of 1934."

Approved, June 19, 1934.

BIBLIOGRAPHY

Collections. Manuscript collections have proved of special value. Collections are identified in the bibliography by letter, as follows:

(C)   Columbia University Oral History Collection, New York.
(M)   Mass Communications History Center of the Wisconsin Historical Society, Madison.
(N)   National Broadcasting Company Library, New York.
(P)   Broadcast Pioneers History Project, New York.

AER Journal.   Chicago, Association for Education by Radio, monthly, 1941–53; became AERT Journal, 1956–59.   See also NAEB Journal.

AFRS Playback.   Los Angeles, Armed Forces Radio Service, weekly, from 1944.   Unpublished.

Allen, Fred.   Treadmill to Oblivion.   Boston, Little, Brown, 1954.

Allen, Frederick Lewis.   The Big Change: America transforms itself 1900–1950.   New York, Bantam, 1952.

Allen, Frederick Lewis.   Since Yesterday: the nineteen-thirties in America. New York, Harper, 1939.

Allport, G. W., and Hadley Cantril.   The Psychology of Radio.   New York, Harper, 1935.

The American Forces Network: serving American forces in Europe.   U. S. Department of Defense memorandum, ca. 1953.   Unpublished.

An Analysis of Negro talent on the Columbia Broadcasting System.   Prepared by the program records division, CBS research department.   New York, Columbia Broadcasting System, 1943.   Unpublished.

And With Lotions of Love: pages from a Jergens journal.   New York, National Broadcasting Company, 1940.

Anderson, Maxwell, *et al.*   See This Is War!

349

Anderson, Robert Gordon.   See McNamee, Graham, in collaboration with—

Annual Report of the Federal Radio Commission.   Washington, Government Printing Office, annual, 1927–34.

Anthony, Edward.   See Schechter, A. A., with—

Archer, Gleason L.   Big Business and Radio.   New York, American Historical Company, 1939.

Ardrey, Robert.   "Hollywood: the toll of the frenzied forties," Reporter, March 21, 1957.

Armed Forces Radio Service.   For Playback, see AFRS Playback.

Armed Forces Radio Service: progress report.   Washington, War Department, 1944.   Unpublished.

Asbell, Bernard.   When F. D. R. Died.   New York, Holt, Rinehart & Winston, 1961.

Bacher, William A. (ed.).   The Treasury Star Parade.   New York, Farrar & Rinehart, 1942.

Bain, Donald.   See Catalog of Sound Effects Made by Donald Bain.

Baldwin, Roger N.   Reminiscences, 2 v., 1954.   Unpublished.   (C)

Bannister, Harry Ray.   Reminiscences, 1951.   Unpublished.   (C)

Barnouw, Erik.   Handbook of Radio Production.   Boston, Little, Brown, 1949.

Barnouw, Erik.   Handbook of Radio Writing.   Boston, Little, Brown, 1947.

Barnouw, Erik.   Mass Communication: television, radio, film, press.   New York, Rinehart, 1956.

Barnouw, Erik (ed.).   Radio Drama in Action: twenty-five plays of a changing world.   New York, Rinehart, 1945.

Barnouw, Erik.   "Radio Programs for Troop Education," Educational Outlook, March 1945.

Barnouw, Erik.   A Tower in Babel: a history of broadcasting in the United States, v. I—to 1933.   New York, Oxford University Press, 1966.

Barrett, Edward W. (ed.).   Journalists in Action.   Manhasset (N.Y.), Channel Press, 1963.

Barry, David W.   See Parker, Everett C., and—

Barth, Alan.   The Loyalty of Free Men.   New York, Viking, 1951.

Barth, Alan.   When Congress Investigates.   Public Affairs Pamphlet No. 227. New York, Public Affairs Committee, 1955.

Beaumont, Charles.   "Requiem for Radio," Playboy, May 1960.

Benét, Stephen Vincent.   They Burned the Books.   New York, Farrar & Rinehart, 1942.

Benét, Stephen Vincent.   We Stand United and other radio scripts.   New York, Farrar & Rinehart, 1945.

Benét, Stephen Vincent, et al.   See This Is War!

Berg, Cherney.   See Berg, Gertrude, with—

Berg, Gertrude, with Cherney Berg.   Molly and Me.   New York, McGraw-Hill, 1961.

Berle, Adolf A., Jr., and Gardiner C. Means. The Modern Corporation and Private Property. New York, Macmillan, 1932, 1948.

Bernays, Edward L. Biography of an Idea: memoirs of a public relations counsel. New York, Simon & Schuster, 1965.

Bettinger, Hoyland. Television Techniques. New York, Harper, 1947.

Biow, Milton H. Butting In: an adman speaks out. Garden City (N.Y.), Doubleday, 1964.

Bliss, Edward, Jr. (ed.). In Search of Light: the broadcasts of Edward R. Murrow 1938–1961. New York, Knopf, 1967.

Bluem, A. William. Documentary in American Television. New York, Hastings House, 1965.

Blum, Daniel C. Pictorial History of TV. Philadelphia, Chilton, 1958.

Bogart, Leo. The Age of Television. New York, Ungar, 1958.

Borkin, Joseph. See Waldrop, Frank C., and—

Bormann, Ernest G. "This is Huey P. Long Talking," Journal of Broadcasting, Spring 1958.

Bouck, Zeh. Making a Living in Radio. New York, McGraw-Hill, 1935.

Boyd, James (ed.). The Free Company Presents. New York, Dodd, Mead, 1941.

Brecher, Edward M. "Whose Radio?" Atlantic Monthly, August, 1946.

Bretz, Rudy. Techniques of Television Production. New York, McGraw-Hill, 1953.

Bretz, Rudy. See also Stasheff, Edward, and—

Brewer, Fred A. See Skornia, Harry T., Robert H. Lee, and—

Bricker, Harry. See Witty, Paul, and—

Briggs, Asa. The Birth of Broadcasting: the history of broadcasting in the United Kingdom, v. I. London, Oxford University Press, 1961.

Briggs, Asa. The Golden Age of Wireless: the history of broadcasting in the United Kingdom, v. II. London, Oxford University Press, 1965.

Briggs, Asa. "Broadcasting and Society," The Listener, November 22, 1962.

Brindze, Ruth. Not To Be Broadcast: the truth about radio. New York, Vanguard, 1937.

Broadcasting. Washington, semimonthly, then weekly, 1931—

Broadcasting in the United States. Washington, National Association of Broadcasters, 1933.

Broadcasting Yearbook. Washington, annual, 1935, etc.

Brome, Vincent. The International Brigades: Spain 1936–1939. New York, Morrow, 1966.

Brooks, William F. Radio News Writing. New York, McGraw-Hill, 1948.

Brown, David, and W. Richard Bruner (eds.). I Can Tell It Now. New York, Dutton, 1964.

Bruner, W. Richard. See Brown, David, and—

Bryce, Oliver. "Thought Control American Style," New Republic, January 13, 1947.

Bryson, Lyman (ed.). The Communication of Ideas. New York, Harper, 1948.

Bryson, Lyman. Reminiscences, 1951. Unpublished. (C)

Bryson, Lyman. Time for Reason About Radio: from a series of broadcasts on CBS. New York, Stewart, 1948.

Buck, Pearl S. My Several Worlds. New York, John Day, 1954.

Buxton, Frank, and Bill Owen. Radio's Golden Age: the programs and the personalities. New York, Easton Valley Press, 1966.

Campbell, Angus. See Smythe, Dallas W., and—

Cantril, Hadley (ed.). Public Opinion: 1935–1946. Princeton, Princeton University Press, 1951.

Cantril, Hadley, with the assistance of Hazel Gaudet and Herta Herzog. The Invasion From Mars: a study in the psychology of panic. Princeton, Princeton University Press, 1940.

Cantril, Hadley. See also Allport, G. W., and—

Catalog of Sound Effects Made by Donald Bain. East Orange, N.J., undated.

Chafee, Zechariah, Jr. Freedom of Speech and Press. New York, Freedom Agenda, 1955.

Chafee, Zechariah, Jr. Government and Mass Communications: a report from the Commission on Freedom of the Press. 2 v. Chicago, University of Chicago Press, 1947.

Chase, Francis, Jr. Sound and Fury: an informal history of broadcasting. New York, Harper, 1942.

Chase, Gilbert. Music in Radio Broadcasting. New York, McGraw-Hill, 1946.

Chester, Giraud. "The Press-Radio War," Public Opinion Quarterly, Summer 1949.

Chester, Giraud. The Radio Commentaries of H. V. Kaltenborn: a case study in persuasion. Ph.D. dissertation. Madison, University of Wisconsin, 1947. Unpublished.

Chester, Giraud. "What Constitutes Irresponsibility on the Air?—a case study," Public Opinion Quarterly, Spring 1949.

Chester, Giraud, Garnet R. Garrison, and Edgar E. Willis. Television and Radio. New York, Appleton-Century-Crofts, 1963.

Cogley, John. Report on Blacklisting. 2 v. Fund for the Republic, 1956.

Columbia Journalism Review. New York, Graduate School of Journalism, Columbia University, quarterly, 1962—

Comden, Betty, and Adolph Green. Reminiscences, 1959. Unpublished. (C)

Commager, Henry Steele (ed.). The Pocket History of the Second World War. New York, Pocket Books, 1945.

Commager, Henry Steele. "Who is Loyal to America?," Harper's, September 1947.

Conant, Michael. Antitrust in the Motion Picture Industry. Berkeley, University of California Press, 1960.

Cook, Fred J. The FBI Nobody Knows. New York, Macmillan, 1964.

Cook, Joe. See Slate, Sam, and—

Cooley, Hazel. Vision in Television. New York, Channel, 1952.

Coons, John E. (ed.). Freedom and Responsibility in Broadcasting. Evanston, Northwestern University Press, 1961.

Corwin, Norman. Interview, 1966. Unpublished. (C)

Corwin, Norman. More By Corwin: 16 radio dramas. New York, Holt, 1944.

Corwin, Norman. On a Note of Triumph. New York, Simon & Schuster, 1945.

Corwin, Norman. The Plot to Overthrow Christmas: a holiday play. Mount Vernon (N.Y.), Peter Pauper Press, 1940.

Corwin, Norman. Seems Radio Is Here to Stay. New York. Columbia Broadcasting System, 1939.

Corwin, Norman. They Fly Through the Air With the Greatest of Ease. Weston (Vt.), Orton, 1939.

Corwin, Norman. Thirteen By Corwin. New York, Holt, 1942.

Corwin, Norman. Untitled and Other Radio Dramas. New York, Holt, 1945.

Corwin, Norman. We Hold These Truths. New York, Howell, Soskin, 1942.

Corwin, Norman, et al. See This Is War!

Coulter, Douglas (ed.). Columbia Workshop Plays: fourteen radio dramas. New York, Whittlesey, 1939.

Counterattack: the newsletter of facts on communism. New York, American Business Consultants, monthly, 1947–55.

Cowan, Louis G. Reminiscences, 1968. Unpublished. (C)

Cowgill, Rome. See Kingston, Walter K., and—

Craig, Walter. Interview by Edwin L. Dunham recorded in Sarasota, Fla., 1965. Unpublished. (P)

Crawford, Kenneth G. The Pressure Boys. New York, Messner, 1939.

Cromwell, John. Reminiscences, 1958. Unpublished. (C)

Crosby, Bing. Call Me Lucky (as told to Pete Martin). New York, Simon & Schuster, 1953.

Crosby, John. Out of the Blue. New York, Simon & Schuster, 1952.

Crowther, Bosley. The Lion's Share: the story of an entertainment empire. New York, Dutton, 1957.

Curtis, Alberta. Listeners Appraise a College Station: station WOI, Iowa State College, Ames, Iowa. Washington, Federal Radio Education Committee, 1940.

David Sarnoff: biographical sketch. New York, Radio Corporation of America, 1945.

Daytime Hours Sell. New York, National Broadcasting Company, 1933.

De Forest, Lee. Father of Radio: the autobiography of Lee de Forest. Chicago, Wilcox and Follett, 1950.

De Lay, Theodore Stuart, Jr. An Historical Study of the Armed Forces Radio Service: to 1946. Ph.D. dissertation. Los Angeles, University of Southern California, 1951. Unpublished.

DeLong, Edmund. Reminiscences, 1962. Unpublished. (C)

Dies Committee Accusations: comments.   (Prepared privately by FCC employees, 1942.)   Unpublished.

Dill, Clarence C.   Interview by Ed Craney recorded in Butte, Montana, 1964.   Unpublished.   (P)

Douglas, Melvyn.   Reminiscences, 1958.   Unpublished.   (C)

Driscoll, John, et al.   See This Is War!

Dryer, Sherman H.   Radio in Wartime.   New York, Greenberg, 1942.

Dunlap, Orrin E., Jr.   The Future of Television.   New York, Harper, 1947.

Dunlap, Orrin E., Jr.   Radio and Television Almanac.   New York, Harper, 1951.

Dupuy, Judy.   Television Show Business.   Schenectady, General Electric, 1945.

Edmerson, Estelle.   A Descriptive Study of the American Negro in United States Professional Radio 1922–1953.   Master's essay.   Los Angeles, University of California at Los Angeles, 1954.   Unpublished.

Education on the Air: yearbook of the Institute for Education by Radio.   Columbus (Ohio), Institute for Education by Radio, annual, 1930—

Education by Radio.   Washington, Information and Education Division, War Department, 1946.   Unpublished.

The Eighth Art.   Introduction by Robert Lewis Shayon.   New York, Holt, Rinehart & Winston, 1962.

Eisenhower, Dwight D.   The White House Years: mandate for change 1953–1956.   New York, Doubleday, 1963.

Emery, Walter B.   Broadcasting and Government: responsibilities and regulations.   East Lansing, Michigan State University Press, 1961.

Ernst, Morris.   The First Freedom.   New York, Macmillan, 1946.

Everson, George.   The Story of Television: the life of Philo T. Farnsworth.   New York, Norton, 1949.

Ewbank, Henry L., and Sherman P. Lawton.   Broadcasting: radio and television.   New York, Harper, 1952.

Faulk, John Henry.   Fear on Trial.   New York, Simon & Schuster, 1964.

Faulkner, George, et al.   See This Is War!

FCC Dockets No. 6536 (transfer of Blue Network licenses), 6767 (transfer of Crosley licenses), 9405 (WGAR renewal), 9468 (KMPC renewal), 9469 (WJR renewal.)   Hearings.   Unpublished.

FCC Log: a chronology of events in the history of the Federal Communications Commission 1934–1956.   Washington, Federal Communications Commission, 1956.

FCC   Reports.   Washington, Government Printing Office, annual, 1935—

Federal Communications Commission: hearings before the committee on interstate commerce, U. S. Senate, 73rd Congress, 2nd session, on S. 2910.   Washington, Government Printing Office, 1935.

Federal Communications Commission.   See also following titles: Graves, Statement of Harold N. Graves, Jr.; Hearings: on order No. 79 and 79A; Leigh, Statement of Robert D. Leigh; New Nazi Portrait of the American Soldier; Proposed Findings of Fact and Conclusions of Law of General Counsel; Public Service Responsibility of Broadcast Licensees; Radio Service Bulletin; Report on Chain Broadcasting; Report on Social and Economic Data.

Fetzer, John Earl. Reminiscences, 1950. Unpublished. (C)

Field, Harry. See Lazarsfeld, Paul F., and—

Flanagan, Hallie. Arena. New York, Duell, Sloan & Pearce, 1940.

Fly, James Lawrence. Papers. Unpublished. (C)

FREC Service Bulletin. Washington, Federal Radio Education Committee, monthly, 1939–50.

Friedrich, Carl J. Controlling Broadcasting in Wartime. Cambridge (Mass.), Studies in the Control of Radio, 1940.

Friedrich, Carl J., and Jeanette Sayre. The Development of the Control of Advertising on the Air. Cambridge (Mass.), Studies in the Control of Radio, 1940.

Friedrich, Carl J., and Jeanette Sayre Smith. Radiobroadcasting and Higher Education. Studies in the Control of Radio, 1942.

Friendly, Fred W. Due to Circumstances Beyond Our Control. . . . New York, Random House, 1967.

Frost, S. E., Jr. Education's Own Stations: the history of broadcast licenses issued to educational institutions. Chicago, University of Chicago Press, 1937.

Frost, S. E., Jr. Is American Radio Democratic? Chicago, University of Chicago Press, 1937.

Gammons, Earl. The Twin Cities Story, 1964. Unpublished. (P)

Gardner, Horace J. See Hayes, John S., and—

Garrison, Garnet R. See Chester, Giraud, and—

Gaudet, Hazel. See Cantril, Hadley, with—

Gingell, George. Interview, recorded 1963. Unpublished. (C)

Goldman, Eric F. Rendezvous With Destiny. New York, Vintage, 1956.

Gordon, Dorothy. All Children Listen. New York, Stewart, 1942.

Graves, Harold N., Jr. Statement of Harold N. Graves, Jr., Formerly Assistant to the Director, FCC Foreign Broadcast Intelligence Service: before the House select committee to investigate the FCC, 1944. Unpublished.

Green, Abel, and Joe Laurie, Jr. Show Biz: from vaude to video. New York, Holt, 1951.

Green, Adolph. See Comden, Betty, and—

Green, Gerald. "What Does the Monkey Do?," in Barrett, Edward W. (ed.), Journalists In Action. Manhasset (N.Y.), Channel Press, 1963.

Greene, Robert S. The Development of Narrative Technique in Radio Drama and Its Relationship to the Rise of News Broadcasting. Master's essay. New York, Columbia University, 1958. Unpublished.

Greene, Robert S. Television Writing: theory and technique. New York, Harper, 1952, 1956.

Gross, Ben.　I Looked and Listened: informal recollections of radio and TV. New York, Random House, 1954.

Gunther, John.　Taken at the Flood: the story of Albert D. Lasker.　New York, Harper, 1960.

Hackett, Albert.　Reminiscences, 1958.　Unpublished.　(C)

Hanser, Richard F.　Reminiscences, 1967.　Unpublished.　(C)

Harmon, Jim.　The Great Radio Heroes.　Garden City (N.Y.), Doubleday, 1967.

Harris, Credo Fitch.　Microphone Memoirs: of the horse and buggy days of radio.　Indianapolis, Bobbs-Merrill, 1937.

Harris, Jack W.　See Kirby, Edward M., and—

Hayes, John S., and Horace J. Gardner.　Both Sides of the Microphone. Philadelphia, Lippincott, 1938.

Hazard, Patrick D. (ed.).　TV as Art: some essays in criticism.　Champaign (Ill.), National Council of Teachers of English, 1966.

Head, Sydney W.　Broadcasting in America: a survey of television and radio. Boston, Houghton Mifflin, 1956.

Hearings: before committee on un-American activities on communist infiltration of Hollywood motion picture industry, 80th Congress, 1st session. Washington, Government Printing Office, 1947.

Hearings: on H. R. 8301, House committee on interstate and foreign commerce, 73rd Congress, 2nd session.　Washington, Government Printing Office, 1934.

Hearings: on order No. 79 and 79A, Federal Communications Commission, July-August 1941.

Hedges, William S.　Reminiscences, 1951.　Unpublished.　(C)

Herring, E. Pendleton.　Federal Commissioners: a study of their careers and qualifications.　Cambridge, Harvard University Press, 1936.

Herring, E. Pendleton.　"Politics and Radio Regulation," Harvard Business Review, January 1935.

Herzog, Herta.　"On Borrowed Experience," in Studies in Philosophy and Social Science, IX, 1.　New York, Institute of Social Research, 1941.

Herzog, Herta.　See also Cantril, Hadley, with the assistance of Hazel Gaudet and—

High, Stanley.　"Not-So-Free Air," Saturday Evening Post, February 11, 1939.

Hill, Frank Ernest.　The Groups Tune In.　Washington, Federal Radio Education Committee, 1940.

Hill, Frank Ernest.　Tune In For Education: eleven years of education by radio.　New York, National Committee on Education by Radio, 1942.

Hilliard, Robert L.　Writing for Television and Radio.　New York, Hastings, 1962.

Hirshberg, Al.　See Nelson, Lindsey, with—

Hofstadter, Richard.　Anti-intellectualism in American life.　New York, Knopf, 1963.

Hohenberg, John. Foreign Correspondence: the great reporters and their times. New York, Columbia University Press, 1964.

Hollywood Quarterly. Berkeley, University of California Press, quarterly, 1945–51. Became Quarterly of Film, Radio, and Television.

Howe, Quincy. The News and How to Understand It: in spite of the newspapers, in spite of the magazines, in spite of the radio. New York, Simon & Schuster, 1940.

Howe, Quincy. Reminiscences, 1962. Unpublished. (C)

Hower, Ralph M. The History of an Advertising Agency: N. W. Ayer & Son at work. Cambridge, Harvard University Press, 1939.

Hubbell, Richard W. 4000 Years of Television: the story of seeing at a distance. New York, Putnam, 1942.

Hummert, Ann. The Woman's Daytime Serial. Lecture, Columbia University, January 11, 1939. Unpublished.

Hutchinson, Thomas H. Here Is Television: your window on the world. New York, Hastings House, 1946.

Ickes, Harold L. The Secret Diary of Harold L. Ickes (v. 1): the first thousand days. New York, Simon & Schuster, 1953.

Innis, Harold A. The Bias of Communication. Toronto, University of Toronto Press, 1951.

Innis, Harold A. Empire and Communications. Oxford, Clarendon Press, 1950.

Investigation of the Federal Communications Commission: final report of the select committee to investigate the FCC pursuant to H. Res. 21, 78th Congress. Washington, Government Printing Office, 1945.

Investigation of Lobbying Activities: hearings before a special committee to investigate lobbying activities, U. S. Senate, 74th, 75th Congress, 1935–1938. 8 v. Washington, Government Printing Office, 1935–38.

Jahoda, Marie. "Anti-Communism and Employment Practices in Radio and Television," in Cogley, Report on Blacklisting (v. 2): radio-television. Fund for the Republic, 1956.

Journal of Broadcasting. Los Angeles, Association for Professional Broadcasting Education, quarterly, 1956—

Judson, Arthur. Reminiscences, 1950. Unpublished. (C)

Kahn, E. J. "The Greenwich Tea Party," New Yorker, April 15, 1950.

Kaland, William. Interview, 1963. Unpublished. (C)

Kaltenborn, H. V. Kaltenborn Edits the News. New York, Modern Age, 1937.

Kaltenborn, H. V. I Broadcast the Crisis. New York, Random House, 1938.

Kaltenborn, H. V. Papers. Unpublished. (M)

Kaltenborn, H. V. Reminiscences, 1950. Unpublished. (C)

Kaplan, Milton A. Radio and Poetry. New York, Columbia University Press, 1949.

Kapp, David. Reminiscences, 1959. Unpublished. (C)

Kelley, Stanley, Jr. Professional Public Relations and Political Power. Baltimore, Johns Hopkins Press, 1966.

Kendall, Patricia L. See Lazarsfeld, Paul F., and—

Kieran, John. Not Under Oath: recollections and reflections. Boston, Houghton Mifflin, 1964.

Kingson, Walter K., Rome Cowgill, and Ralph Levy. Broadcasting: television and radio. New York, Prentice-Hall, 1955.

Kirby, Edward M., and Jack W. Harris. Star-Spangled Radio. Chicago, Ziff-Davis, 1948.

Knight, Arthur. The Liveliest Art: a panoramic history of the movies. New York, Macmillan, 1957.

Knight, Kirk. Reminiscences, 1951. Unpublished. (C)

KNX-CBS Radio: continuity, growth and creativity. Los Angeles, KNX, 1961. Unpublished.

Lacy, Dan. Freedom and Communications. Urbana, University of Illinois Press, 1961.

Lampell, Millard. The Lonesome Train. Music by Earl Robinson. LP album. Decca Records, 1945.

Landry, Robert J. Magazines and Radio Criticism. Washington, National Association of Broadcasters, 1942.

Landry, Robert J. This Fascinating Radio Business. Indianapolis, Bobbs-Merrill, 1946.

Landry, Robert J. "Wanted: Radio Critics," Public Opinion Quarterly, December 1940.

Landry, Robert J. Who, What, Why Is Radio? New York, Stewart, 1942.

LaPrade, Ernest. Broadcasting Music. New York, Rinehart, 1947.

Lasker, Albert Davis. Reminiscences, 1950. Unpublished. (C)

Latouche, John, and Earl Robinson. Ballad for Americans. New York, Robbins Music, 1939.

Laurie, Joe, Jr. See Green, Abel, and—

Lawrence, Jerome (ed.). Off Mike: radio writing by the nation's top radio writers. New York, Essential Books, 1944.

Lawton, Sherman P. See Ewbank, Henry L., and—

Lazarsfeld, Paul F. "The Change of Opinion During a Political Discussion," Journal of Applied Psychology, February, 1939.

Lazarsfeld, Paul F. The People's Choice. New York, Duell, Sloan & Pearce, 1944.

Lazarsfeld, Paul F. Radio and the Printed Page. New York, Duell, Sloan & Pearce, 1940.

Lazarsfeld, Paul F., and Harry Field. The People Look At Radio. Chapel Hill, University of North Carolina Press, 1946.

Lazarsfeld, Paul F., and Patricia L. Kendall. Radio Listening in America: the people look at radio—again. New York, Prentice-Hall, 1948.

Lazarsfeld, Paul F., and Frank N. Stanton (eds.). Communications Research 1948–1949. New York, Harper, 1949.

Lazarsfeld, Paul F., and Frank N. Stanton (eds.). Radio Research 1941. New York, Duell, Sloan & Pearce, 1941.

Lazarsfeld, Paul F., and Frank N. Stanton (eds.). Radio Research 1942–1943. New York, Duell, Sloan & Pearce, 1944.

Lee, Robert H. See Skornia, Harry T., and—

Leigh, Robert D. "Politicians vs. Bureaucrats," Harper's Magazine," January, 1945.

Leigh, Robert D. Statement of Robert D. Leigh, Director of FCC Foreign Broadcast Intelligence Service: before the House select committee to investigate the FCC, 1944. Unpublished.

Lessing, Lawrence. Man of High Fidelity: Edwin Howard Armstrong. Philadelphia, Lippincott, 1956.

Levenson, William B. Teaching Through Radio. New York, Farrar & Rinehart, 1945.

Levy, I. D., and Leon Levy. Conversation: text of recording, ca. 1964. Unpublished. (P)

Levy, Ralph. See Kingson, Walter K., Rome Cowgill, and—

Lichtenfield, Leon. Interview, 1963. Unpublished. (C)

Lichty, Lawrence W. The Nation's Station: a history of radio station WLW. Ph.D. dissertation. Columbus, Ohio State University, 1964. Unpublished.

Lichty, Lawrence W. A Study of the Careers and Qualifications of Members of the Federal Radio Commission and Federal Communications Commission, 1937–1961. Master's essay. Columbus, Ohio State University, 1961. Unpublished.

Liss, Joseph (ed.). Radio's Best Plays. New York, Greenberg, 1947.

The Listener. London, British Broadcasting Corporation, weekly, 1930—

Longstreet, Stephen. See Oboler, Arch, and—

Love, Edgar J. Reminiscences, 1951. Unpublished. (C)

Lyons, Eugene. David Sarnoff: a biography. New York, Harper & Row, 1966.

Mabley, Jack. What Educational TV Offers You. Public Affairs Pamphlet No. 203. New York, Public Affairs Committee, 1954.

MacDougall, Ranald, et al. See This Is War!

Mackey, David R. Drama On the Air. New York, Prentice-Hall, 1951.

MacLeish, Archibald. The American Story. New York, Duell, Sloan & Pearce, 1944.

MacLeish, Archibald. The Fall of the City: a verse play for radio. New York, Farrar & Rinehart, 1937.

MacLeish, Archibald. Poetry and Journalism. Minneapolis, University of Minnesota, 1958.

Martin, Pete. See Crosby, Bing, as told to—

Mayer, Martin. Madison Avenue, U. S. A. New York, Harper, 1958.

Mazo, Earl. Richard Nixon: a political and personal portrait. New York, Harper, 1959.

McBride, Mary Margaret.   Out of the Air.   New York, Doubleday, 1960.

McGill, Earle.   Radio Directing.   New York, McGraw-Hill, 1940.

McLuhan, Marshall.   The Gutenberg Galaxy.   Toronto, University of Toronto Press, 1962.

McLuhan, Marshall.   Understanding Media: the extensions of man.   New York, McGraw-Hill, 1965.

McMahon, Robert S.   For the "McMahon Report," see Regulation of Broadcasting.

McNamee, Graham, in collaboration with Robert Gordon Anderson.   You're On the Air.   New York, Harper, 1926.

Means, Gardiner C.   See Berle, Adolf A., Jr., and—

Merton, Robert K.   Mass Persuasion.   New York, Harper, 1946.

Meyer, Richard J.   "The Blue Book," Journal of Broadcasting, Summer 1962.

Meyer, Richard J.   "Reaction to the Blue Book," Journal of Broadcasting, Fall 1962.

Michie, Allan A., and Frank Ryhlick.   Dixie Demagogues.   New York, Vanguard, 1939.

Millay, Edna St. Vincent.   Poem and Prayer for an Invading Army.   New York, National Broadcasting Company, 1944.

Miller, Arthur.   Reminiscences, 1959.   Unpublished.   (C)

Miller, Merle.   The Judges and the Judged.   Garden City (N.Y.), Doubleday, 1952.

Miller, William Burke.   Interview by Edwin Dunham: text of recording, ca. 1964.   Unpublished.   (P)

Mills, John.   A Fugue in Cycles and Bells.   New York, Van Nostrand, 1935.

Morris, Lloyd.   Not So Long Ago.   New York, Random House, 1949.

Morse, Carlton.   Interview, 1963.   Unpublished.   (C)

Munitions Industry: report of the special committee on investigation of the munitions industry, U. S. Senate, pursuant to S. Res. 206 (73rd Congress). Report No. 944, U. S. Senate, 74th Congress, 2nd session.   Washington, Government Printing Office, 1936.

Murrow, Edward R.   A Reporter Remembers.   LP Album.

Murrow, Edward R.   This Is London.   New York, Simon & Schuster, 1941.

Murrow, Edward R.   See also Bliss, Edward, Jr. (ed.), In Search of Light: the broadcasts of Edward R. Murrow 1938–1961.

NAEB Journal.   Bimonthly, successor to AERT Journal.   Urbana (Ill.), National Association of Educational Broadcasters, 1957—

NAEB Monitoring Studies.   See Smythe, Dallas W., New York Television January 4–10, 1951, 1952; Smythe, Dallas W., Three Years of New York Television 1951–1953; Smythe, Dallas W., and Angus Campbell, Los Angeles Television May 23–29, 1951.

NBC and You.   New York, National Broadcasting Company, 1944.

Nelson, Lindsey, with Al Hirshberg.   "A Stadium Inside a Studio," Sports Illustrated, March 28, 1966.

Network Broadcasting: report of the committee on interstate and foreign commerce. Report No. 1297, House of Representatives, 85th Congress, 2nd session. Washington, Government Printing Office, 1958.

New Nazi Portrait of the American Soldier. Special report No. 104, FCC Foreign Broadcast Intelligence Service, 1943. Unpublished.

New Policies. New York, Columbia Broadcasting System, 1935.

Nixon, Richard M. Six Crises. Garden City (N.Y.), Doubleday, 1962.

Nizer, Louis. The Jury Returns. Garden City (N.Y.), Doubleday, 1966.

Nobel, Milton. The Municipal Broadcasting System: its history, organization and activities. Master's essay. New York, City College of New York, 1953. Unpublished.

Noble, Peter. The Fabulous Orson Welles. London, Hutchinson, 1956.

Oboler, Arch. Fourteen Radio Plays. New York, Random House, 1940.

Oboler, Arch. New Radio Plays. New York, Random House, 1941.

Oboler, Arch. Oboler Omnibus: radio plays and personalities. New York, Duell, Sloan & Pearce, 1945.

Oboler, Arch, and Stephen Longstreet (eds.). Free World Theatre: nineteen new radio plays. New York, Random House, 1944.

Overstreet, Harry A., and Bonaro W. Overstreet. Town Meeting Comes To Town. New York, Harper, 1938.

Owen, Bill. See Buxton, Frank, and—

Parker, Dorothy. Reminiscences, 1959. Unpublished. (C)

Parker, Everett C., David W. Barry, and Dallas W. Smythe. The Television-Radio Audience and Religion. New York, Harper, 1955.

Pastore, John O. The Story of Communications: from beacon light to Telstar. New York, Macfadden-Bartell, 1964.

Patt, John F. Reminiscences, 1960. Unpublished. (C)

Payne, George Henry. The Federal Communications Act: a lecture at Harvard University Graduate School of Business Administration, May 14, 1935. New York, Ritz Tower, 1935.

Payne, George Henry. The Story of Journalism in the United States. New York, Appleton, 1920.

Payne, Robert (ed.). The Civil War in Spain: 1936–1939. New York, Putnam, 1962.

Perkins, Frances. The Roosevelt I Knew. New York, Harper, 1946.

Peterson, H. Austin. Hitchhiker on AFRS Road to Tokyo: extracts from Major Peterson's reports. Los Angeles, Armed Forces Radio Service, ca. 1944–45. Undated, unpublished.

Pogue, Forrest C. George C. Marshall: ordeal and hope 1939–1942. New York, Viking, 1966.

Political Broadcasts: a series of letters exchanged between the Columbia Broadcasting System and the Republican National Committee. New York, Columbia Broadcasting System, 1936.

Poole, Lynn. Science Via Television. Baltimore, Johns Hopkins Press, 1950.

Porterfield, John, and Kay Reynolds (eds.). We Present Television. New York, Norton, 1940.

Powdermaker, Hortense. Hollywood: the dream factory. Boston, Little, Brown, 1950.

Powell, John Walker. Channels of Learning: the story of educational television. Washington, Public Affairs Press, 1962.

Power, Leonard. College Radio Workshops. Washington, Federal Radio Education Committee, 1940.

Power, Leonard. Local Cooperative Broadcasting: a summary and appraisal. Washington, Federal Radio Education Committee, 1940.

Power, Leonard. Public Service Broadcasting: station WMBC, Peoria, Ill. Washington, Federal Radio Education Committee, 1940.

Program Ratings: boon or menace? Chicago, A. C. Nielsen, 1947.

Proposed Findings of Fact and Conclusions of Law of General Counsel of the Federal Communications Commission. Dockets No. 9405 (WGAR renewal), 9468 (KMPC renewal), 9469 (WJR renewal). Washington, Federal Communications Commission, 1951. Unpublished.

Prospects for NBC Telecasting 1946–1950. New York, NBC Research Department, 1946. Unpublished. In Hedges, Papers. (M)

Public Service Responsibility of Broadcast Licensees (the "blue book"). Washington, Federal Communications Commission, 1946.

Publicity and Psychological Warfare, 12th Army Group: history, January 1943–August 1945. European Theater of Operations. Undated.

Quarterly of Film, Radio, and Television. Berkeley, University of California Press, quarterly, 1951–57. Successor to Hollywood Quarterly; became Film Quarterly.

QST. Hartford (Conn.), American Radio Relay League, monthly, 1915—

Radio Annual. New York, Radio Daily, annual, 1938–64.

Radio Art. New York, semimonthly, then quarterly, 1923–39.

Radio as a Cultural Agency. See Tyler, Tracy (ed.).

Radio Daily. New York, daily, 1937–65.

Radio Service Bulletin. Washington, U. S. Department of Commerce, monthly, 1915–34; Federal Communications Commission, 1934—

RCA Annual Report. New York, annual, 1921—

Red Channels: the report of communist influence in radio and television. New York, American Business Consultants, 1950.

Regulation of Broadcasting: half a century of government regulation of broadcasting and the need for further legislative action. Study for the committee on interstate and foreign commerce, U. S. House of Representatives, 85th Congress, 2nd session (The "McMahon report"). Washington, Government Printing Office, 1958.

Reinsch, J. Leonard. Radio Station Management. New York, Harper, 1948.

Report on Chain Broadcasting: commission order No. 37, Docket No. 5060. Washington, Federal Communications Commission, 1941.

A Report on the Results of Paul Draper's Appearance on "Toast of the Town" Sunday, January 22, 1950. New York, Kenyon & Eckhardt, 1950. Unpublished.

Report on Social and Economic Data Pursuant to the Informal Hearing on Broadcasting, Docket 4063, beginning October 5, 1936. Washington, Government Printing Office, 1938.

Report of the Special Subcommittee of the Committee on Appropriations: pursuant to H. Res. 105, 78th Congress, 1st session (re Watson, Dodd, Schuman), April 21, 1943. Washington, Government Printing Office, 1943.

Reporter Political Yearbook. New York, Reporter, 1951.

Reynolds, Kay. See Porterfield, John, and—

Robinson, Earl. See Lampell, Millard, with music by—

Robinson, Earl. See Latouche, John, and—

Robinson, Thomas Porter. Radio Networks and the Federal Government. New York, Columbia University Press, 1943.

Robson, William N. Reminiscences, 1966. Unpublished. (C)

Robson, William N., et al. See This Is War!

Rolo, Charles J. Radio Goes to War: the "fourth front." New York, Putnam, 1942.

Roosevelt, Franklin D. Selected Speeches, Messages, Press Conferences, and Letters. New York, Rinehart, 1957.

Rorty, James. "Advertising Rides the War," Common Sense, December, 1943.

Rorty, James. Order in the Air! New York, John Day, 1934.

Rorty, James. Our Master's Voice: advertising. New York, John Day, 1934.

Rorty, James. "Radio Comes Through," Nation, October 15, 1938.

Ross, Murray. Stars and Strikes: unionization of Hollywood. New York, Columbia University Press, 1941.

Rosten, Leo C. Hollywood: the movie colony and the movie makers. New York, Harcourt, Brace, 1941.

Rovere, Richard H. Senator Joe McCarthy. Cleveland, World, 1960.

Royal, John F. (ed.). Television Production Problems. New York, McGraw-Hill, 1948.

Ryan, J. Harold. Reminiscences, 1960. Unpublished. (C)

Ryhlick, Frank. See Michie, Allan A., and—

Saerchinger, César. Hello America! radio adventures in Europe. Boston, Houghton Mifflin, 1938.

Saerchinger, César. "Radio as a Political Instrument," Foreign Affairs, January 1938.

Sarnoff, David. Radio and Education: an address . . . at the 75th annual convocation of the University of the State of New York. New York, National Broadcasting Company, 1939.

Sarnoff, David. See also title David Sarnoff.

Sayre, Jeanette. See Friedrich, Carl J., and—

Schacht, Hjalmar. Account Settled. London, Weidenfeld & Nicolson, 1949.

Schairer, Otto S. Patent Policies of the Radio Corporation of America. New York, RCA Institutes Technical Press, 1939.

Schechter, A. A. Reminiscences, 1950. Unpublished. (C)

Schechter, A. A., with Edward Anthony. I Live on Air. New York, Stokes, 1941.

Schlesinger, Arthur M., Jr. The Coming of the New Deal. Boston, Houghton Mifflin, 1959.

Schlesinger, Arthur M., Jr. The Crisis of the Old Order. Boston, Houghton Mifflin, 1957.

Schlesinger, Arthur M., Jr. The Politics of Upheaval. Boston, Houghton Mifflin, 1960.

Schramm, Wilbur. Communications in Modern Society. Urbana, University of Illinois Press, 1948.

Schramm, Wilbur (ed.). Mass Communications. Urbana, University of Illinois Press, 1949, 1960.

Schramm, Wilbur (ed.). The Process and Effects of Mass Communications. Urbana, University of Illinois Press, 1954.

Schramm, Wilbur. Responsibility in Mass Communication. New York, Harper, 1957.

The Screen Writer. Hollywood, Screen Writers Guild, monthly, 1945–48.

Seldes, Gilbert. The Great Audience. New York, Viking, 1950.

Seldes, Gilbert. The Public Arts. New York, Simon & Schuster, 1956.

Seldes, Gilbert. Writing for Television. Garden City (N.Y.), Doubleday, 1952.

Settel, Irving. A Pictorial History of Radio. New York, Citadel, 1960.

Sevareid, Eric. In One Ear. New York, Knopf, 1952.

Sevareid, Eric. Not So Wild a Dream. New York, Knopf, 1946.

Shannon, David A. (ed.). The Great Depression. New York, Prentice-Hall, 1960.

Shayon, Robert Lewis. Reminiscences, 1967. Unpublished. (C)

Shayon, Robert Lewis. Television and Our Children. New York, Longmans, Green, 1951.

Shayon, Robert Lewis. See also The Eighth Art.

Sheats, Paul H. Forums on the Air: a report of plans and procedures developed in the broadcasting of public affairs discussion programs over local radio stations. Washington, Federal Radio Education Committee, 1939.

Sherwood, Robert E. Roosevelt and Hopkins: an intimate history. 2 v. New York, Harper, 1950.

Shirer, William L. Berlin Diary: the journal of a foreign correspondent 1934–1941. New York, Knopf, 1941.

Shirer, William L. Midcentury Journey: the western world through its years of conflict. New York, Farrar, Straus & Cudahy, 1952.

Shirer, William L. The Rise and Fall of the Third Reich: a history of nazi Germany. New York, Simon & Schuster, 1960.

Shurick, E. P. J. The First Quarter-Century of American Broadcasting. Kansas City, Midland, 1946.

Siepmann, Charles A. Radio in Wartime. Pamphlet No. 26, America in a world at war. New York, Oxford University Press, 1942.

Siepmann, Charles A. The Radio Listener's Bill of Rights: democracy, radio, and you. New York, Anti-Defamation League of B'nai B'rith, 1948.

Siepmann, Charles A. Radio's Second Chance. Boston, Little, Brown, 1946.

Siepmann, Charles A. Radio, Television and Society. New York, Oxford University Press, 1950.

Siepmann, Charles A. Television and Education in the United States. Paris, UNESCO, 1952.

Sill, Jerome. The Radio Station: management, functions, future. New York, Stewart, 1946.

Sinclair, Upton. I, Candidate for Governor: and how I got licked. Pasadena, 1934.

Skornia, Harry T. Television and Society: an inquest and agenda for improvement. New York, McGraw-Hill, 1965.

Skornia, Harry T., Robert H. Lee, and Fred A. Brewer. Creative Broadcasting. New York, Prentice-Hall, 1950.

Slate, Sam J., and Joe Cook. It Sounds Impossible. New York, Macmillan, 1963.

Slaton, John L. Interview, 1963. Unpublished. (C)

Smiley, Robert. Interview, 1963. Unpublished. (C)

Smith, Jeanette Sayre. See Friedrich, Carl J., and—

Smythe, Dallas W. New York Television January 4–10, 1951, 1952: monitoring study No. 4. Urbana (Ill.), National Association of Educational Broadcasters, 1952.

Smythe, Dallas W. Three Years of New York Television 1951–1953: monitoring study No. 6. Urbana (Ill.), National Association of Educational Broadcasters, 1953.

Smythe, Dallas W., and Angus Campbell. Los Angeles Television May 23–29, 1951: monitoring study No. 2. Urbana (Ill.), National Association of Educational Broadcasters, 1951.

Smythe, Dallas W. See also Parker, Everett C., David W. Barry, and—

Sparks, Jefferson. Interview, 1963. Unpublished. (C)

Speedy-Q Sound Effects: catalog. Los Angeles, Starr Piano, 1938.

Sponsor. New York, bi-weekly, then weekly, 1948—

Stanton, Frank N. See Lazarsfeld, Paul F., and—

Stasheff, Edward, and Rudy Bretz. The Television Program: its writing, direction, and production. New York, Wyn, 1951.

Stearns, Marshall W. The Story of Jazz. New York, Oxford University Press, 1958.

Storer, George B. The Storer Story. Memorandum, 1964. Unpublished. (P)

The Story of WOR. Newark, Bamberger, 1934.

Suber, Howard. The 1947 Hearings of the House Committee on Un-American

Activities into Communism in the Hollywood Motion Picture Industry. Master's essay. Los Angeles, University of California, 1966. Unpublished.

Subversive Infiltration of Radio, Television and the Entertainment Industry: hearings before the subcommittee to investigate the administration of the internal security act and other internal security laws of the committee on the judiciary, U. S. Senate, 82nd Congress. Washington, Government Printing Office, 1952.

Suggestions for Radio Playwrights: Campana's *First Nighter* broadcast. Chicago, Aubrey, Moore & Wallace, 1939. Unpublished.

Summers, Harrison B. (ed.). Radio Censorship. New York, Wilson, 1939.

Summers, Harrison B. (ed.). A Thirty-Year History of Programs Carried on National Radio Networks in the United States 1926–1956. Columbus, Ohio State University, 1958.

Summers, Harrison B. See also Summers, Robert E., and—

Summers, Robert E., and Harrison B. Summers. Broadcasting and the Public. Belmont (Calif.), Wadsworth, 1966.

Swing, Raymond Gram. Forerunners of American Fascism. New York, Messner, 1935.

Swing, Raymond (Gram). Good Evening! a professional memoir. New York, Harcourt Brace, 1964.

Swing, Raymond (Gram). In the Name of Sanity. New York, Harper, 1946.

Talks. New York, Columbia Broadcasting System, quarterly, 1936–49.

Taylor, Davidson. Reminiscences, 1967. Unpublished. (C)

Taylor, Telford. Grand Inquest: the story of congressional investigations. New York, Simon & Schuster, 1955.

Tebbel, John. David Sarnoff: putting electrons to work. Chicago, Encyclopaedia Britannica Press, 1963.

Television Digest. Washington, Triangle, weekly, 1945—

Television Factbook. Supplements to Television Digest. Radnor (Pa.), Triangle, 1945—

Television in education: a summary report . . . of the educational television program institute held at Pennsylvania State College April 20–24, 1952. Washington, American Council on Education, 1952.

Television Network Program Procurement: report of the committee on interstate and foreign commerce. House report No. 281, 88th Congress, 1st session. Washington, Government Printing Office, 1963.

Television Quarterly: journal of the National Academy of Television Arts and Sciences. Syracuse, Syracuse University, quarterly, 1962—

This Is an Army Hitler Forgot! Washington, National Association of Broadcasters, ca. 1943. Undated.

This Is War! a collection of plays about America on the march, by Norman Corwin, Stephen Vincent Benét, Philip Wylie, William N. Robson, Maxwell Anderson, George Faulkner, Ranald MacDougall, John Driscoll. New York, Dodd, Mead, 1942.

Thought Control in U.S.A.; the collected proceedings of the conference on thought control. Hollywood, Progressive Citizens of America, 1947.

Thurber, James. "Soapland," in The Beast in Me and Other Animals. New York, Harcourt, Brace, 1948.

Trammell, Niles. A Free Radio and the Law: a statement . . . before a sub-committee of the Senate committee on interstate and foreign commerce. Washington, National Broadcasting Company, 1947.

Trammell, Niles. Radio Must Remain Free: a statement . . . before the Senate interstate commerce committee. New York, National Broadcasting Company, 1943.

Truman, Harry S. Memoirs (v. 1): year of decisions. Garden City (N.Y.), Doubleday, 1955.

Truman, Harry S. Memoirs (v. 2): years of trial and hope 1946–1952. Garden City (N.Y.), Doubleday, 1956.

Tull, Charles J. Father Coughlin and the New Deal. Syracuse, Syracuse University Press, 1965.

TV Guide. Philadelphia, Triangle, weekly, 1948—

Tyler, Tracy F. An Appraisal of Radio Broadcasting in the Land-Grant Colleges and State Universities. Washington, National Committee on Education by Radio, 1933.

Tyler, Tracy F. (ed.). Radio as a Cultural Agency: proceedings of a national conference on the use of radio as a cultural agency in a democracy. Washington, National Committee on Education by Radio, 1934.

Tyson, Levering (ed.). Radio and Education. Chicago, University of Chicago Press, 1933.

Ulanov, Barry. The Incredible Crosby. New York, Whittlesey, 1948.

United States Department of Commerce. See Radio Service Bulletin.

United States Department of Defense. See The American Forces Network.

United States House of Representatives, committee on appropriations. See Report of the Special Subcommittee of the Committee on Appropriations.

United States House of Representatives, committee on interstate and foreign commerce. See following titles: Hearings: on H. R. 8301; Network Broadcasting; Regulation of Broadcasting; Television Network Program Procurement.

United States House of Representatives, committee on un-American activities. See Hearings: before committee on un-American activities.

United States House of Representatives, select committee to investigate the Federal Communications Commission. See Investigation of the Federal Communications Commission.

United States Office of War Information. See When Radio Writes for War.

United States Senate, committee on interstate commerce. See Federal Communications Commission.

United States Senate, committee on the judiciary. See Subversive Infiltration of Radio, Television and the Entertainment Industry.

United States Senate, special committee to investigate lobbying activities.   See Investigation of Lobbying Activities.

United States Senate, special committee to investigate the munitions industry. See Munitions Industry.

United States War Department.   See following titles: AFRS Playback; Armed Forces Radio Service; Education by Radio; Peterson, Hitchhiker on AFRS Road to Tokyo; Publicity and Psychological Warfare.

Variety.   New York, weekly, 1905—

Variety Radio Directory.   New York, Variety, annual, 1937–41.

Wade, Robert J.   Designing for TV.   New York, Pelligrini & Cudahy, 1952.

Wakeman, Frederic.   The Hucksters.   New York, Rinehart, 1946.

Wald, Jerry.   Reminiscences, 1959.   Unpublished.   (C)

Waldrop, Frank C., and Joseph Borkin.   Television: a struggle for power. New York, Morrow, 1938.

Waller, George.   Kidnap: the story of the Lindbergh trial.   New York, Dial, 1961.

Waller, Judith C.   Radio, the Fifth Estate.   Boston, Houghton, Mifflin, 1950.

Watson, Goodwin.   Reminiscences, 1963.   Unpublished.   (C)

Wecter, Dixon.   "Hearing is Believing," Atlantic Monthly, June-August 1945.

Weiser, Norman S. (ed.).   The Writer's Radio Theater 1940–41.   New York, Harper, 1941.

Weiser, Norman S. (ed.).   The Writer's Radio Theater 1941.   New York, Harper, 1942.

Whalen, Grover A.   Reminiscences, 1951.   Unpublished.   (C)

Whalen, Richard J.   The Founding Father: the story of Joseph P. Kennedy. New York, New American Library, 1964.

When Radio Writes for War: a digest of practical suggestions on wartime radio scripts.   Washington, Office of War Information, 1943.

White, Llewellyn.   The American Radio: a report on the broadcasting industry in the United States from the Commission on Freedom of the Press. Chicago, University of Chicago Press, 1947.

White, Paul W.   News on the Air.   New York, Harcourt, Brace, 1947.

Wile, Frederic William.   News Is Where You Find It: forty years' reporting at home and abroad.   Indianapolis, Bobbs-Merrill, 1939.

Willey, Roy DeVerl, and Helen Ann Young.   Radio in Elementary Education. Boston, Heath, 1948.

Williams, Albert N.   Listening.   Denver, University of Denver Press, 1948.

Willis, Edgar E.   Foundations in Broadcasting.   New York, Oxford University Press, 1951.

Willis, Edgar E.   See Chester, Giraud, Garnet R. Garrison, and—

Willkie, Wendell L.   One World.   New York, Simon & Schuster, 1943.

Wilson, H. H.   Congress: corruption and compromise.   New York, Rinehart, 1951.

Wishengrad, Morton.   The Eternal Light: twenty-six radio plays from the *Eternal Light* program.   New York, Crown, 1947.

Wishengrad, Morton. "The Last Inca," in Liss, Joseph (ed.), Radio's Best Plays. New York, Greenberg, 1947.

Witty, Paul, and Harry Bricker. Your Child and Radio, TV, Comics and Movies. Chicago, Science Research Associates, 1952.

Wood, William A. Electronic Journalism. New York, Columbia University Press, 1967.

Woods, Mark. Reminiscences, 1951. Unpublished. (C)

Woolley, Thomas Russell, Jr. A Rhetorical Study: the radio speaking of Edward R. Murrow. Ph.D. dissertation. Evanston, Northwestern University, 1957. Unpublished.

Writers' War Board: first annual report. New York, Writers' War Board, 1942.

Wylie, Max. "Amos 'n' Andy—Loving Remembrance," Television Quarterly, Summer 1963.

Wylie Max (ed.). Best Broadcasts of 1938–39. New York, Whittlesey, 1939.

Wylie, Max (ed.). Best Broadcasts of 1939–40. New York, Whittlesey, 1940.

Wylie, Max. Radio and Television Writing. New York, Rinehart, 1950.

Wylie, Philip, et al. See This Is War!

You Do What You're Told. New York, Columbia Broadcasting System, 1935.

Young, Helen Ann. See Willey, Roy DeVerl, and—

The Zenith Story: a history from 1919. Chicago, Zenith, 1955.

Zolotov, Maurice. "Washboard Weepers," Saturday Evening Post, May 29, 1943.

INDEX

AAA, 7, 14

Abraham, George, 114

ABSIE, 198

Ace, Goodman, 290

actor: in television, 43, 126; in radio, 108–11, 229; development of blacklists, 246–82; photographs, following 90, 186, 282

ad lib programming: at first discouraged by networks, 92; increase of, 92–3; wartime problems, 156; encouraged by magnetic recording, 199, 240–41; by rise of disk-jockey, 218–19; by economic decline of radio, 288–9

Adam hats, 128

Adams, Joe, 290

Adler, Larry, 262–3, 266n.

advertising: rising influence of, 8–18, 61–2; complaints against, 24–5, 32, 35, 60–61, 234; trends in radio, 82, 92, 148, 188–9, 219, 227–8, 234–5; merchandising techniques, 97–8, 112; Federal Trade Commission review, 111–12; advertising in wartime, 165–7; television experiments, 243

advertising agency, role of: in politics, 14–18, 47, 51–4, 144, 298–9; in radio, 16–17, 90, 94, 103–4, 108, 111, 114, 282; in wartime, 165–7, 193–5; activity in television, 243, 263–4, 270, 276–80

affiliation agreements, network-station, 57–8, 171–2

AFM, 194, 218

AFRA, 108

Agricultural Adjustment Administration, 7, 14

Aldrich Family, television series, 268, 297

Aherne, Brian, 70

Albert, Eddie, photograph, following 186

Alexander, A. L., 112

Allen, Fred, 99–100, 104, 286–90

Allen, George, 298

Allen, Gracie, 17, 99

Allen, Robert S., 233

Allis Chalmers, 166

Alpine, N. J., 42, 129, 284; photographs of transmitter, following 90

Amahl and the Night Visitors, television opera, 297

Amalgamated Broadcasting System, 31n.

amateur stations, 30, 41, 131, 156

America First, 138, 144

American Album of Familiar Music, radio series, 94

American Association of Advertising Agencies, 114

American Bar Association, 112

American Broadcasting Company: formation, 190; early history, 199, 242, 244–5, 258, 276, 287, 290

371

XGOY, Chungking, 186

Yankee Network, 52, 129
Yeh Chien-ying, 240
You Are There, radio drama series, 238
You Bet Your Life, radio series, 290
You Can't Cheat an Honest Man, film, 104
You Do What You're Told, promotion brochure, 61–2
Young, Loretta, 193
Young, Owen D., 125

Young & Rubicam, advertising agency, 17n., 103–4, 160, 193, 195, 214, 268–9, 276, 278, 283
Young Widder Brown, radio serial, 94n.
Your Family and Mine, radio serial, 94n.
Your Show of Shows, television series, 296

Zenith radio, 130, 283
Zoomar lens, 244
Zukor, Adolph, 58–9
Zworykin, Vladimir K., 38–9